CLAMP's

MAGIC·KNIGHT
RAYEARTH

Volume 1 (of 3)

TOKYOPOP®

LOS ANGELES * TOKYO * LONDON

ALSO AVAILABLE FROM 🐢 TOKYOPOP®

11.20.03 T

Translator - Anita Sengupta
English Adaption - Jamie S. Rich
Copy Editors - Bryce Coleman, Carol Fox
Retouch - Paul Morrissey
Lettering - Monalisa de Asis
Cover Layout - Patrick Hook

Editor - Jake Forbes
Managing Editor - Jill Freshney
Production Coordinator - Antonio DePietro
Production Manager - Jennifer Miller, Mutsumi Miyazaki
Art Director - Matt Alford
Editorial Director - Jeremy Ross
VP of Production - Ron Klamert
President & C.O.O. - John Parker
Publisher & C.E.O. - Stuart Levy

Email: editor@TOKYOPOP.com
Come visit us online at www.TOKYOPOP.com

A  Manga

TOKYOPOP Inc.
5900 Wilshire Blvd. Suite 2000
Los Angeles, CA 90036

Magic Knight Rayearth II Vol. 1

Magic Knight Rayearth II Vol. 1 ©1995 CLAMP.
First published in 1995 by Kodansha Ltd., Tokyo.
English publication rights arranged through Kodansha Ltd.

English text © 2003 by Mixx Entertainment, Inc.
TOKYOPOP is a registered trademark of Mixx Entertainment, Inc.

ISBN: 1-59182-266-1

First TOKYOPOP printing: February 2004

10 9 8 7 6 5 4 3 2 1
Printed in the USA

Introduction...

Welcome to Magic Knight Rayearth II! Here begins Hikaru, Umi and Fuu's second adventure in the magical realm of Cephiro. This new adventure stands on its own, but it does help if you know a bit about the first series before you begin. For those of you who are new to Rayearth, or if you just need a little refresher course, here's what happened in the first series...

Hikaru, Umi and Fuu were three Tokyo schoolgirls with nothing in common, that is until they were magically summoned to the land of Cephiro. An ancient wizard (with a childlike body) named Guru Clef told the girls that they were the Magic Knights, the legendary heroes from another world who were prophesized to save Cephiro from Zagato, a sinister man who held the land's ruler captive. After receiving some magical armor, called "guards," the girls began their quest.

Along the way they befriended Presea, the blacksmith, Ferio, a wandering swordsman, and Mokona, a bizarre white puffball who became their guide. In order to become true Magic Knights, the girls first had to unlock the Mashin (or Rune Gods, as they're called in the anime). These ancient spirits function like "mecha" in combat, as well as providing guidance to the girls from within their own souls.

Armed with new powerful weapons and even more powerful Mashin, the girls journeyed to Zagato's fortress to rescue Princess Emeraude. Much to their surprise, the Magic Knights discovered that Emeraude wanted the Magic Knights to slay her. Zagato was bent on destroying the knights only to protect Emeraude, the woman he loved. The tragic nature of Cephiro's existence is based on the leader, or "Pillar," devoting herself 100% to her country. When Emeraude fell in love with Zagato, she could not be with him because of her duty, and so she chose to die rather than live in sorrow. The Magic Knights defeated Emeraude, but it left the three girls scarred for life and sent them back to earth in tears.

Now we rejoin the girls one year later, more mature for their experiences, holding many regrets for what they were forced to do. Perhaps the future holds happier times for these young ladies from another world who are so pure of heart.

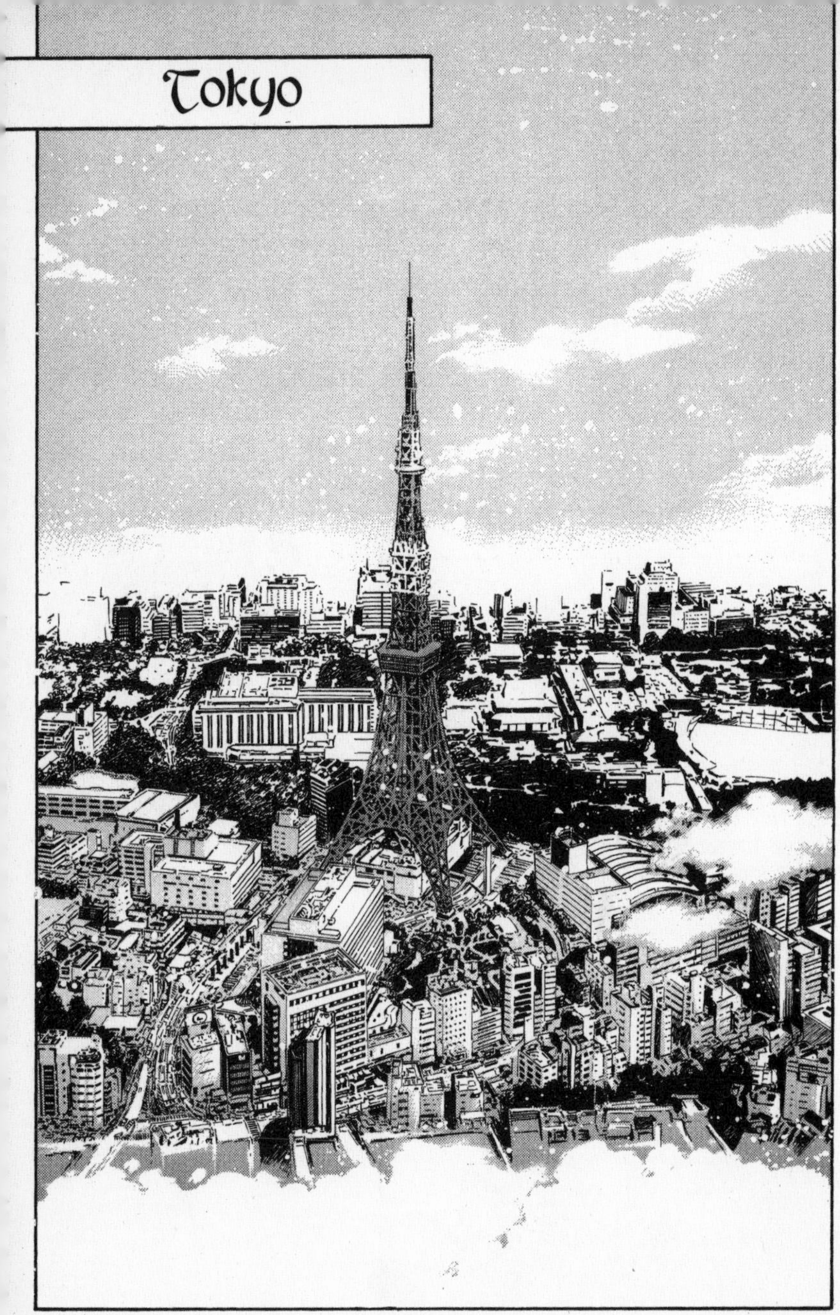
Tokyo

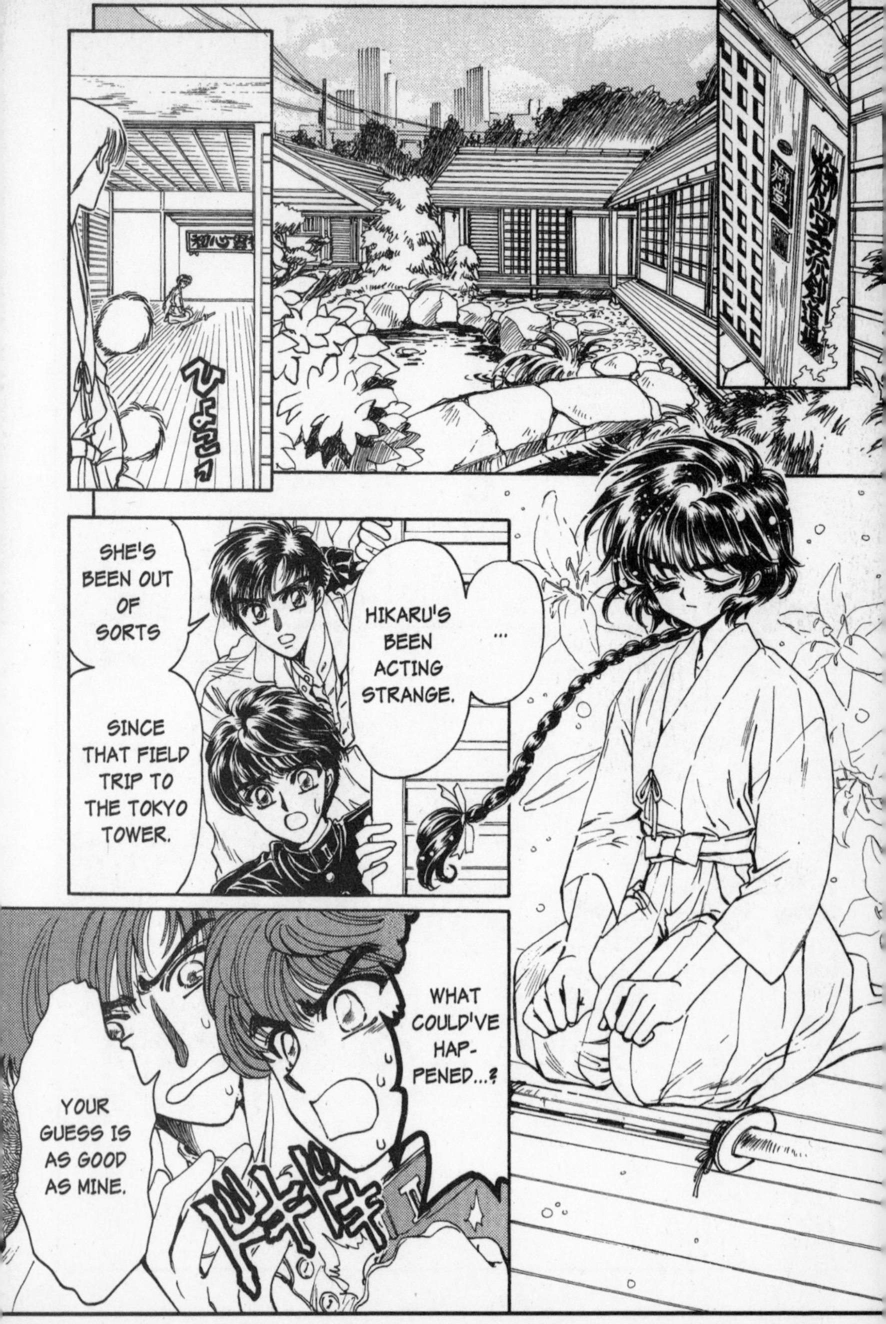
...
HIKARU'S BEEN ACTING STRANGE.
SHE'S BEEN OUT OF SORTS
SINCE THAT FIELD TRIP TO THE TOKYO TOWER.
WHAT COULD'VE HAP-PENED...?
YOUR GUESS IS AS GOOD AS MINE.

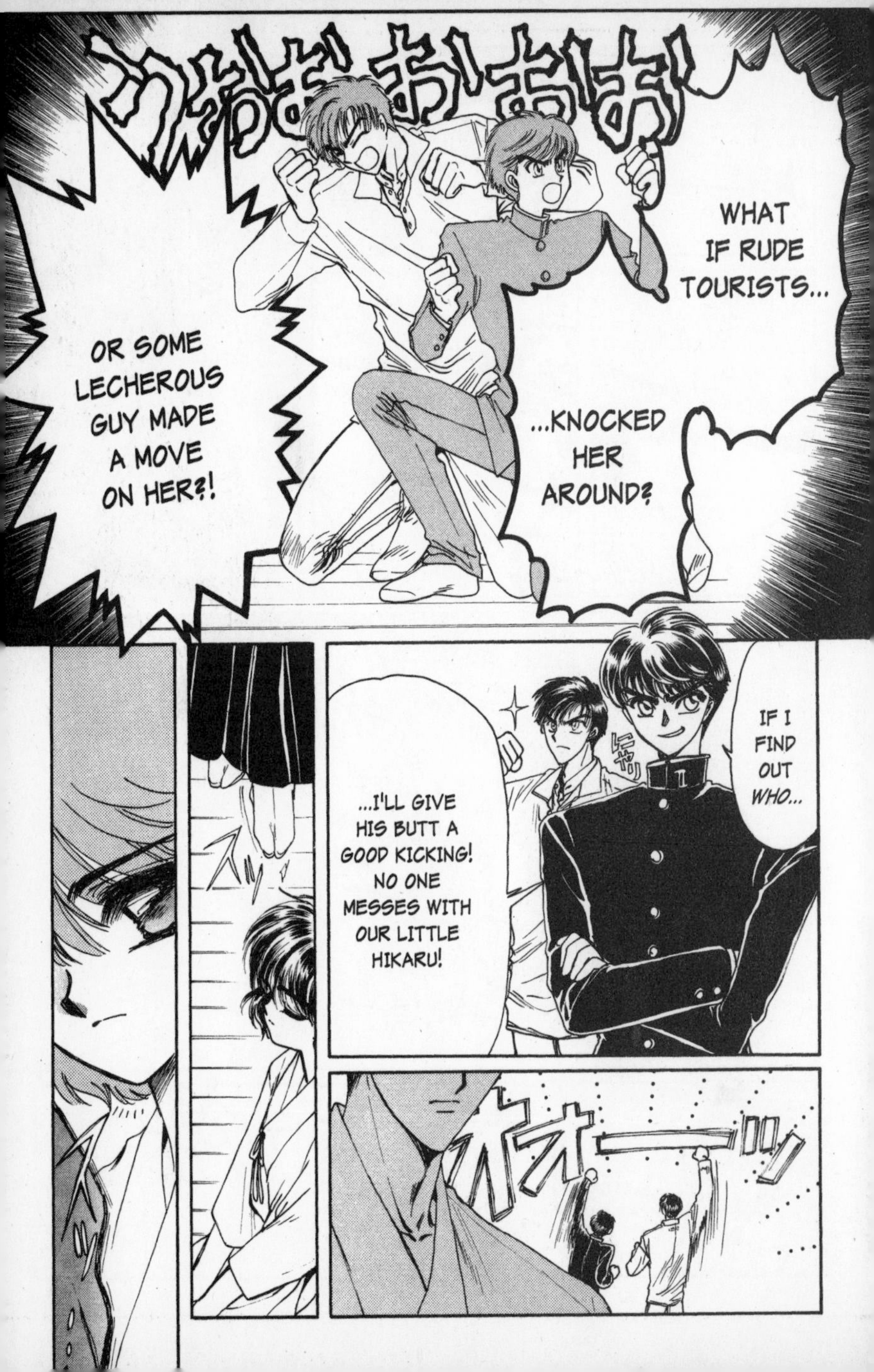

WHAT IF RUDE TOURISTS...
...KNOCKED HER AROUND?
OR SOME LECHEROUS GUY MADE A MOVE ON HER?!
IF I FIND OUT WHO...
...I'LL GIVE HIS BUTT A GOOD KICKING! NO ONE MESSES WITH OUR LITTLE HIKARU!
...

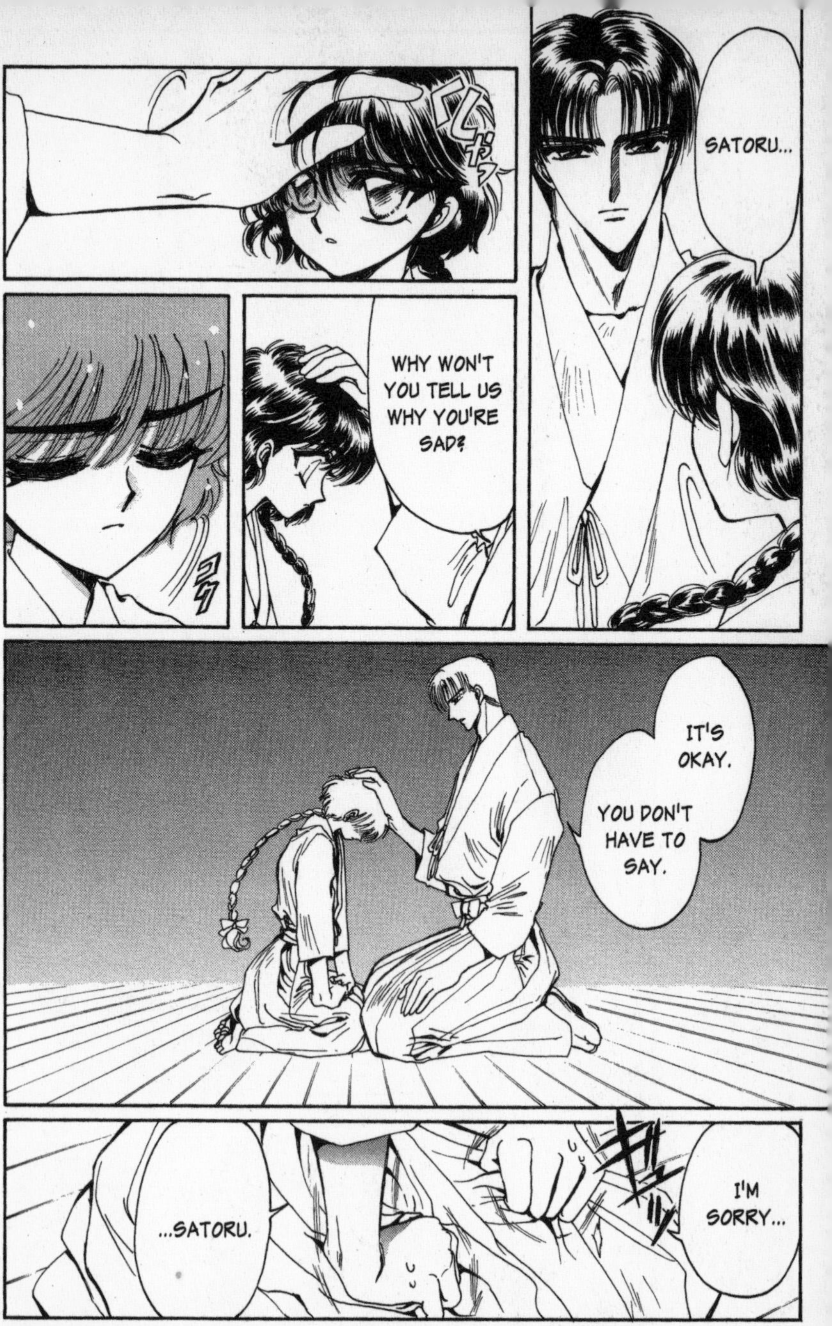
SATORU...
WHY WON'T YOU TELL US WHY YOU'RE SAD?
IT'S OKAY.
YOU DON'T HAVE TO SAY.
I'M SORRY...
...SATORU.

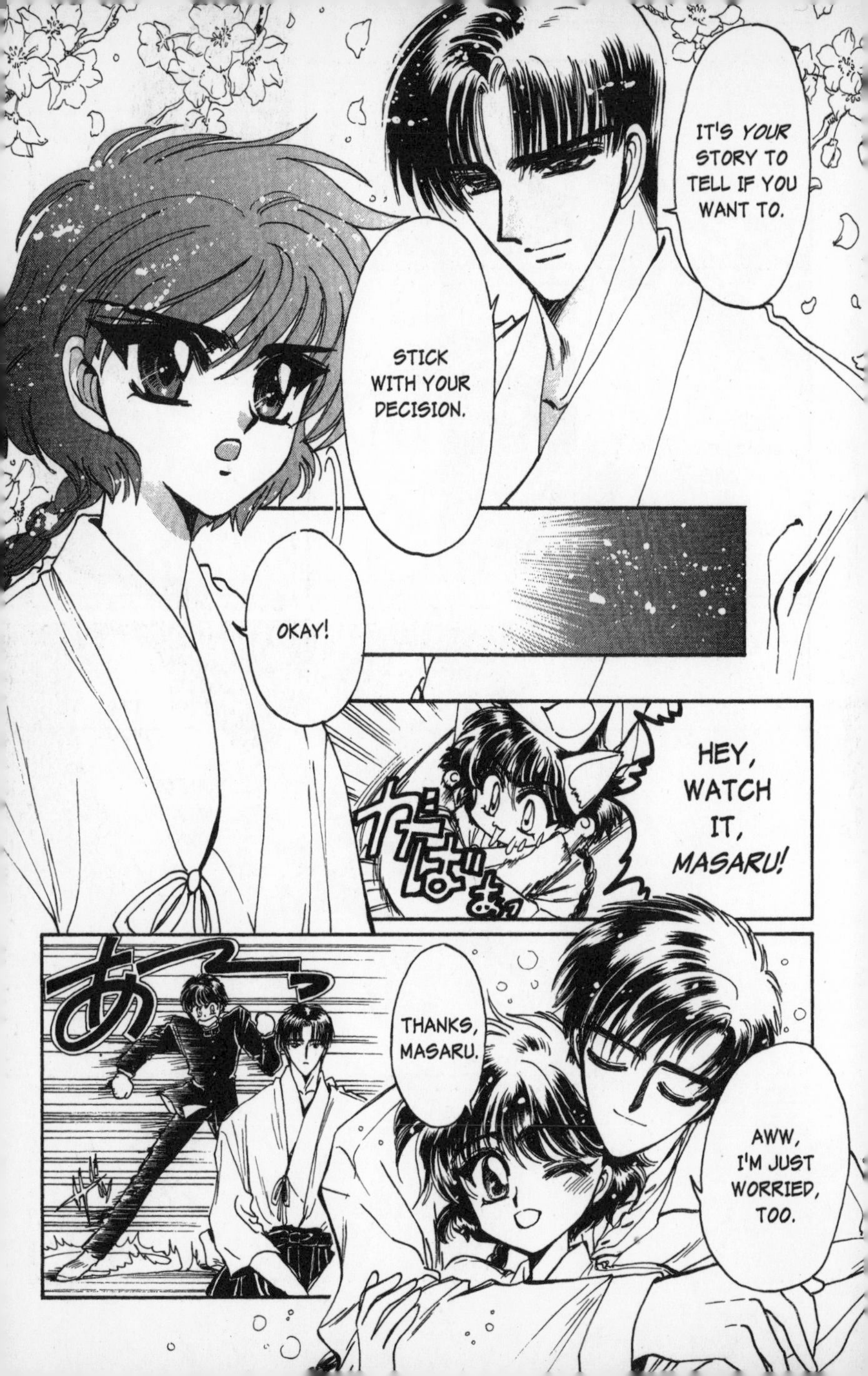
IT'S *YOUR* STORY TO TELL IF YOU WANT TO.
STICK WITH YOUR DECISION.
OKAY!
HEY, WATCH IT, *MASARU!*
THANKS, MASARU.
AWW, I'M JUST WORRIED, TOO.

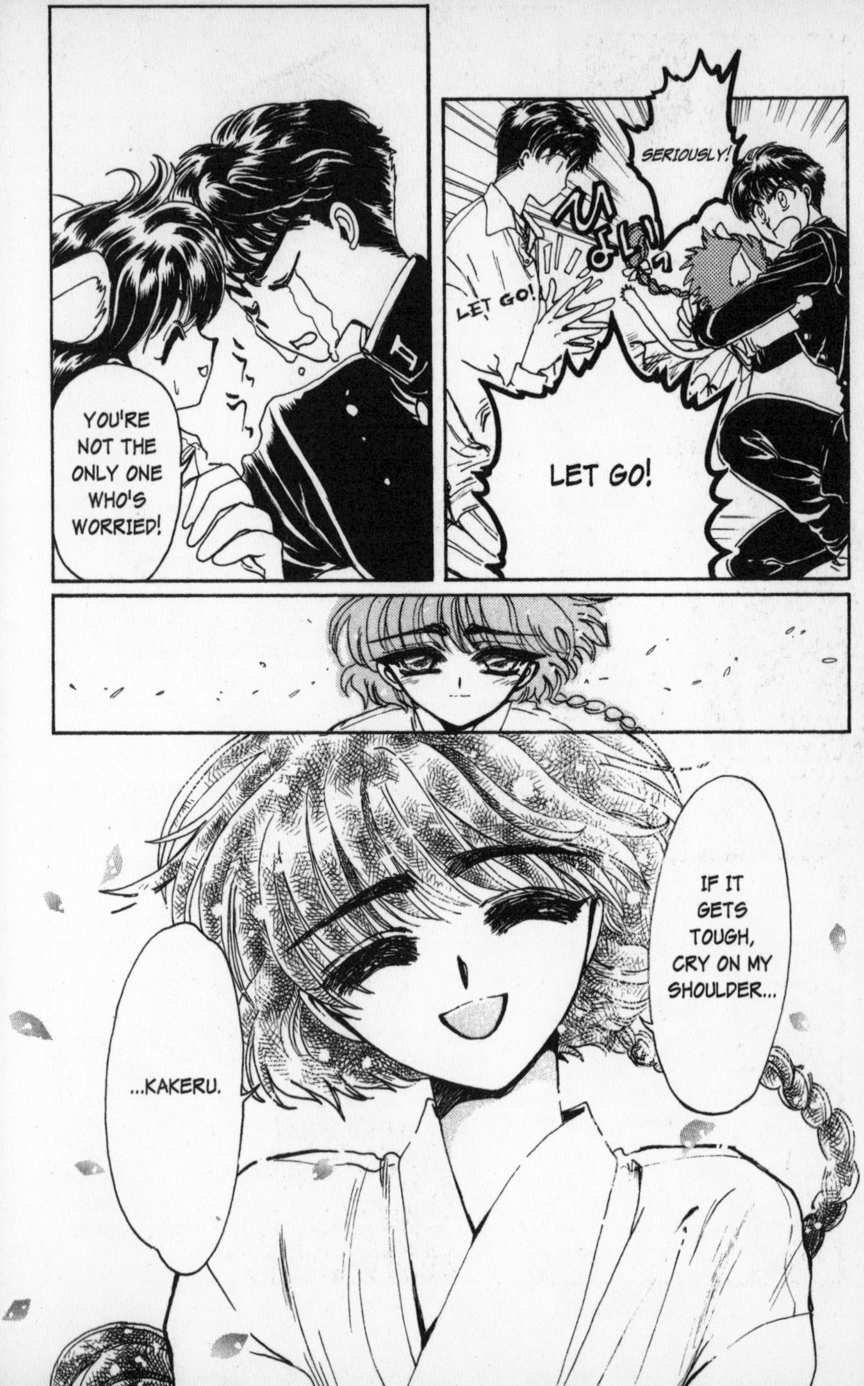
SERIOUSLY!
ひょいっ
LET GO!
LET GO!
YOU'RE NOT THE ONLY ONE WHO'S WORRIED!
IF IT GETS TOUGH, CRY ON MY SHOULDER...
...KAKERU.

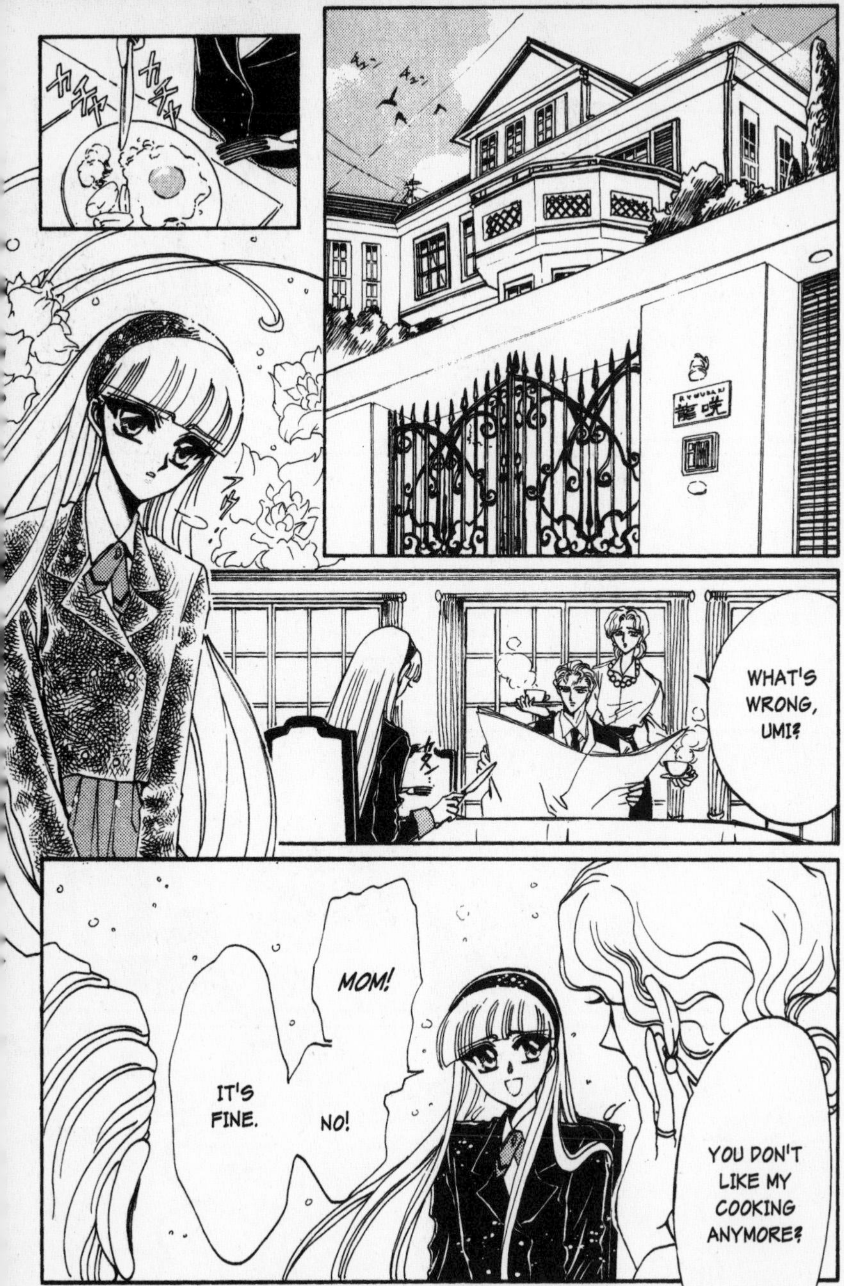
龍咲
カチャ
カチャ
WHAT'S WRONG, UMI?
YOU DON'T LIKE MY COOKING ANYMORE?
MOM!
NO!
IT'S FINE.

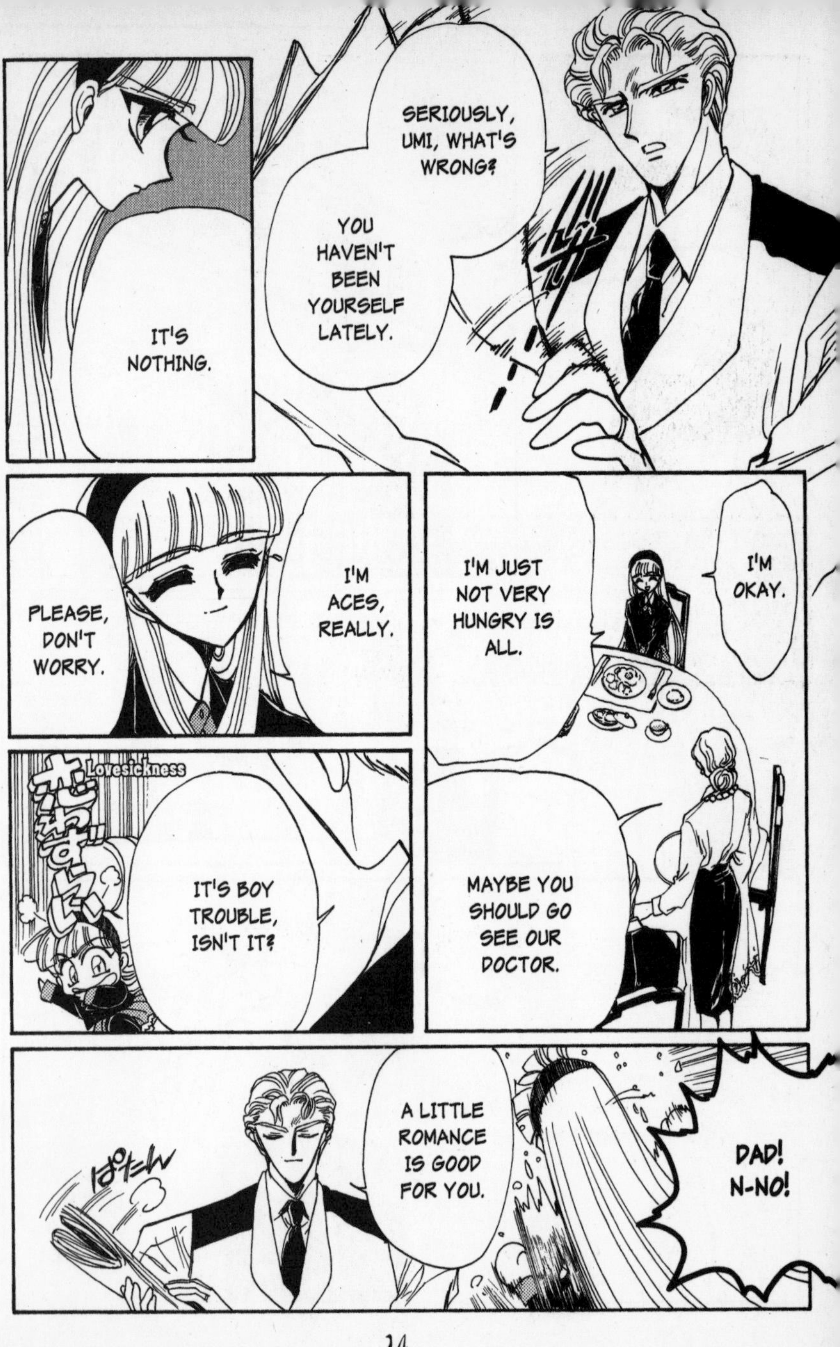
SERIOUSLY, UMI, WHAT'S WRONG?
YOU HAVEN'T BEEN YOURSELF LATELY.
IT'S NOTHING.
I'M OKAY.
I'M JUST NOT VERY HUNGRY IS ALL.
MAYBE YOU SHOULD GO SEE OUR DOCTOR.
I'M ACES, REALLY.
PLEASE, DON'T WORRY.
Lovesickness
IT'S BOY TROUBLE, ISN'T IT?
A LITTLE ROMANCE IS GOOD FOR YOU.
DAD! N-NO!

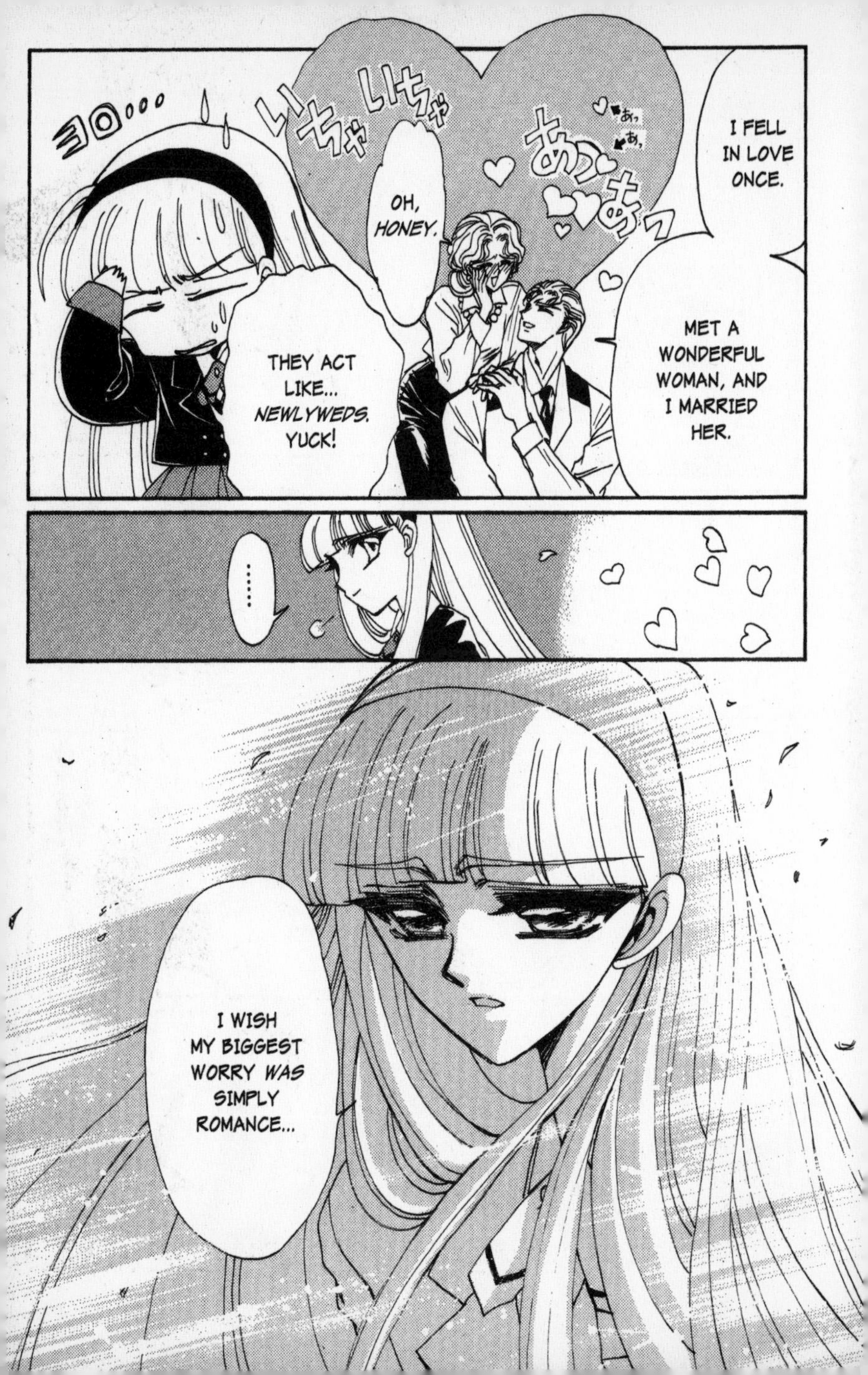
I FELL IN LOVE ONCE.
MET A WONDERFUL WOMAN, AND I MARRIED HER.
あっあっ
OH, HONEY.
いちゃいちゃ
THEY ACT LIKE... NEWLYWEDS. YUCK!
......
I WISH MY BIGGEST WORRY WAS SIMPLY ROMANCE...

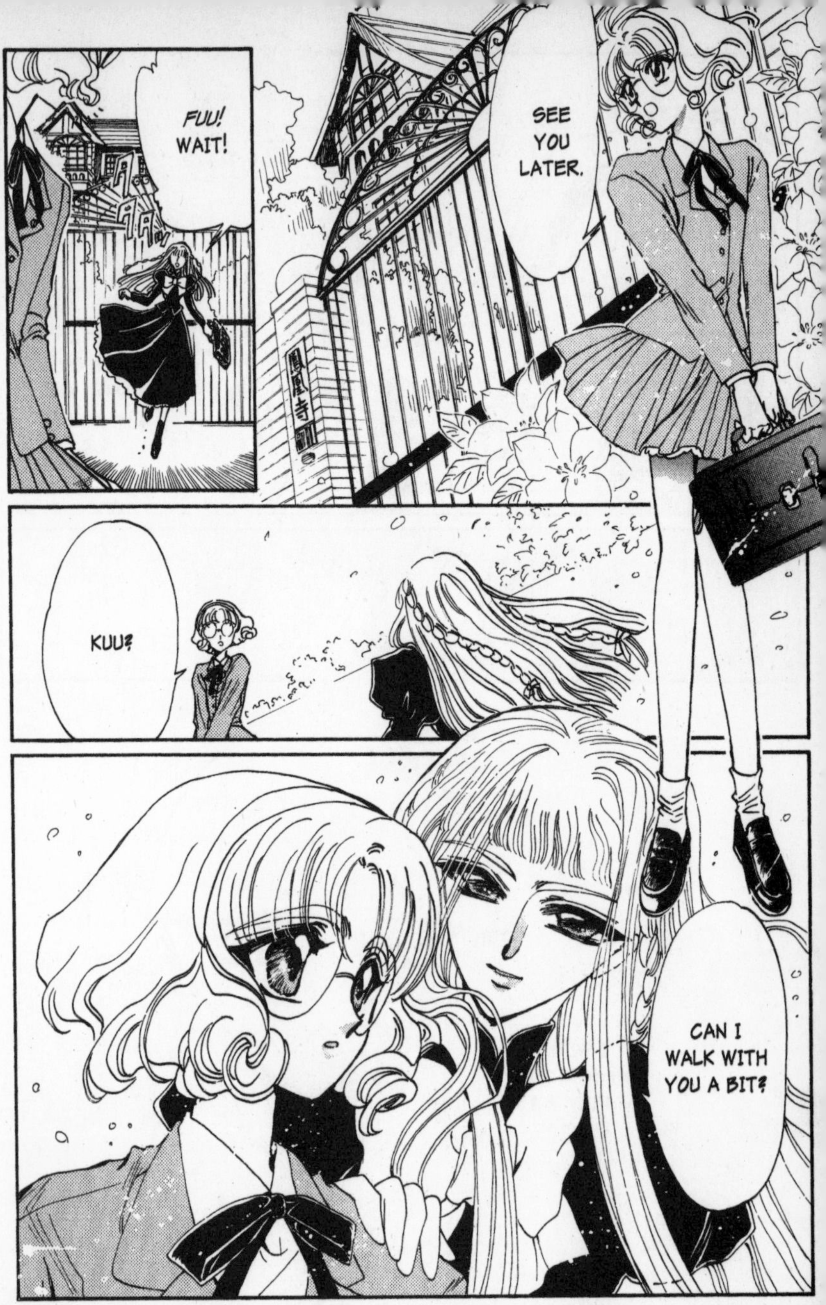
SEE YOU LATER.
FUU! WAIT!
KUU?
CAN I WALK WITH YOU A BIT?

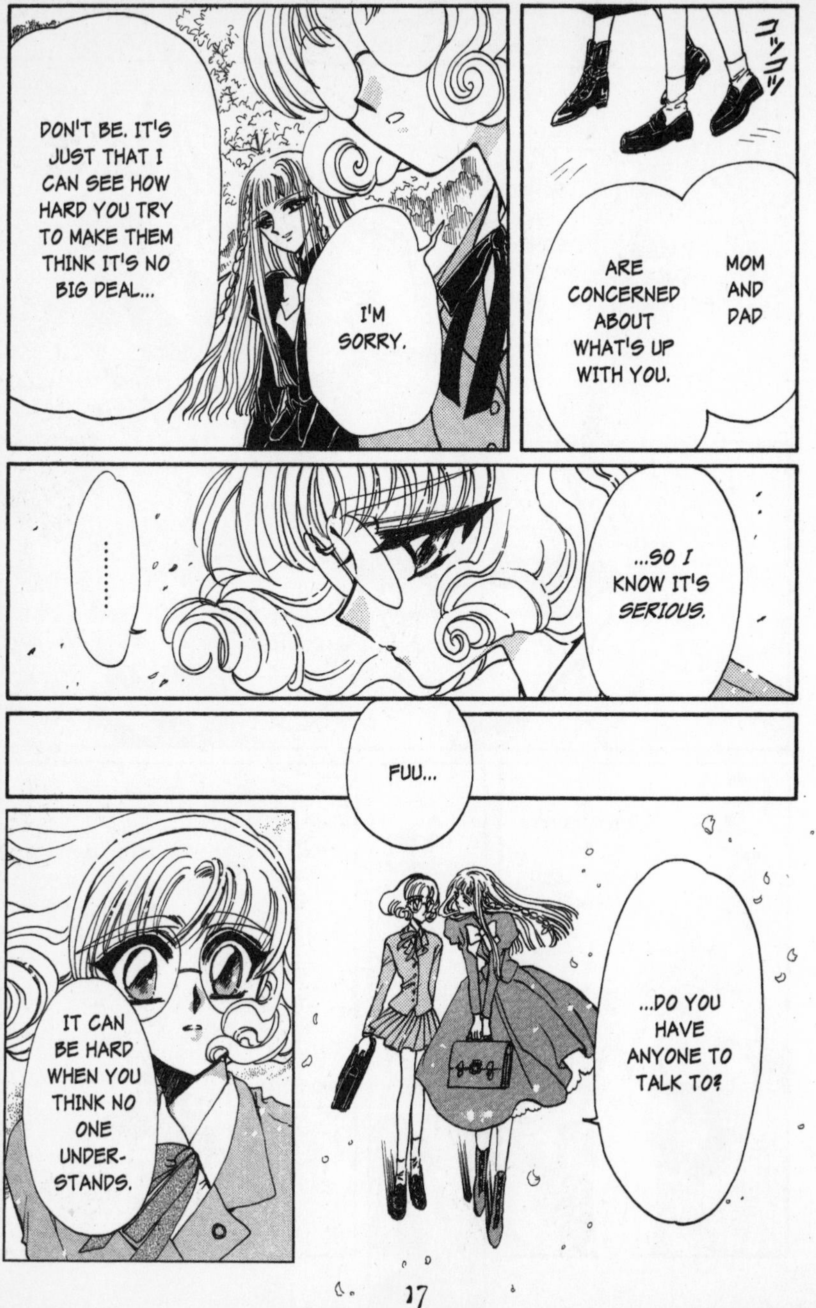
コッコッ
MOM AND DAD
ARE CONCERNED ABOUT WHAT'S UP WITH YOU.
I'M SORRY.
DON'T BE. IT'S JUST THAT I CAN SEE HOW HARD YOU TRY TO MAKE THEM THINK IT'S NO BIG DEAL...
...SO I KNOW IT'S *SERIOUS.*
......
FUU...
...DO YOU HAVE ANYONE TO TALK TO?
IT CAN BE HARD WHEN YOU THINK NO ONE UNDER-STANDS.

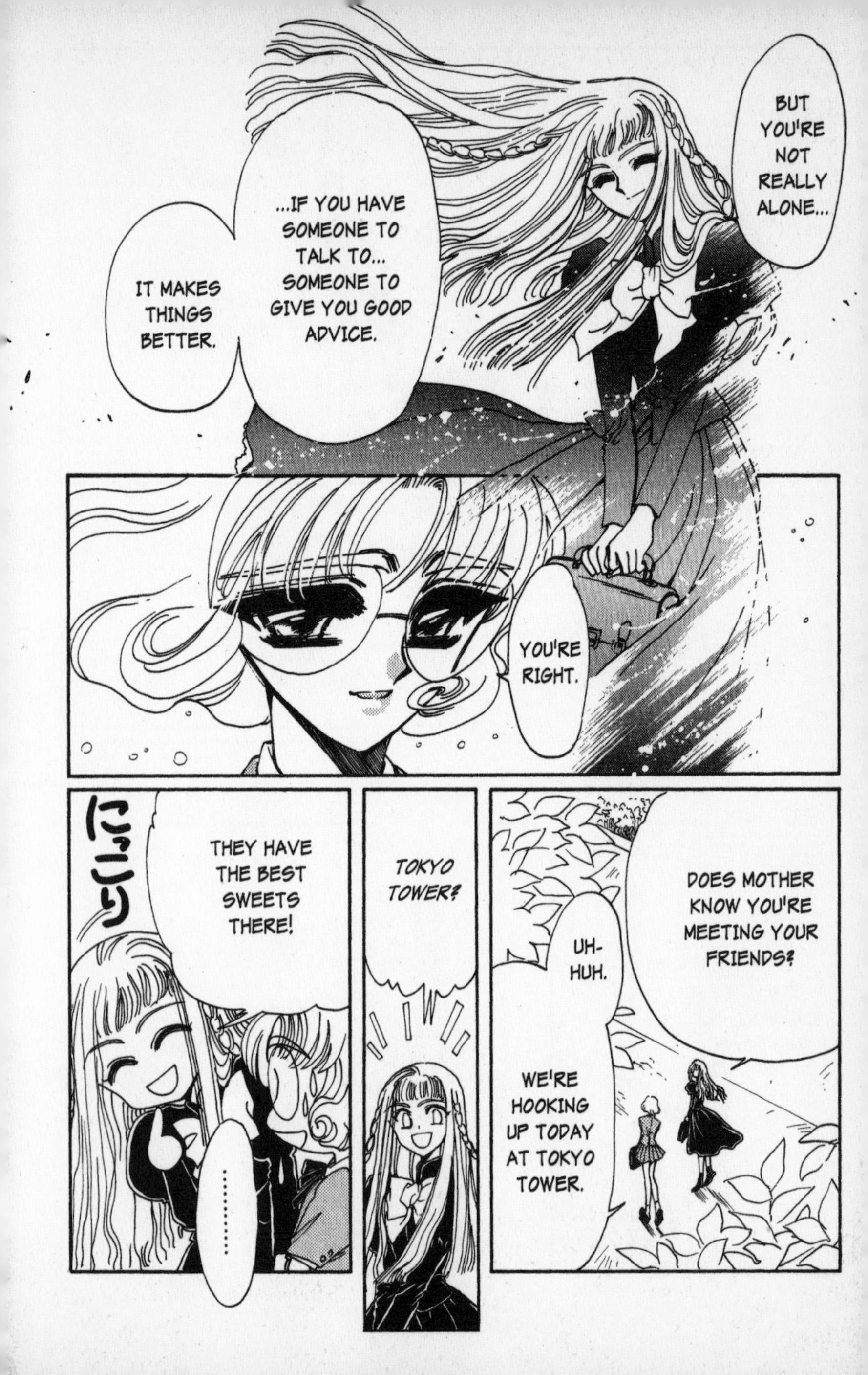
BUT YOU'RE NOT REALLY ALONE...
...IF YOU HAVE SOMEONE TO TALK TO... SOMEONE TO GIVE YOU GOOD ADVICE.
IT MAKES THINGS BETTER.
YOU'RE RIGHT.
DOES MOTHER KNOW YOU'RE MEETING YOUR FRIENDS?
UH-HUH.
WE'RE HOOKING UP TODAY AT TOKYO TOWER.
TOKYO TOWER?
THEY HAVE THE BEST SWEETS THERE!
にっこり
....

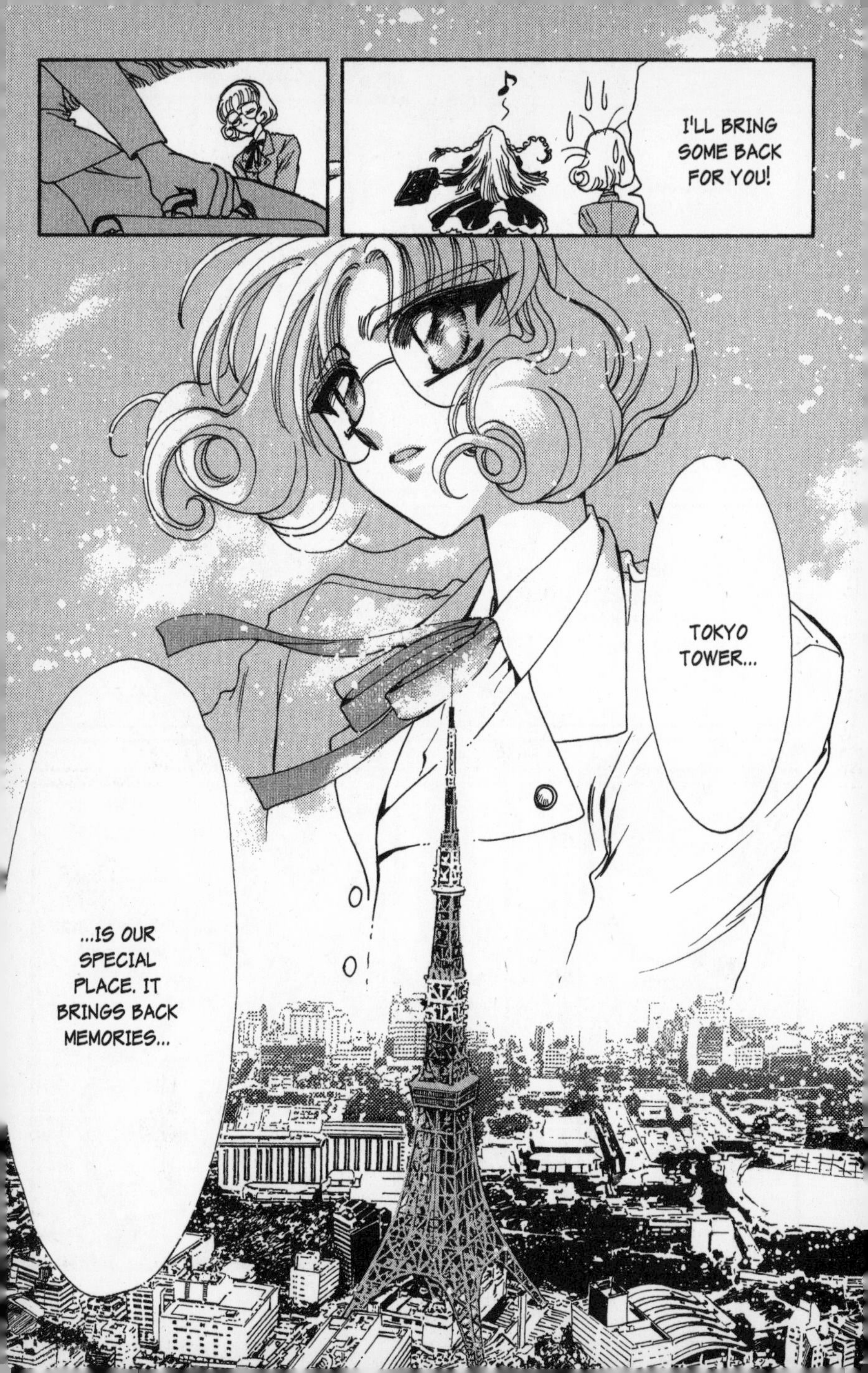
I'LL BRING SOME BACK FOR YOU!
TOKYO TOWER...
...IS OUR SPECIAL PLACE. IT BRINGS BACK MEMORIES...

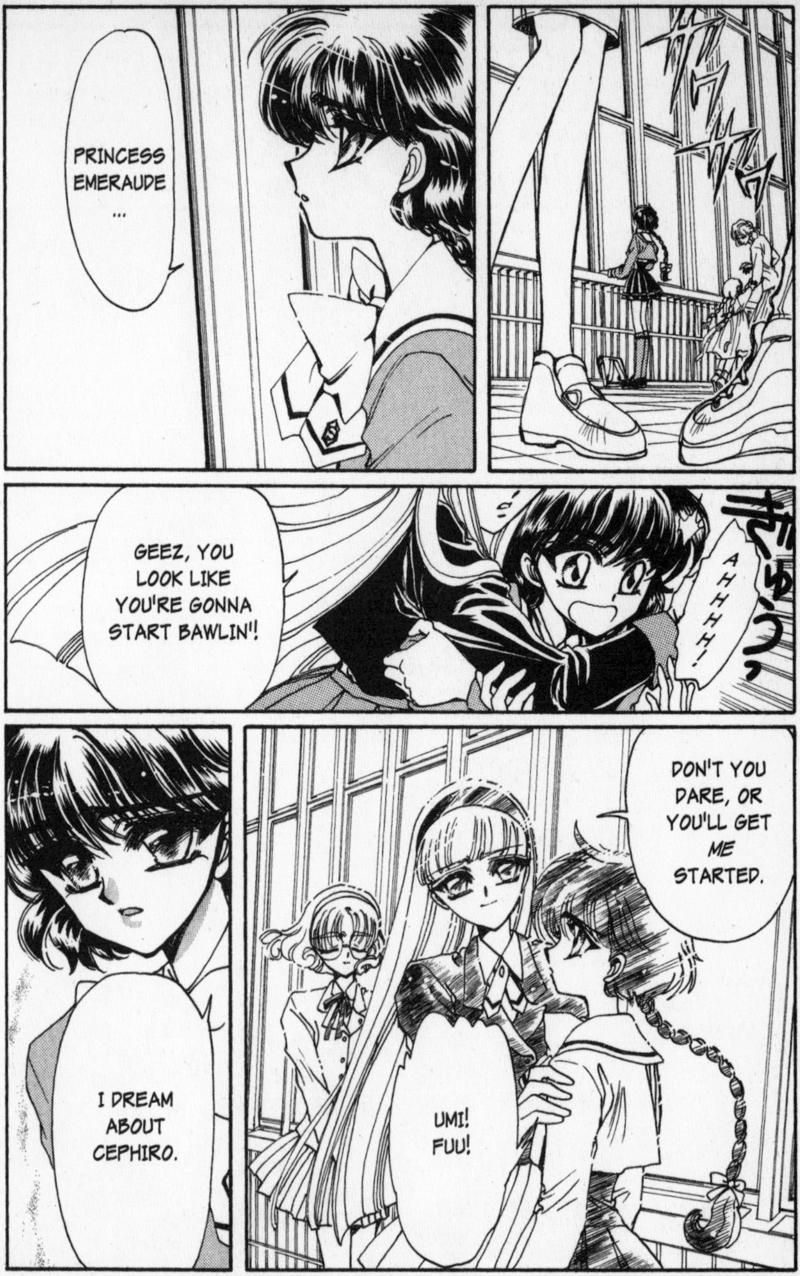
PRINCESS EMERAUDE ...
AHHHH!
GEEZ, YOU LOOK LIKE YOU'RE GONNA START BAWLIN'!
DON'T YOU DARE, OR YOU'LL GET *ME* STARTED.
UMI! FUU!
I DREAM ABOUT CEPHIRO.

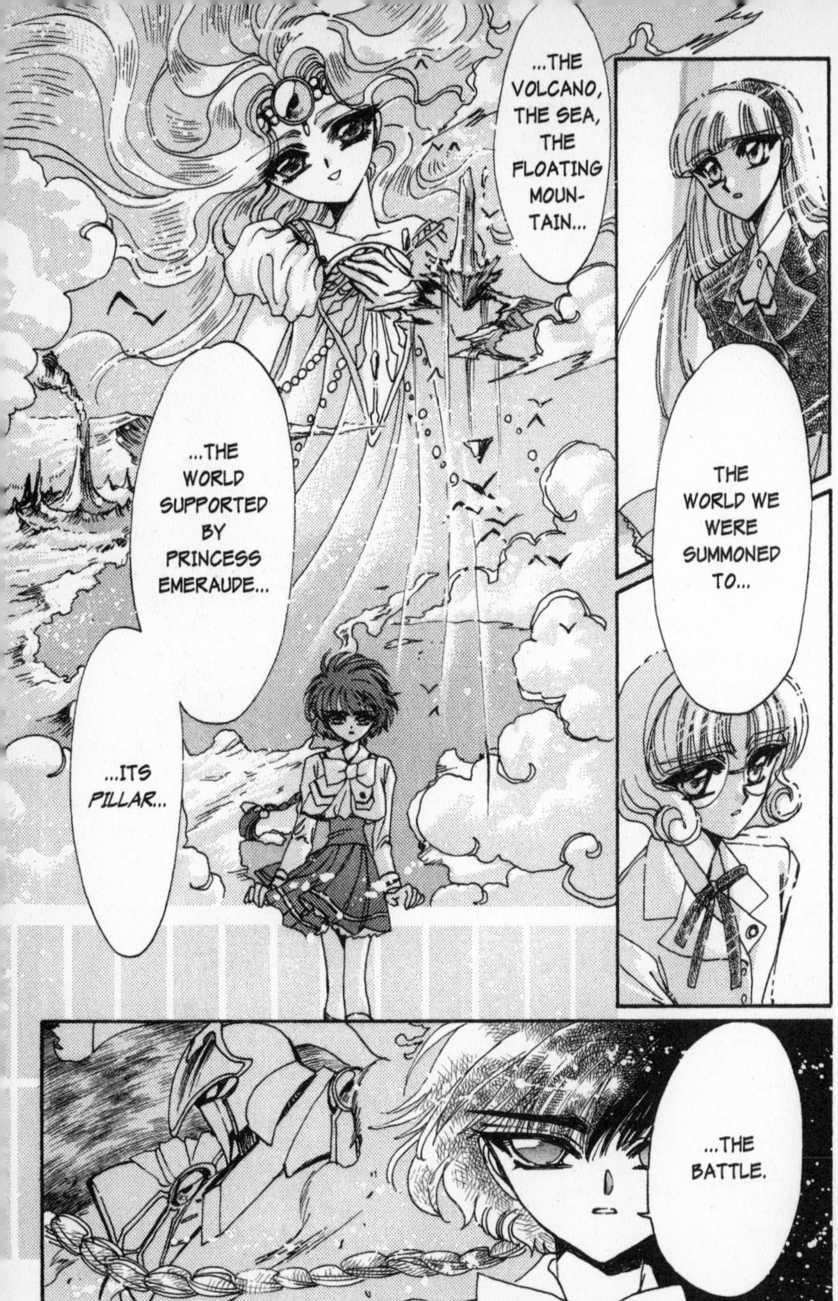
THE WORLD WE WERE SUMMONED TO...
...THE VOLCANO, THE SEA, THE FLOATING MOUN-TAIN...
...THE WORLD SUPPORTED BY PRINCESS EMERAUDE...
...ITS PILLAR...
...THE BATTLE.

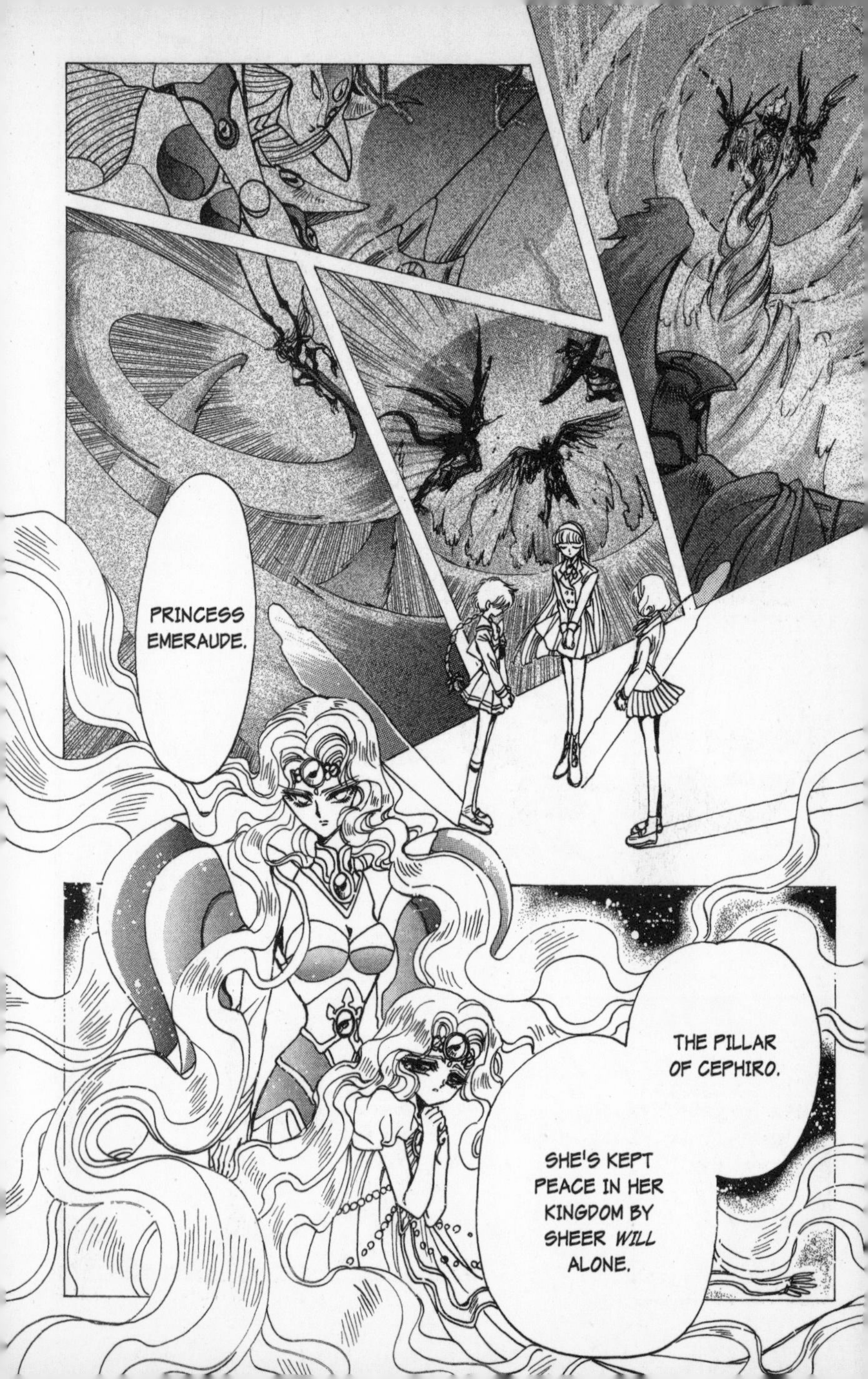
PRINCESS EMERAUDE.
THE PILLAR OF CEPHIRO.
SHE'S KEPT PEACE IN HER KINGDOM BY SHEER *WILL* ALONE.

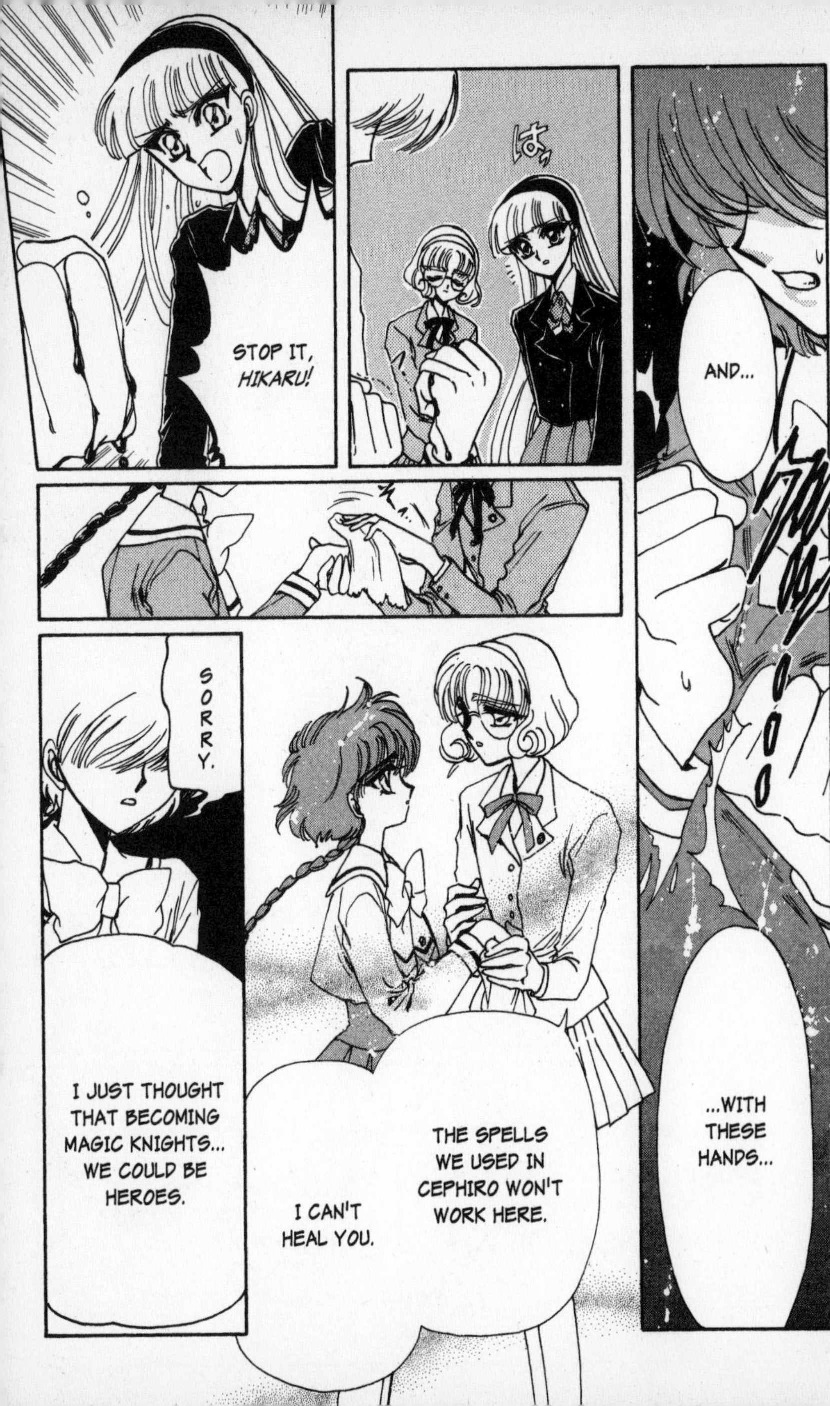
AND...
...WITH THESE HANDS...
はっ
STOP IT, HIKARU!
SORRY.
THE SPELLS WE USED IN CEPHIRO WON'T WORK HERE.
I CAN'T HEAL YOU.
I JUST THOUGHT THAT BECOMING MAGIC KNIGHTS... WE COULD BE HEROES.

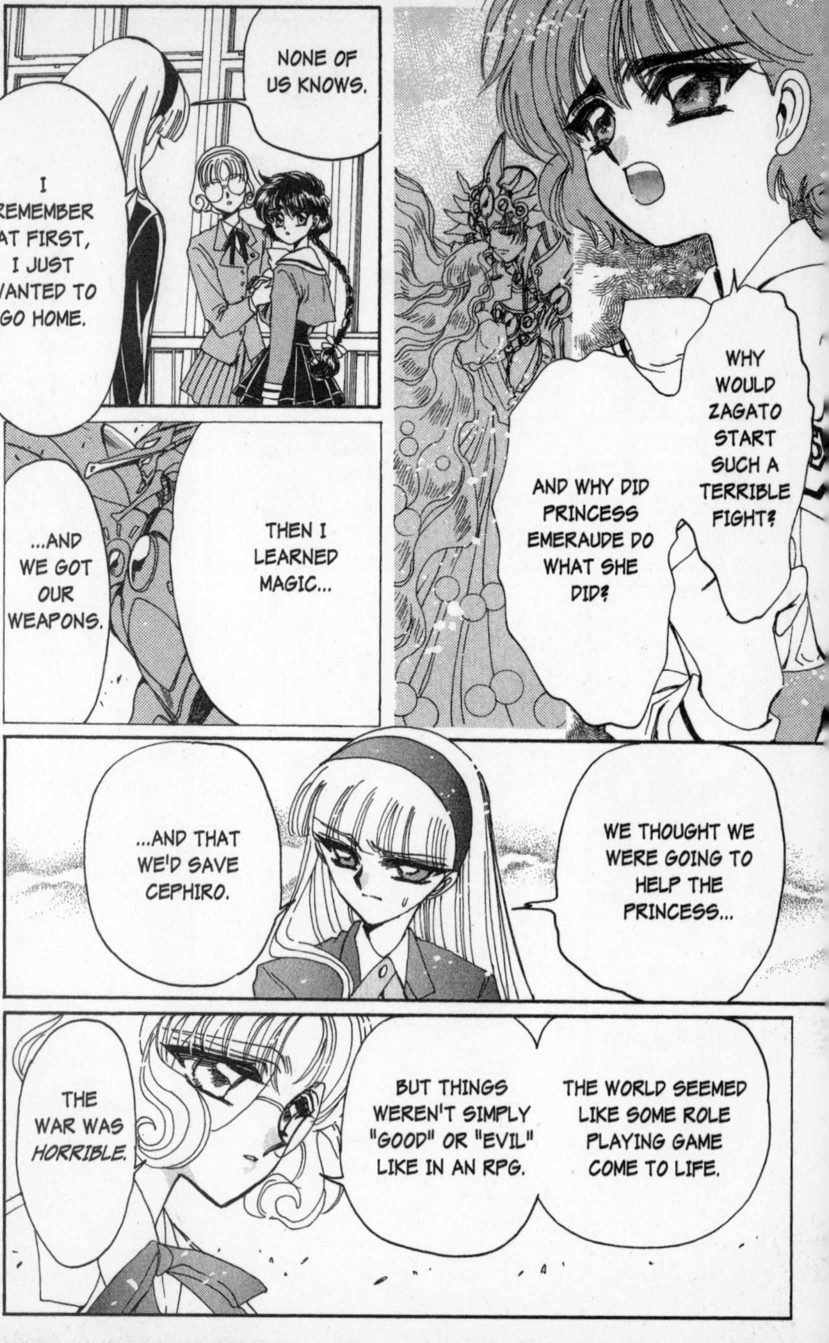
WHY WOULD ZAGATO START SUCH A TERRIBLE FIGHT?
AND WHY DID PRINCESS EMERAUDE DO WHAT SHE DID?
NONE OF US KNOWS.
I REMEMBER AT FIRST, I JUST WANTED TO GO HOME.
THEN I LEARNED MAGIC...
...AND WE GOT OUR WEAPONS.
WE THOUGHT WE WERE GOING TO HELP THE PRINCESS...
...AND THAT WE'D SAVE CEPHIRO.
THE WORLD SEEMED LIKE SOME ROLE PLAYING GAME COME TO LIFE.
BUT THINGS WEREN'T SIMPLY "GOOD" OR "EVIL" LIKE IN AN RPG.
THE WAR WAS *HORRIBLE.*

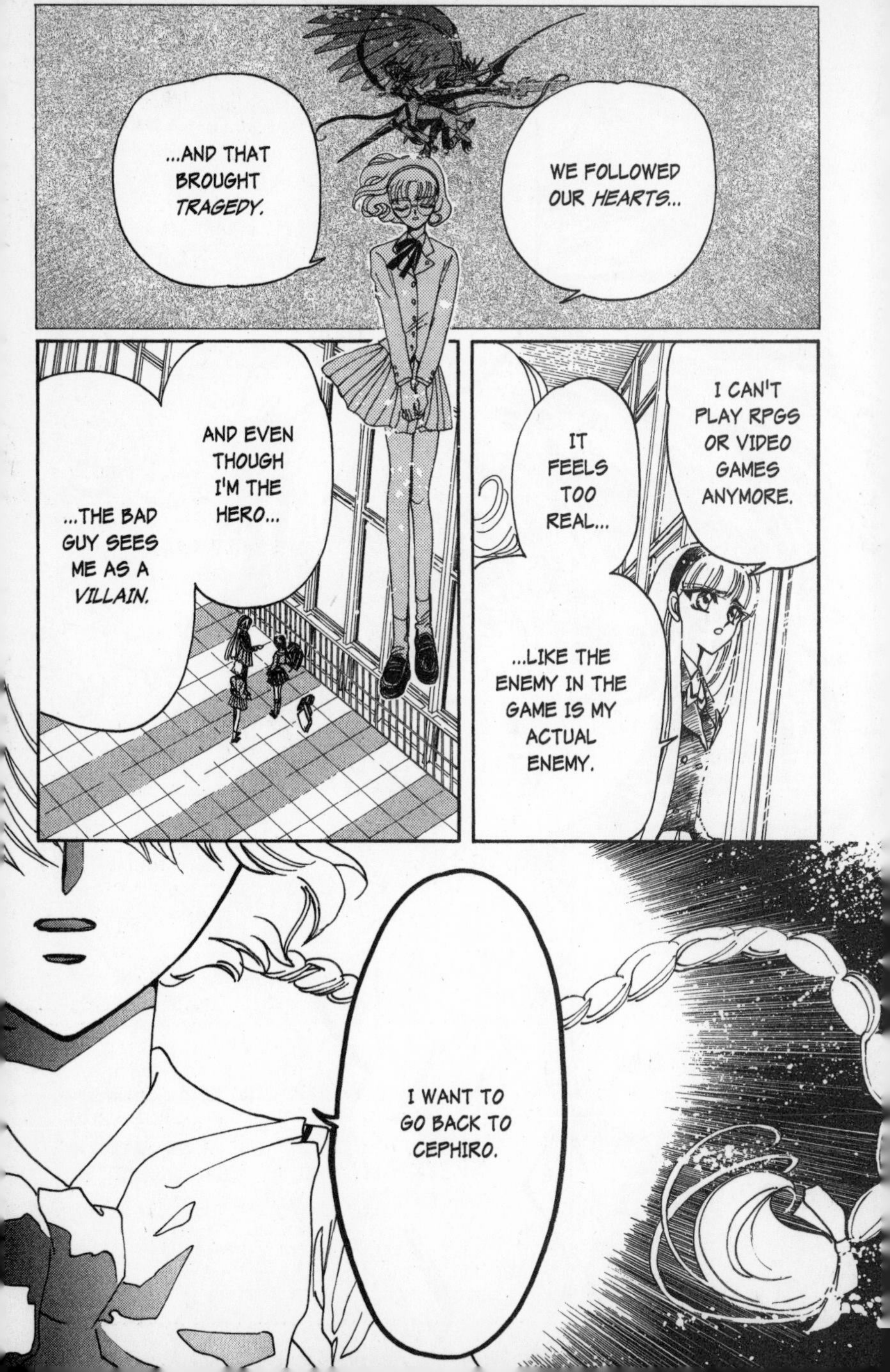
WE FOLLOWED OUR *HEARTS*...
...AND THAT BROUGHT *TRAGEDY.*
I CAN'T PLAY RPGS OR VIDEO GAMES ANYMORE.
IT FEELS TOO REAL...
...LIKE THE ENEMY IN THE GAME IS MY ACTUAL ENEMY.
AND EVEN THOUGH I'M THE HERO...
...THE BAD GUY SEES ME AS A *VILLAIN.*
I WANT TO GO BACK TO CEPHIRO.

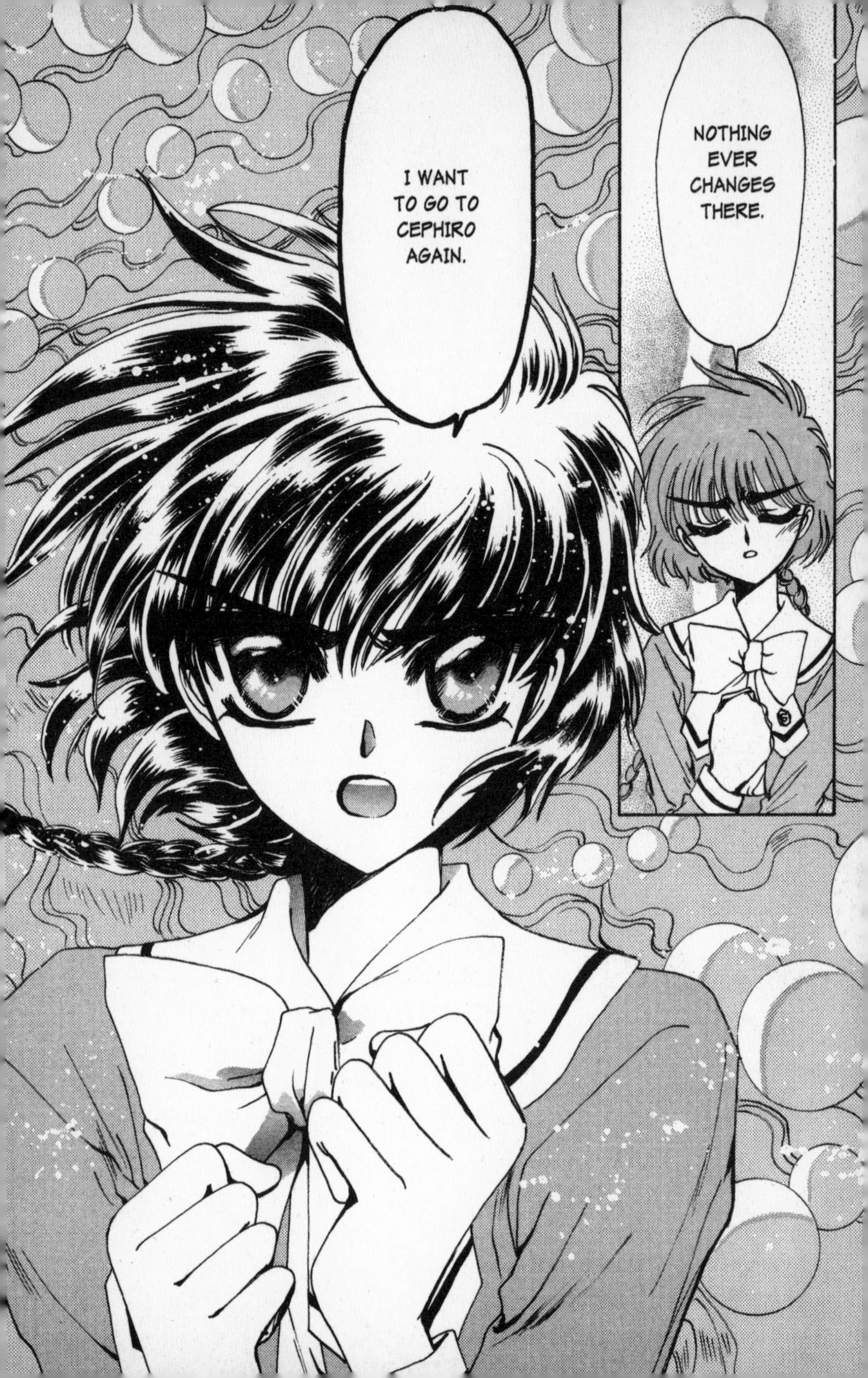
NOTHING EVER CHANGES THERE.
I WANT TO GO TO CEPHIRO AGAIN.

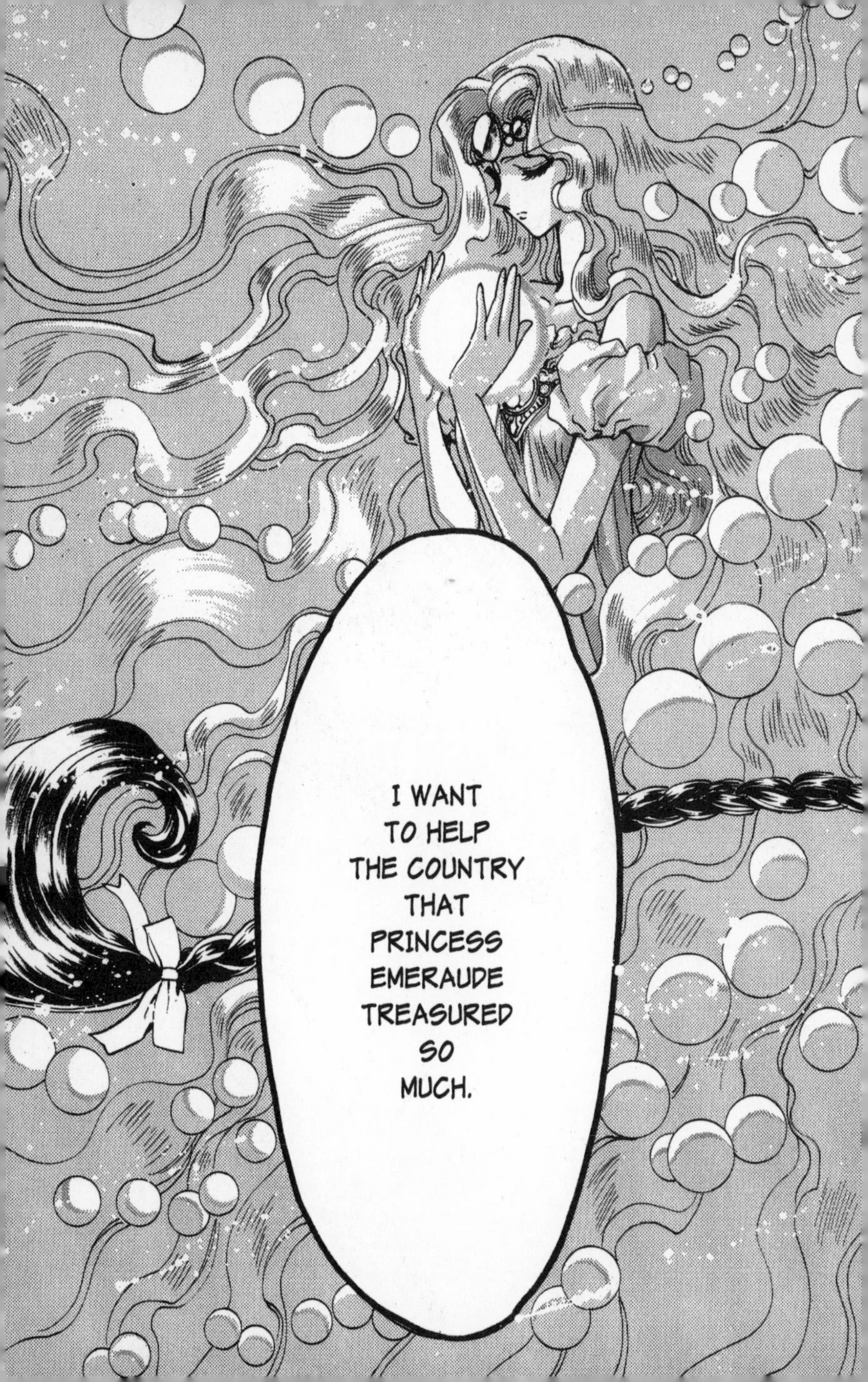
I WANT TO HELP THE COUNTRY THAT PRINCESS EMERAUDE TREASURED SO MUCH.

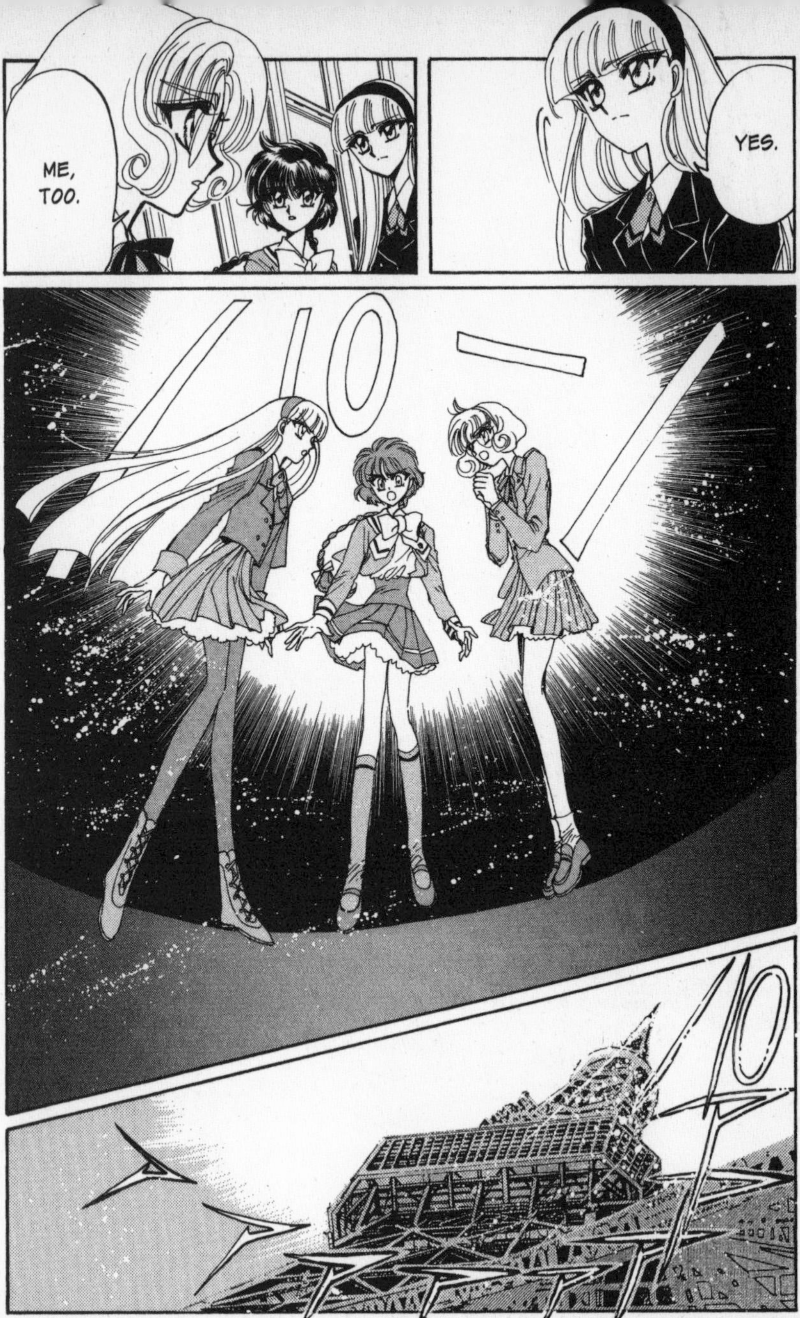
YES.
ME, TOO.

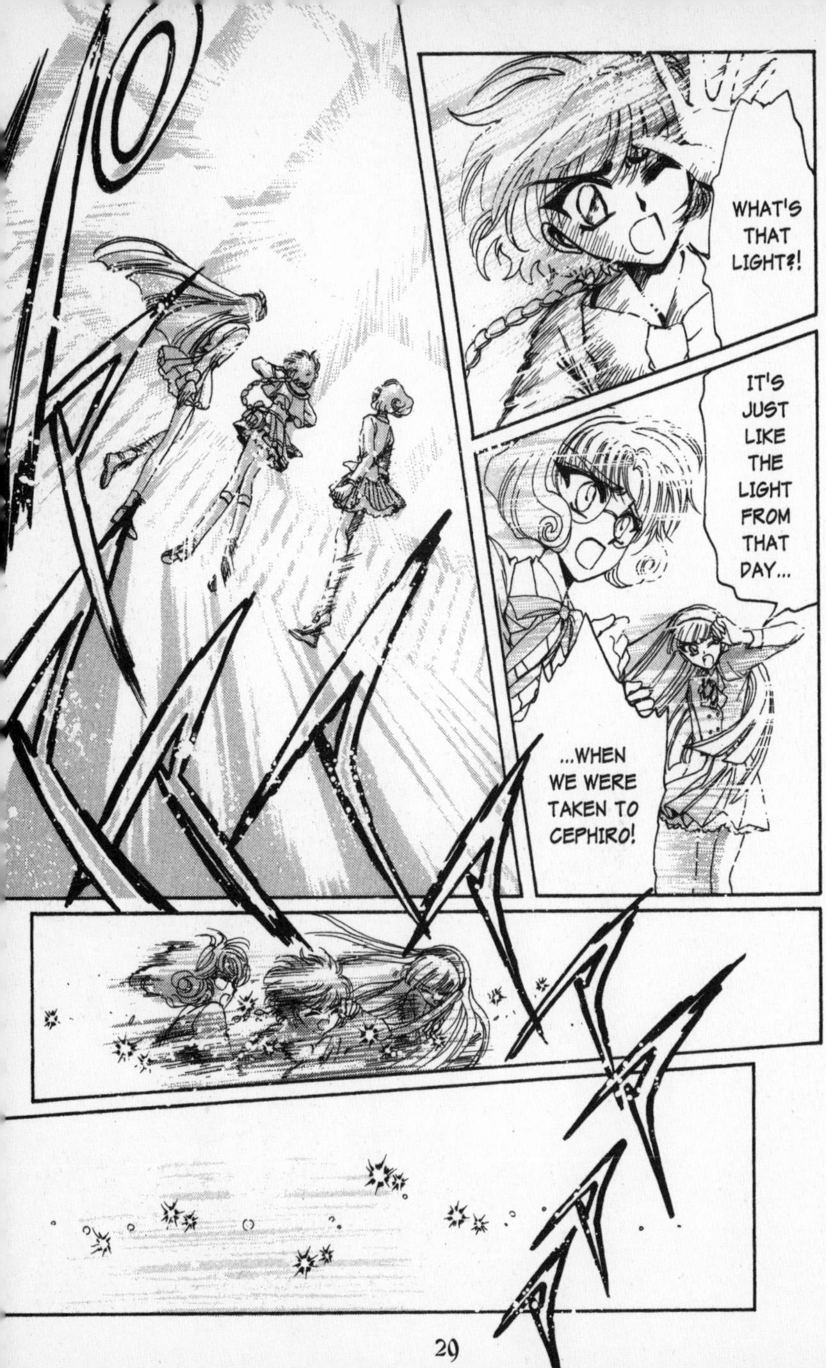

WHAT'S THAT LIGHT?!
IT'S JUST LIKE THE LIGHT FROM THAT DAY...
...WHEN WE WERE TAKEN TO CEPHIRO!

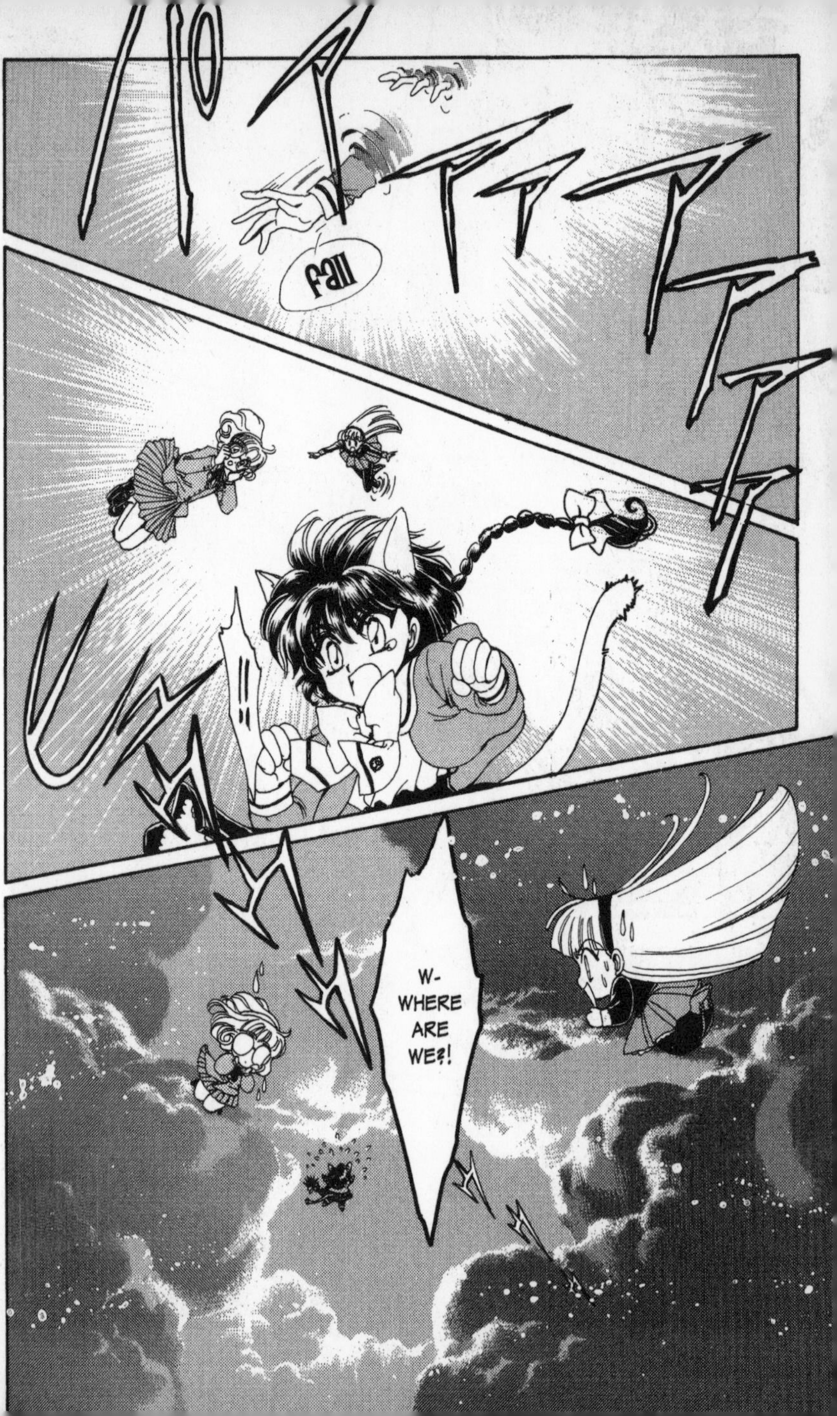
パアアアアアア
fall
いいいいい
W-
WHERE
ARE
WE?!

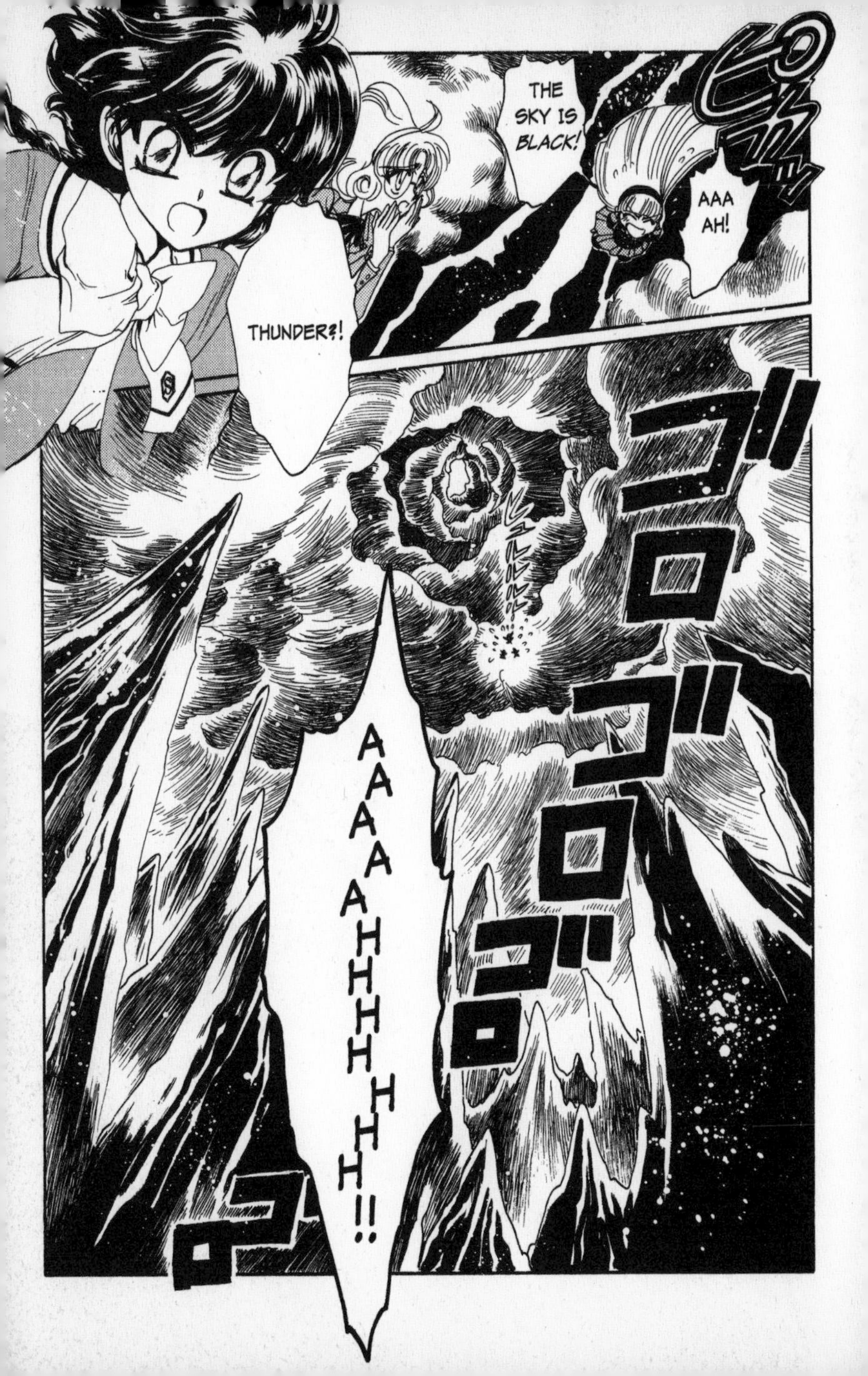
AAA AH!
THE SKY IS BLACK!
THUNDER?!
ゴロゴロゴロ
AAAAAHHHHHHH!!

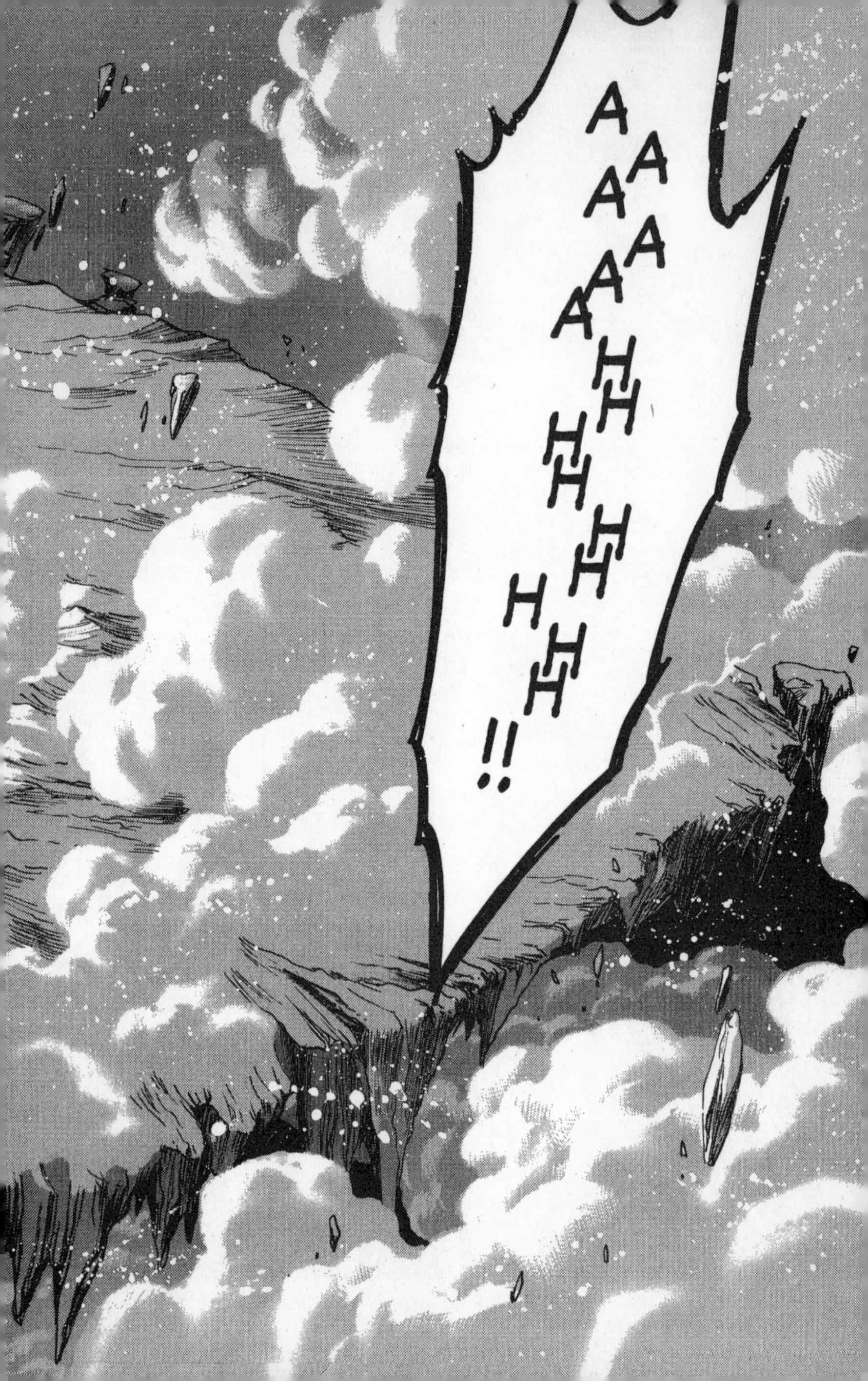
AAAAAAHHHHHHHHHHH!!

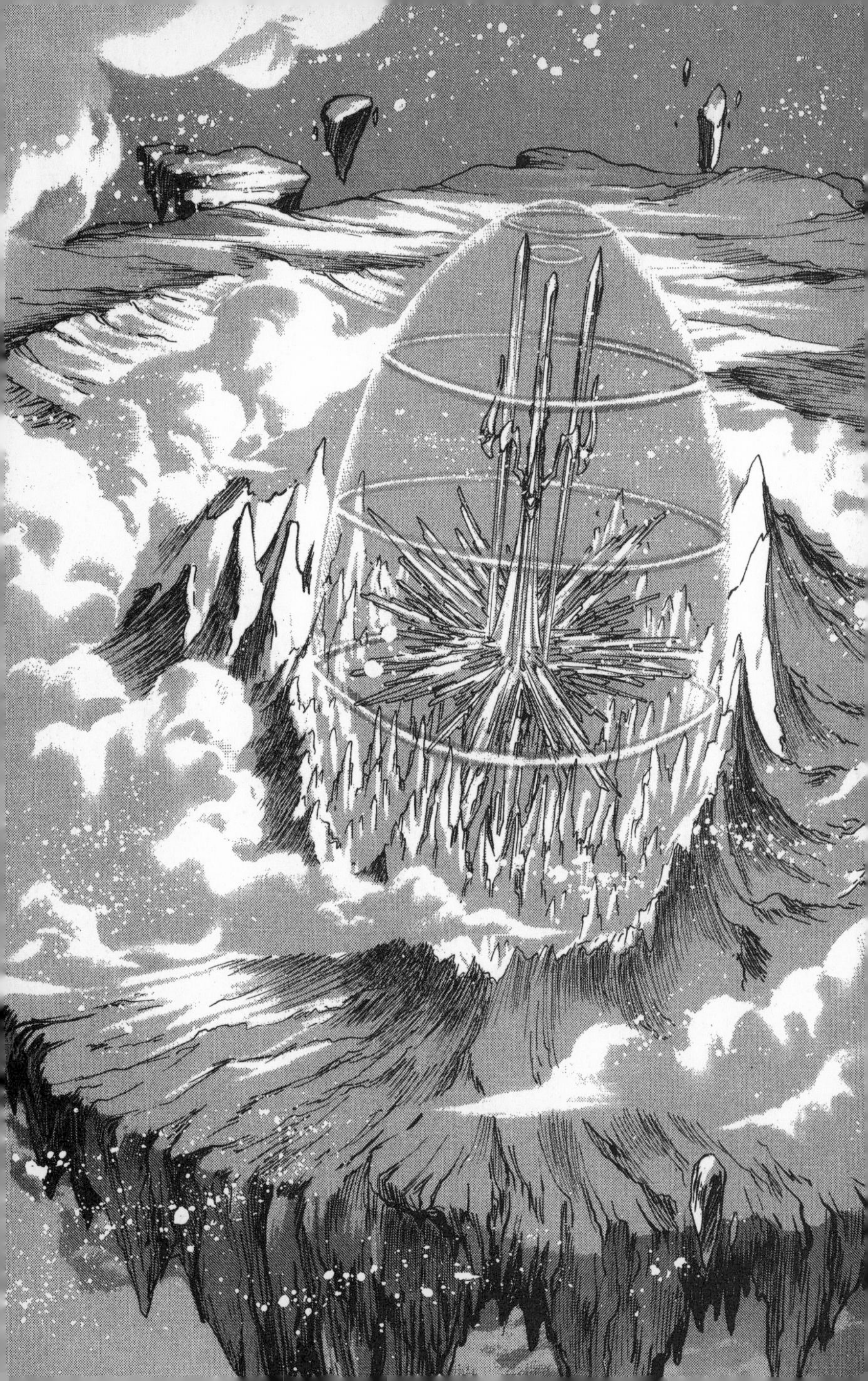

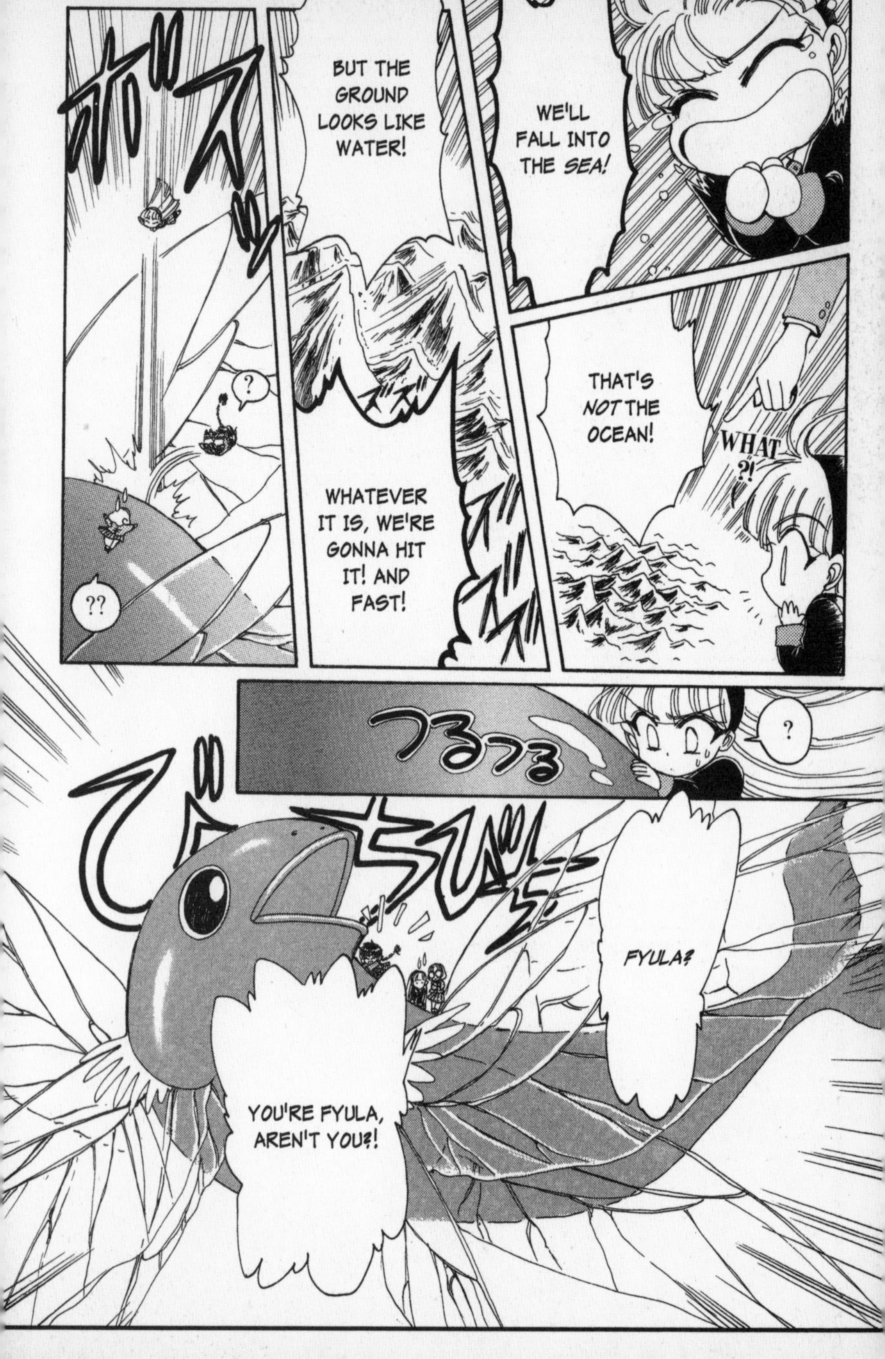

WE'LL FALL INTO THE *SEA!*
THAT'S *NOT* THE OCEAN!
WHAT?!
BUT THE GROUND LOOKS LIKE WATER!
WHATEVER IT IS, WE'RE GONNA HIT IT! AND FAST!
ボズ
?
??
?
つるつる
FYULA?
YOU'RE FYULA, AREN'T YOU?!

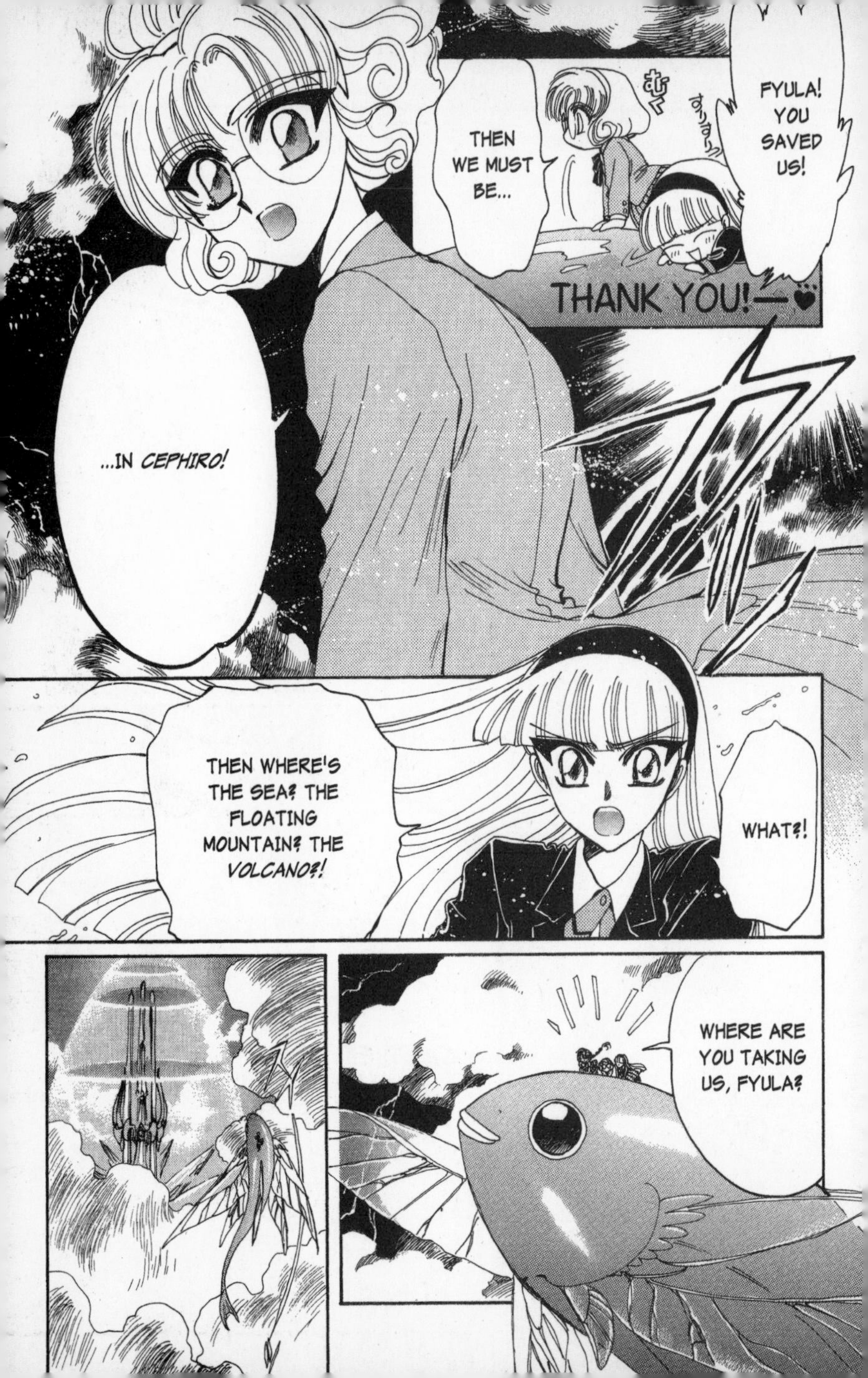
FYULA! YOU SAVED US!
THANK YOU!—♥
THEN WE MUST BE...
...IN *CEPHIRO!*
WHAT?!
THEN WHERE'S THE SEA? THE FLOATING MOUNTAIN? THE *VOLCANO?!*
WHERE ARE YOU TAKING US, FYULA?

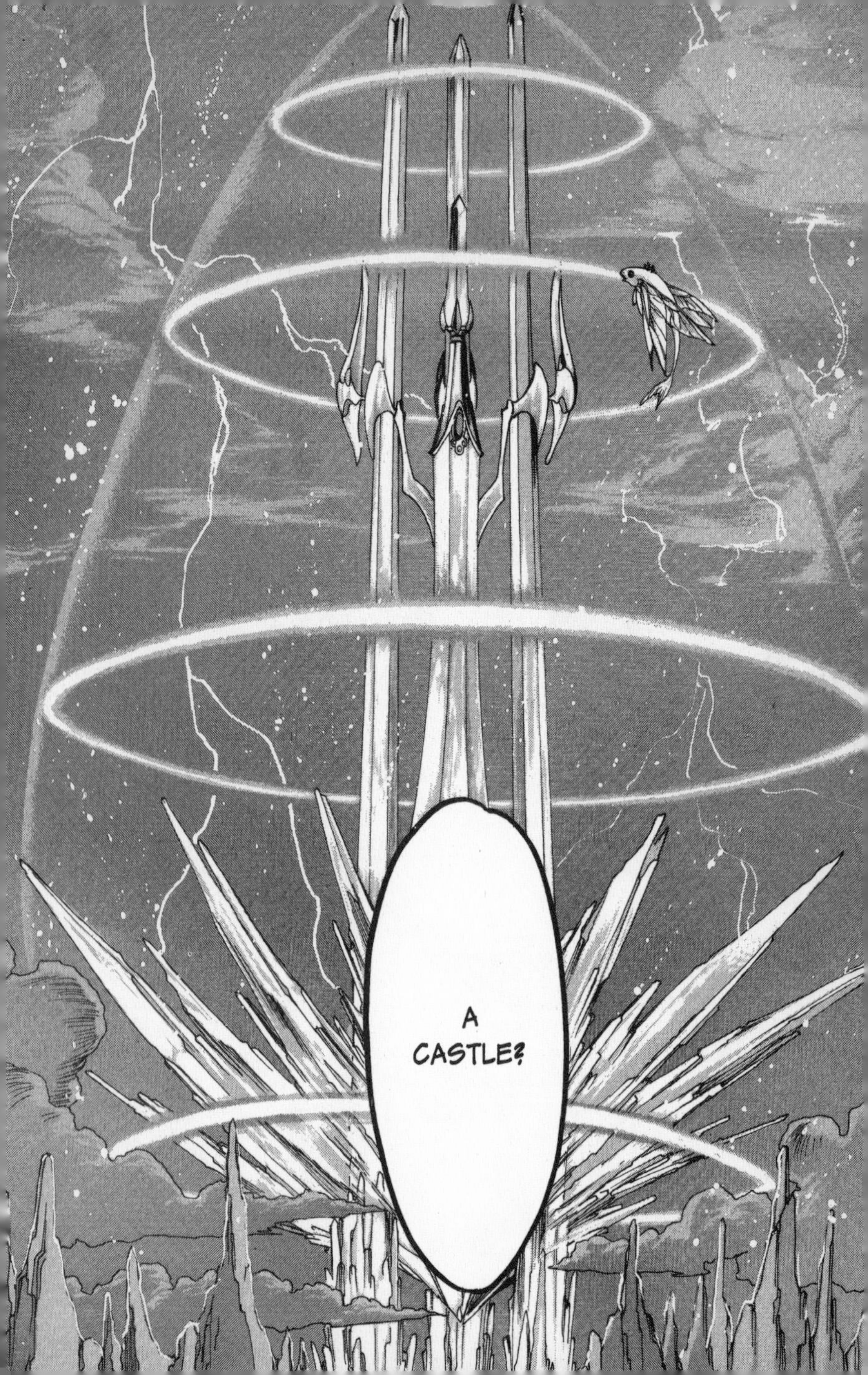
A CASTLE?

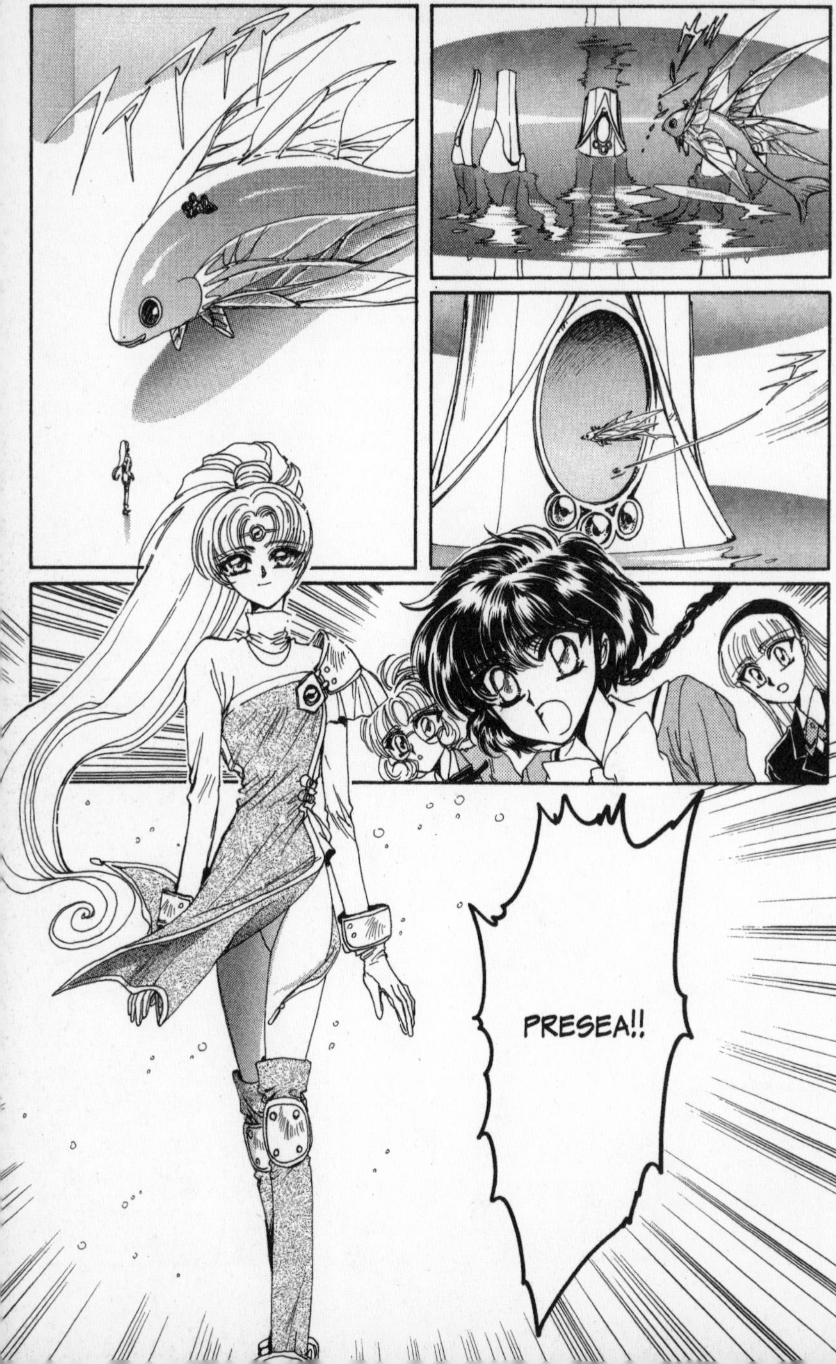
PRESEA!!

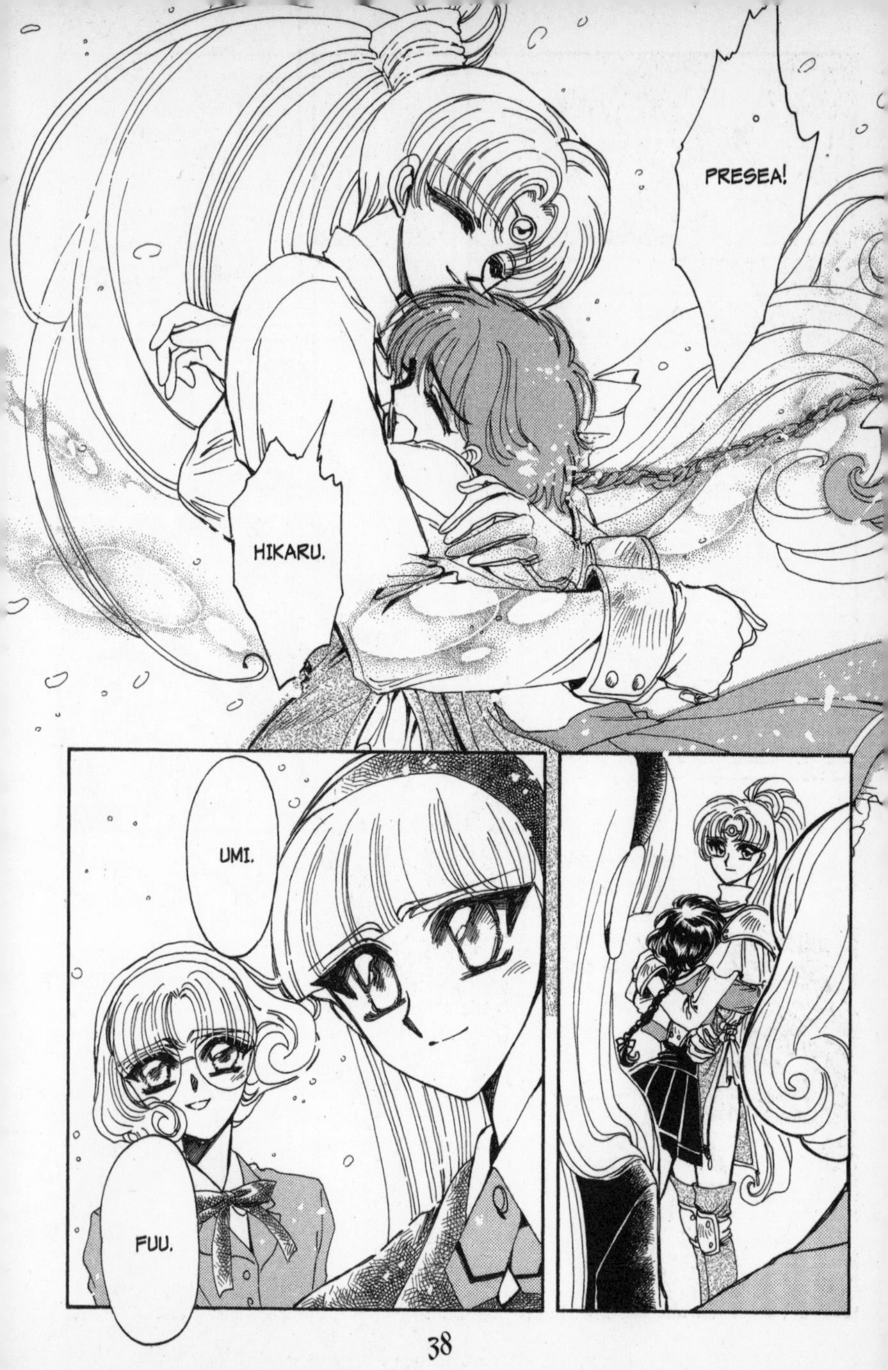
PRESEA!
HIKARU.
UMI.
FUU.

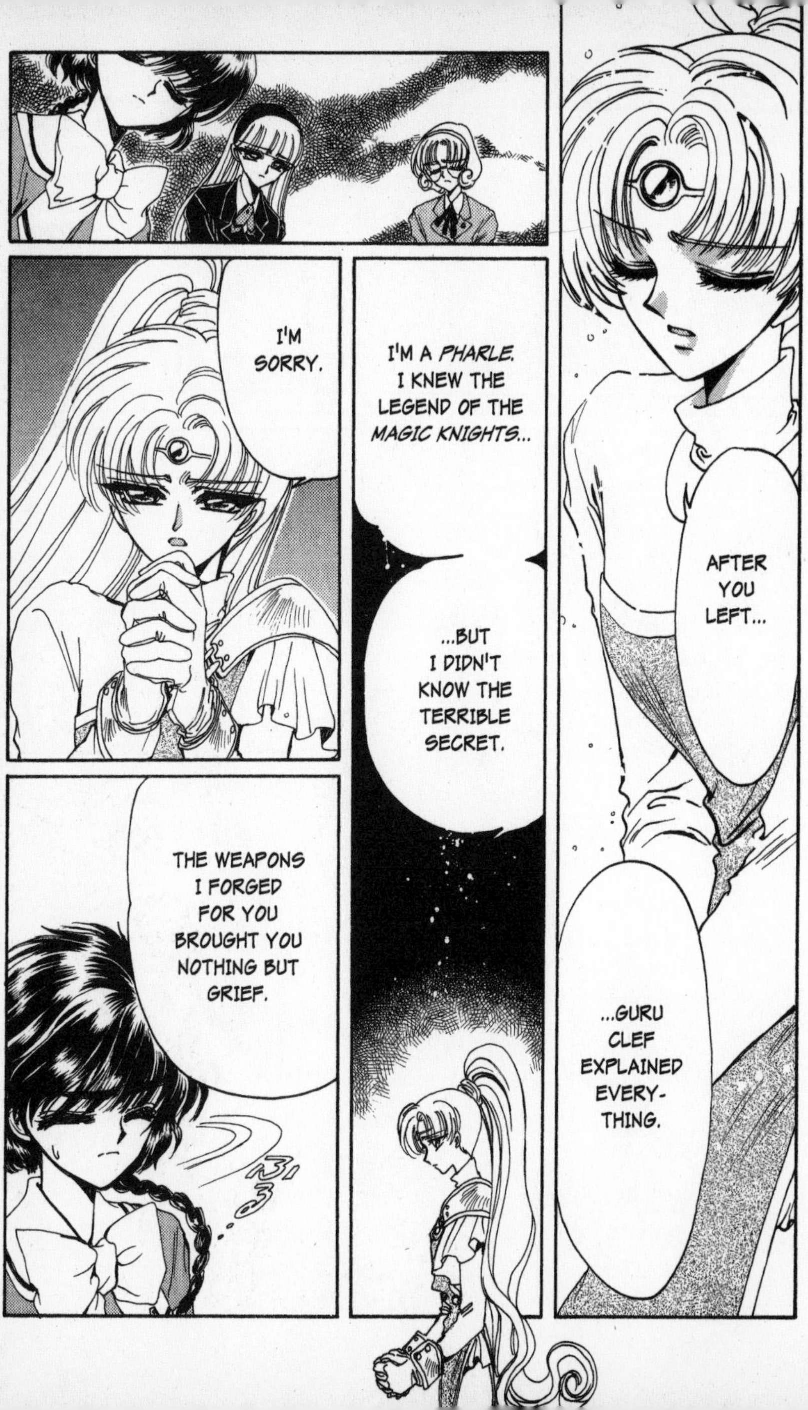
AFTER YOU LEFT...
...GURU CLEF EXPLAINED EVERY-THING.
I'M A *PHARLE.* I KNEW THE LEGEND OF THE *MAGIC KNIGHTS*...
...BUT I DIDN'T KNOW THE TERRIBLE SECRET.
I'M SORRY.
THE WEAPONS I FORGED FOR YOU BROUGHT YOU NOTHING BUT GRIEF.

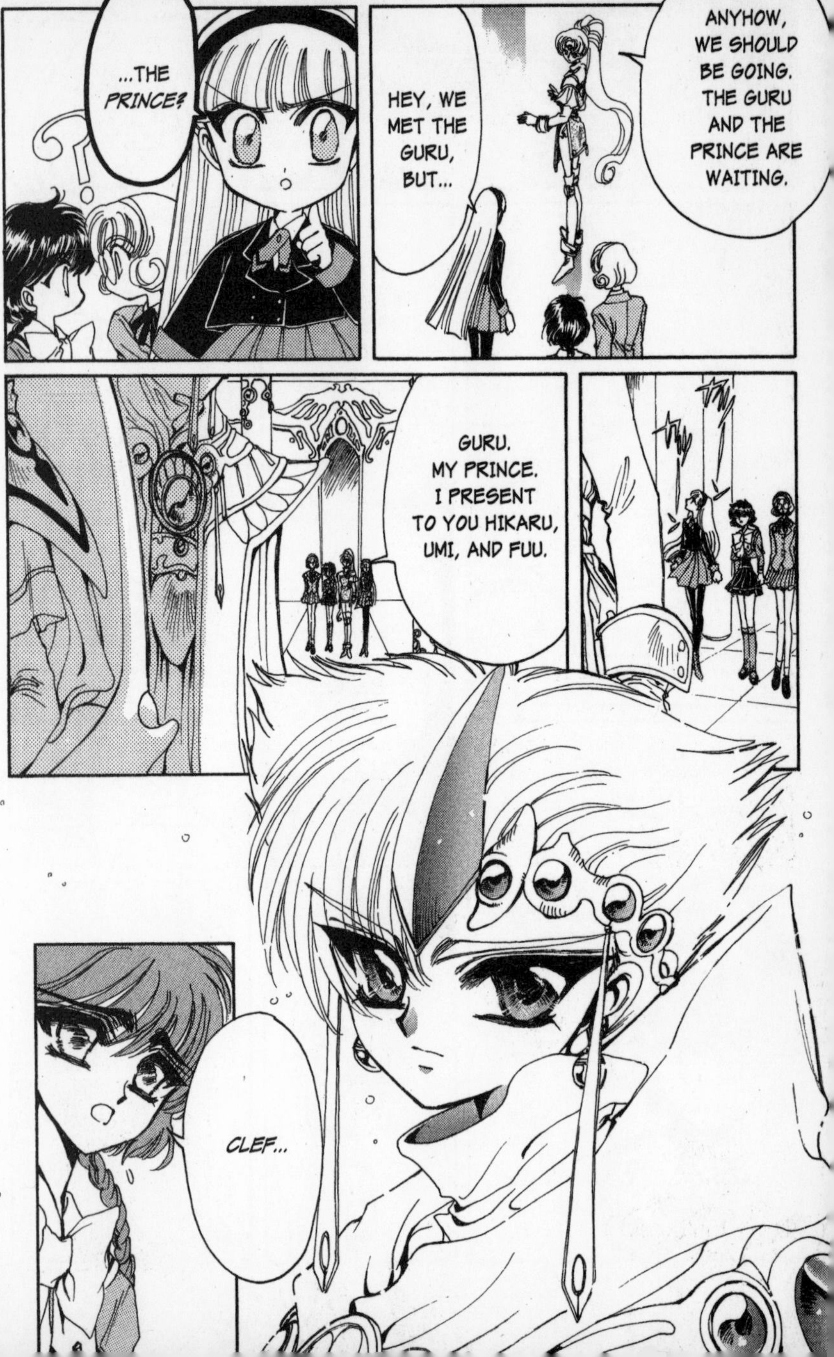
ANYHOW, WE SHOULD BE GOING. THE GURU AND THE PRINCE ARE WAITING.
HEY, WE MET THE GURU, BUT...
...THE *PRINCE?*
GURU. MY PRINCE. I PRESENT TO YOU HIKARU, UMI, AND FUU.
CLEF...

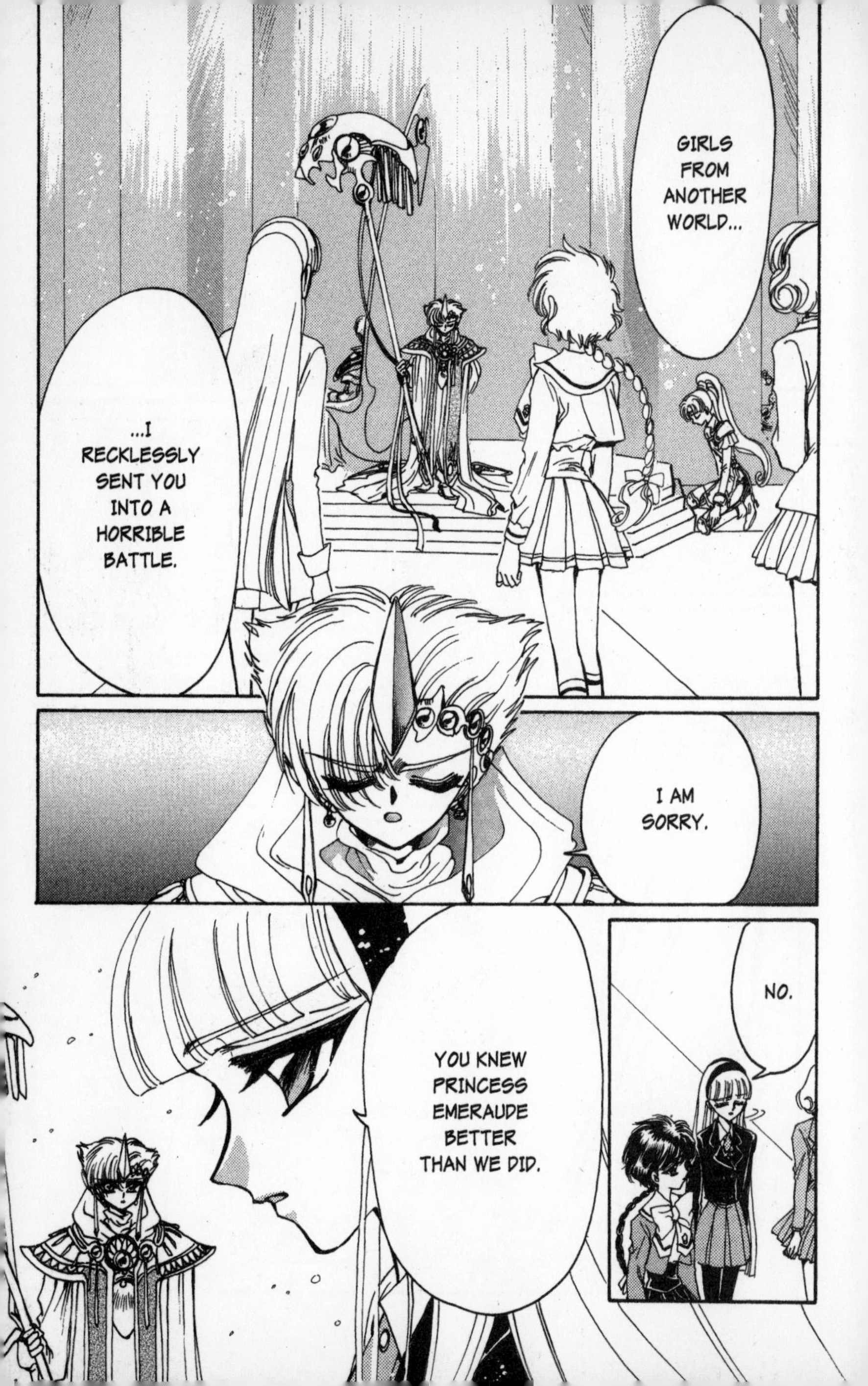
GIRLS FROM ANOTHER WORLD...
...I RECKLESSLY SENT YOU INTO A HORRIBLE BATTLE.
I AM SORRY.
NO.
YOU KNEW PRINCESS EMERAUDE BETTER THAN WE DID.

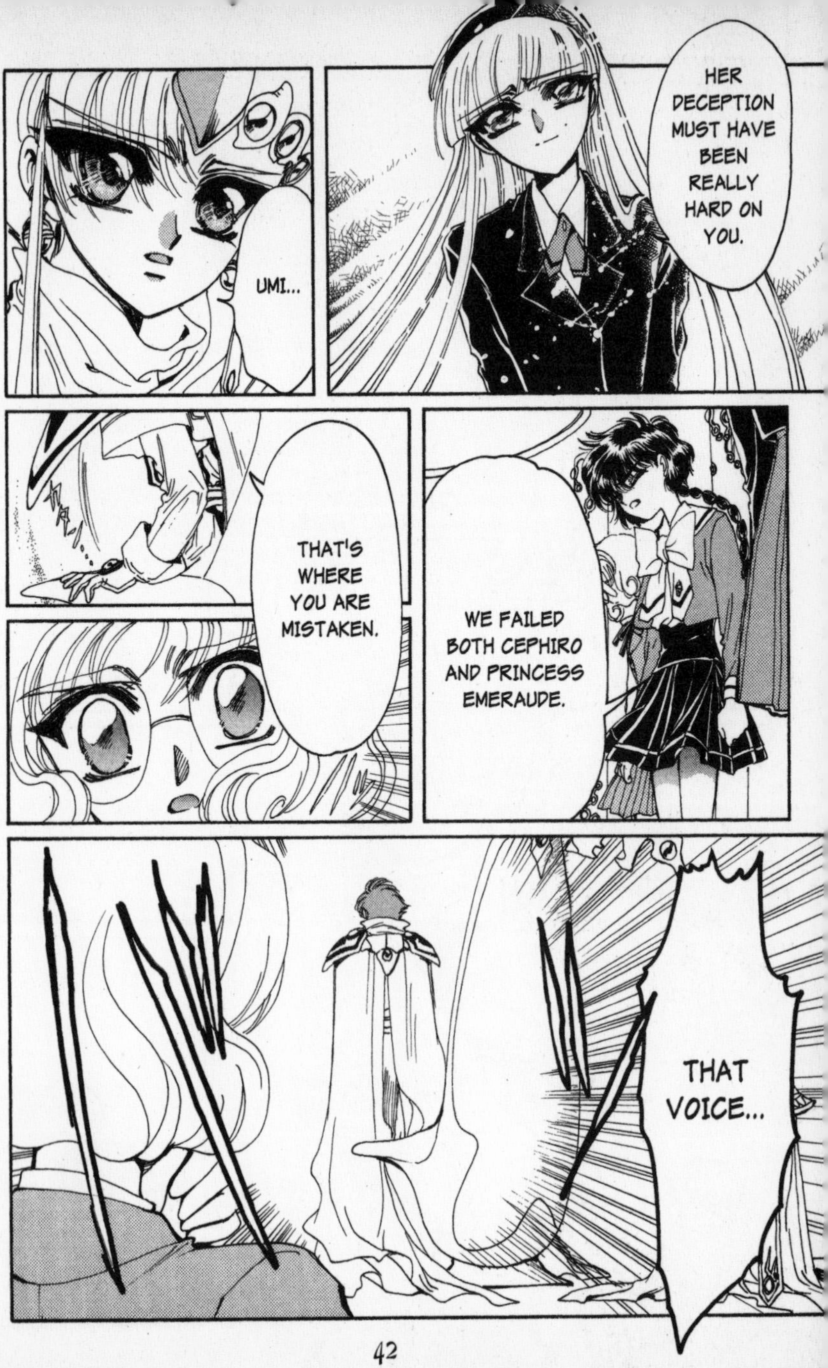
HER DECEPTION MUST HAVE BEEN REALLY HARD ON YOU.
UMI...
WE FAILED BOTH CEPHIRO AND PRINCESS EMERAUDE.
THAT'S WHERE YOU ARE MISTAKEN.
THAT VOICE...

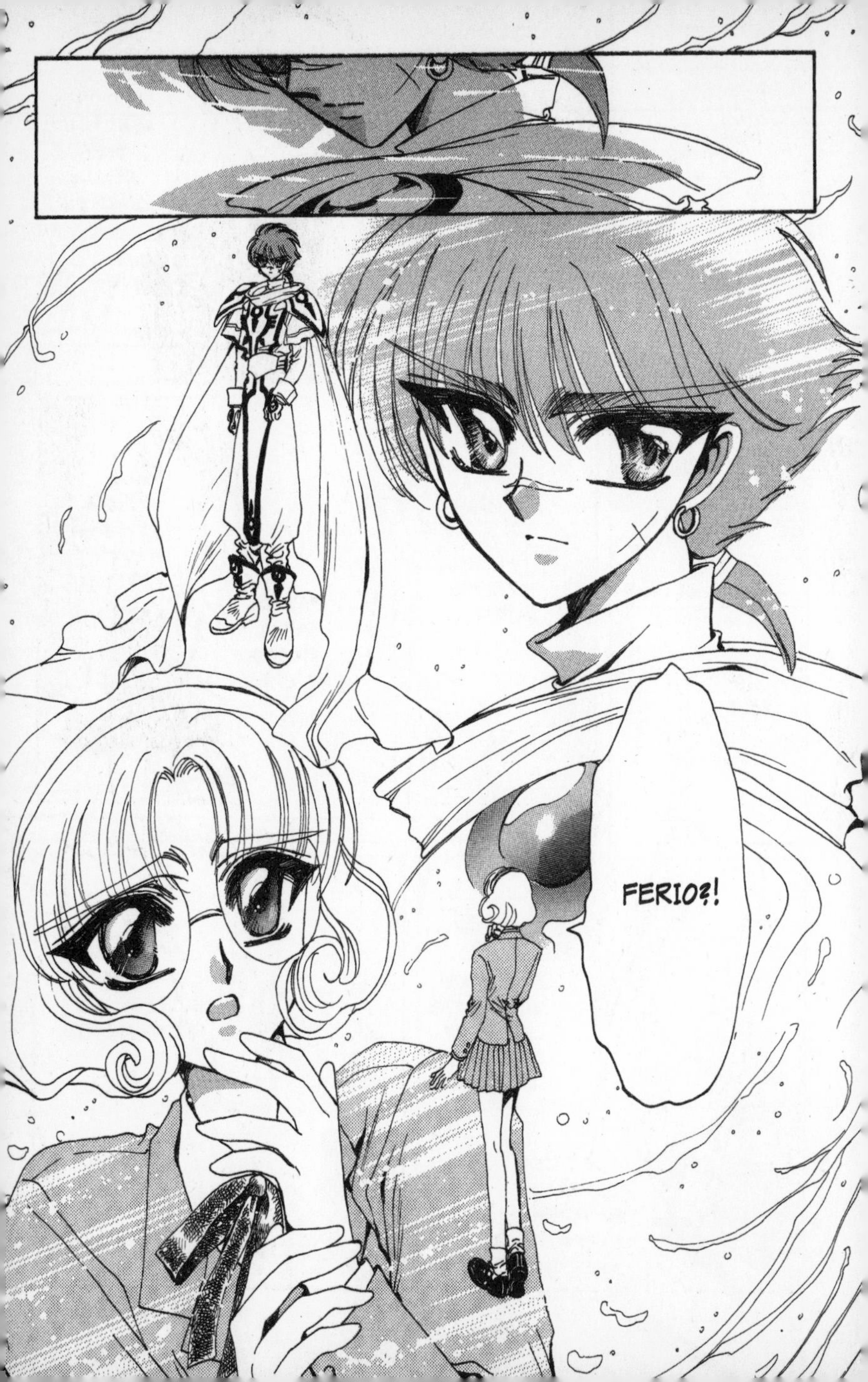
FERIO?!

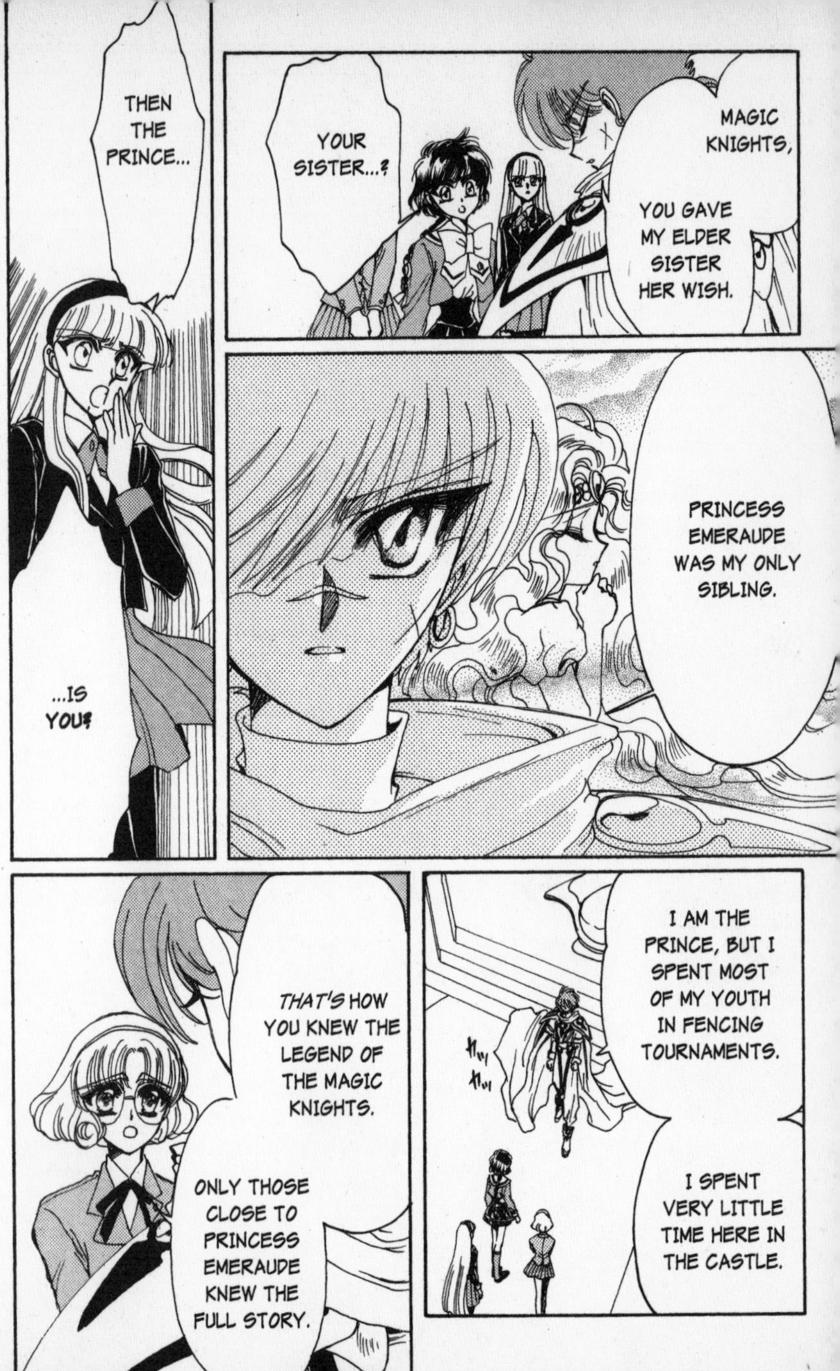
MAGIC KNIGHTS,
YOU GAVE MY ELDER SISTER HER WISH.
YOUR SISTER...?
PRINCESS EMERAUDE WAS MY ONLY SIBLING.
THEN THE PRINCE...
...IS YOU?
I AM THE PRINCE, BUT I SPENT MOST OF MY YOUTH IN FENCING TOURNAMENTS.
I SPENT VERY LITTLE TIME HERE IN THE CASTLE.
THAT'S HOW YOU KNEW THE LEGEND OF THE MAGIC KNIGHTS.
ONLY THOSE CLOSE TO PRINCESS EMERAUDE KNEW THE FULL STORY.

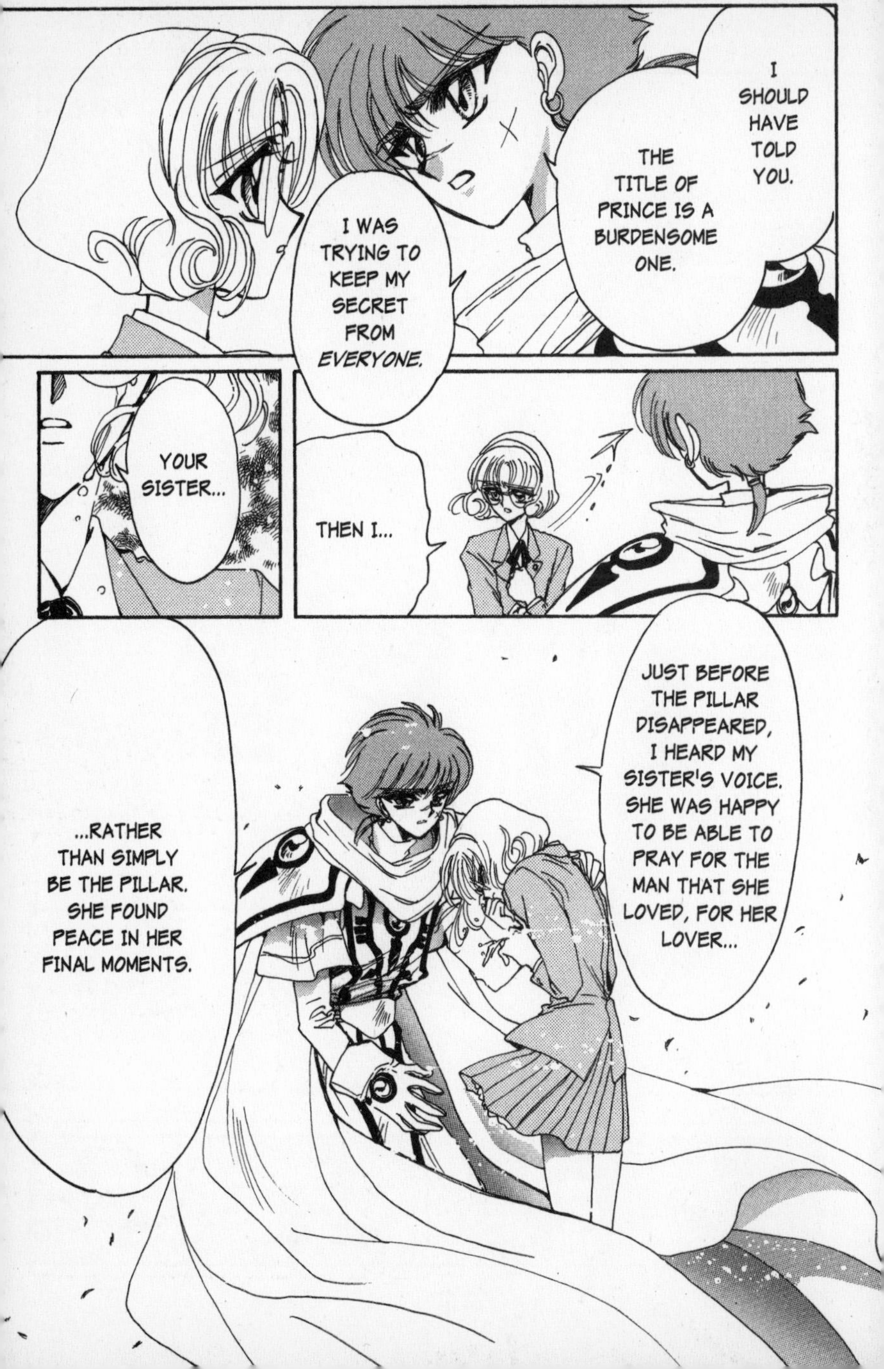
I SHOULD HAVE TOLD YOU.
THE TITLE OF PRINCE IS A BURDENSOME ONE.
I WAS TRYING TO KEEP MY SECRET FROM *EVERYONE.*
THEN I...
YOUR SISTER...
JUST BEFORE THE PILLAR DISAPPEARED, I HEARD MY SISTER'S VOICE. SHE WAS HAPPY TO BE ABLE TO PRAY FOR THE MAN THAT SHE LOVED, FOR HER LOVER...
...RATHER THAN SIMPLY BE THE PILLAR. SHE FOUND PEACE IN HER FINAL MOMENTS.

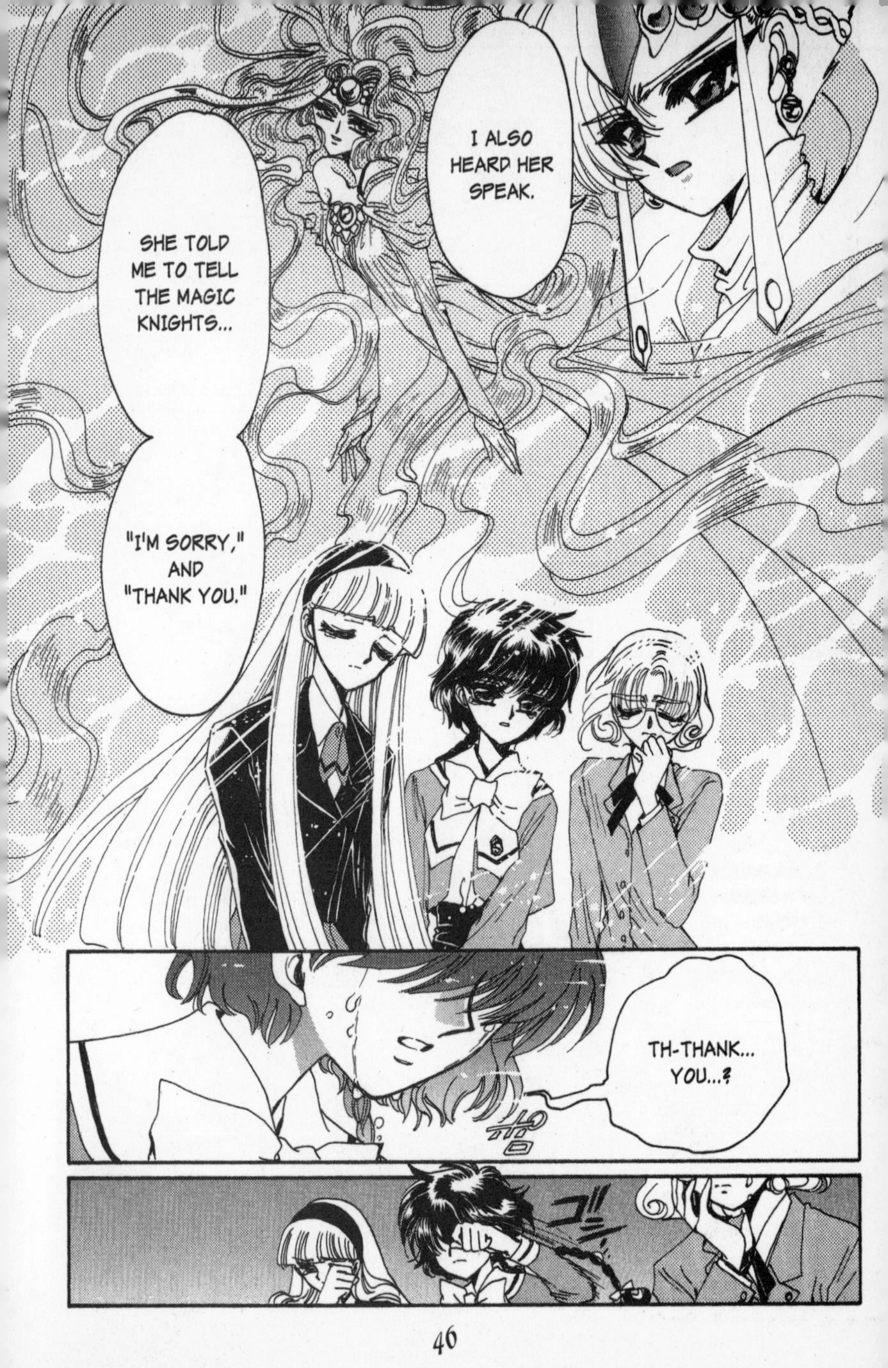
I ALSO HEARD HER SPEAK.
SHE TOLD ME TO TELL THE MAGIC KNIGHTS...
"I'M SORRY," AND "THANK YOU."
TH-THANK... YOU...?

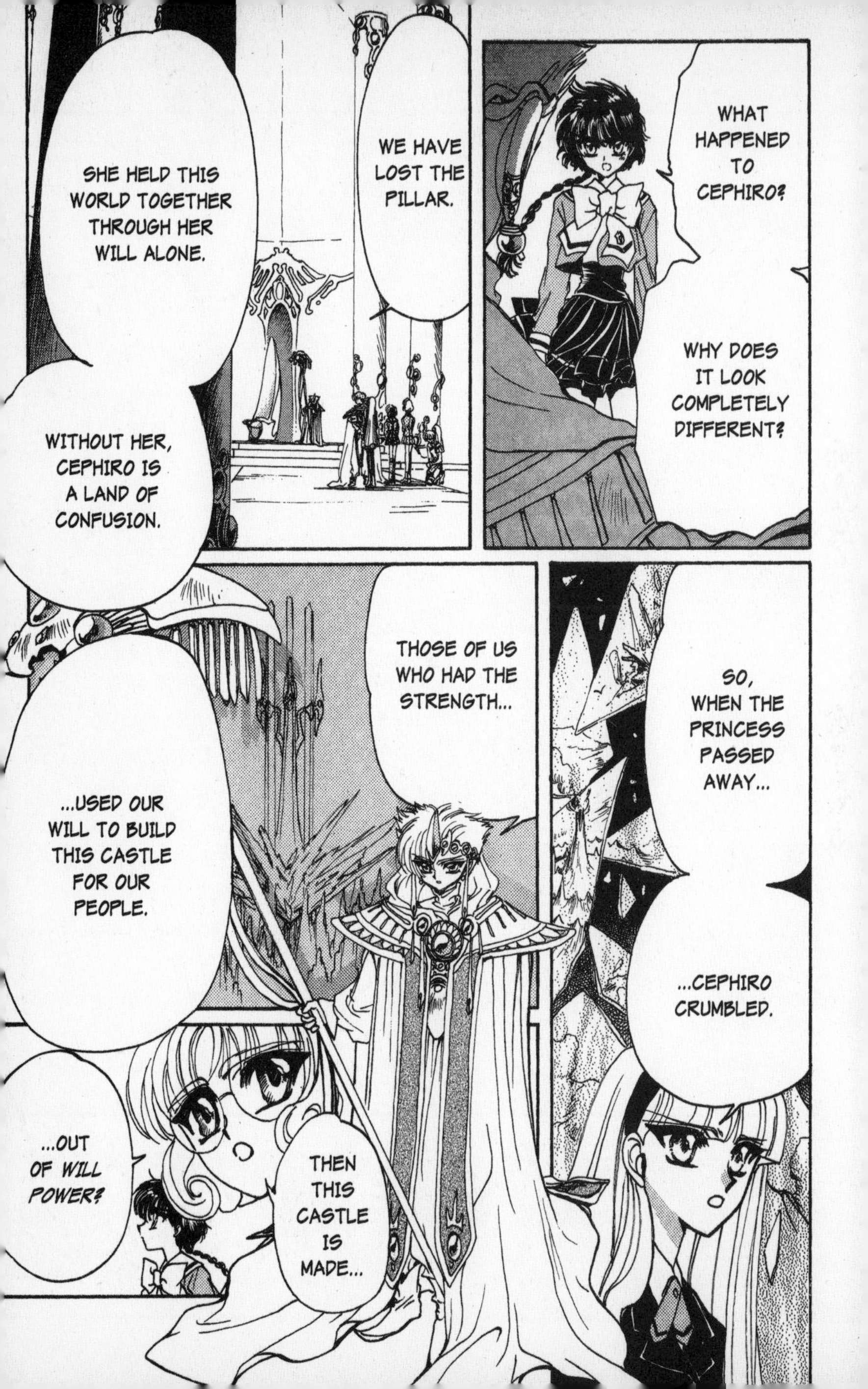
WHAT HAPPENED TO CEPHIRO?
WHY DOES IT LOOK COMPLETELY DIFFERENT?
WE HAVE LOST THE PILLAR.
SHE HELD THIS WORLD TOGETHER THROUGH HER WILL ALONE.
WITHOUT HER, CEPHIRO IS A LAND OF CONFUSION.
SO, WHEN THE PRINCESS PASSED AWAY...
...CEPHIRO CRUMBLED.
THOSE OF US WHO HAD THE STRENGTH...
...USED OUR WILL TO BUILD THIS CASTLE FOR OUR PEOPLE.
THEN THIS CASTLE IS MADE...
...OUT OF WILL POWER?

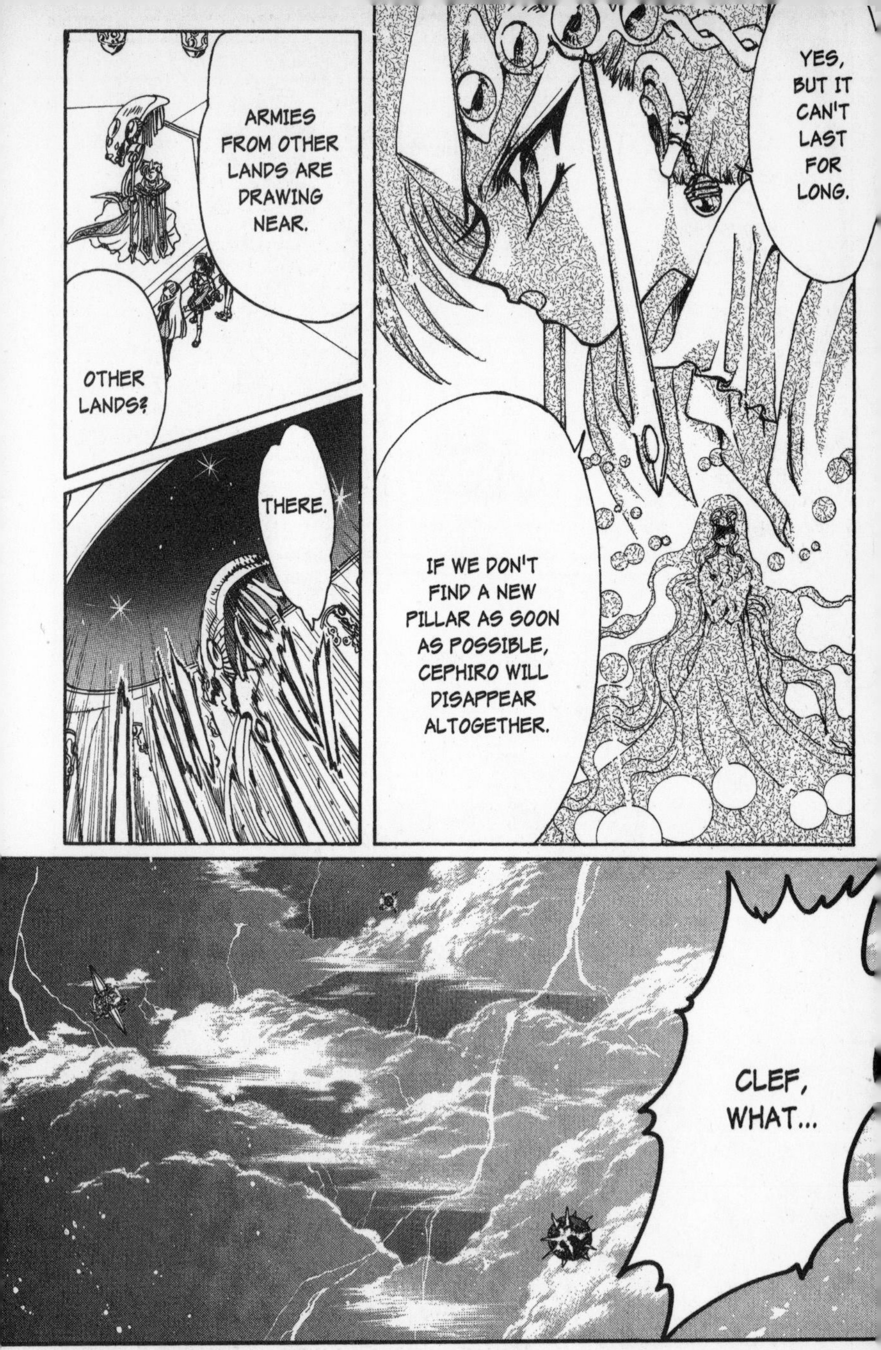
YES, BUT IT CAN'T LAST FOR LONG.
IF WE DON'T FIND A NEW PILLAR AS SOON AS POSSIBLE, CEPHIRO WILL DISAPPEAR ALTOGETHER.
ARMIES FROM OTHER LANDS ARE DRAWING NEAR.
OTHER LANDS?
THERE.
CLEF, WHAT...

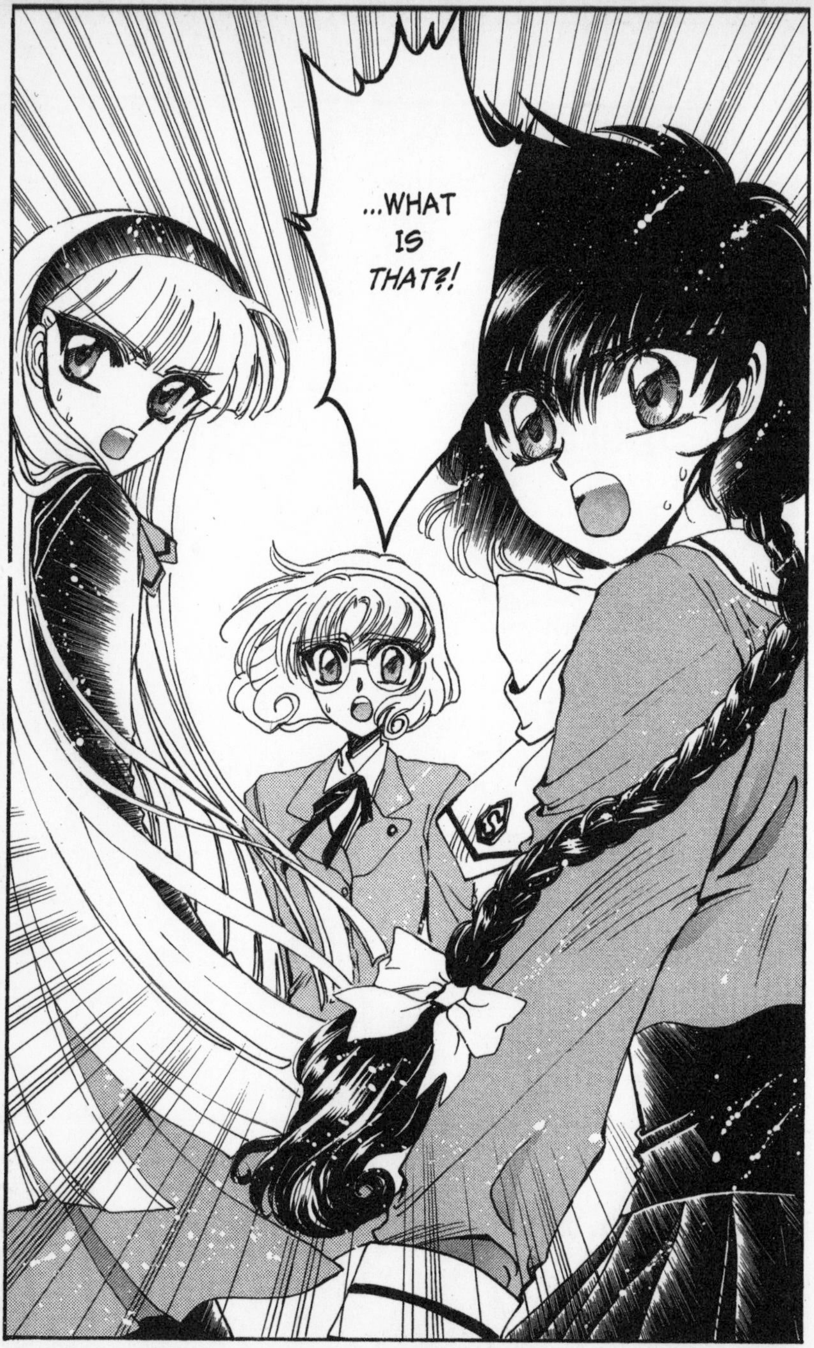
...WHAT IS THAT?!

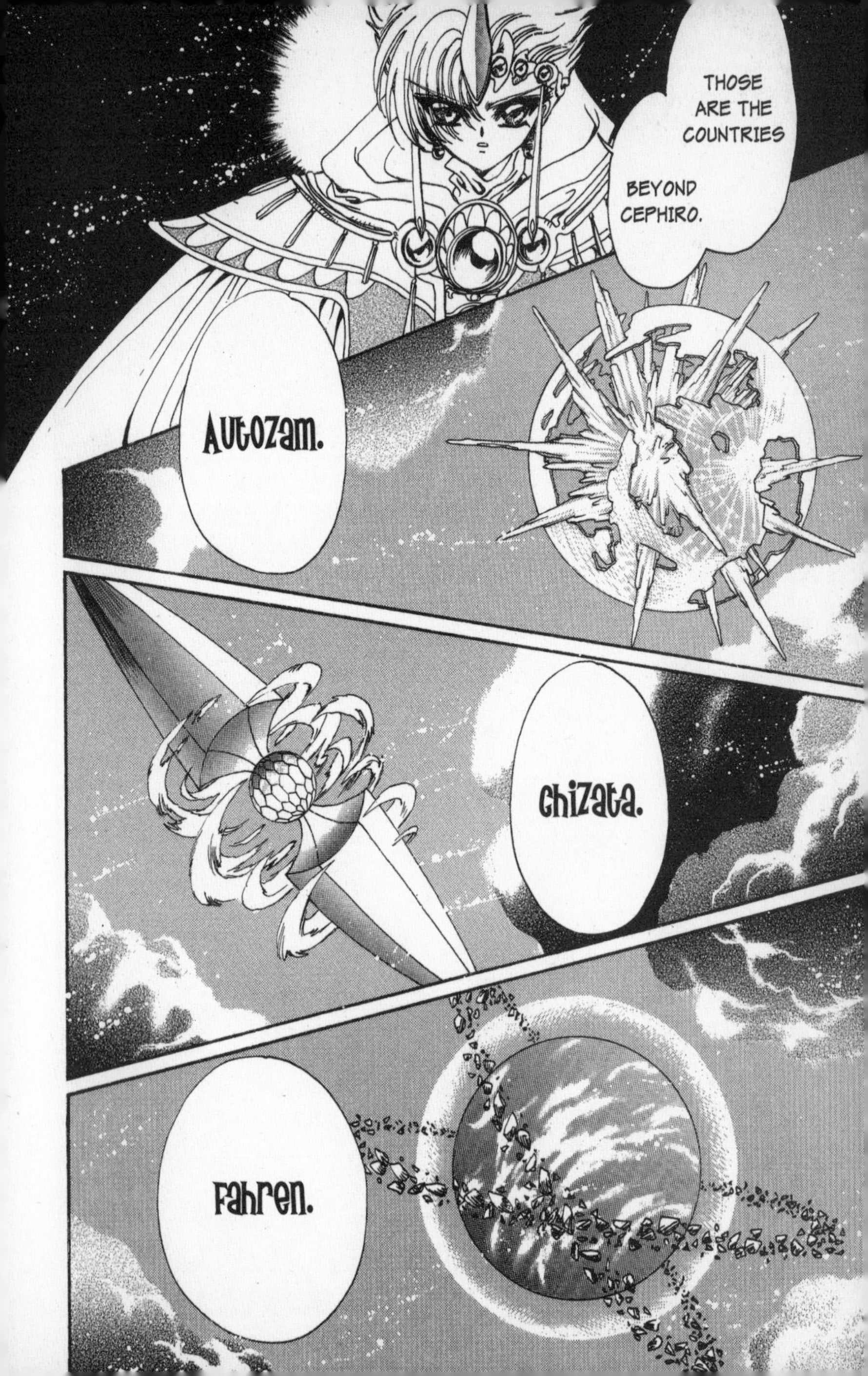
THOSE ARE THE COUNTRIES
BEYOND CEPHIRO.
Autozam.
Chizata.
Fahren.

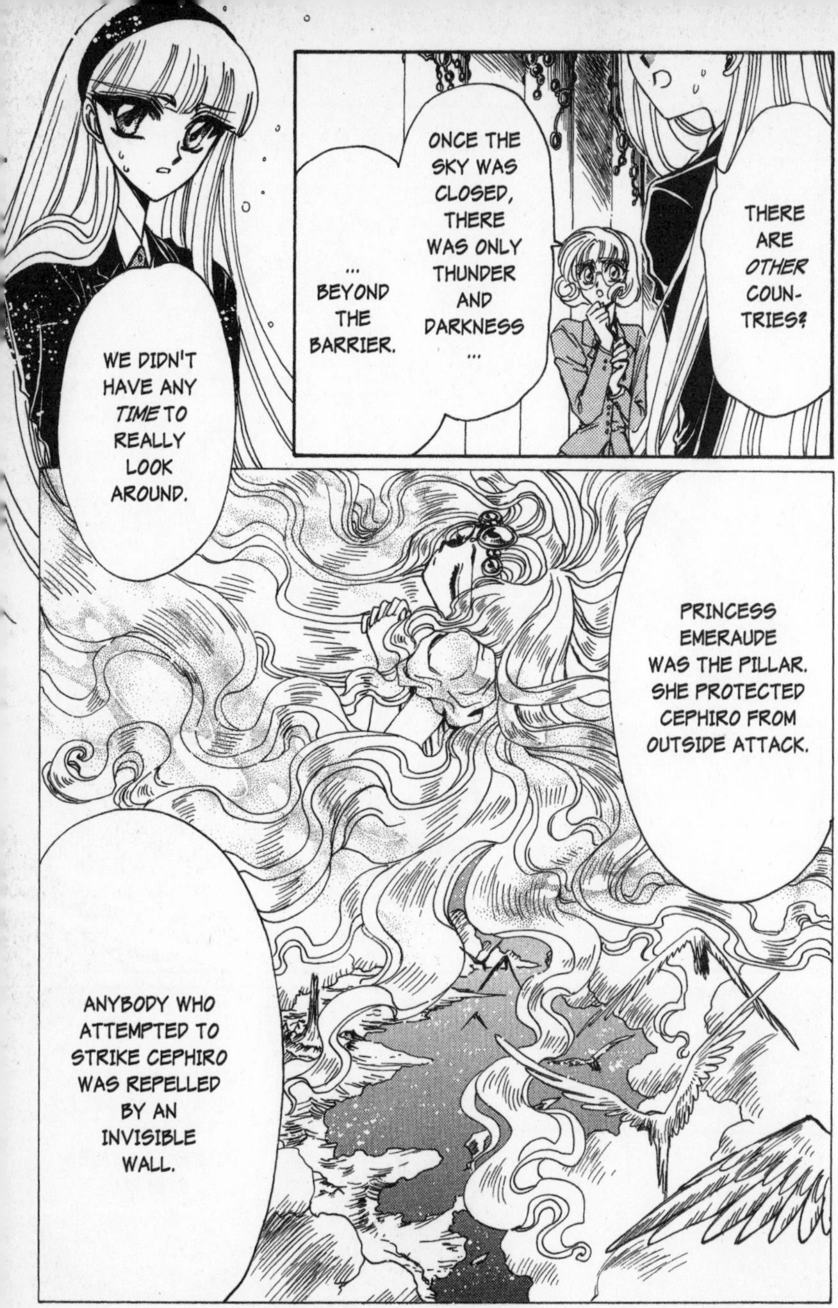
THERE ARE *OTHER* COUNTRIES?
ONCE THE SKY WAS CLOSED, THERE WAS ONLY THUNDER AND DARKNESS ...
... BEYOND THE BARRIER.
WE DIDN'T HAVE ANY *TIME* TO REALLY LOOK AROUND.
PRINCESS EMERAUDE WAS THE PILLAR. SHE PROTECTED CEPHIRO FROM OUTSIDE ATTACK.
ANYBODY WHO ATTEMPTED TO STRIKE CEPHIRO WAS REPELLED BY AN INVISIBLE WALL.

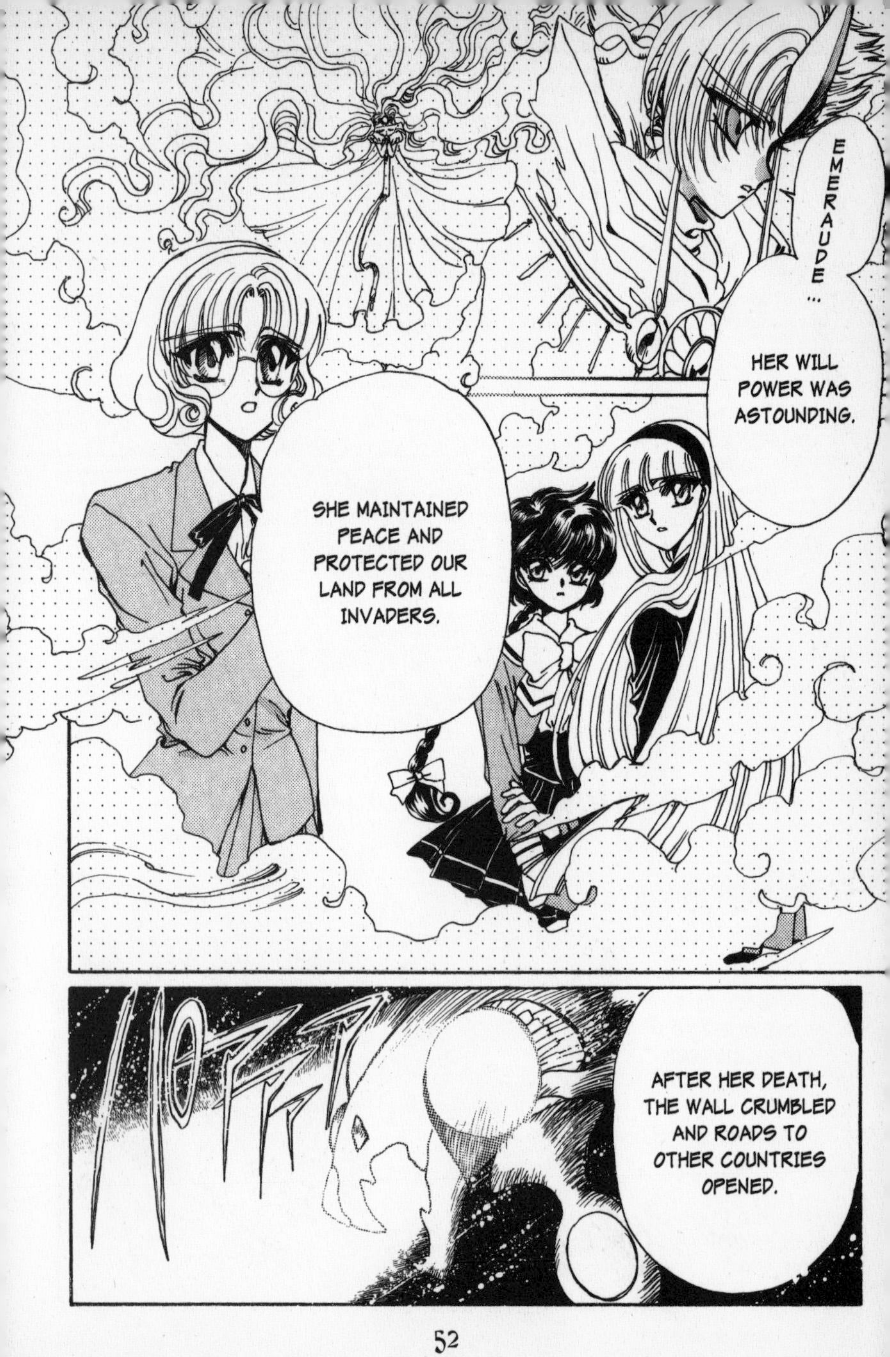
EMERAUDE...
HER WILL POWER WAS ASTOUNDING.
SHE MAINTAINED PEACE AND PROTECTED OUR LAND FROM ALL INVADERS.
AFTER HER DEATH, THE WALL CRUMBLED AND ROADS TO OTHER COUNTRIES OPENED.

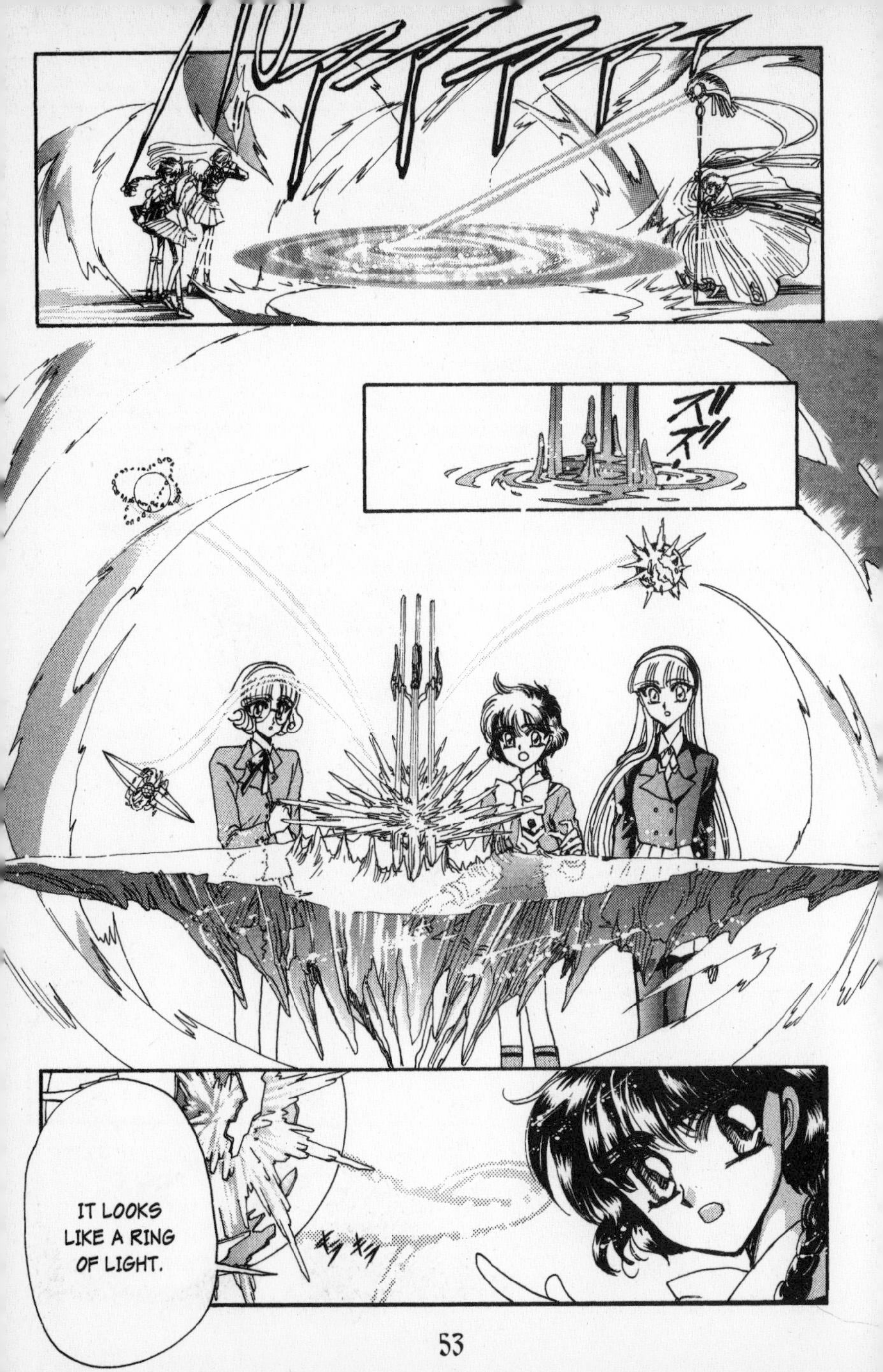
IT LOOKS LIKE A RING OF LIGHT.

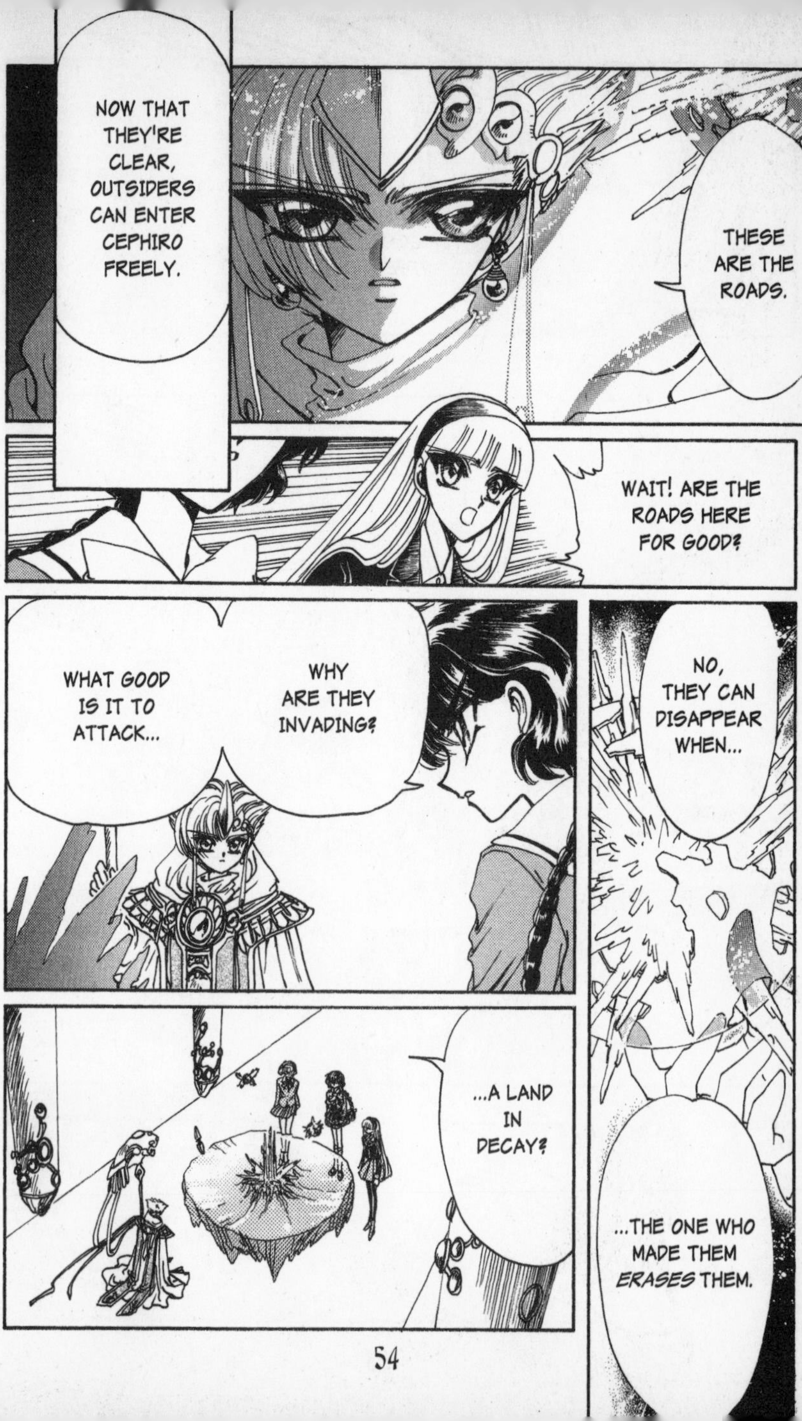
THESE ARE THE ROADS.
NOW THAT THEY'RE CLEAR, OUTSIDERS CAN ENTER CEPHIRO FREELY.
WAIT! ARE THE ROADS HERE FOR GOOD?
NO, THEY CAN DISAPPEAR WHEN...
...THE ONE WHO MADE THEM *ERASES* THEM.
WHY ARE THEY INVADING?
WHAT GOOD IS IT TO ATTACK...
...A LAND IN DECAY?

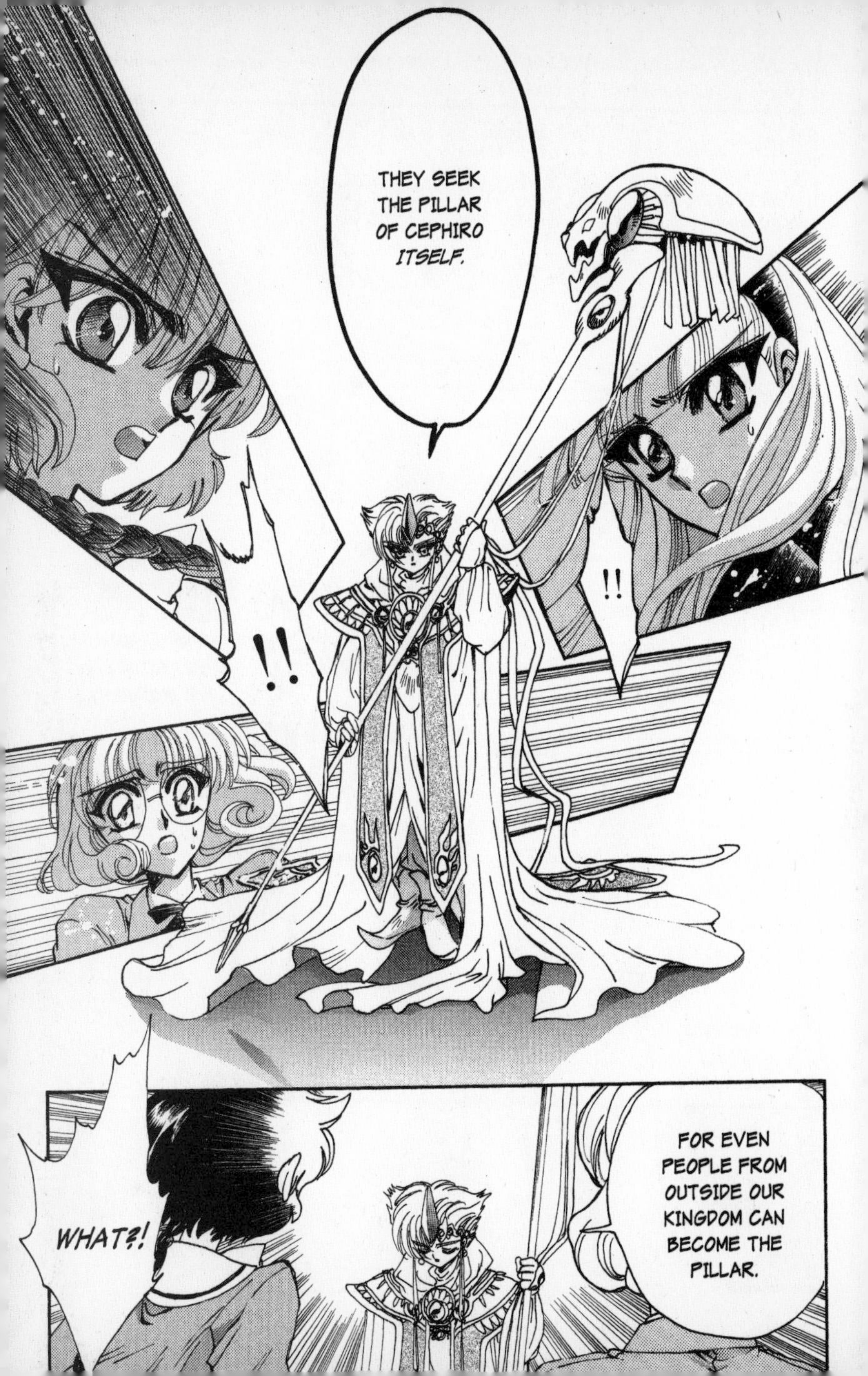
THEY SEEK THE PILLAR OF CEPHIRO ITSELF.
!!
!!
FOR EVEN PEOPLE FROM OUTSIDE OUR KINGDOM CAN BECOME THE PILLAR.
WHAT?!

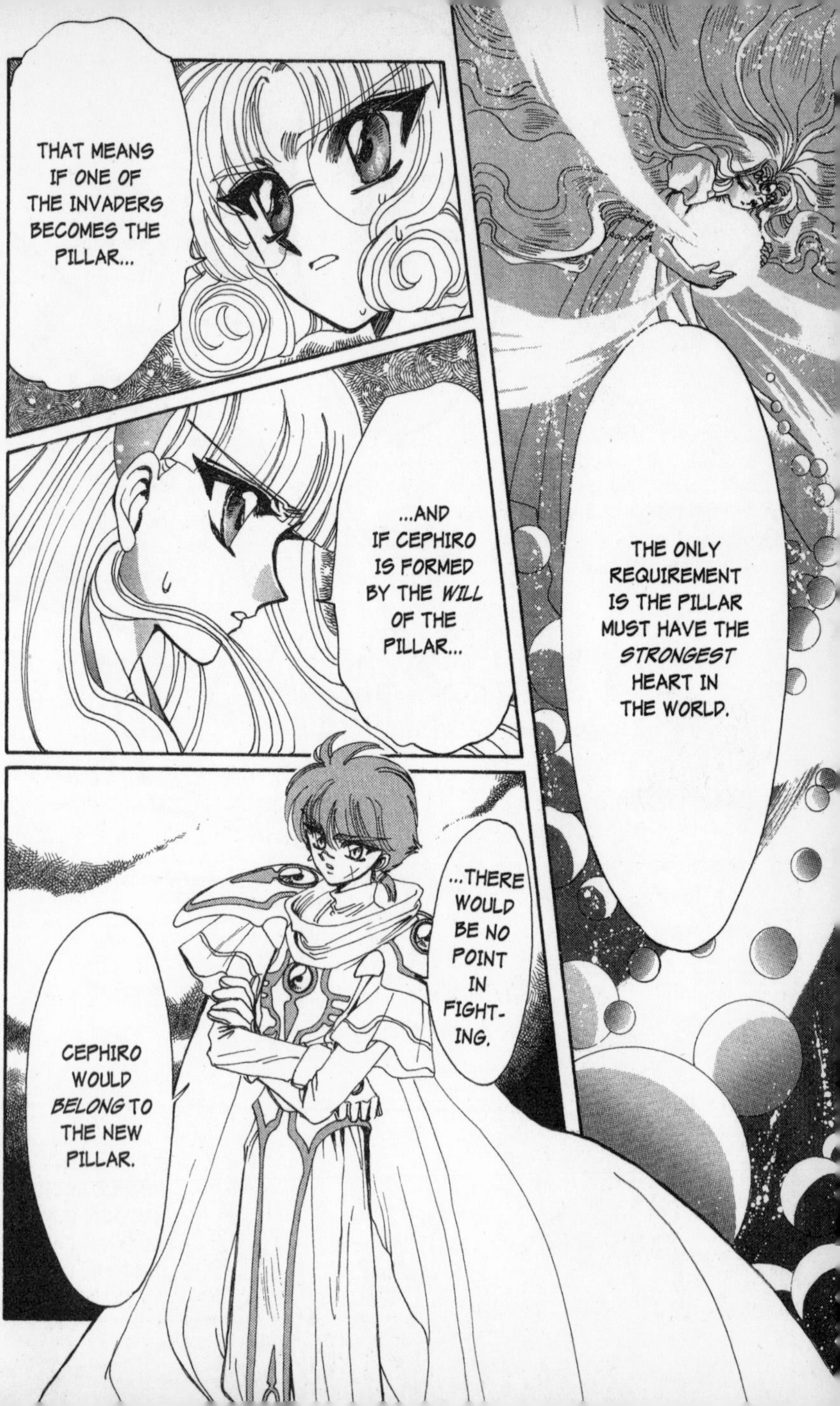
THE ONLY REQUIREMENT IS THE PILLAR MUST HAVE THE *STRONGEST* HEART IN THE WORLD.
THAT MEANS IF ONE OF THE INVADERS BECOMES THE PILLAR...
...AND IF CEPHIRO IS FORMED BY THE *WILL* OF THE PILLAR...
...THERE WOULD BE NO POINT IN FIGHT-ING.
CEPHIRO WOULD *BELONG* TO THE NEW PILLAR.

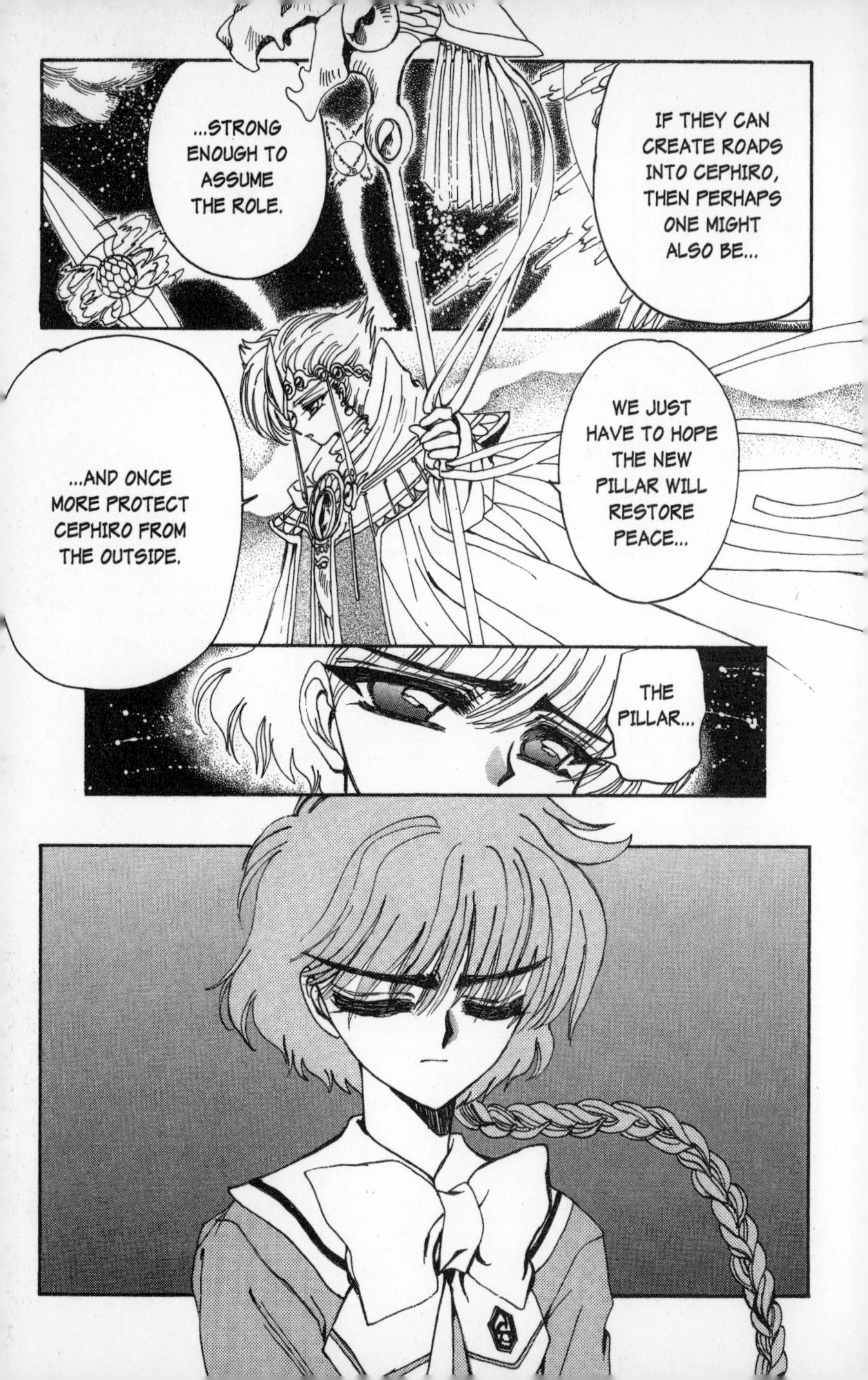
IF THEY CAN CREATE ROADS INTO CEPHIRO, THEN PERHAPS ONE MIGHT ALSO BE...
...STRONG ENOUGH TO ASSUME THE ROLE.
WE JUST HAVE TO HOPE THE NEW PILLAR WILL RESTORE PEACE...
...AND ONCE MORE PROTECT CEPHIRO FROM THE OUTSIDE.
THE PILLAR...

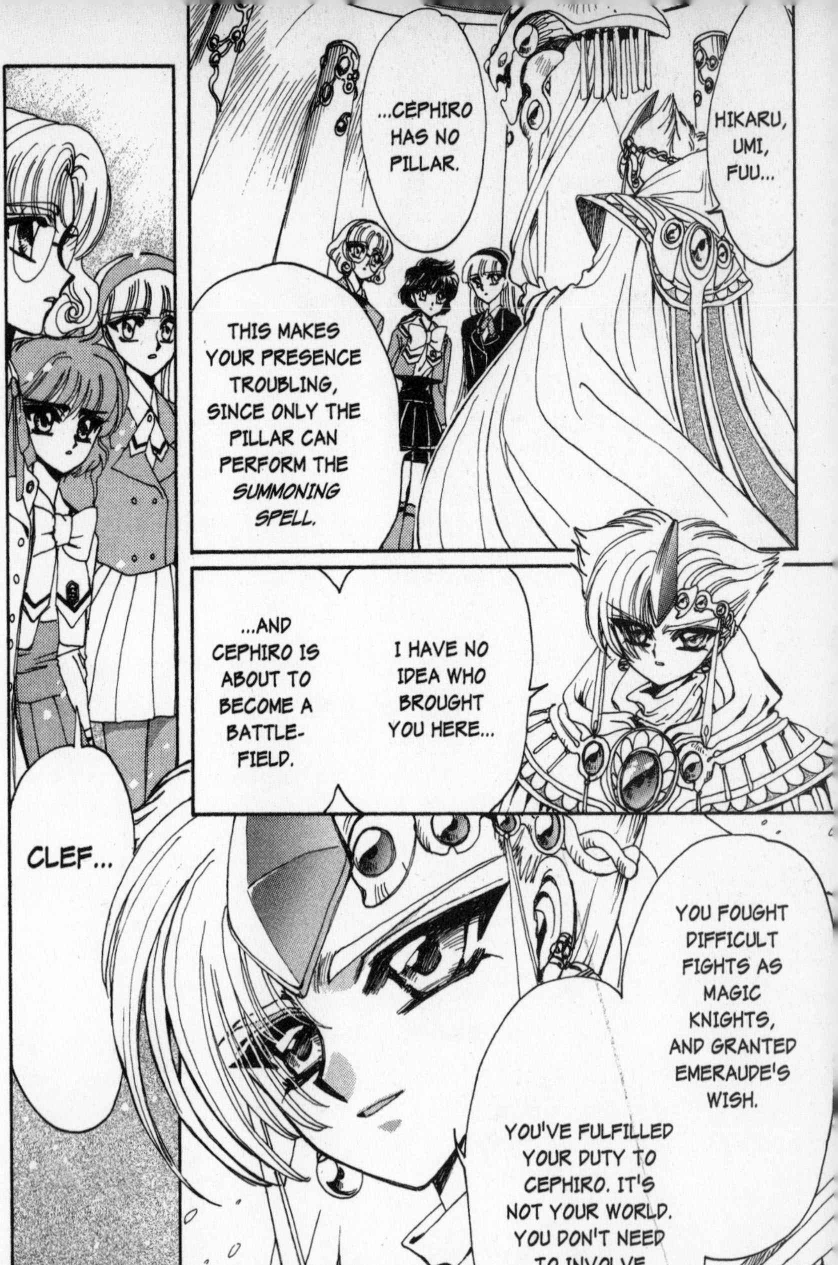
HIKARU, UMI, FUU...
...CEPHIRO HAS NO PILLAR.
THIS MAKES YOUR PRESENCE TROUBLING, SINCE ONLY THE PILLAR CAN PERFORM THE *SUMMONING SPELL*.
I HAVE NO IDEA WHO BROUGHT YOU HERE...
...AND CEPHIRO IS ABOUT TO BECOME A BATTLE-FIELD.
YOU FOUGHT DIFFICULT FIGHTS AS MAGIC KNIGHTS, AND GRANTED EMERAUDE'S WISH.
YOU'VE FULFILLED YOUR DUTY TO CEPHIRO. IT'S NOT YOUR WORLD. YOU DON'T NEED TO INVOLVE YOURSELVES IN OUR WAR.
CLEF...

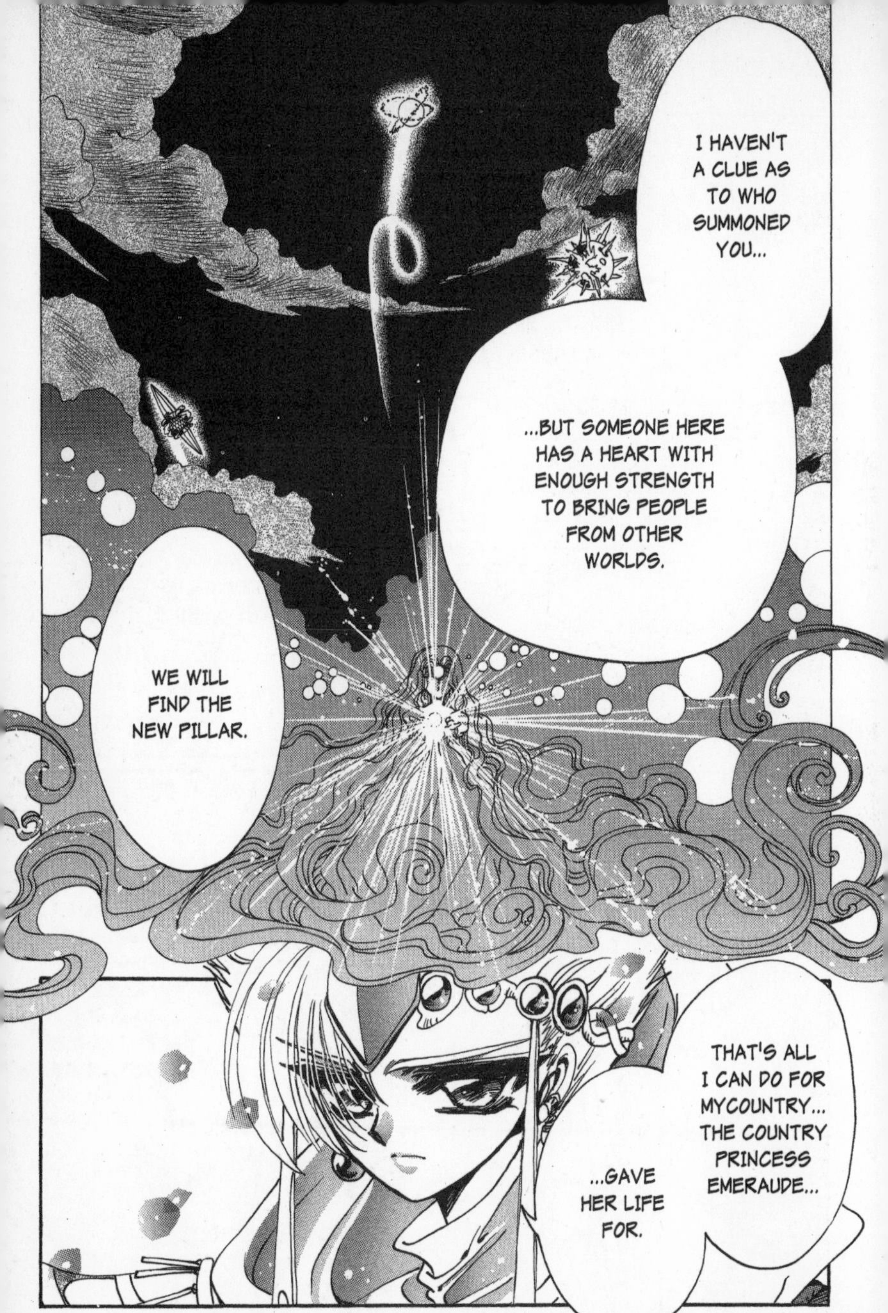
I HAVEN'T A CLUE AS TO WHO SUMMONED YOU...
...BUT SOMEONE HERE HAS A HEART WITH ENOUGH STRENGTH TO BRING PEOPLE FROM OTHER WORLDS.
WE WILL FIND THE NEW PILLAR.
THAT'S ALL I CAN DO FOR MYCOUNTRY... THE COUNTRY PRINCESS EMERAUDE...
...GAVE HER LIFE FOR.

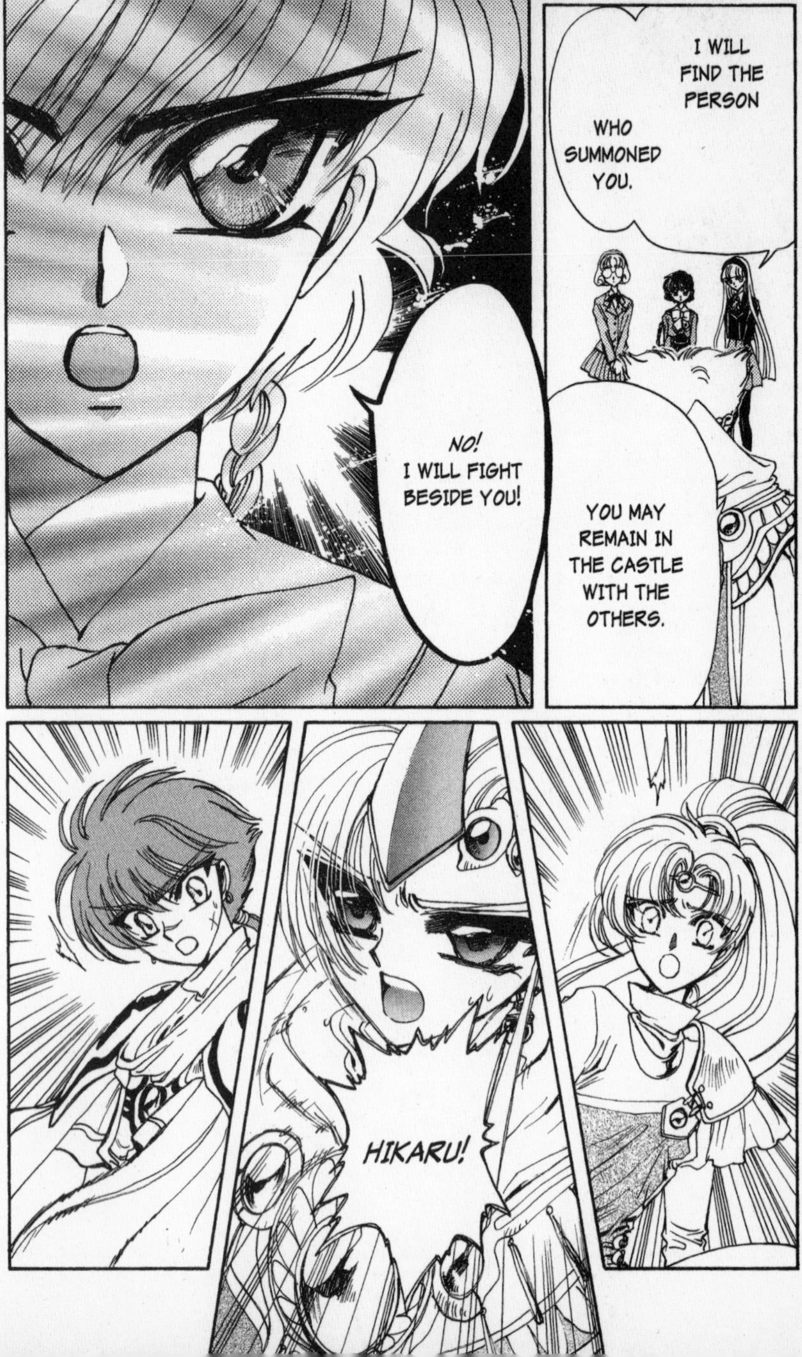
I WILL FIND THE PERSON WHO SUMMONED YOU.
YOU MAY REMAIN IN THE CASTLE WITH THE OTHERS.
NO! I WILL FIGHT BESIDE YOU!
HIKARU!

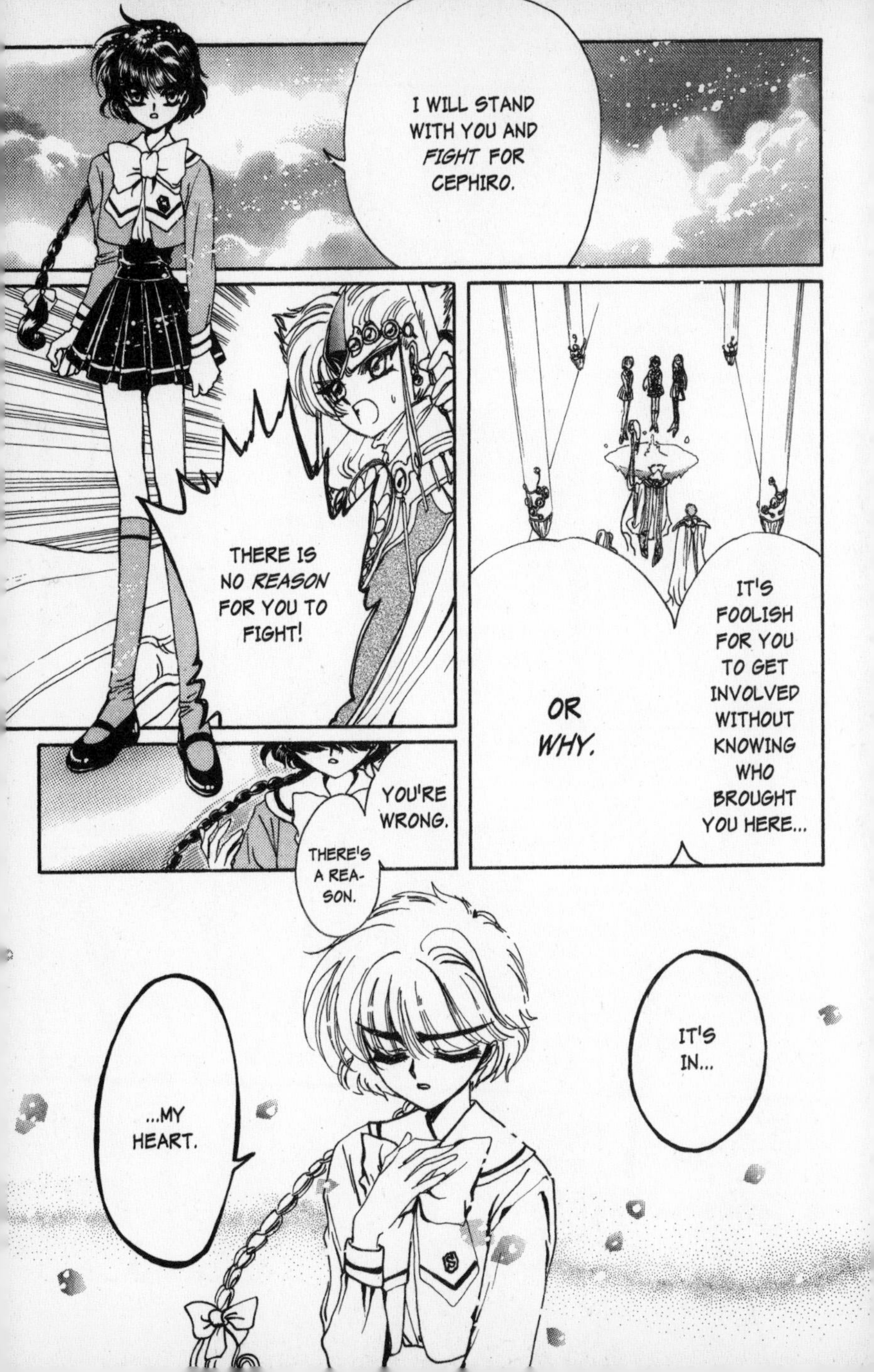
I WILL STAND WITH YOU AND *FIGHT* FOR CEPHIRO.
IT'S FOOLISH FOR YOU TO GET INVOLVED WITHOUT KNOWING WHO BROUGHT YOU HERE...
OR *WHY.*
THERE IS NO *REASON* FOR YOU TO FIGHT!
YOU'RE WRONG.
THERE'S A REA-SON.
IT'S IN...
...MY HEART.

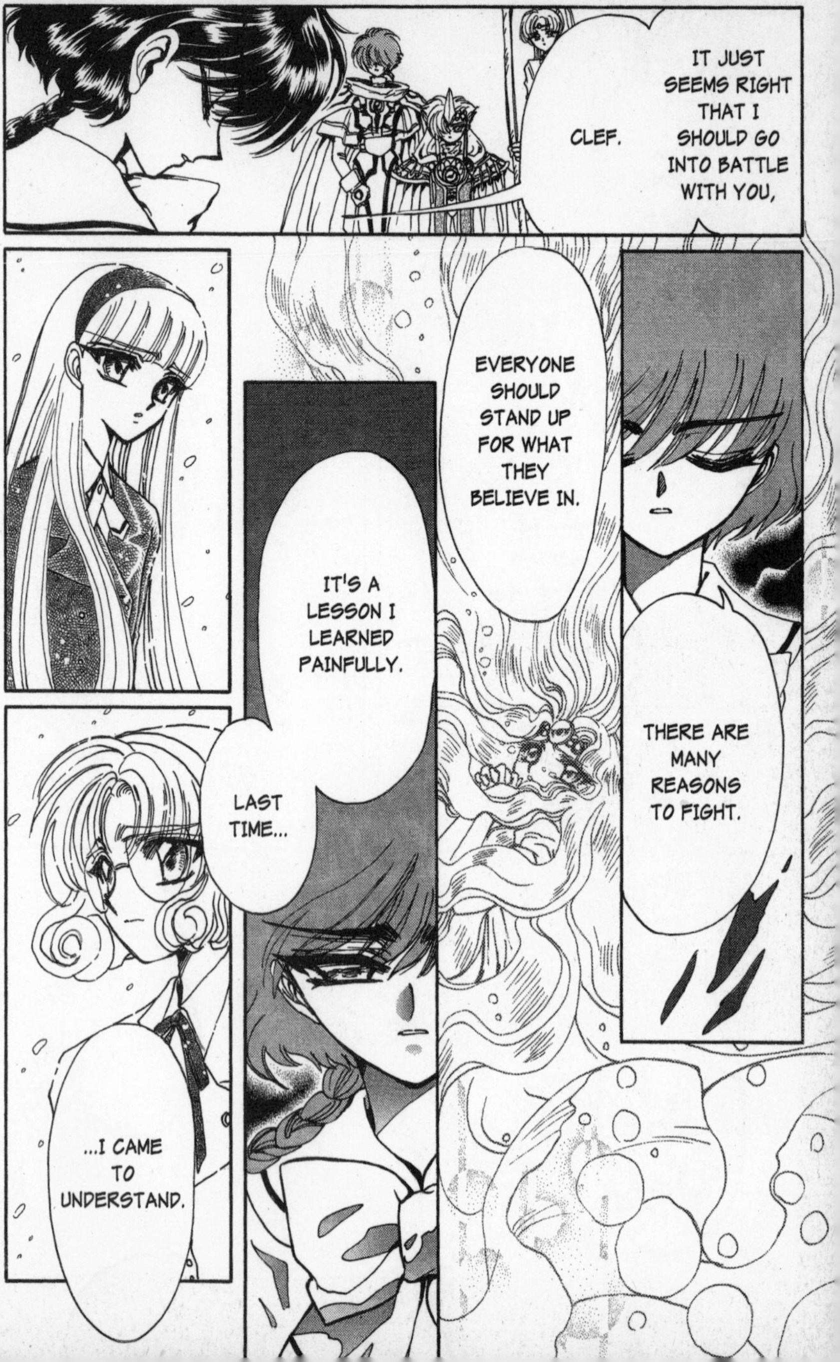
IT JUST SEEMS RIGHT THAT I SHOULD GO INTO BATTLE WITH YOU,
CLEF.
EVERYONE SHOULD STAND UP FOR WHAT THEY BELIEVE IN.
THERE ARE MANY REASONS TO FIGHT.
IT'S A LESSON I LEARNED PAINFULLY.
LAST TIME...
...I CAME TO UNDERSTAND.

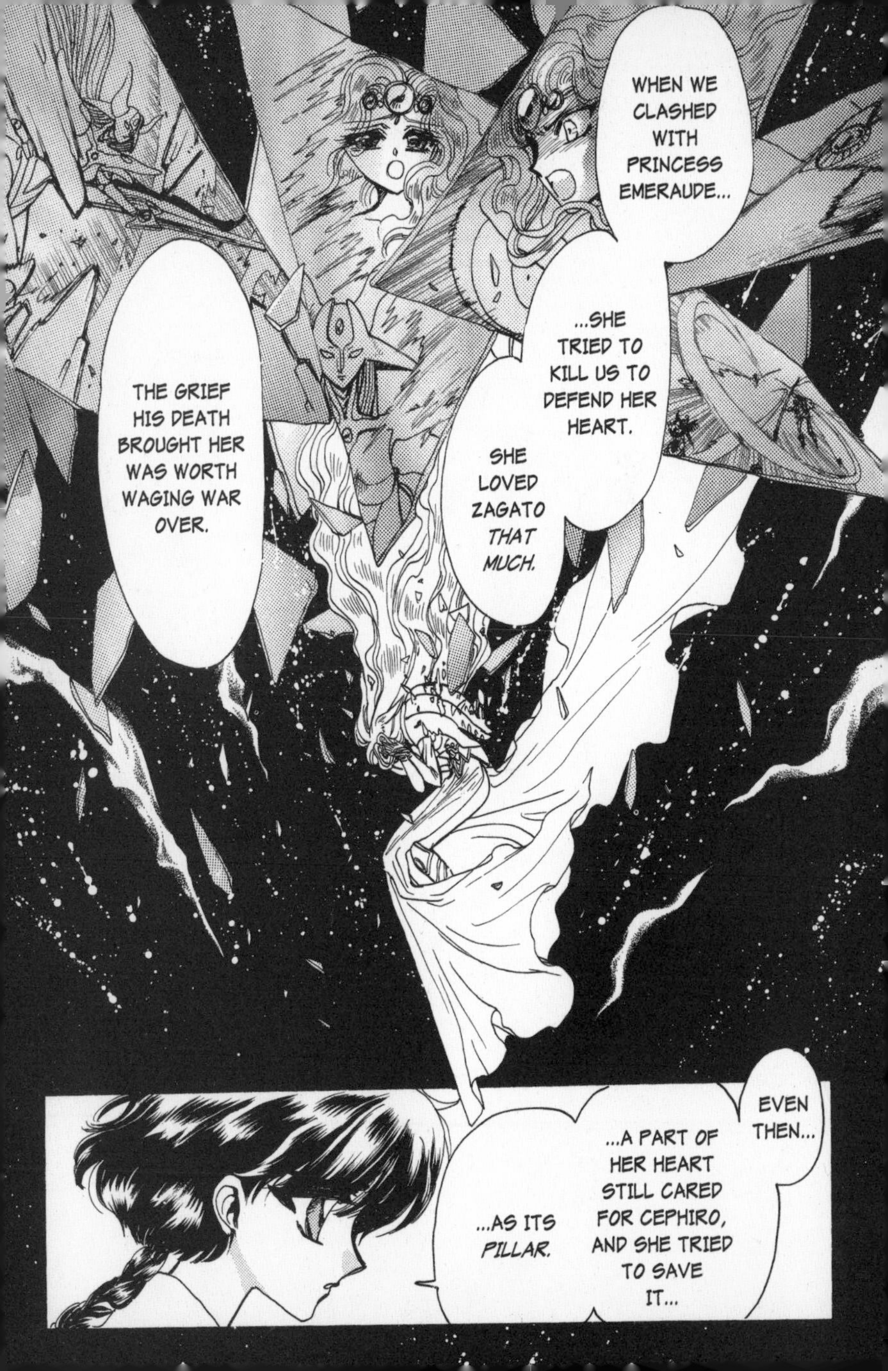
WHEN WE CLASHED WITH PRINCESS EMERAUDE...
...SHE TRIED TO KILL US TO DEFEND HER HEART.
SHE LOVED ZAGATO *THAT* MUCH.
THE GRIEF HIS DEATH BROUGHT HER WAS WORTH WAGING WAR OVER.
EVEN THEN...
...A PART OF HER HEART STILL CARED FOR CEPHIRO, AND SHE TRIED TO SAVE IT...
...AS ITS *PILLAR.*

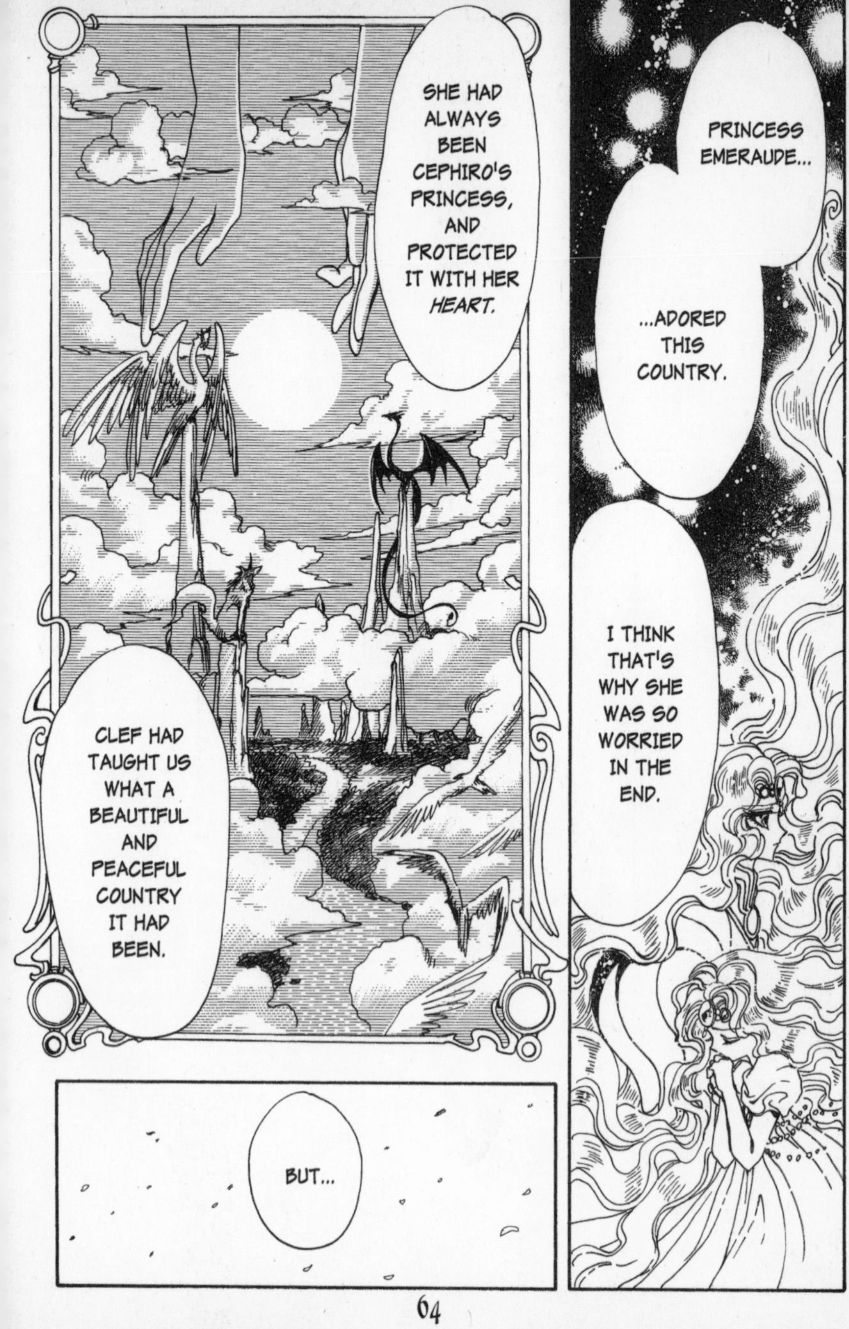
PRINCESS EMERAUDE...
...ADORED THIS COUNTRY.
I THINK THAT'S WHY SHE WAS SO WORRIED IN THE END.
SHE HAD ALWAYS BEEN CEPHIRO'S PRINCESS, AND PROTECTED IT WITH HER *HEART.*
CLEF HAD TAUGHT US WHAT A BEAUTIFUL AND PEACEFUL COUNTRY IT HAD BEEN.
BUT...

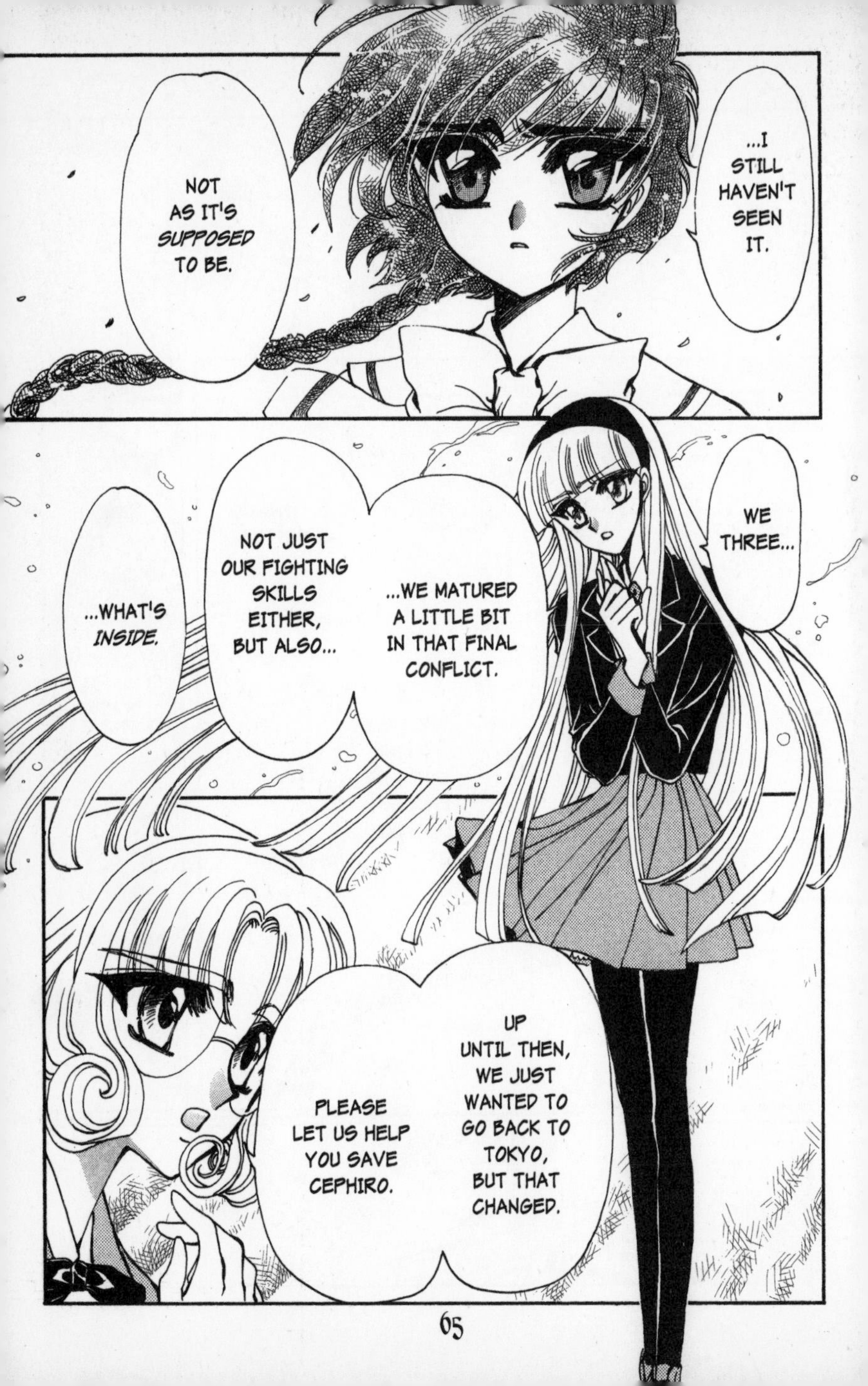
...I STILL HAVEN'T SEEN IT.
NOT AS IT'S *SUPPOSED* TO BE.
WE THREE...
...WE MATURED A LITTLE BIT IN THAT FINAL CONFLICT.
NOT JUST OUR FIGHTING SKILLS EITHER, BUT ALSO...
...WHAT'S *INSIDE.*
UP UNTIL THEN, WE JUST WANTED TO GO BACK TO TOKYO, BUT THAT CHANGED.
PLEASE LET US HELP YOU SAVE CEPHIRO.

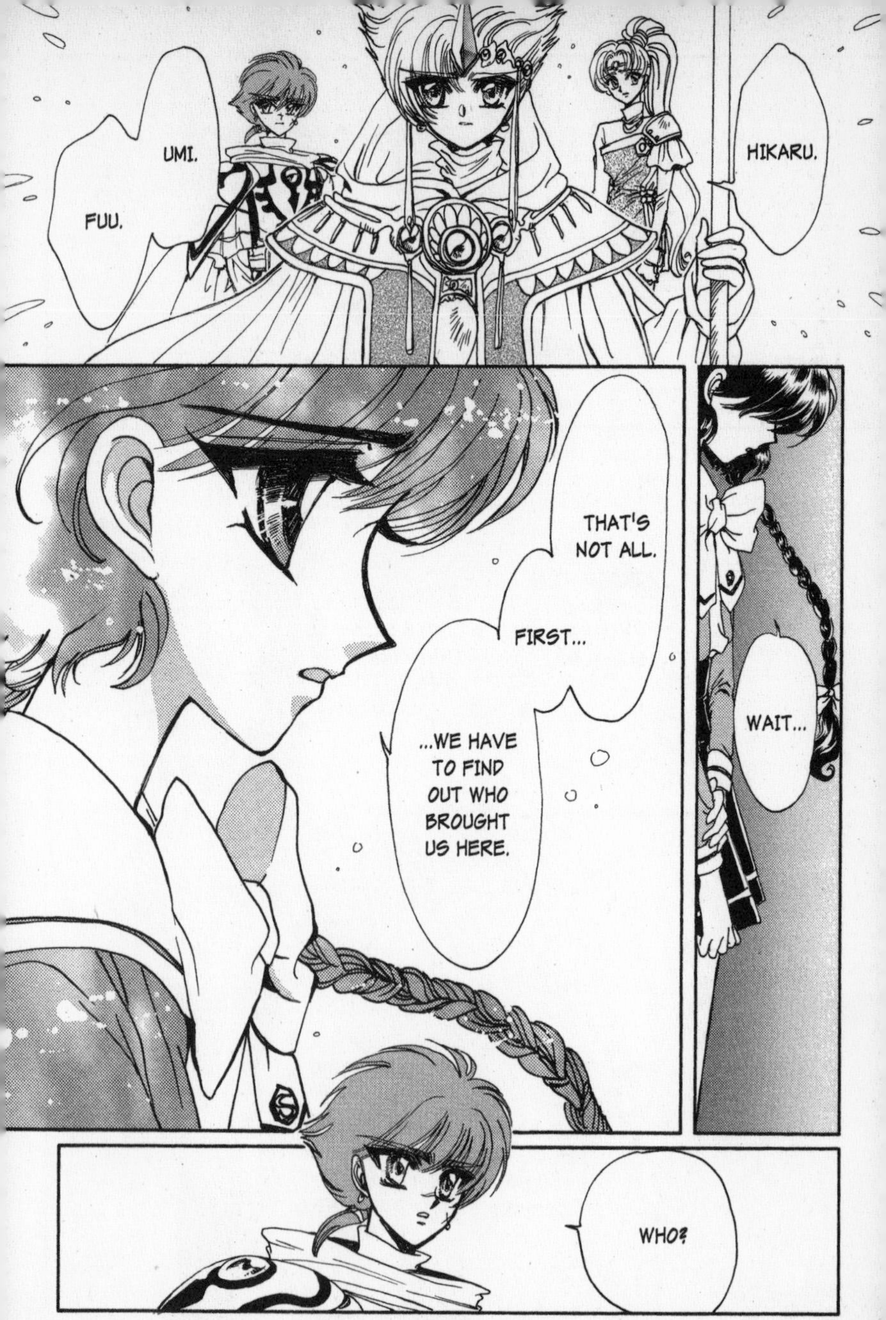
HIKARU.
UMI.
FUU.
WAIT...
THAT'S NOT ALL.
FIRST...
...WE HAVE TO FIND OUT WHO BROUGHT US HERE.
WHO?

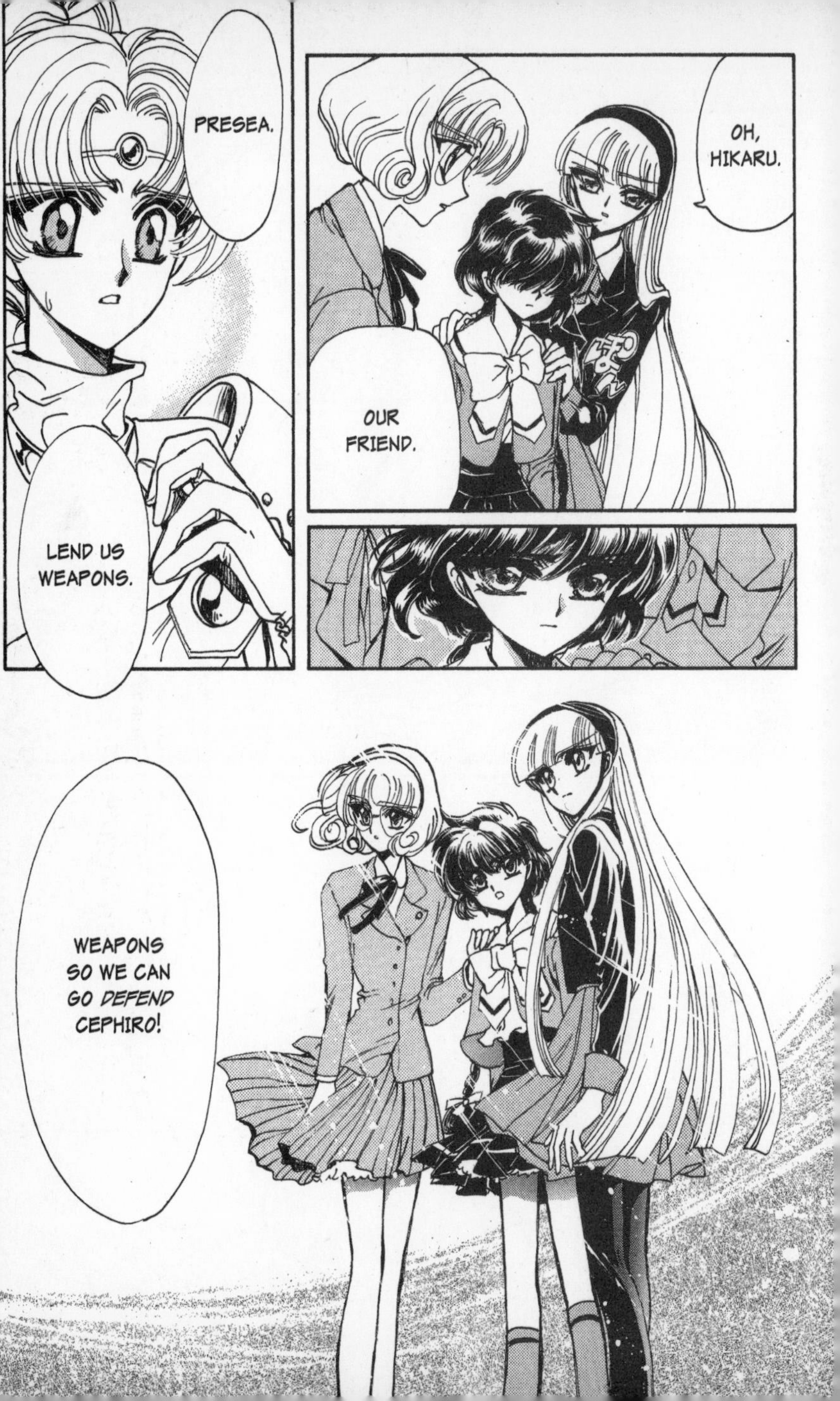
OH, HIKARU.
OUR FRIEND.
PRESEA.
LEND US WEAPONS.
WEAPONS SO WE CAN GO *DEFEND* CEPHIRO!

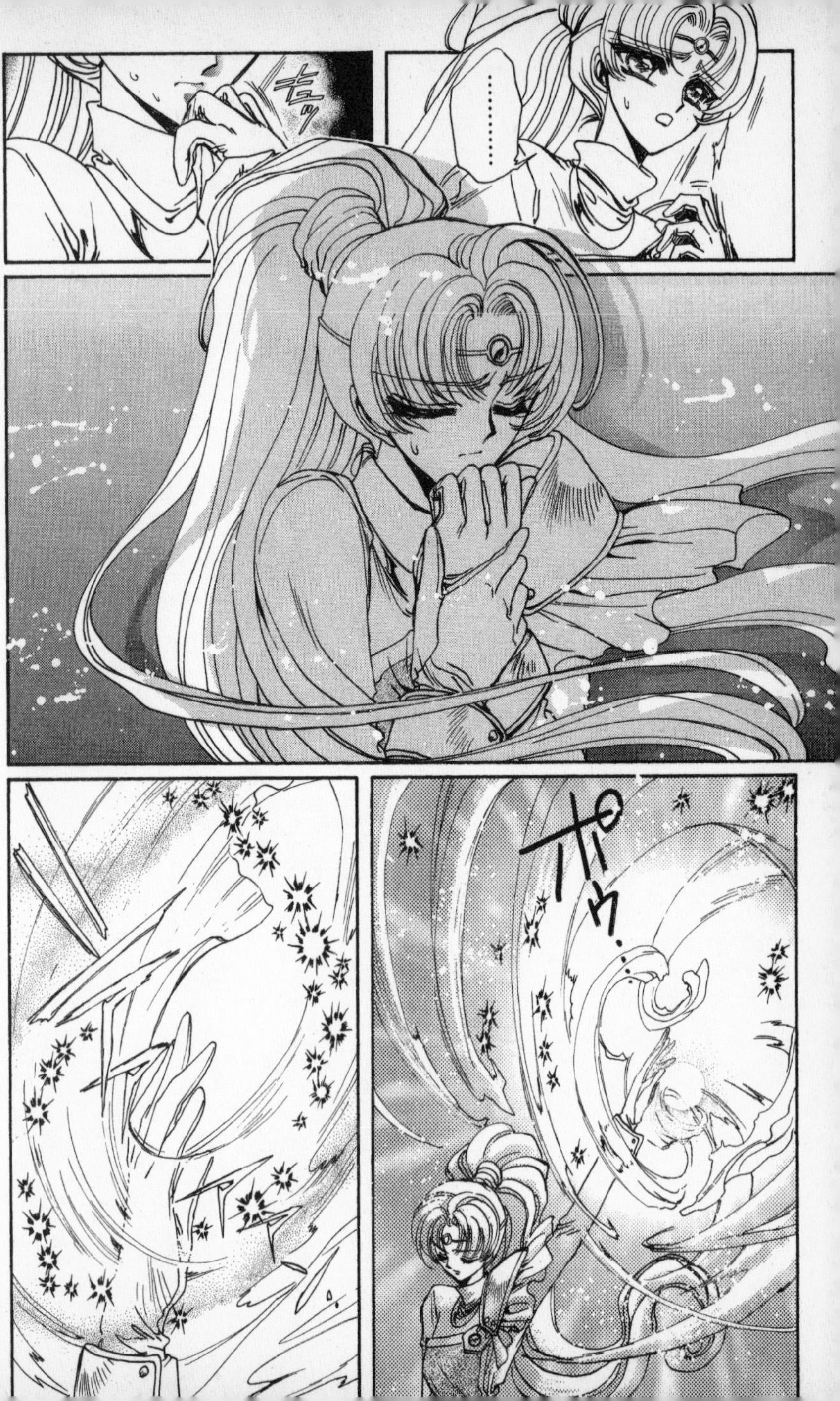
……
キュッ
ポゥ…

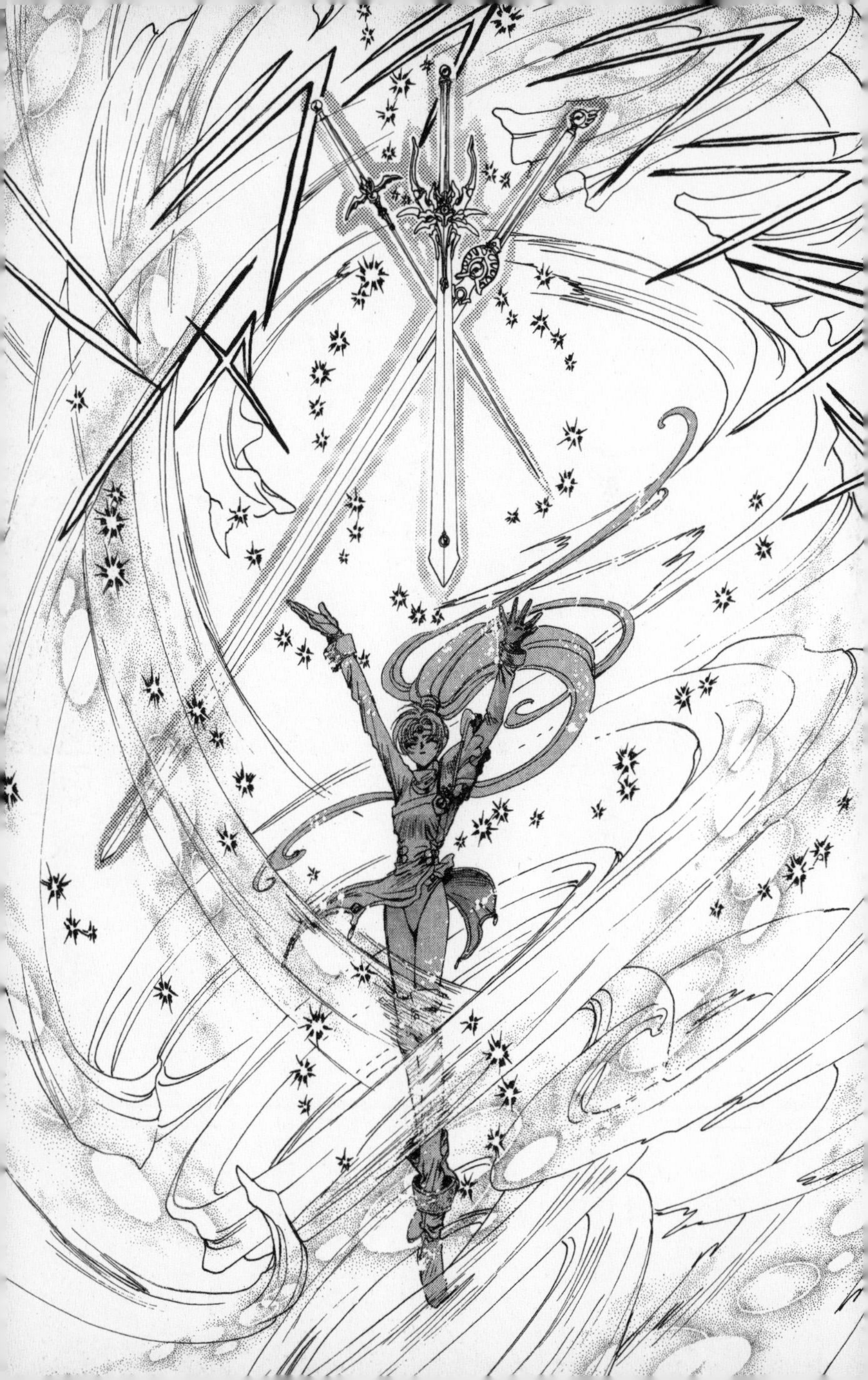

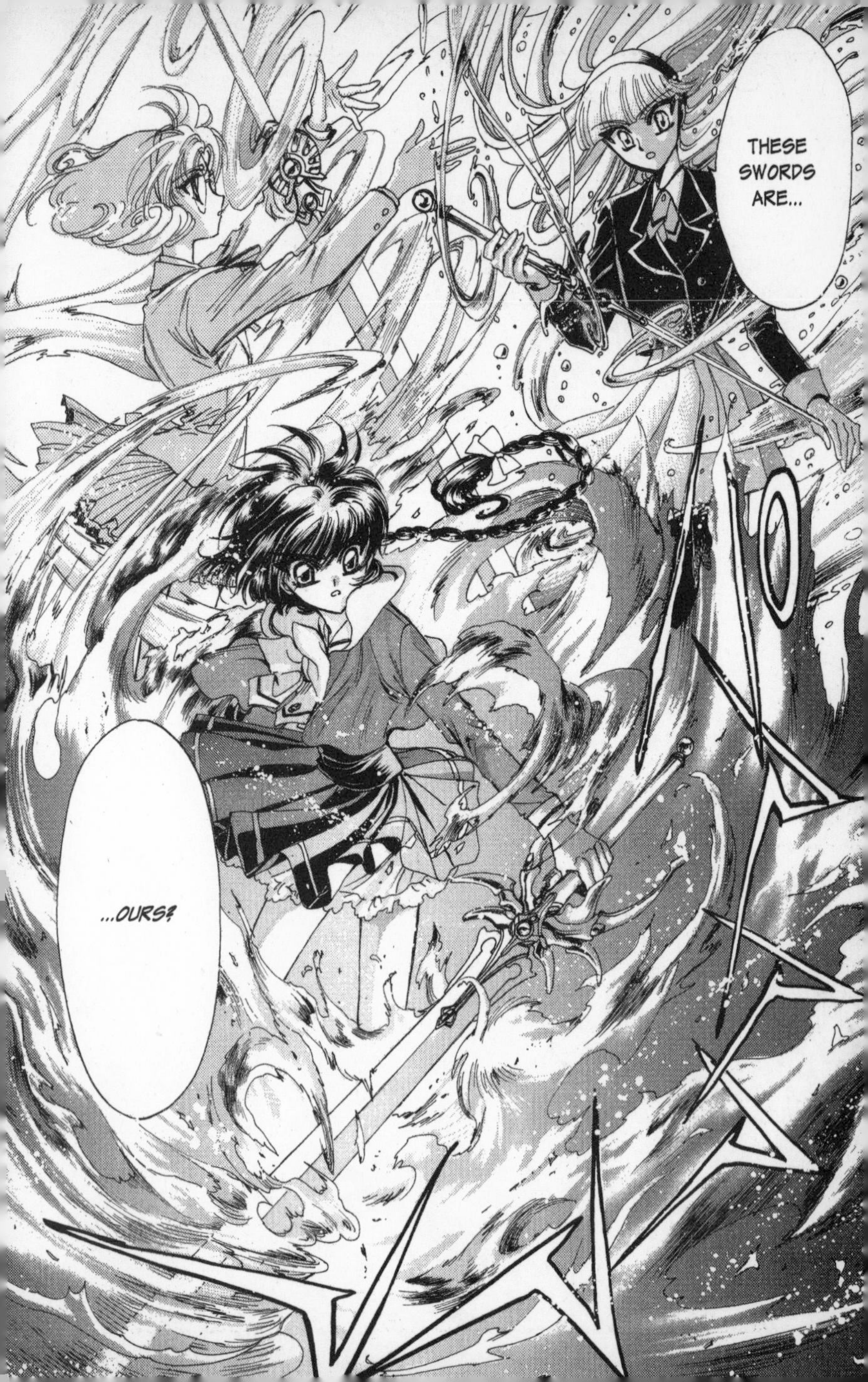
THESE SWORDS ARE...
...OURS?

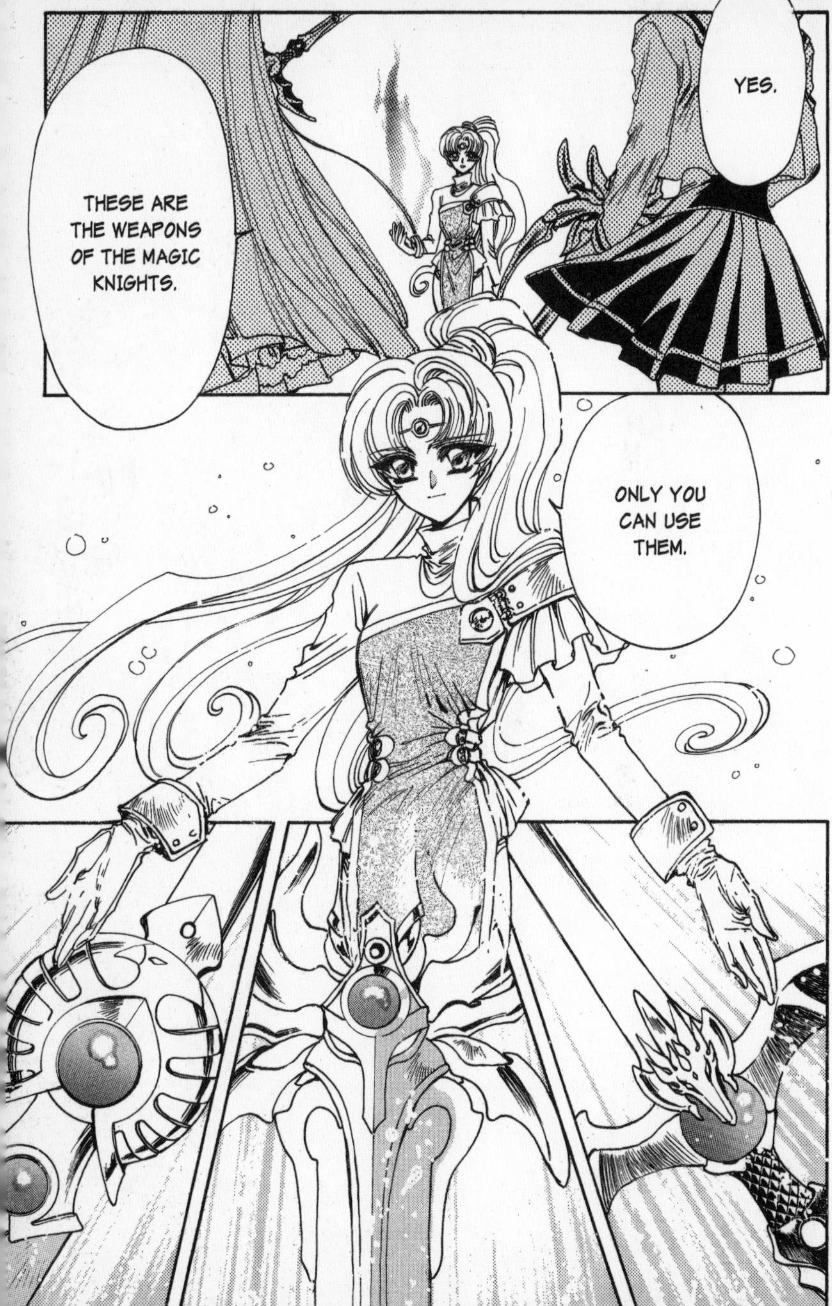
YES.
THESE ARE THE WEAPONS OF THE MAGIC KNIGHTS.
ONLY YOU CAN USE THEM.

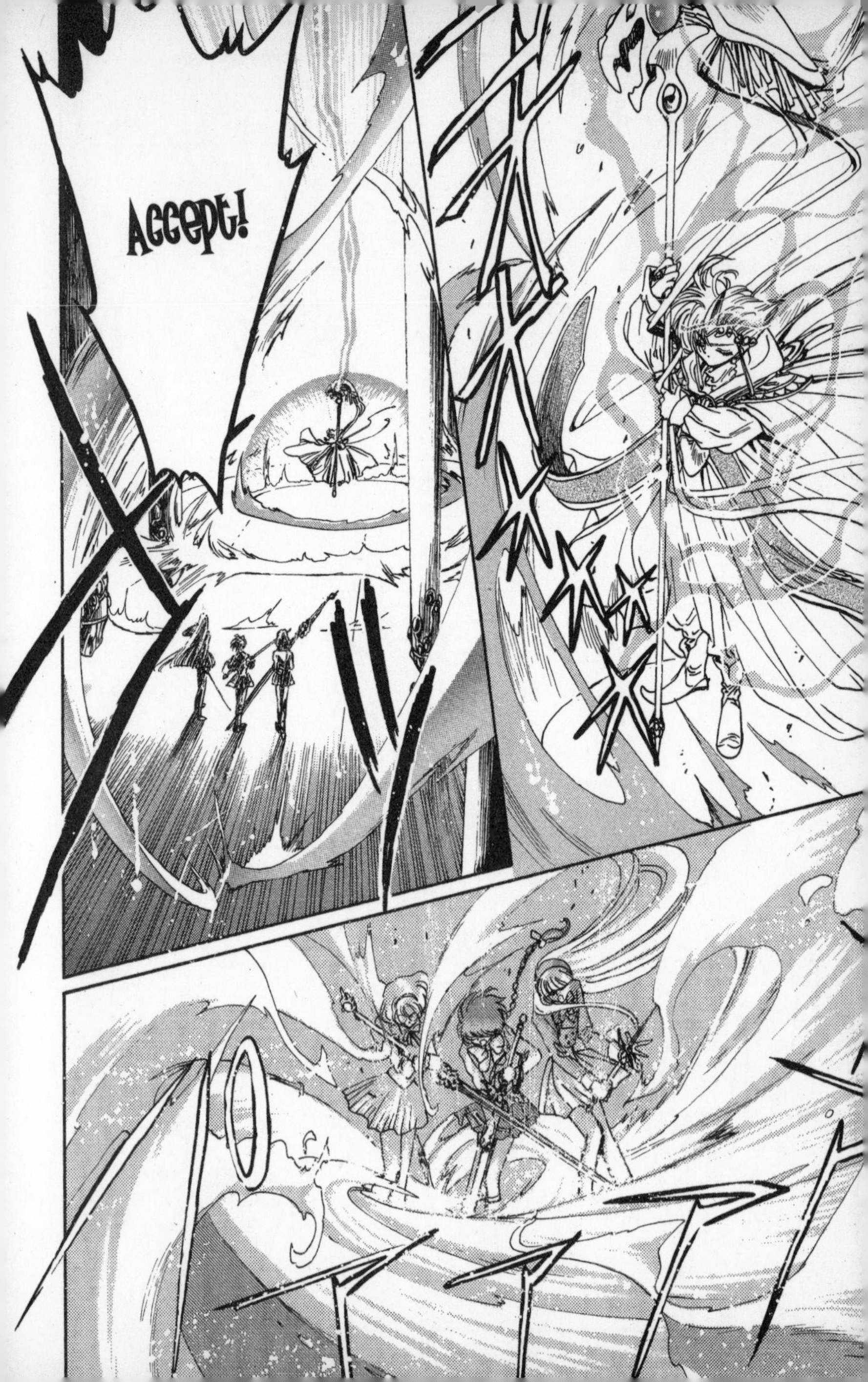
Accept!

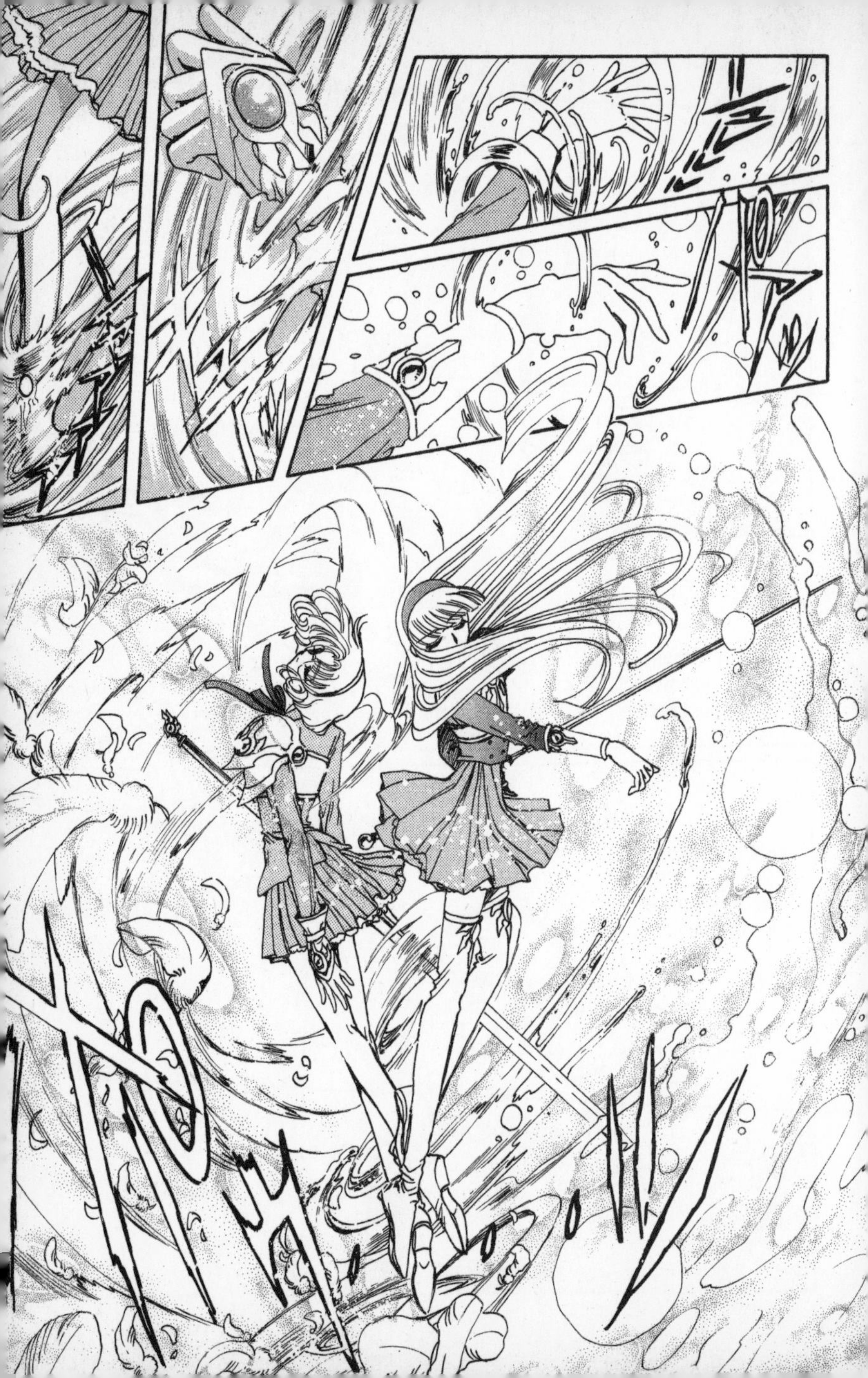

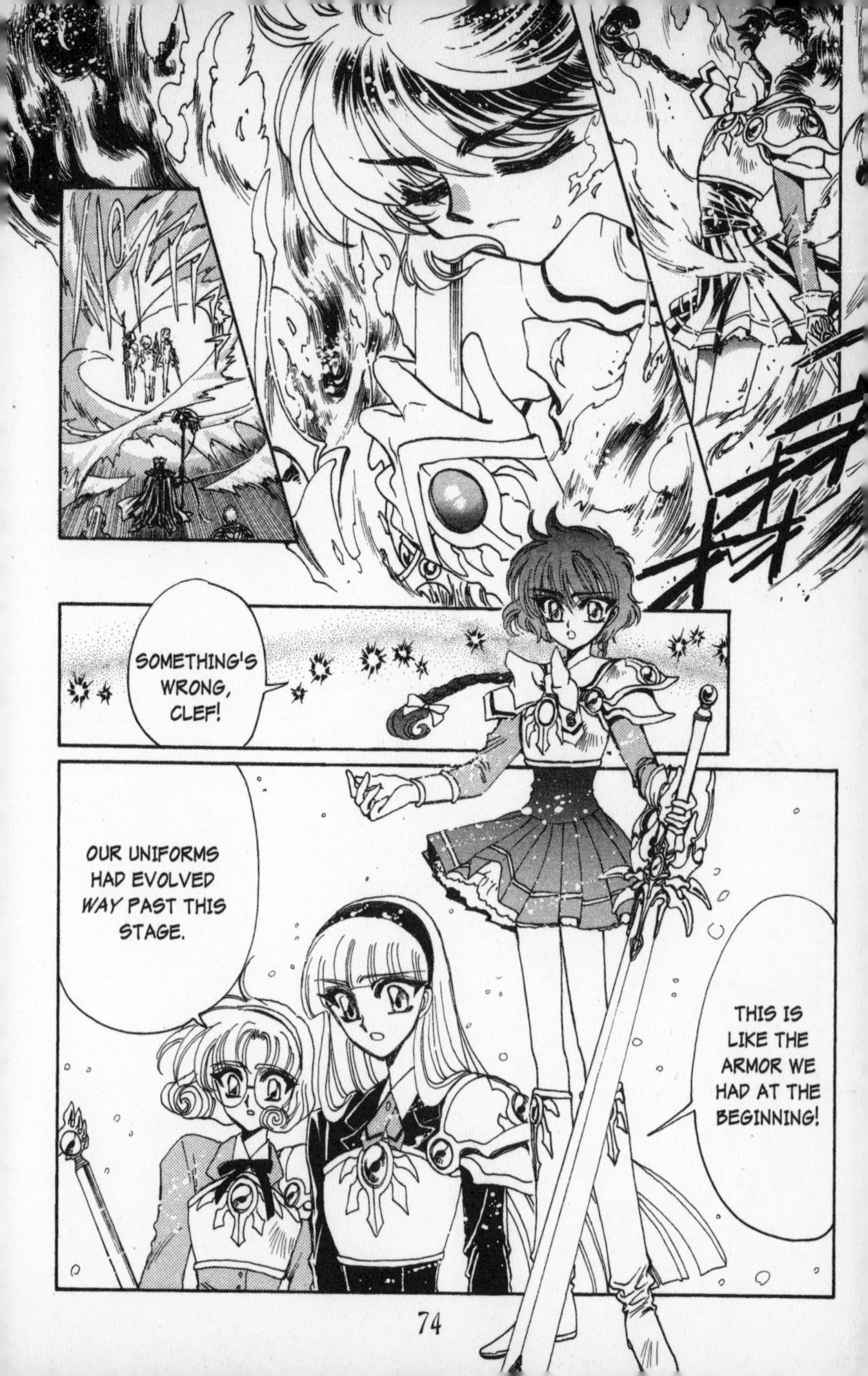
SOMETHING'S WRONG, CLEF!
THIS IS LIKE THE ARMOR WE HAD AT THE BEGINNING!
OUR UNIFORMS HAD EVOLVED *WAY* PAST THIS STAGE.

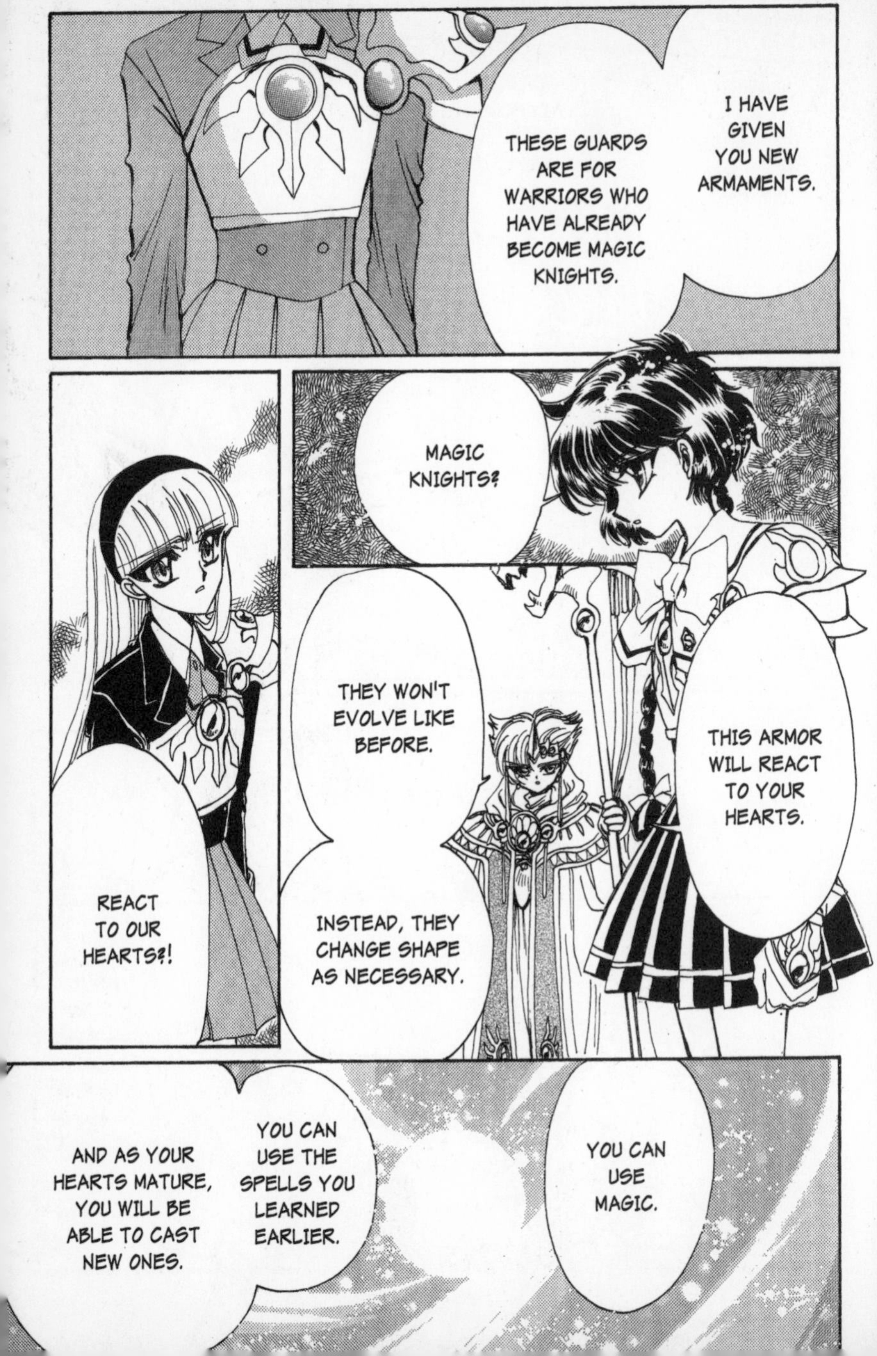
I HAVE GIVEN YOU NEW ARMAMENTS.
THESE GUARDS ARE FOR WARRIORS WHO HAVE ALREADY BECOME MAGIC KNIGHTS.
MAGIC KNIGHTS?
THIS ARMOR WILL REACT TO YOUR HEARTS.
THEY WON'T EVOLVE LIKE BEFORE.
INSTEAD, THEY CHANGE SHAPE AS NECESSARY.
REACT TO OUR HEARTS?!
YOU CAN USE MAGIC.
YOU CAN USE THE SPELLS YOU LEARNED EARLIER.
AND AS YOUR HEARTS MATURE, YOU WILL BE ABLE TO CAST NEW ONES.

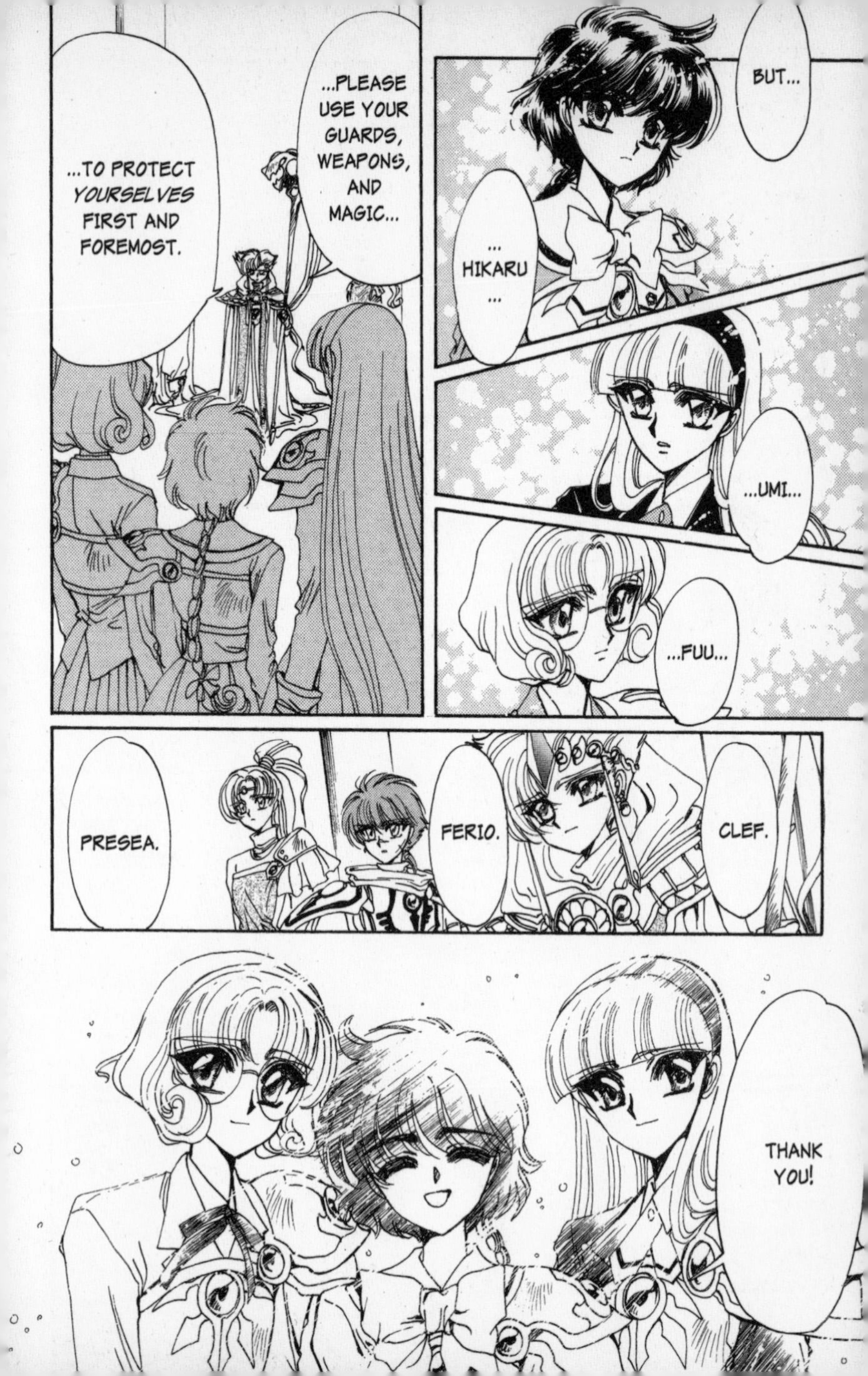
BUT...
... HIKARU ...
...UMI...
...FUU...
...PLEASE USE YOUR GUARDS, WEAPONS, AND MAGIC...
...TO PROTECT *YOURSELVES* FIRST AND FOREMOST.
CLEF.
FERIO.
PRESEA.
THANK YOU!

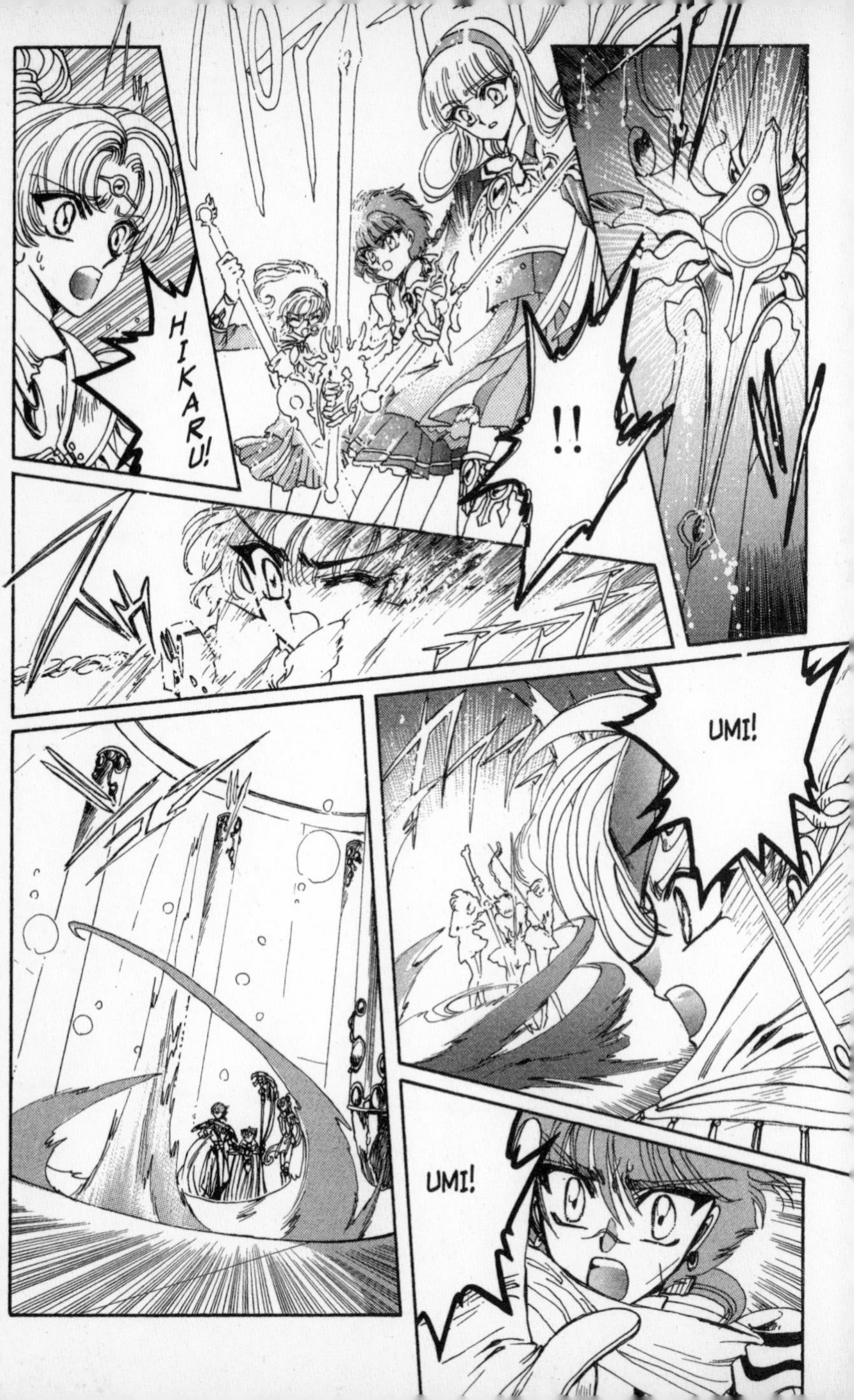
!!
HIKARU!
UMI!
UMI!

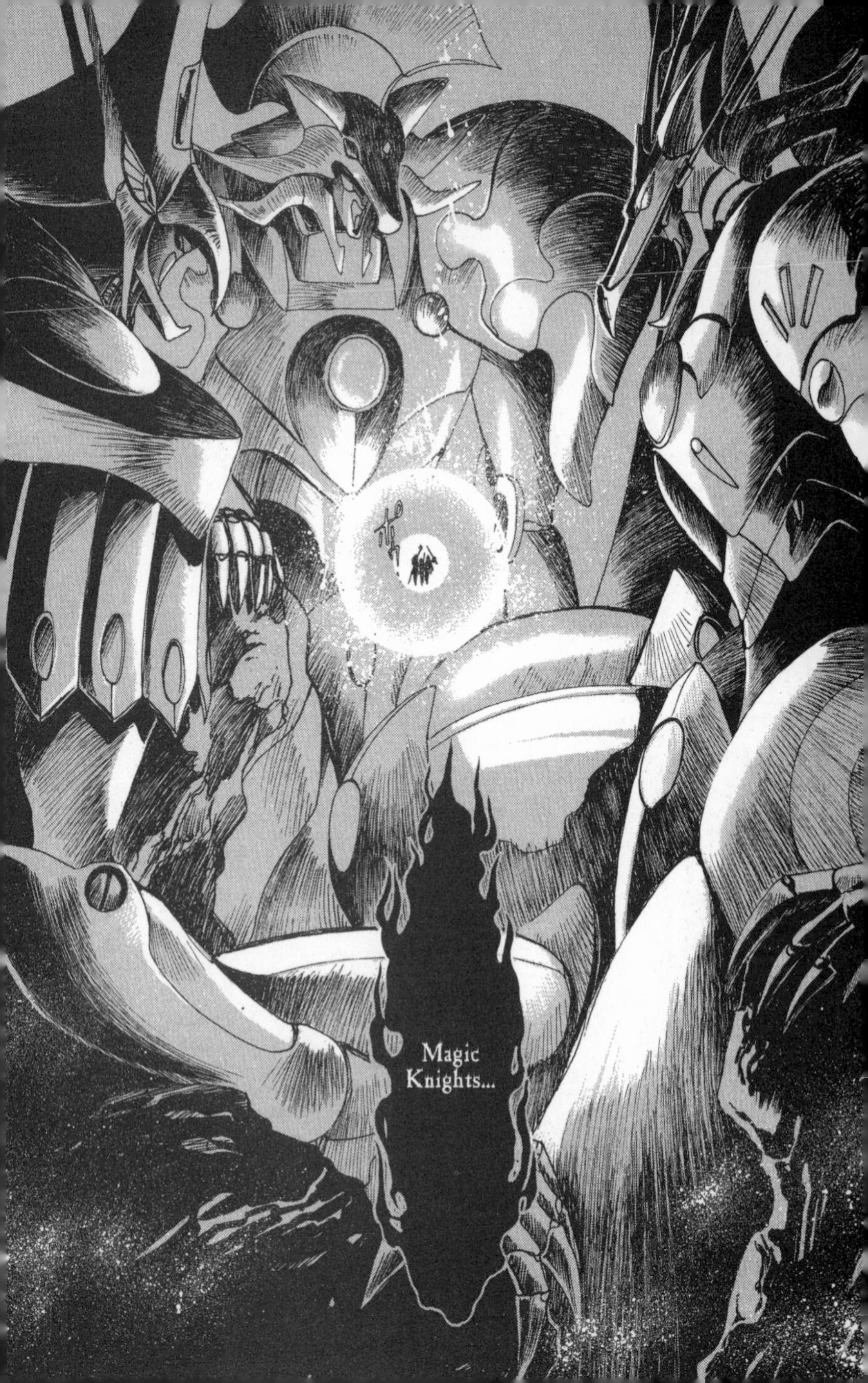
Magic Knights...

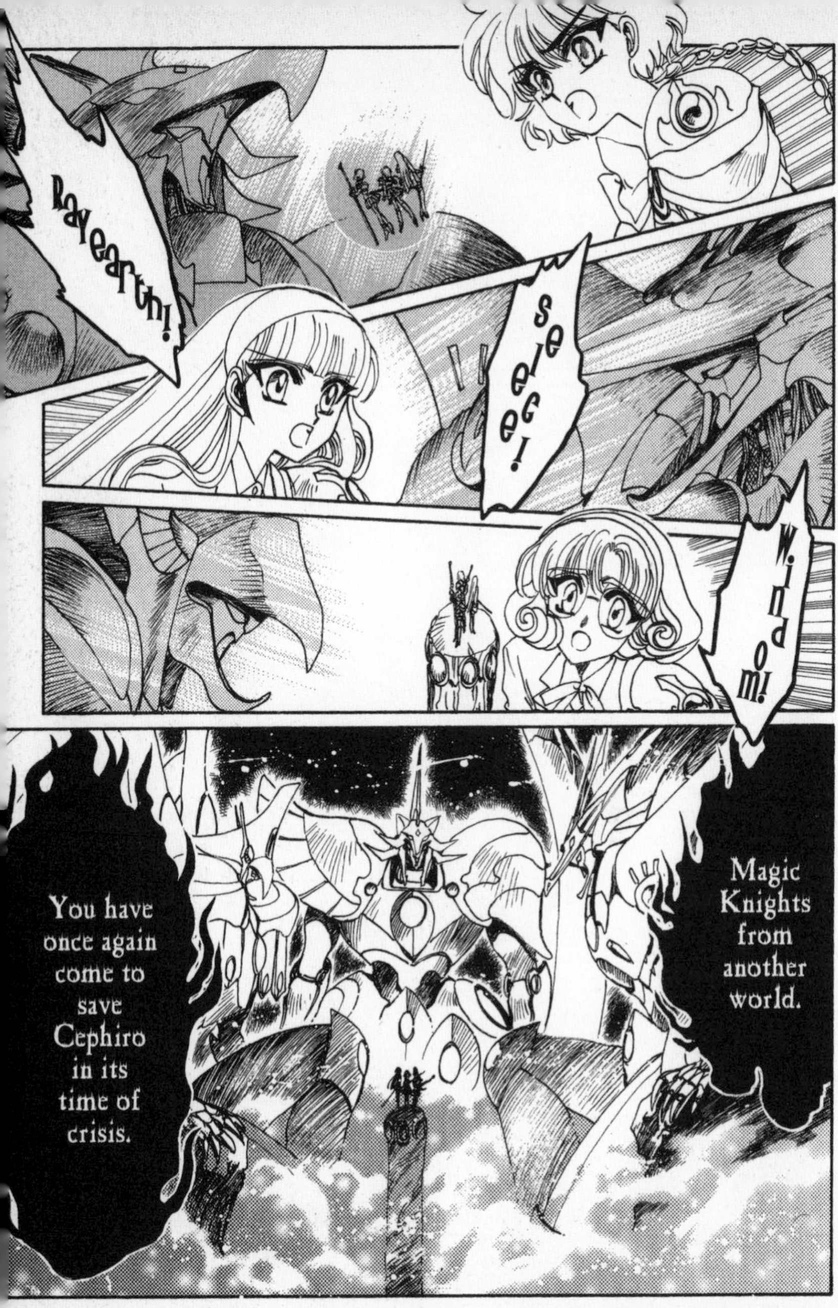
Rayearth!
Selece!
Windom!
Magic Knights from another world.
You have once again come to save Cephiro in its time of crisis.

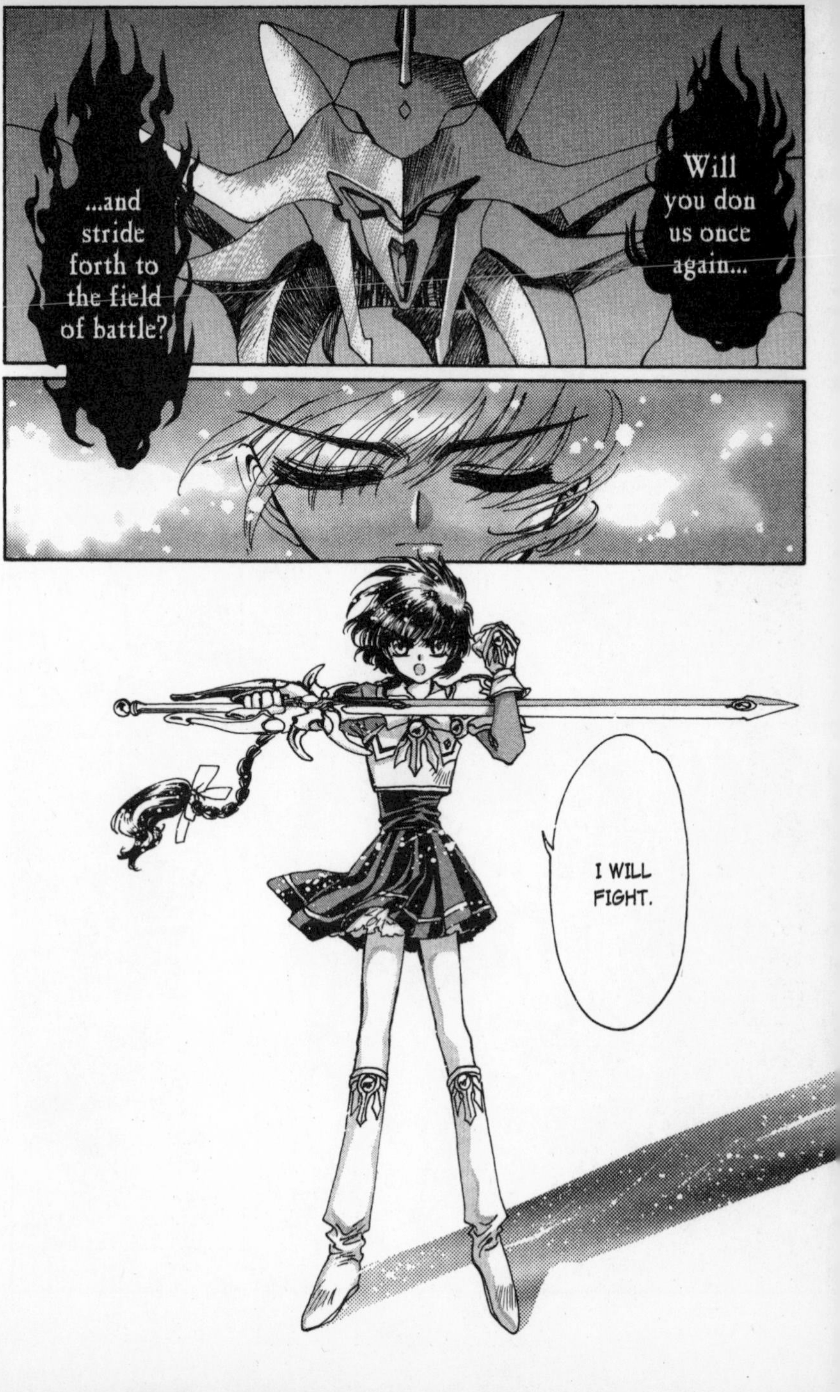
Will you don us once again...
...and stride forth to the field of battle?
I WILL FIGHT.

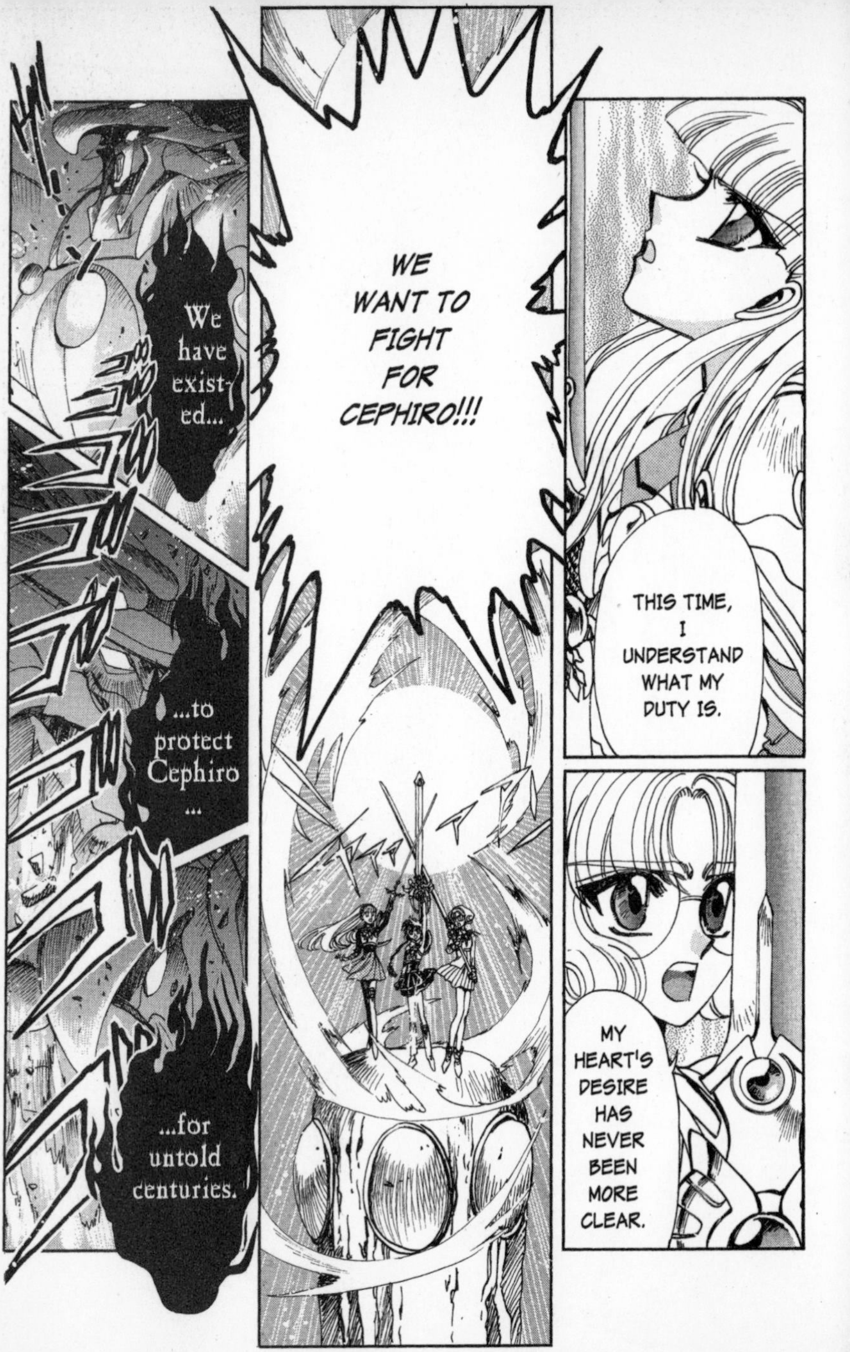
THIS TIME, I UNDERSTAND WHAT MY DUTY IS.
MY HEART'S DESIRE HAS NEVER BEEN MORE CLEAR.
WE WANT TO FIGHT FOR CEPHIRO!!!
We have exist-ed...
...to protect Cephiro...
...for untold centuries.

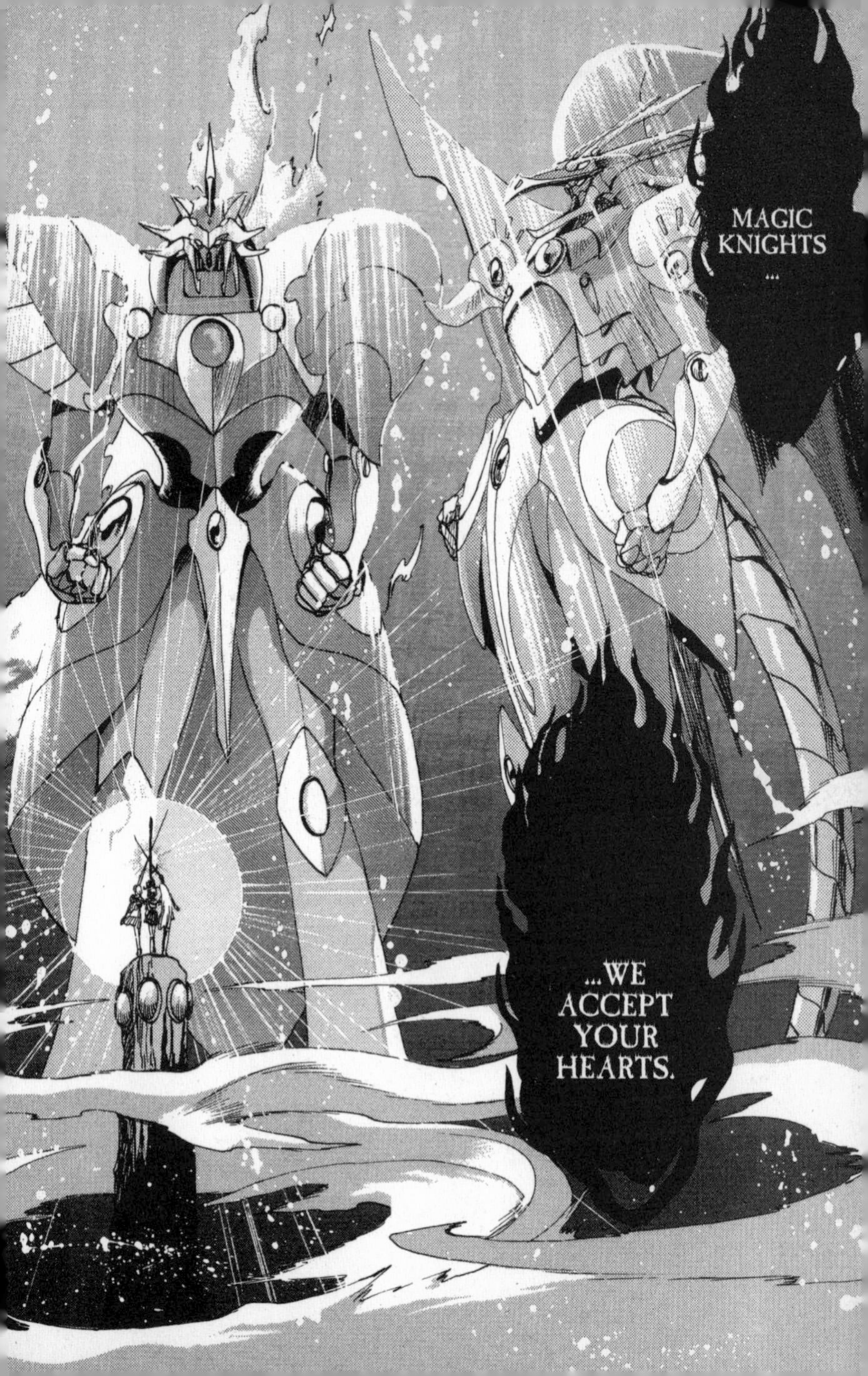
MAGIC KNIGHTS ...
...WE ACCEPT YOUR HEARTS.

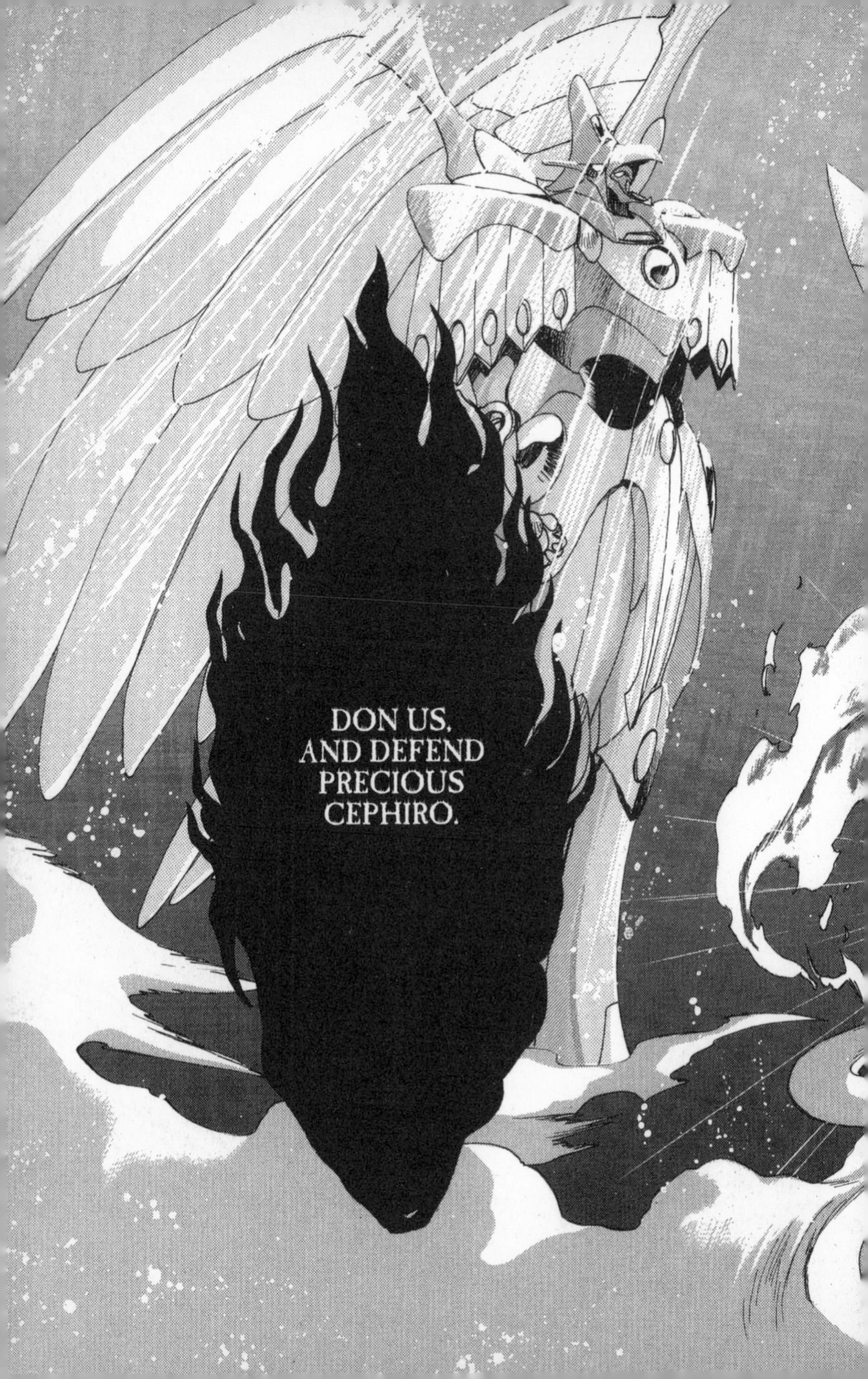
DON US. AND DEFEND PRECIOUS CEPHIRO.

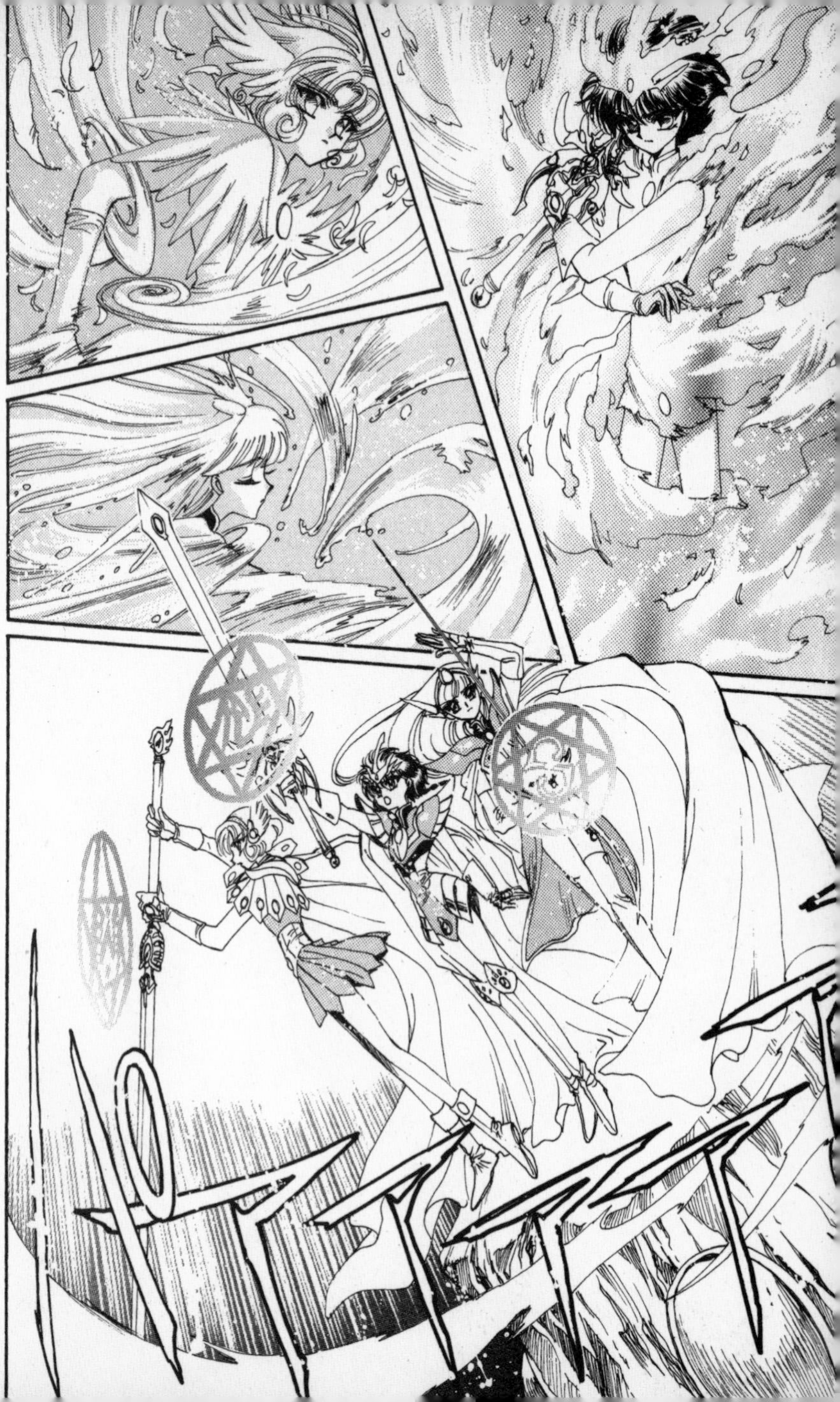

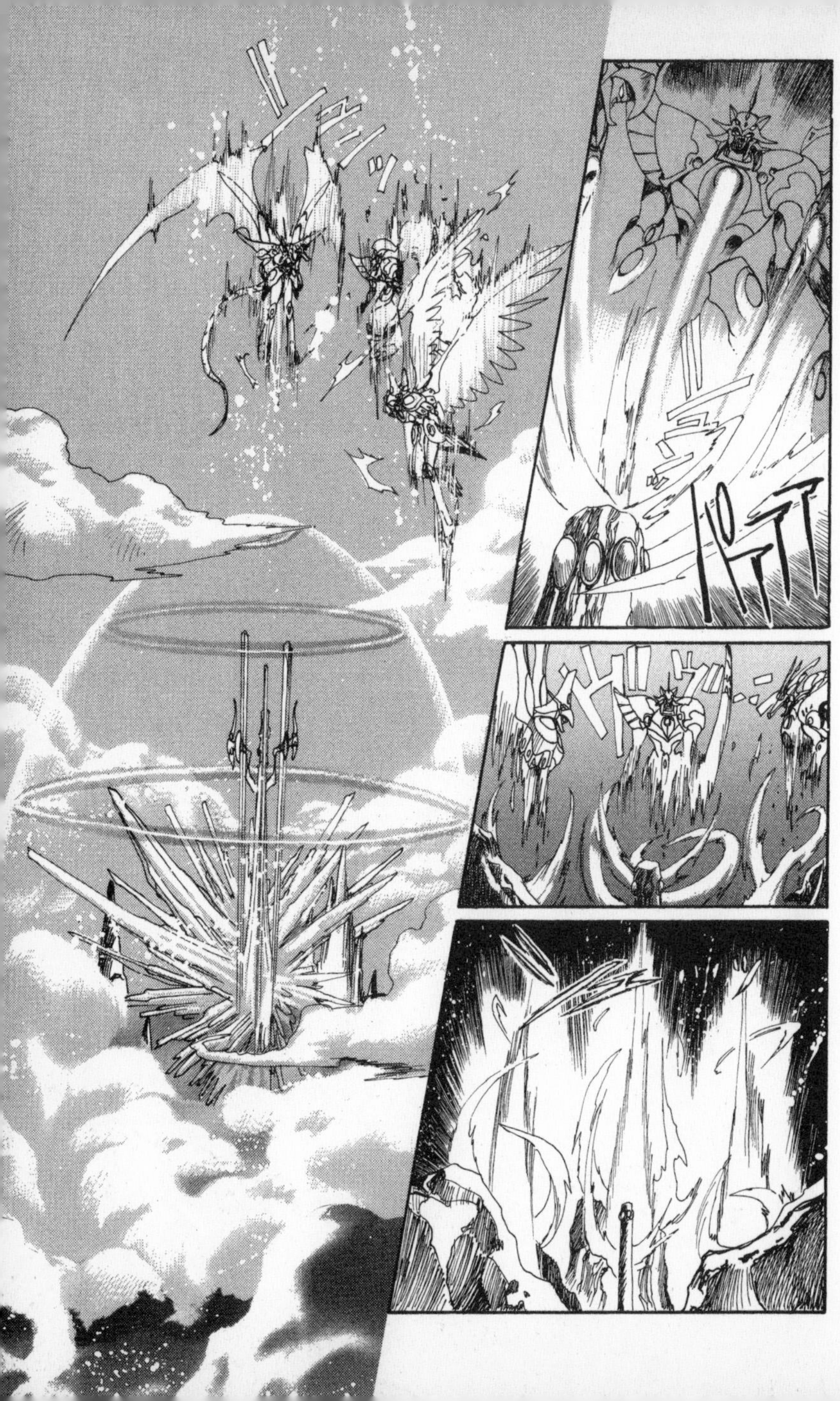
パァァァ

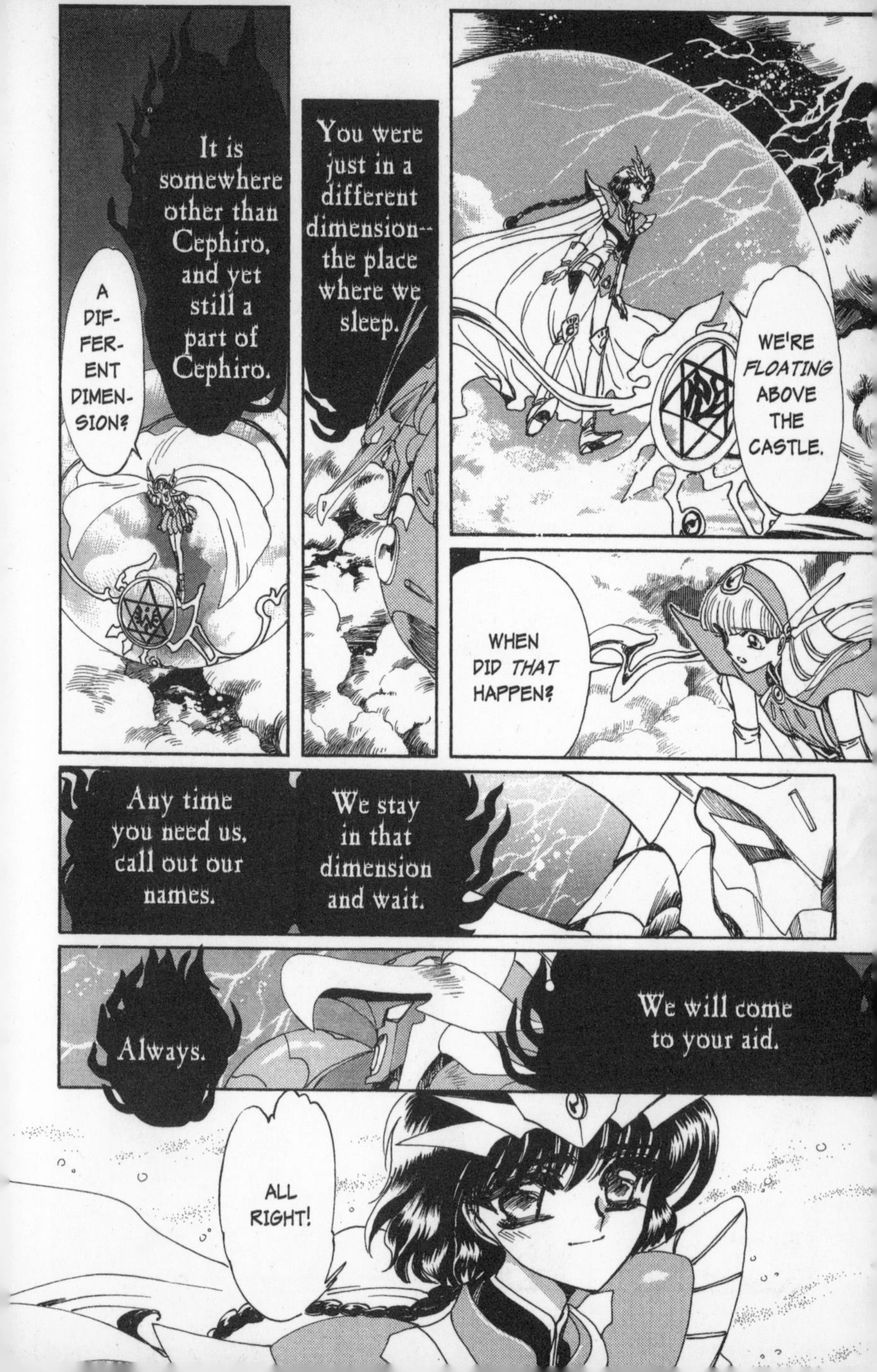
WE'RE *FLOATING* ABOVE THE CASTLE.
WHEN DID *THAT* HAPPEN?
You were just in a different dimension-- the place where we sleep.
It is somewhere other than Cephiro, and yet still a part of Cephiro.
A DIF-FER-ENT DIMEN-SION?
We stay in that dimension and wait.
Any time you need us, call out our names.
We will come to your aid.
Always.
ALL RIGHT!

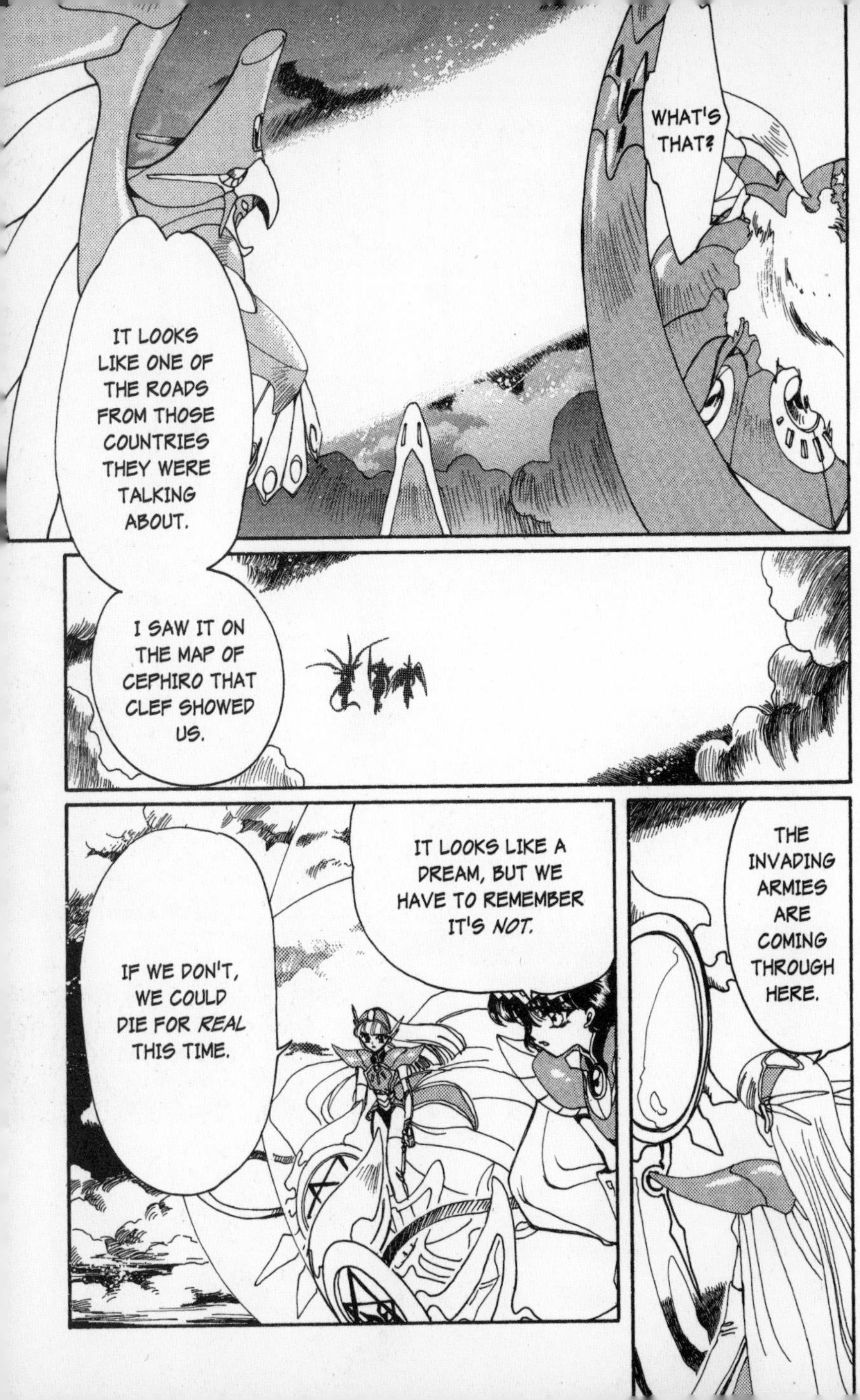
WHAT'S THAT?
IT LOOKS LIKE ONE OF THE ROADS FROM THOSE COUNTRIES THEY WERE TALKING ABOUT.
I SAW IT ON THE MAP OF CEPHIRO THAT CLEF SHOWED US.
THE INVADING ARMIES ARE COMING THROUGH HERE.
IT LOOKS LIKE A DREAM, BUT WE HAVE TO REMEMBER IT'S *NOT.*
IF WE DON'T, WE COULD DIE FOR *REAL* THIS TIME.

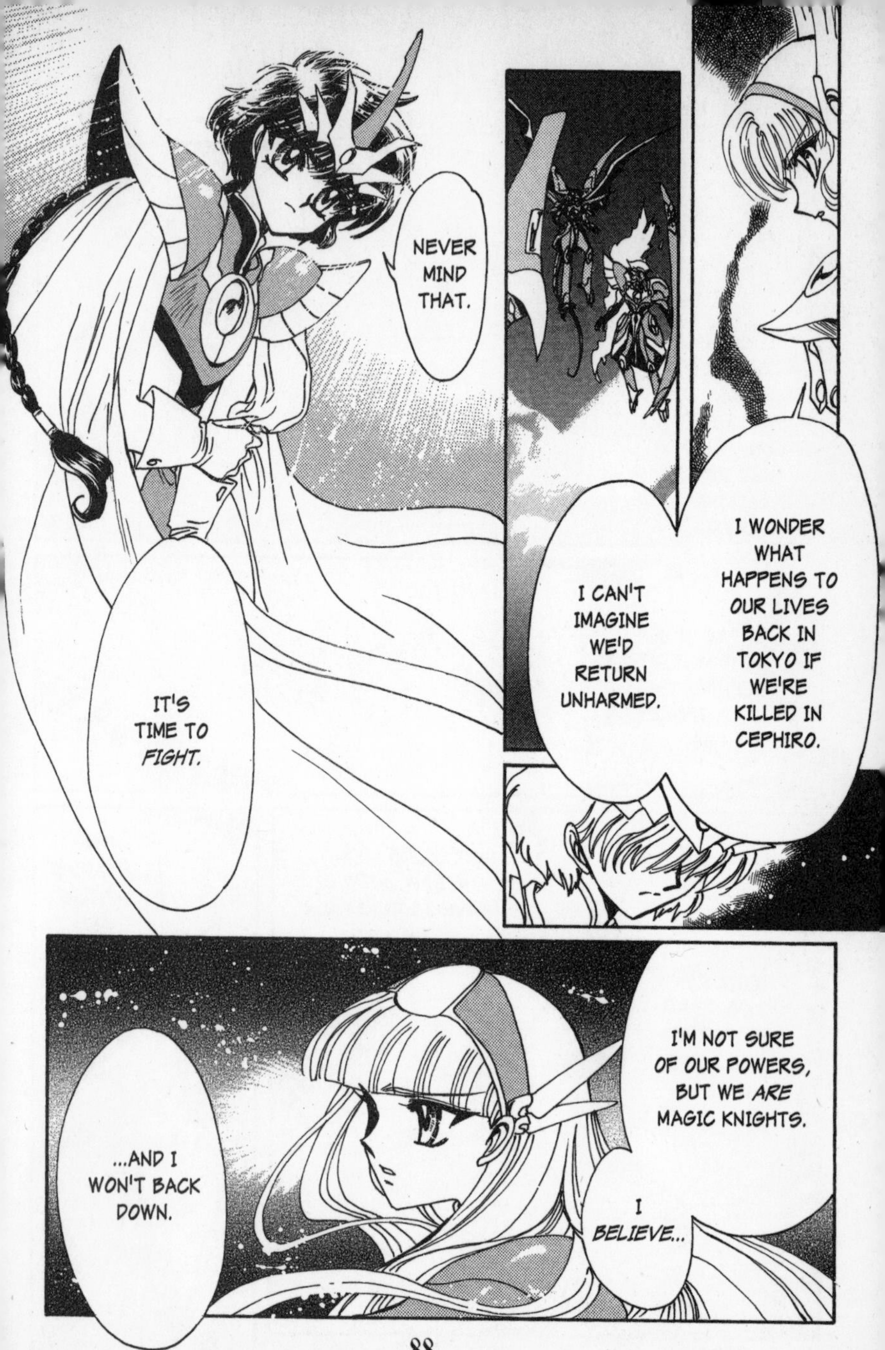
I WONDER WHAT HAPPENS TO OUR LIVES BACK IN TOKYO IF WE'RE KILLED IN CEPHIRO.
I CAN'T IMAGINE WE'D RETURN UNHARMED.
NEVER MIND THAT.
IT'S TIME TO *FIGHT.*
I'M NOT SURE OF OUR POWERS, BUT WE *ARE* MAGIC KNIGHTS.
I *BELIEVE...*
...AND I WON'T BACK DOWN.

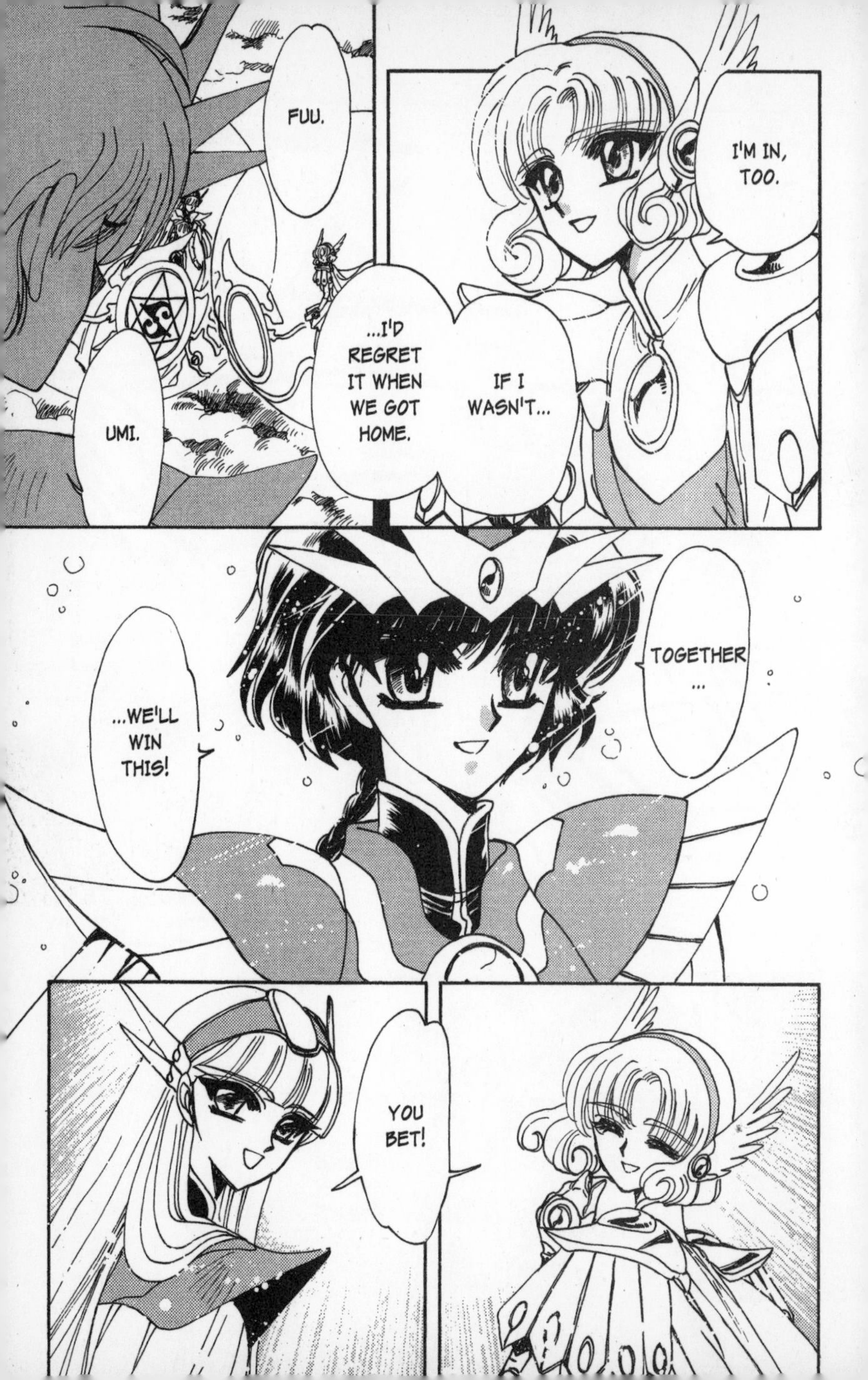
I'M IN, TOO.
IF I WASN'T...
...I'D REGRET IT WHEN WE GOT HOME.
FUU.
UMI.
TOGETHER...
...WE'LL WIN THIS!
YOU BET!

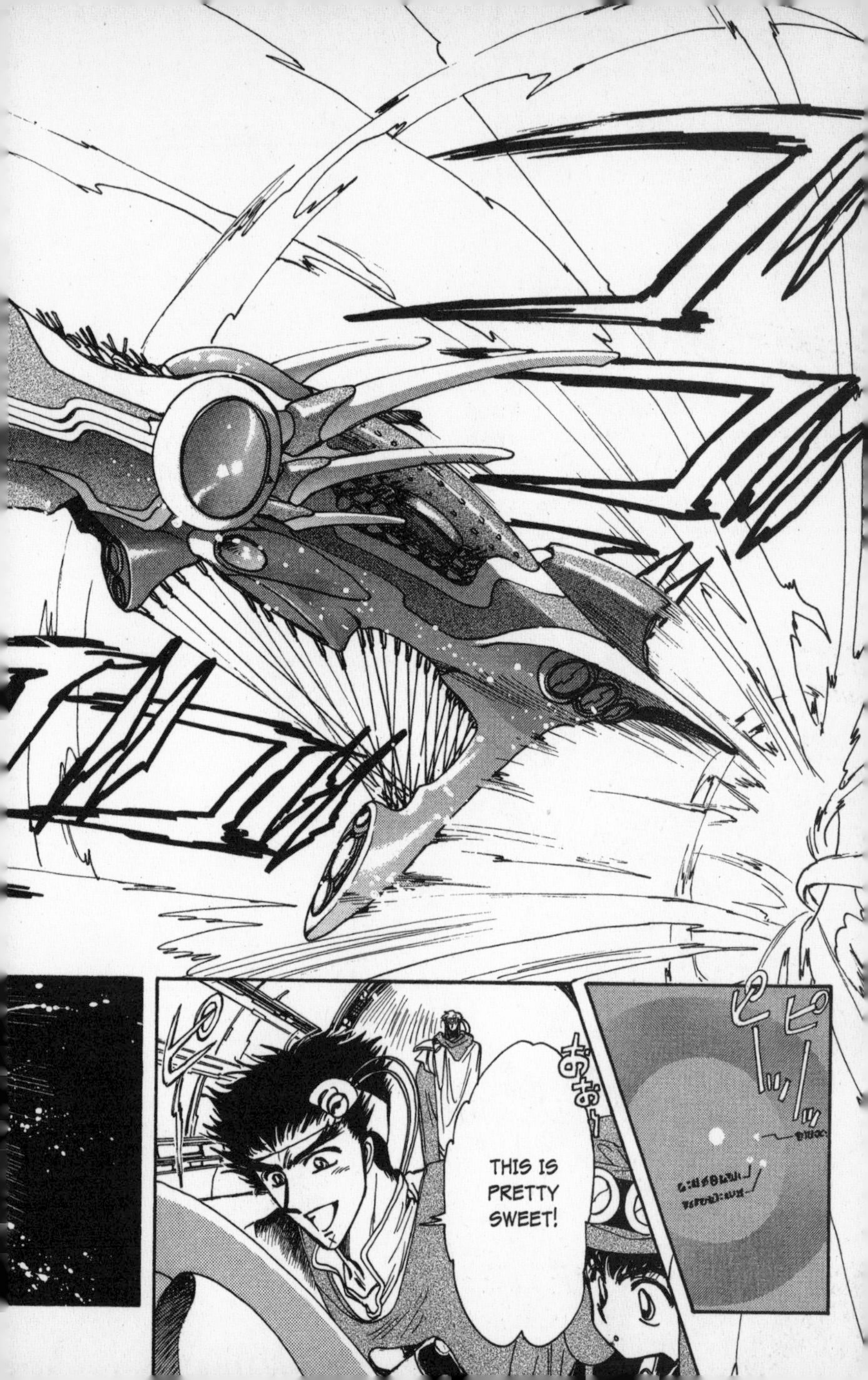
THIS IS PRETTY SWEET!

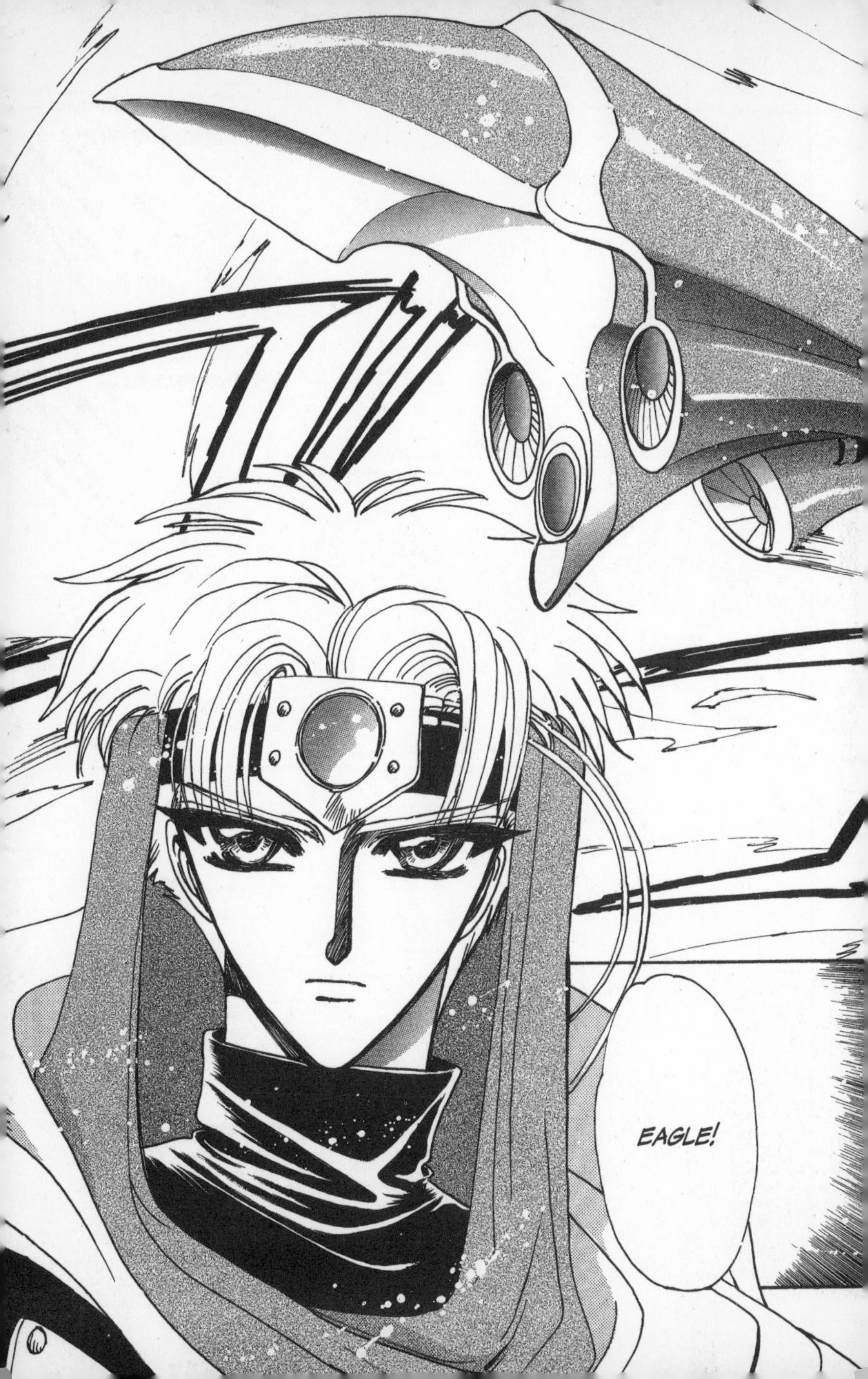
EAGLE!

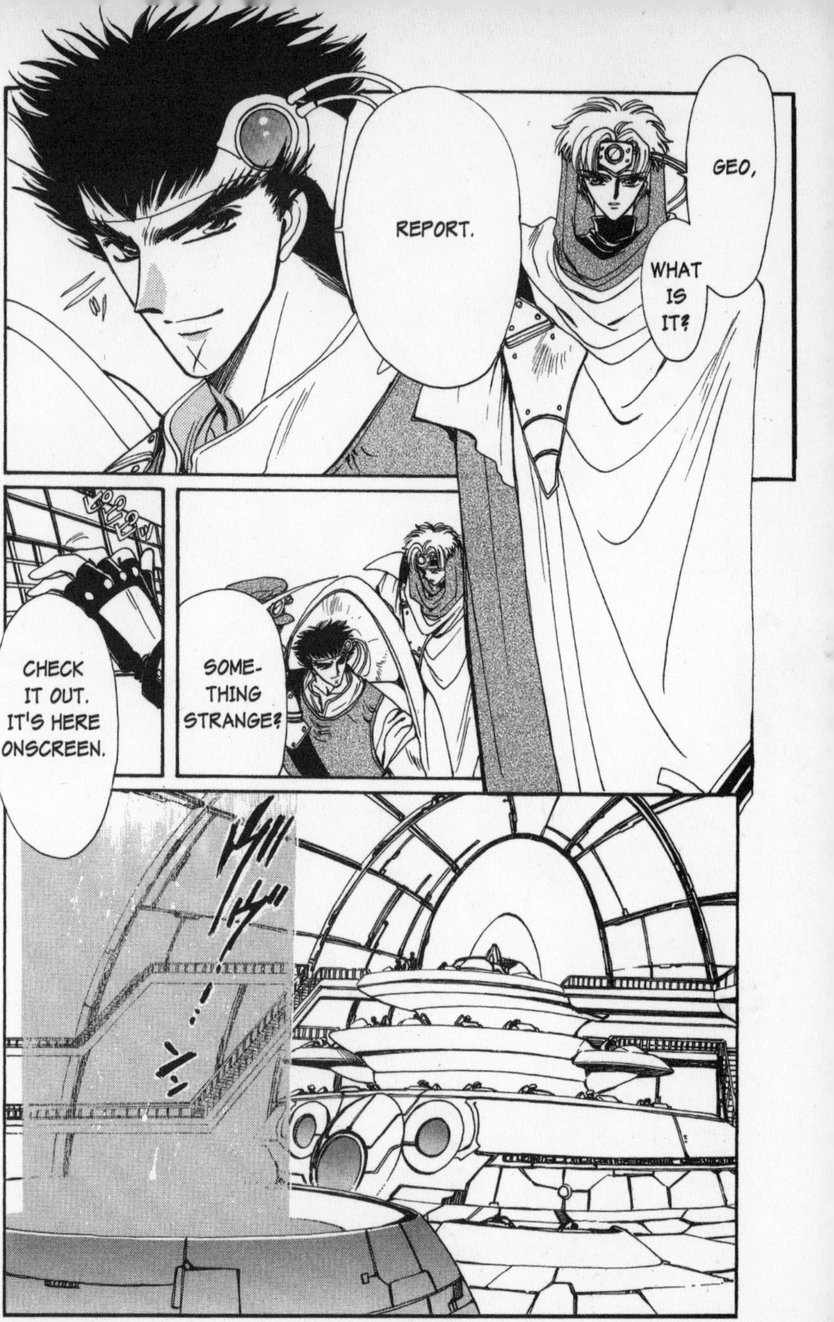
GEO,
WHAT IS IT?
REPORT.
SOME-THING STRANGE?
CHECK IT OUT. IT'S HERE ONSCREEN.

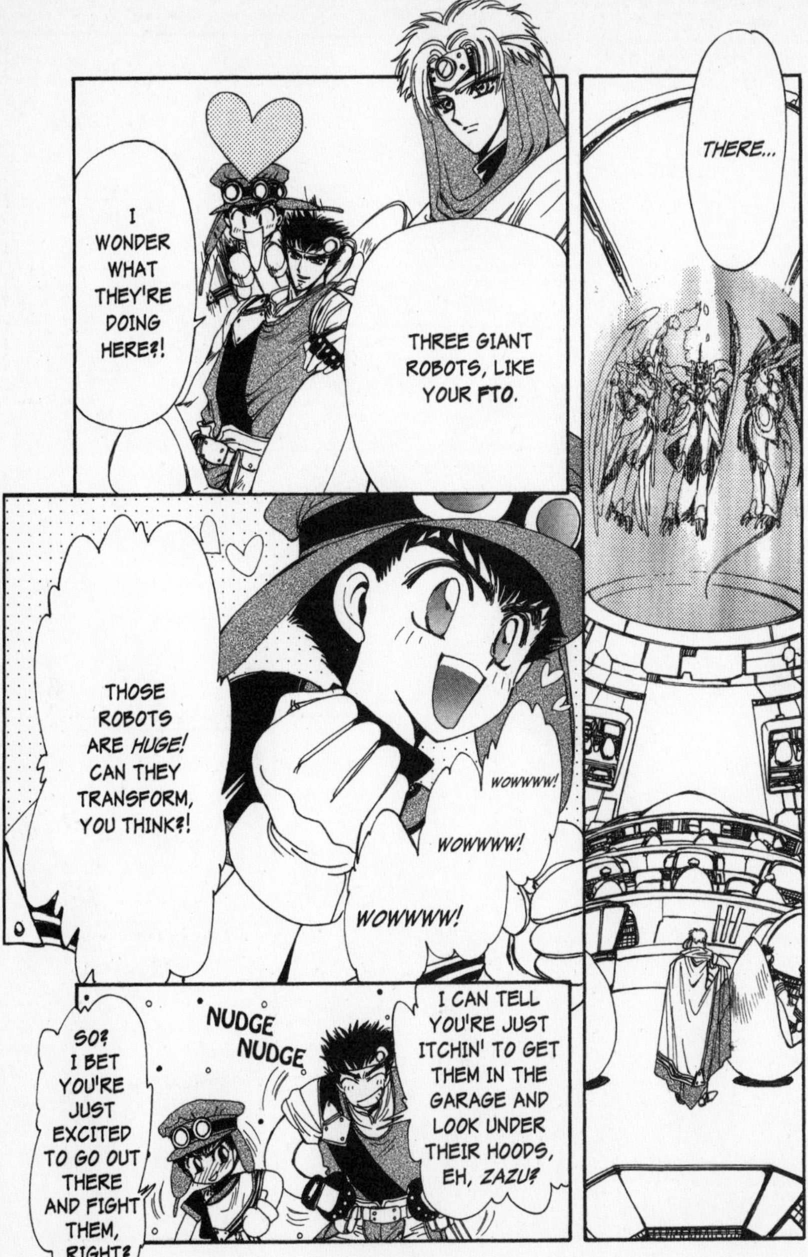
THERE...
THREE GIANT ROBOTS, LIKE YOUR FTO.
I WONDER WHAT THEY'RE DOING HERE?!
THOSE ROBOTS ARE *HUGE*! CAN THEY TRANSFORM, YOU THINK?!
WOWWWW!
WOWWWW!
WOWWWW!
I CAN TELL YOU'RE JUST ITCHIN' TO GET THEM IN THE GARAGE AND LOOK UNDER THEIR HOODS, EH, ZAZU?
NUDGE NUDGE
SO? I BET YOU'RE JUST EXCITED TO GO OUT THERE AND FIGHT THEM, RIGHT?

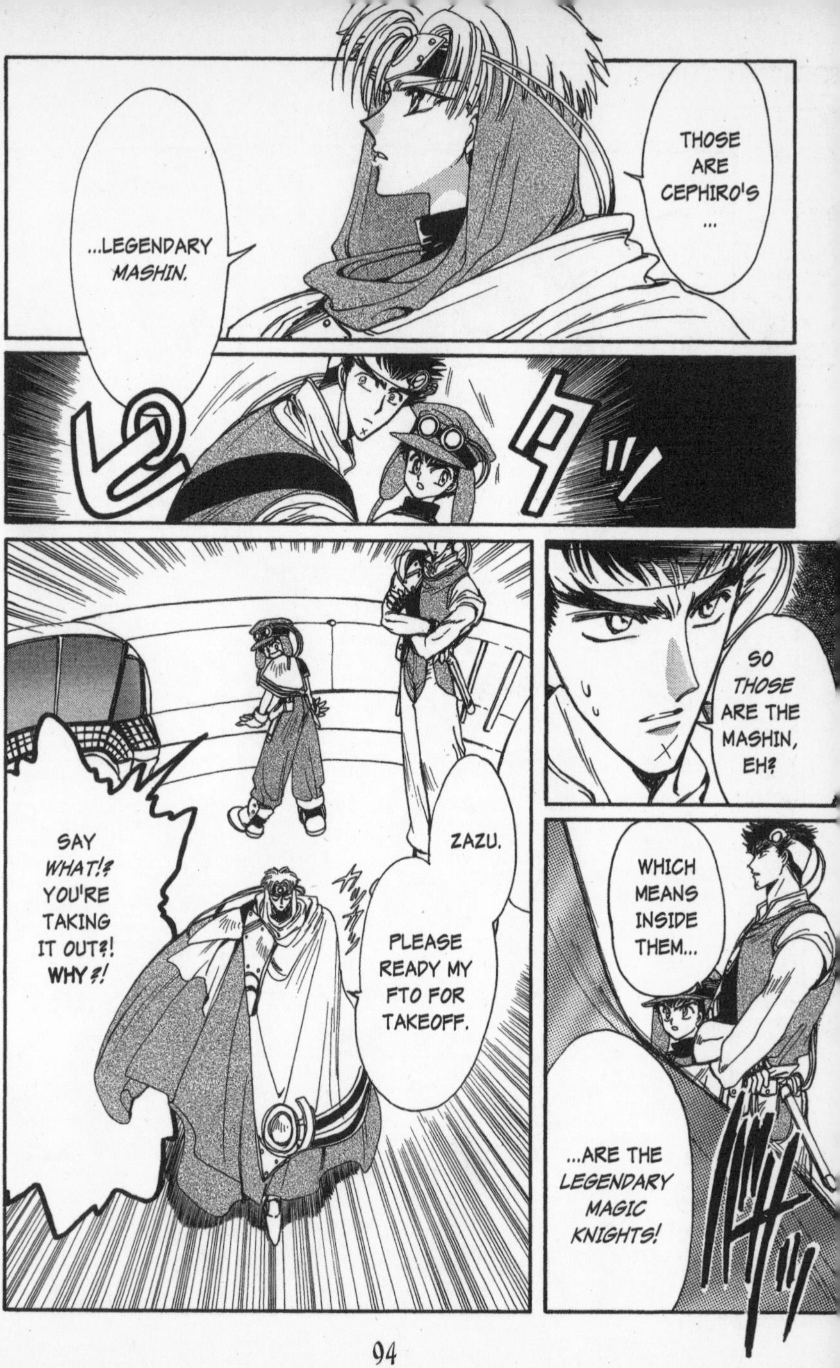
THOSE ARE CEPHIRO'S ...
...LEGENDARY MASHIN.
SO THOSE ARE THE MASHIN, EH?
WHICH MEANS INSIDE THEM...
...ARE THE LEGENDARY MAGIC KNIGHTS!
ZAZU.
PLEASE READY MY FTO FOR TAKEOFF.
SAY WHAT!? YOU'RE TAKING IT OUT?! WHY?!

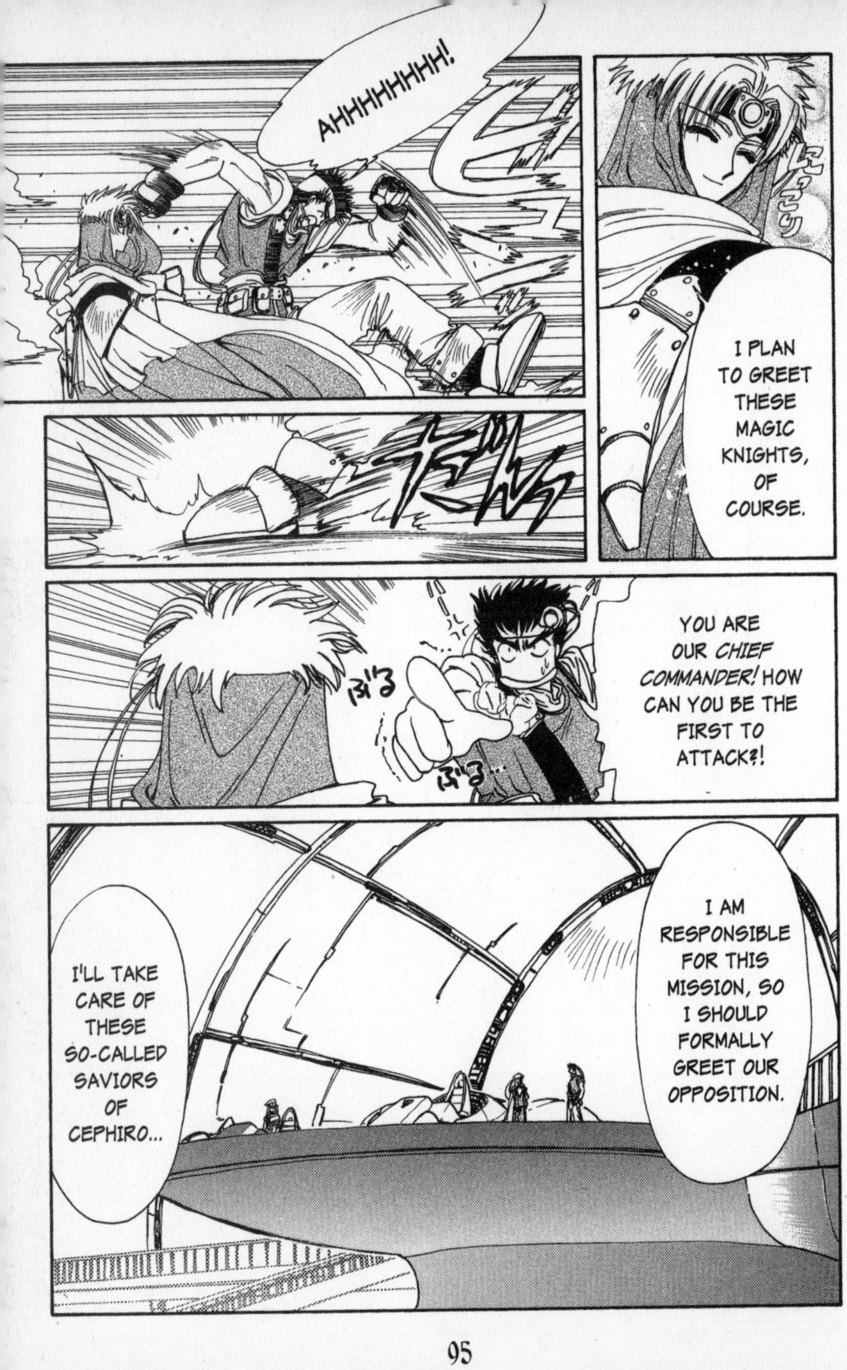
I PLAN TO GREET THESE MAGIC KNIGHTS, OF COURSE.
AHHHHHHHH!
YOU ARE OUR *CHIEF COMMANDER!* HOW CAN YOU BE THE FIRST TO ATTACK?!
ぶる
ぶる…
I AM RESPONSIBLE FOR THIS MISSION, SO I SHOULD FORMALLY GREET OUR OPPOSITION.
I'LL TAKE CARE OF THESE SO-CALLED SAVIORS OF CEPHIRO...

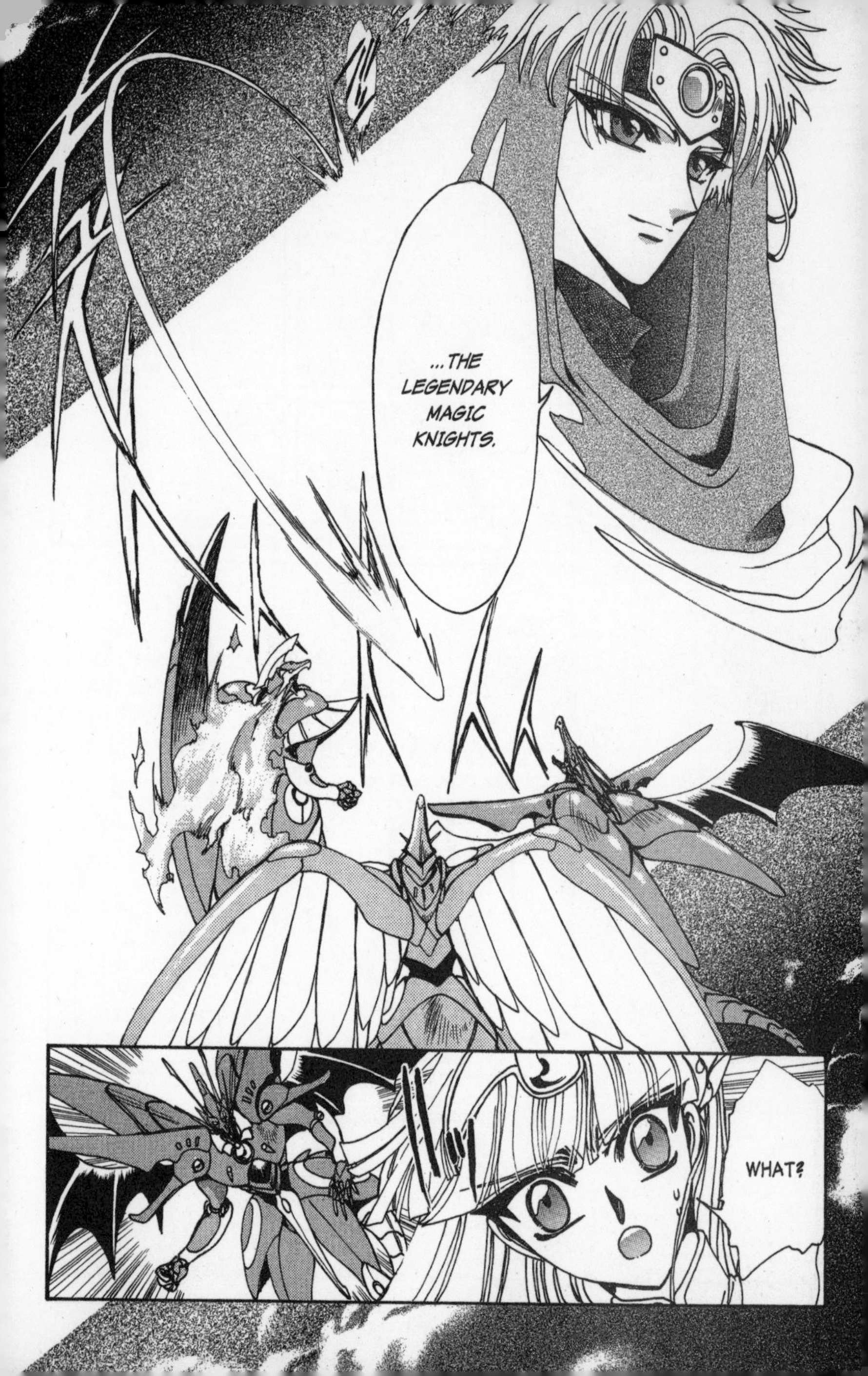
...THE LEGENDARY MAGIC KNIGHTS.
WHAT?

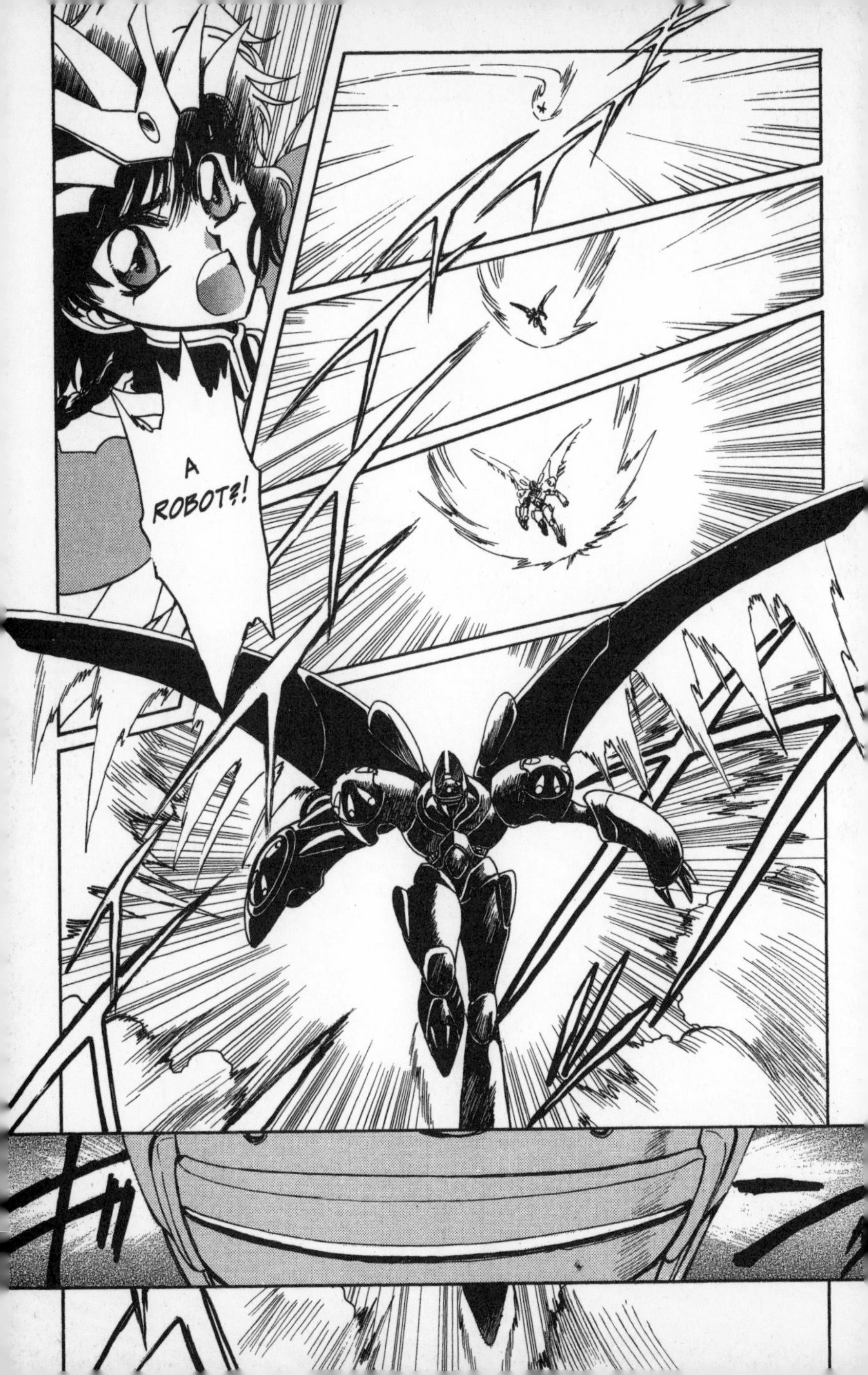
A ROBOT?!

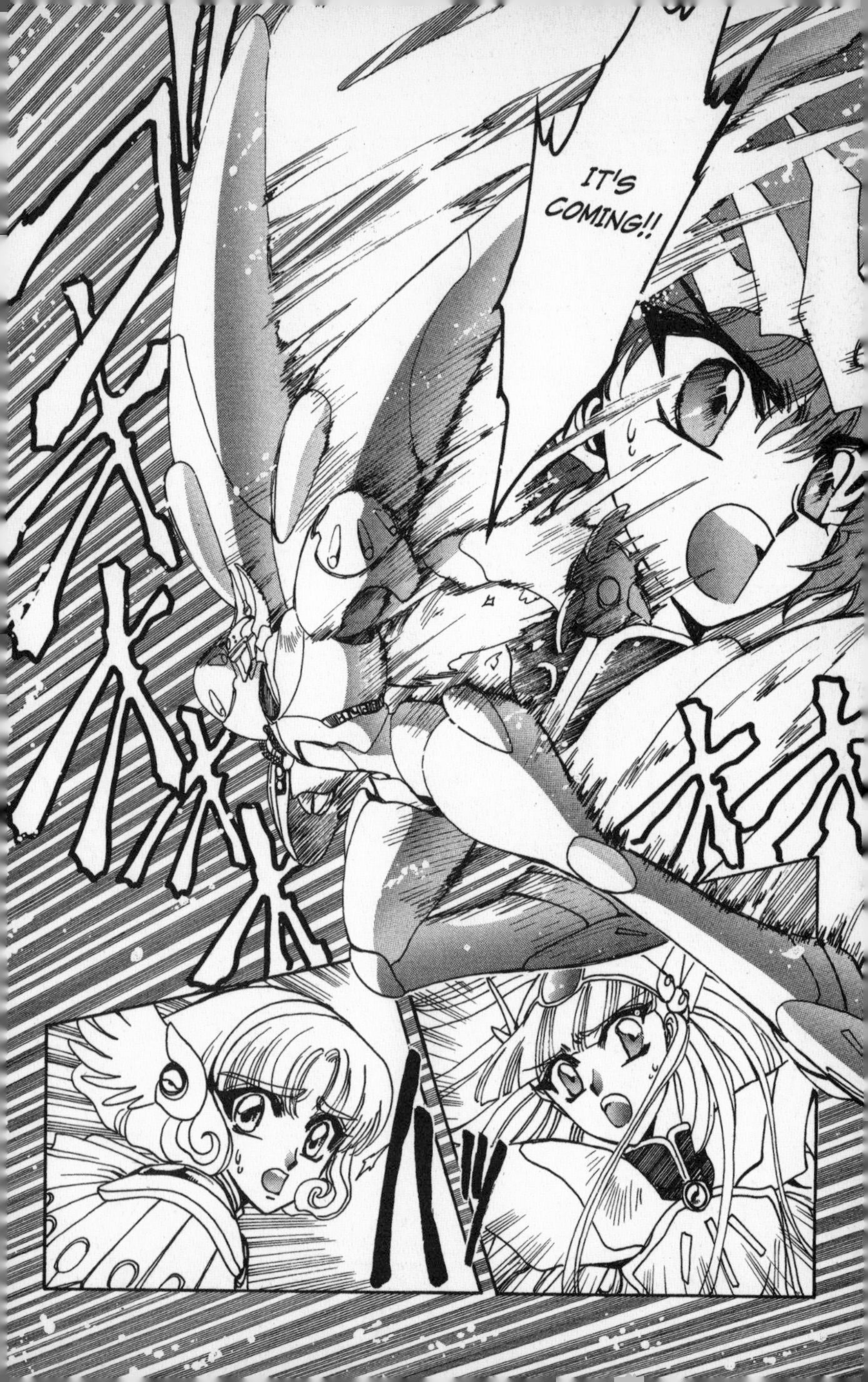
IT'S COMING!!

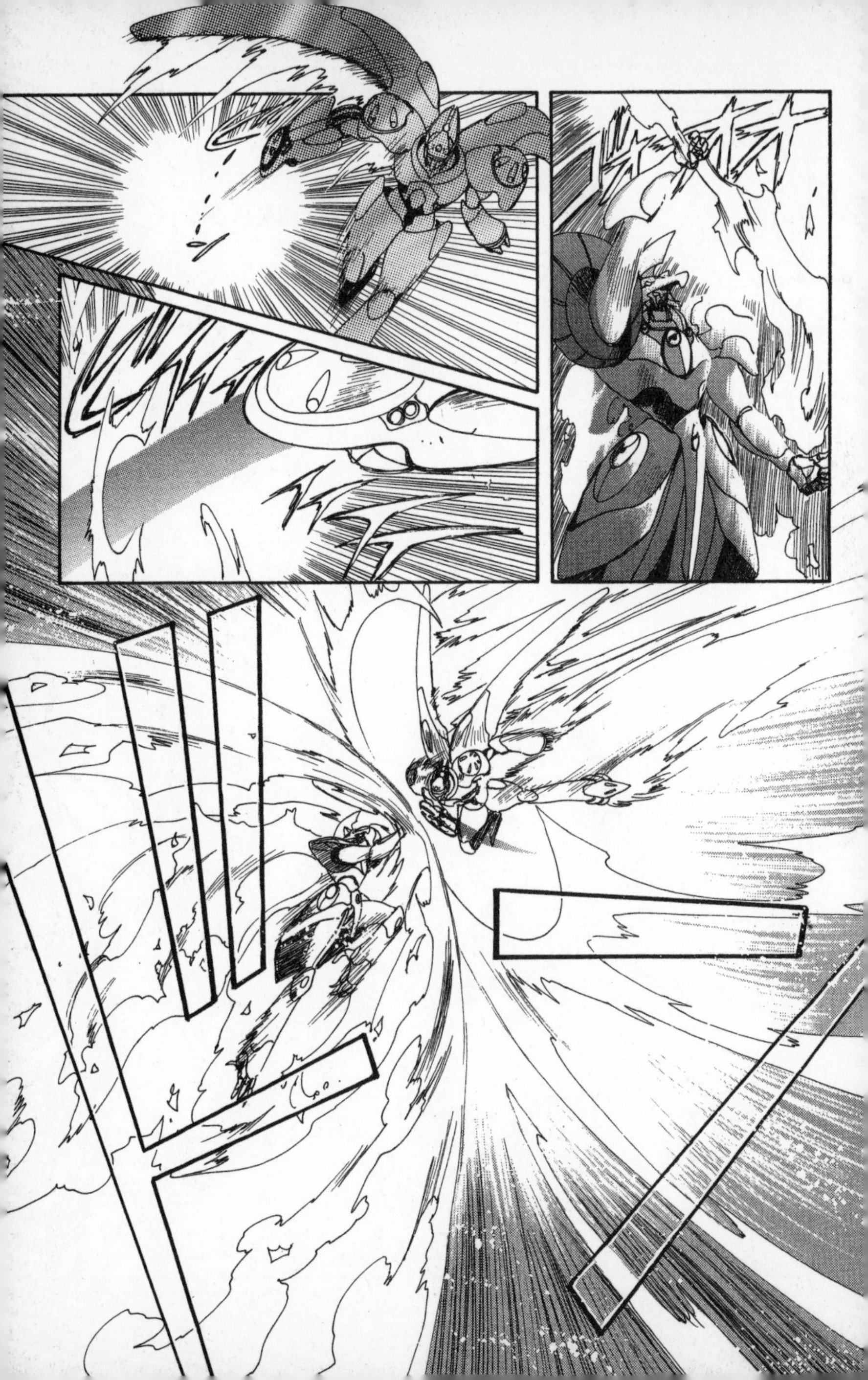

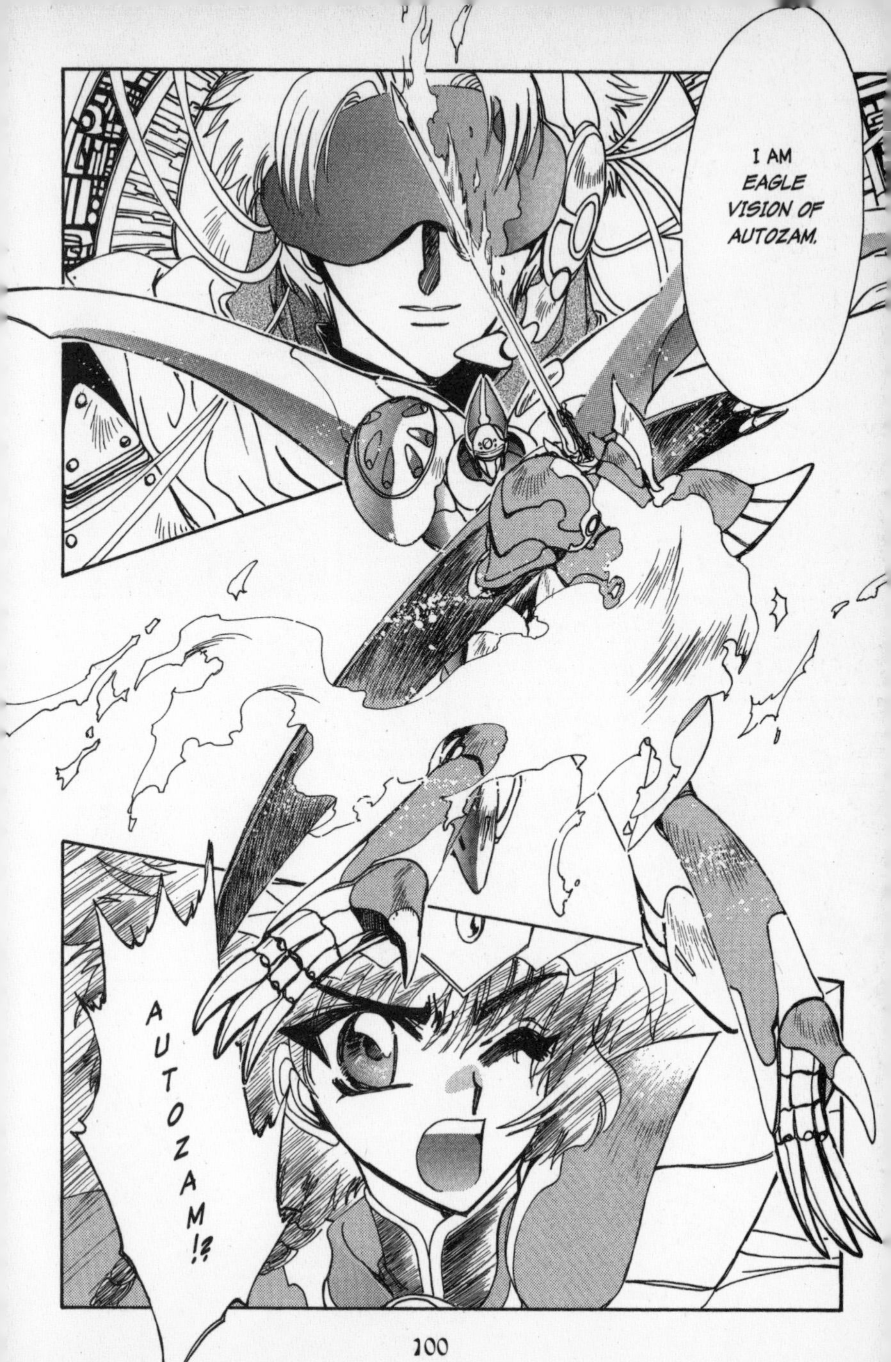
I AM EAGLE VISION OF AUTOZAM.
AUTOZAM!?

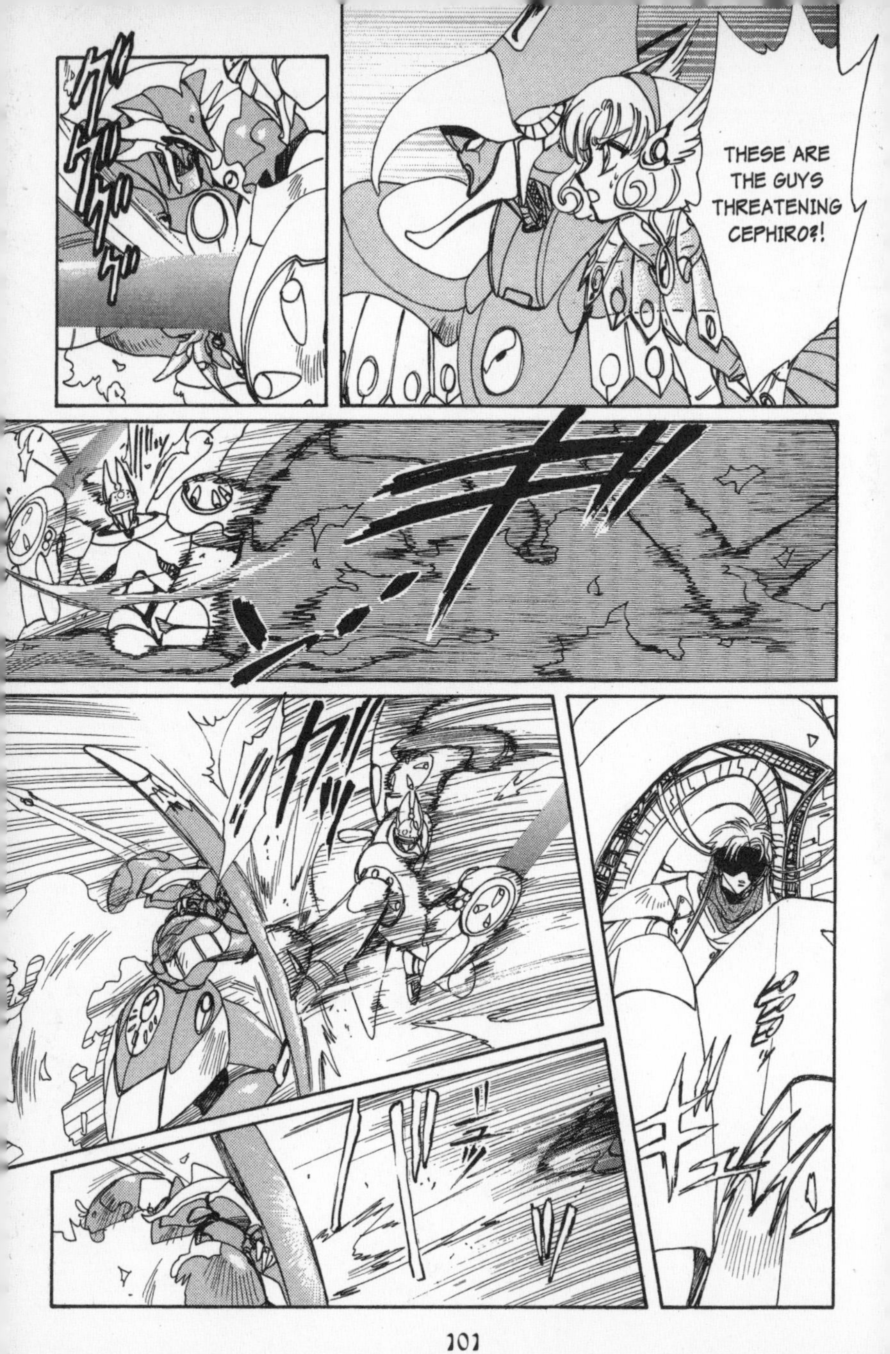
THESE ARE THE GUYS THREATENING CEPHIRO?!

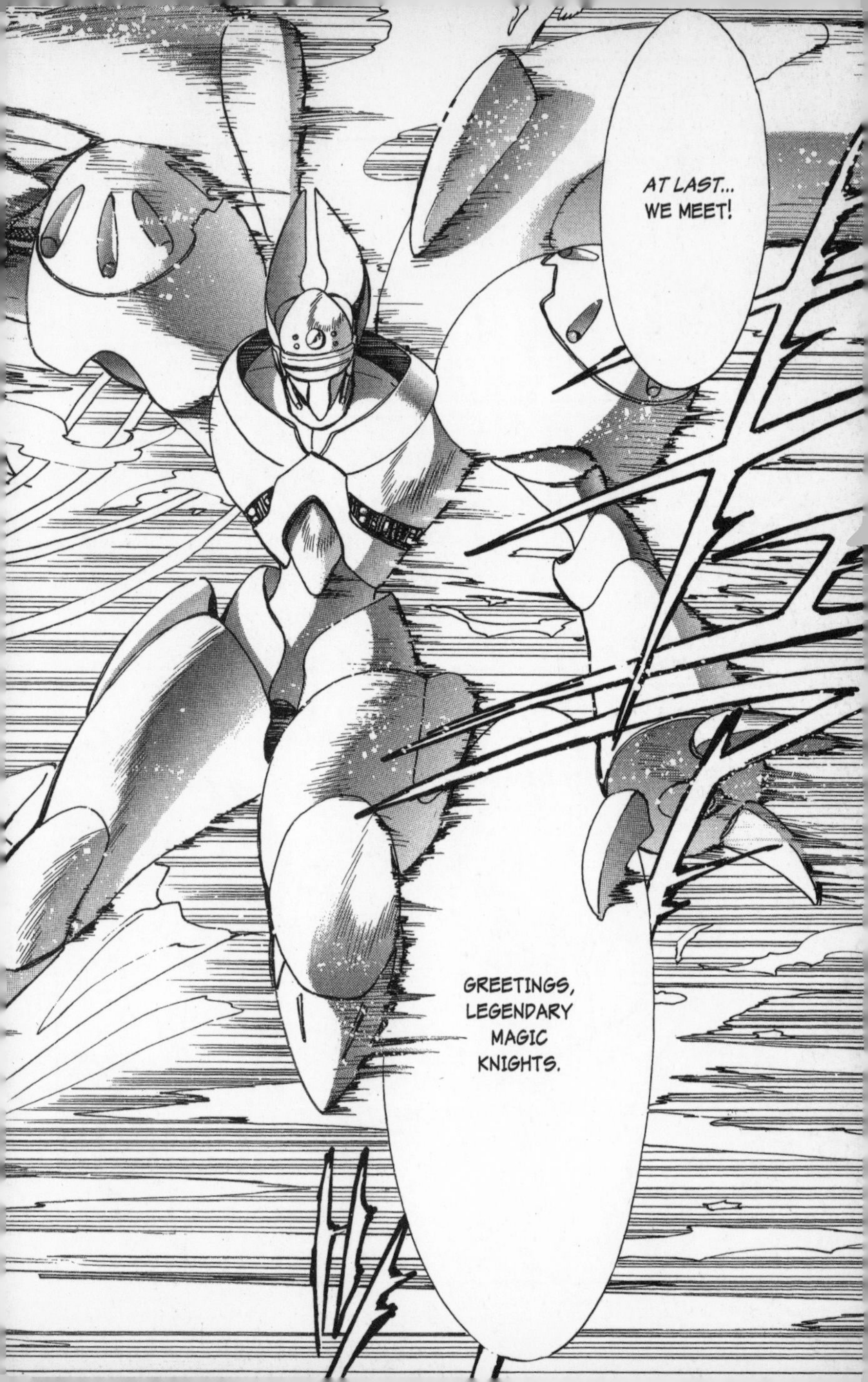
AT LAST... WE MEET!
GREETINGS, LEGENDARY MAGIC KNIGHTS.

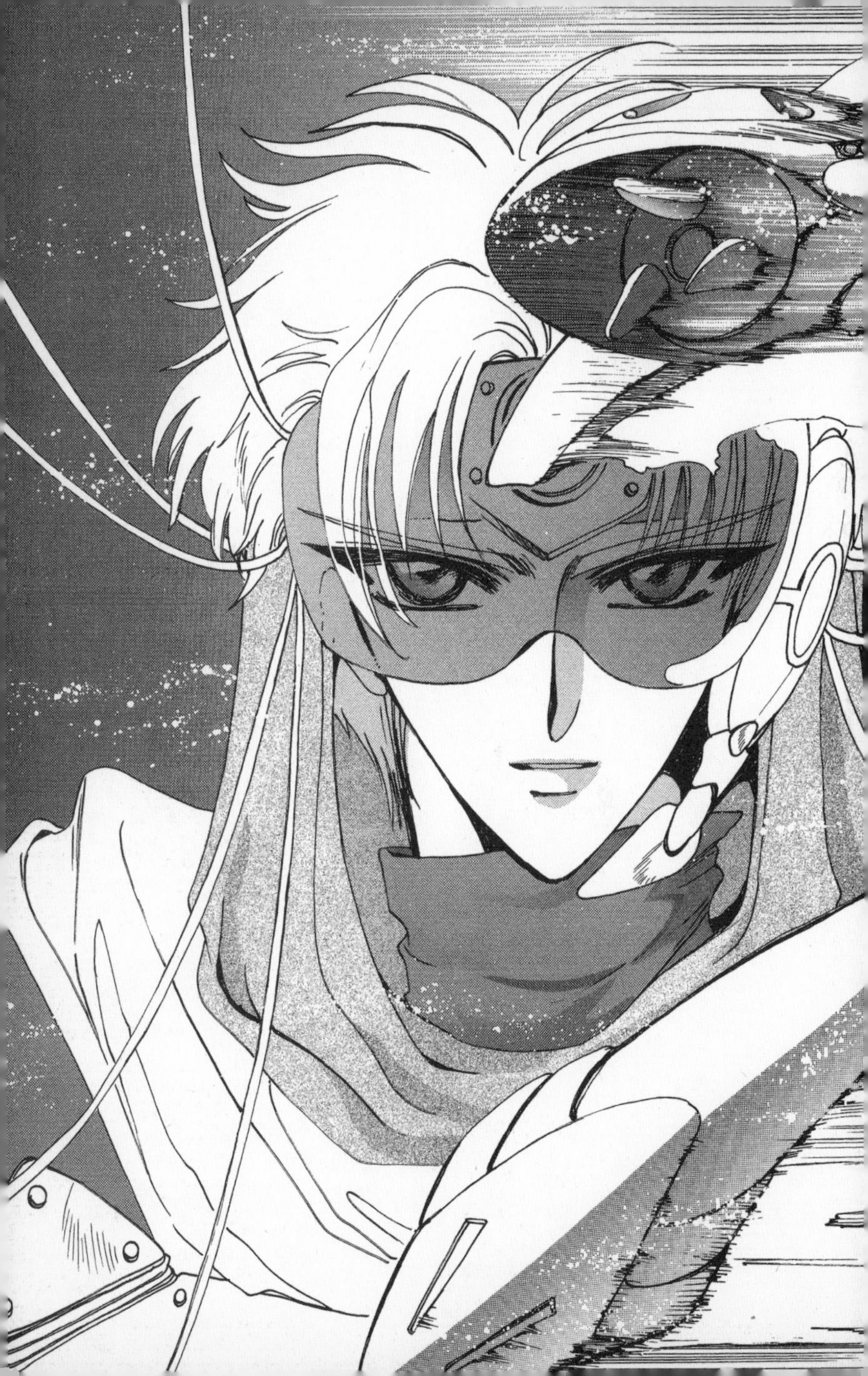

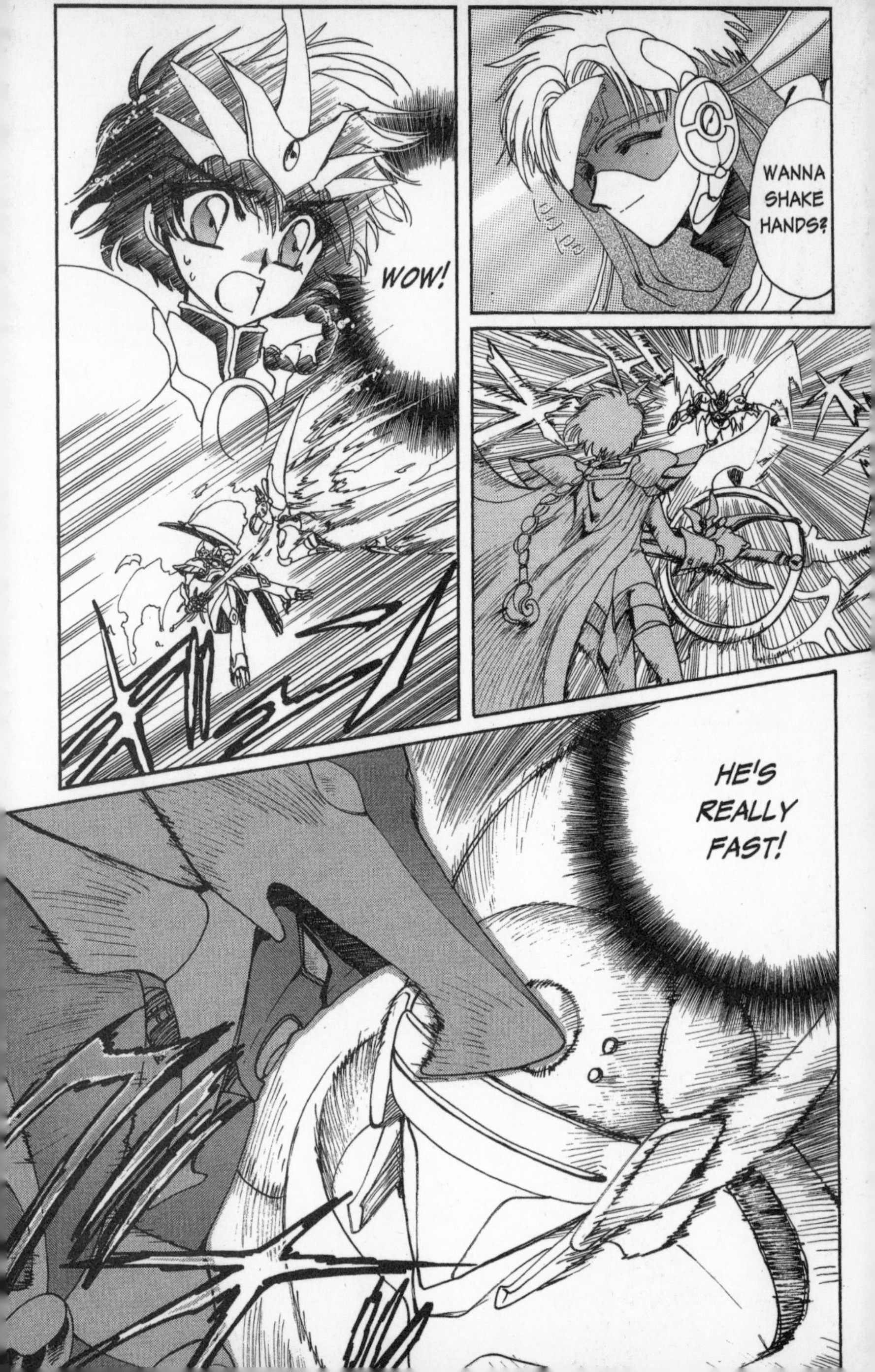
WANNA SHAKE HANDS?
WOW!
HE'S REALLY FAST!

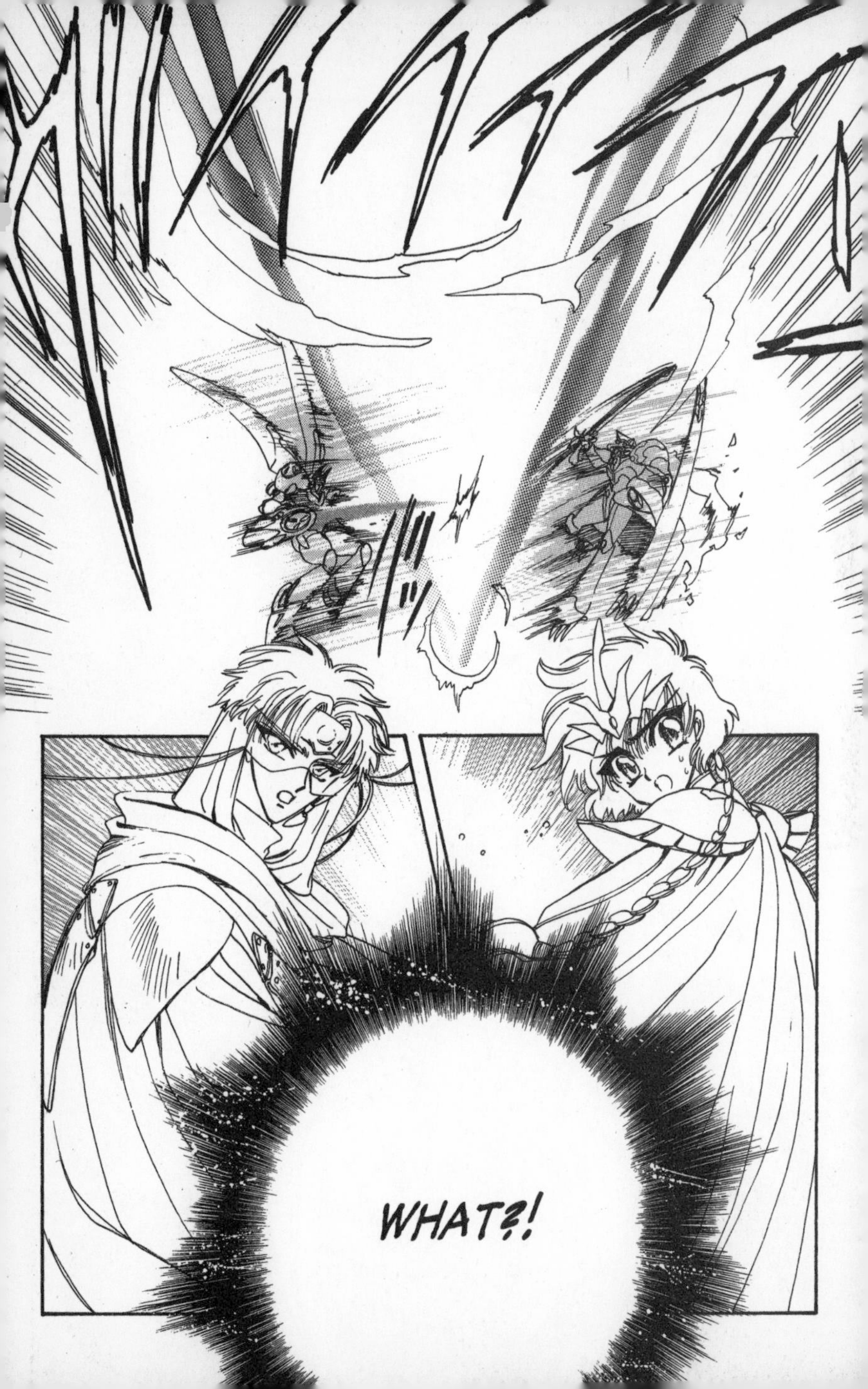
WHAT?!

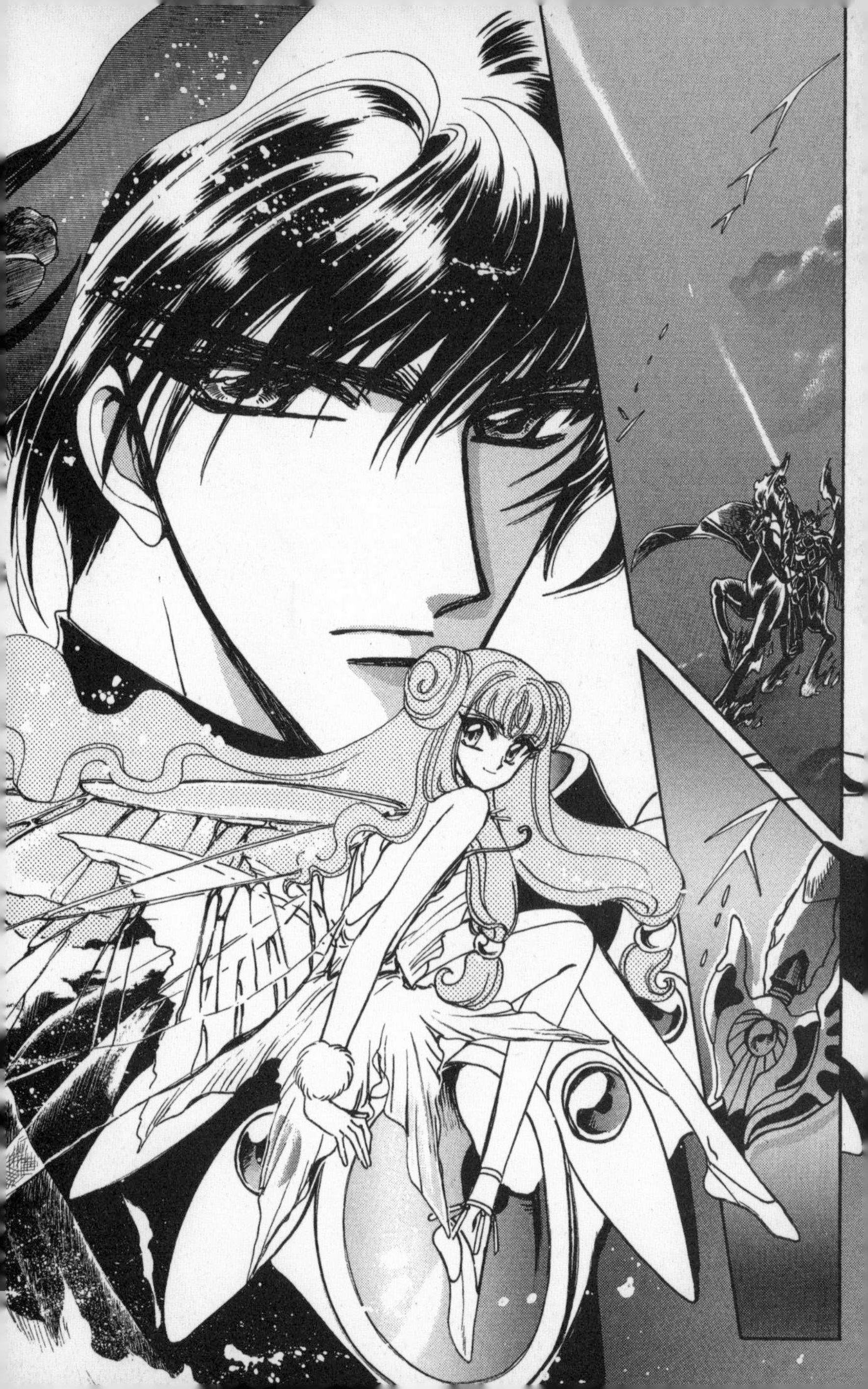

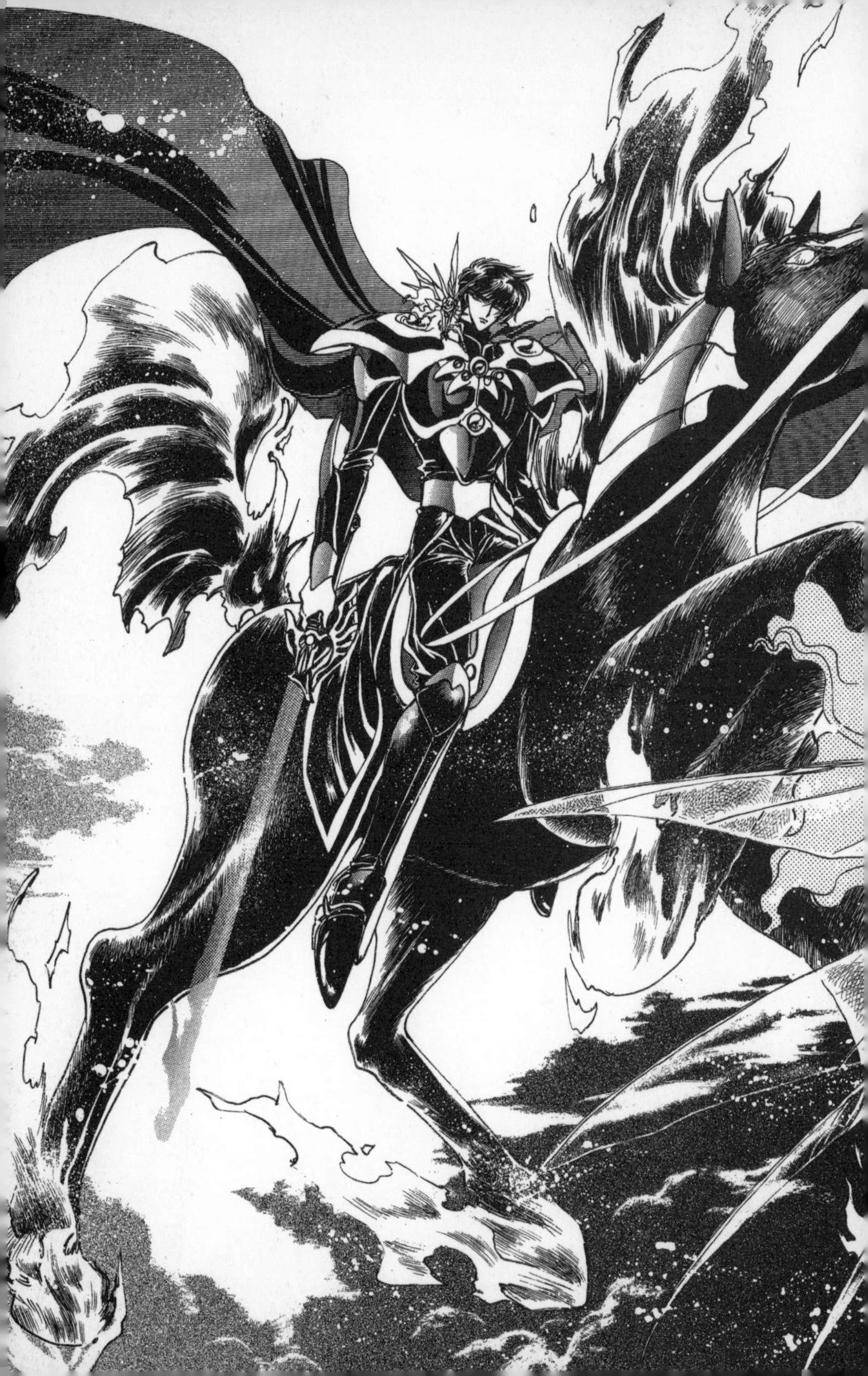

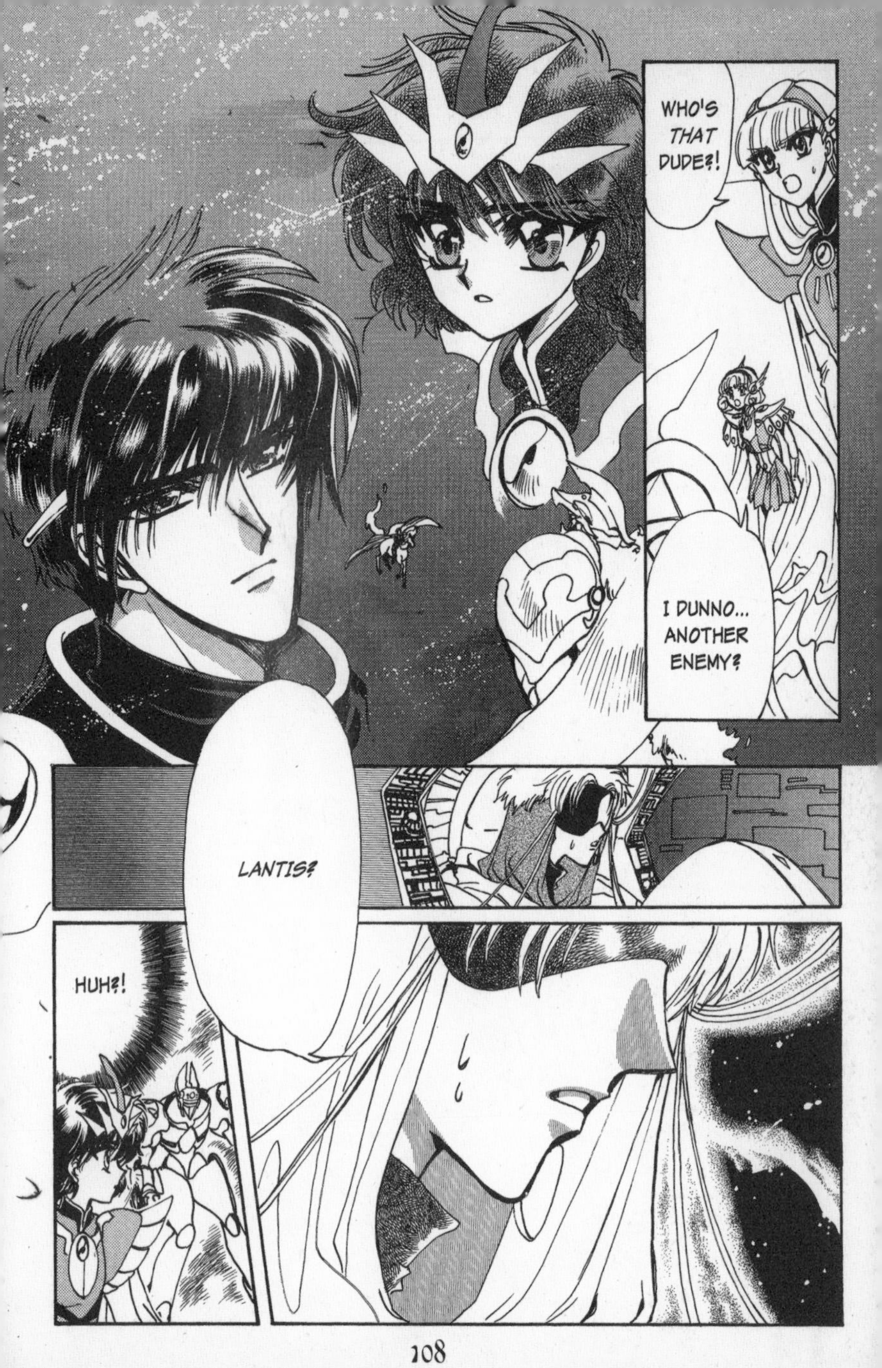
WHO'S *THAT* DUDE?!
I DUNNO... ANOTHER ENEMY?
LANTIS?
HUH?!

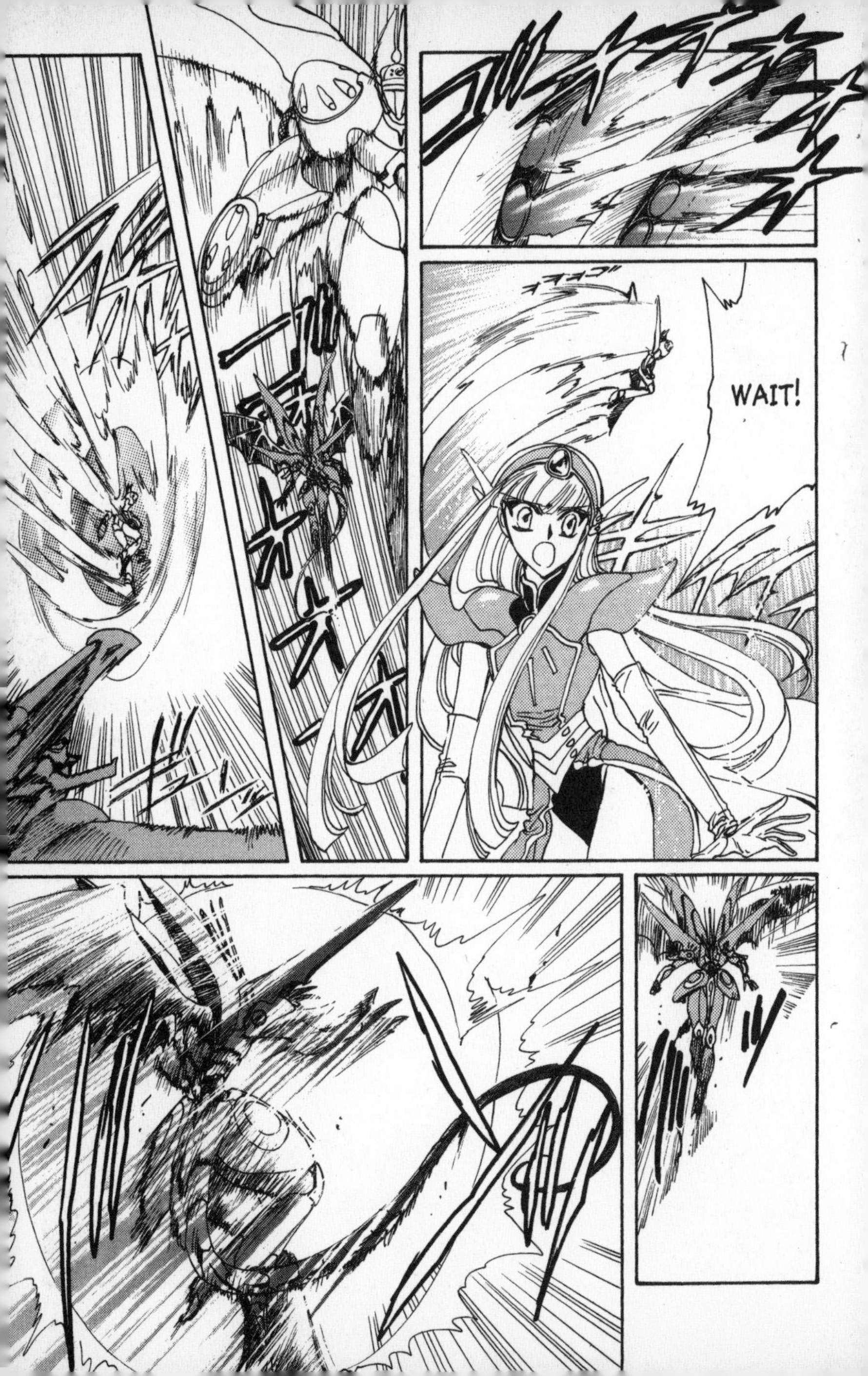
WAIT!

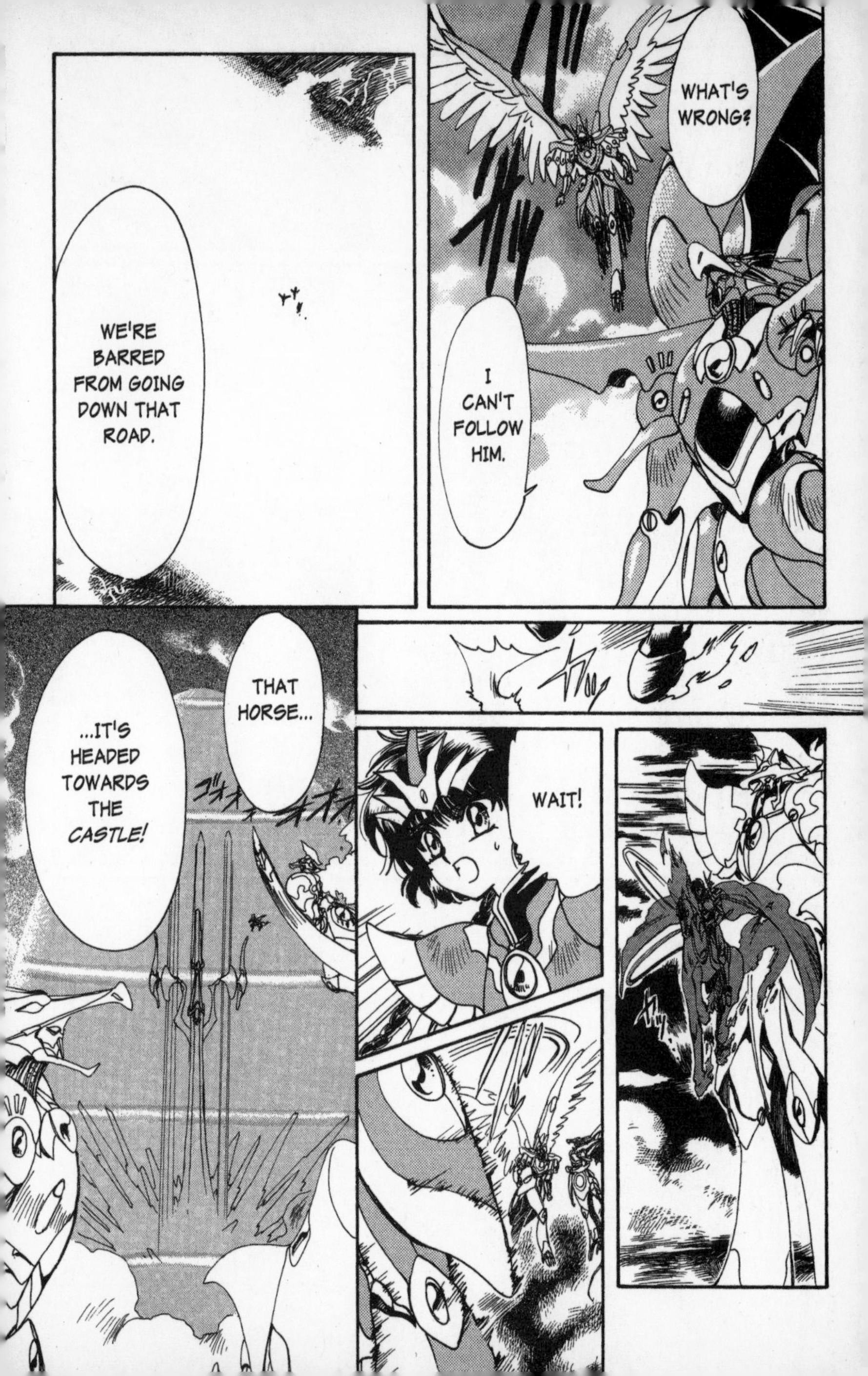
WHAT'S WRONG?
I CAN'T FOLLOW HIM.
WE'RE BARRED FROM GOING DOWN THAT ROAD.
WAIT!
THAT HORSE...
...IT'S HEADED TOWARDS THE CASTLE!

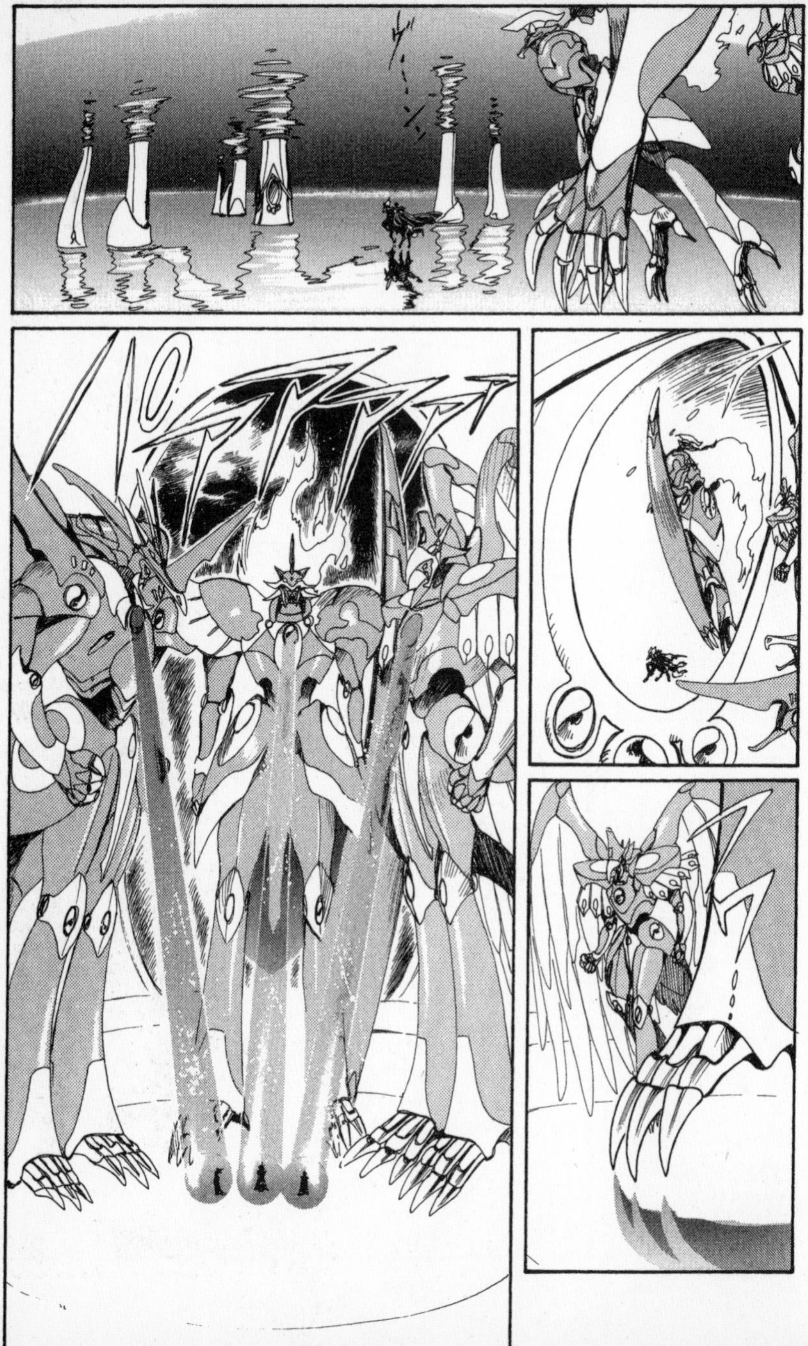

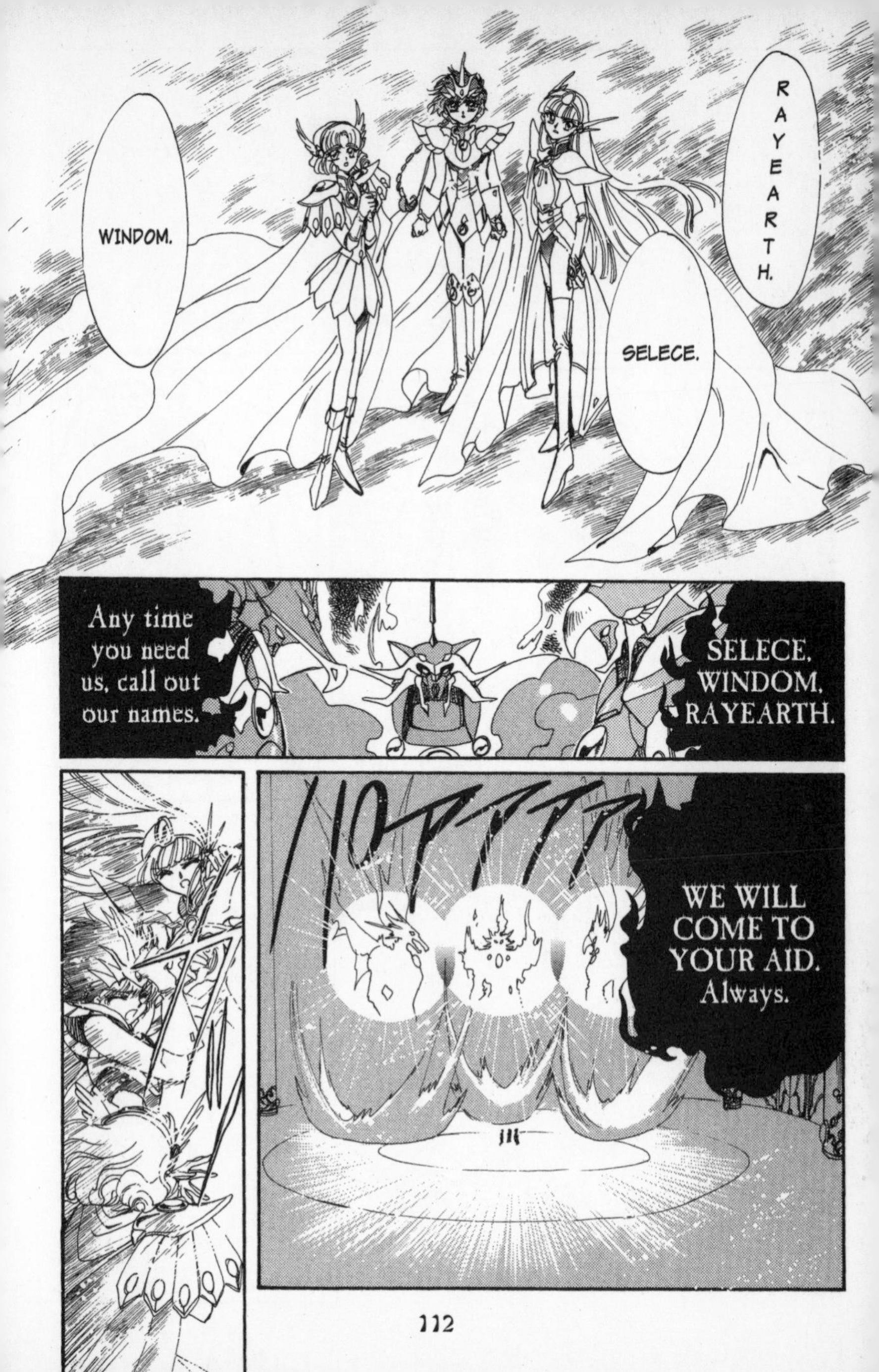
RAYEARTH.
SELECE.
WINDOM.
SELECE. WINDOM. RAYEARTH.
Any time you need us, call out our names.
WE WILL COME TO YOUR AID. Always.

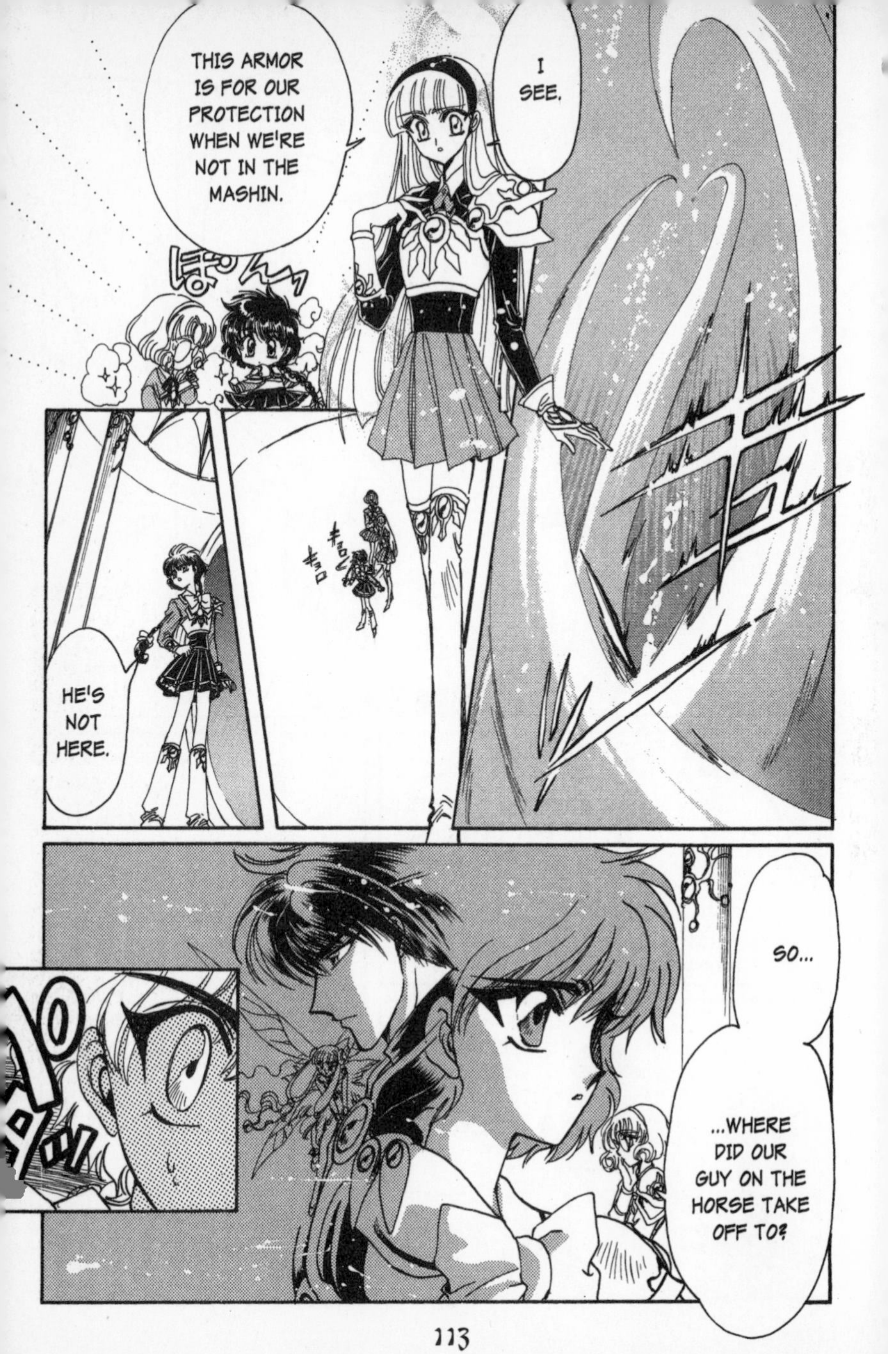
I SEE.
THIS ARMOR IS FOR OUR PROTECTION WHEN WE'RE NOT IN THE MASHIN.
ぽんっ
HE'S NOT HERE.
SO...
...WHERE DID OUR GUY ON THE HORSE TAKE OFF TO?

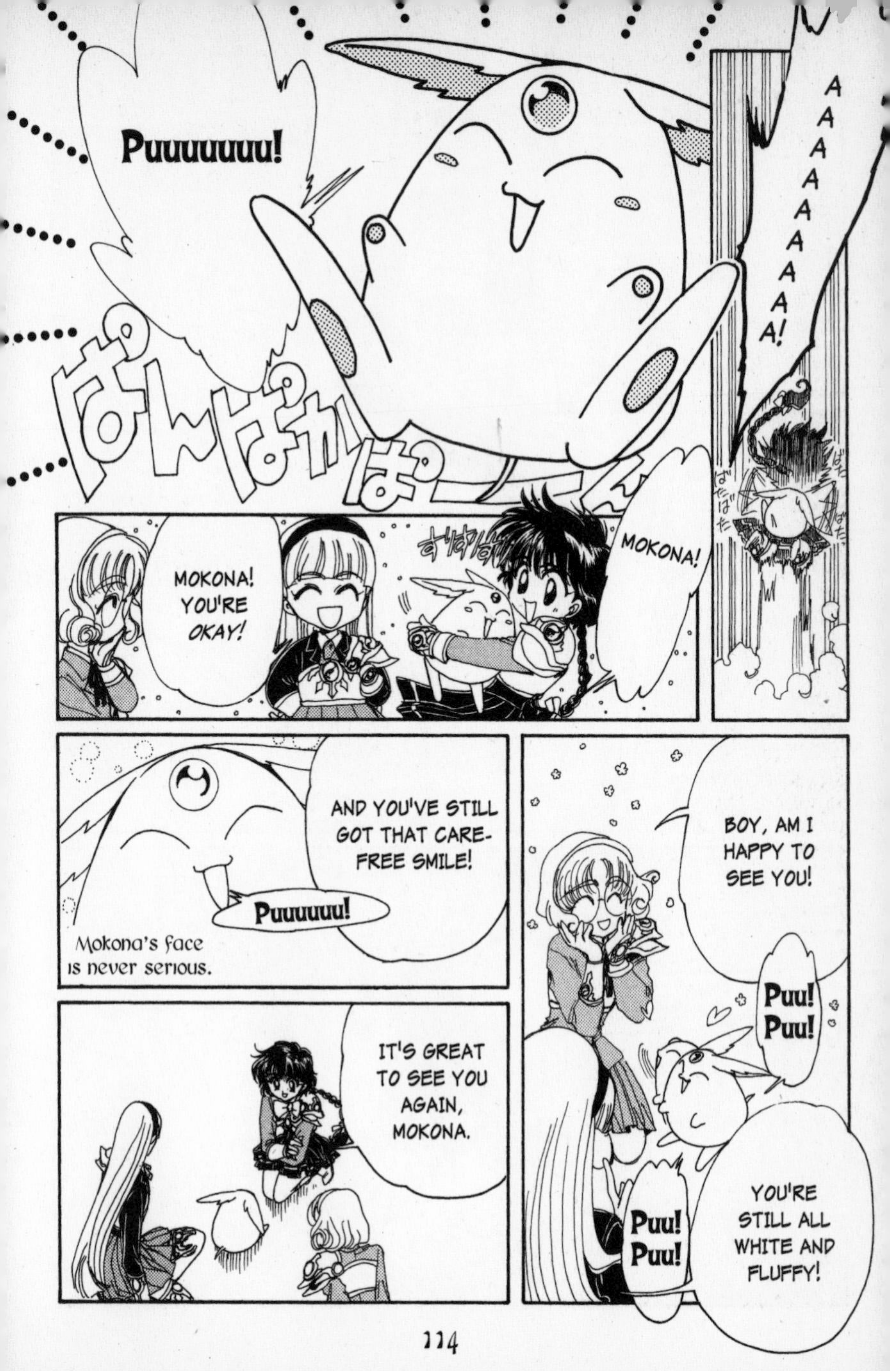
AAAAAAAAAAA!
ばたばた
Puuuuuuu!
ぱんぱかぱーん
MOKONA!
MOKONA! YOU'RE OKAY!
BOY, AM I HAPPY TO SEE YOU!
Puu! Puu!
YOU'RE STILL ALL WHITE AND FLUFFY!
Puu! Puu!
AND YOU'VE STILL GOT THAT CARE-FREE SMILE!
Puuuuuu!
Mokona's face is never serious.
IT'S GREAT TO SEE YOU AGAIN, MOKONA.

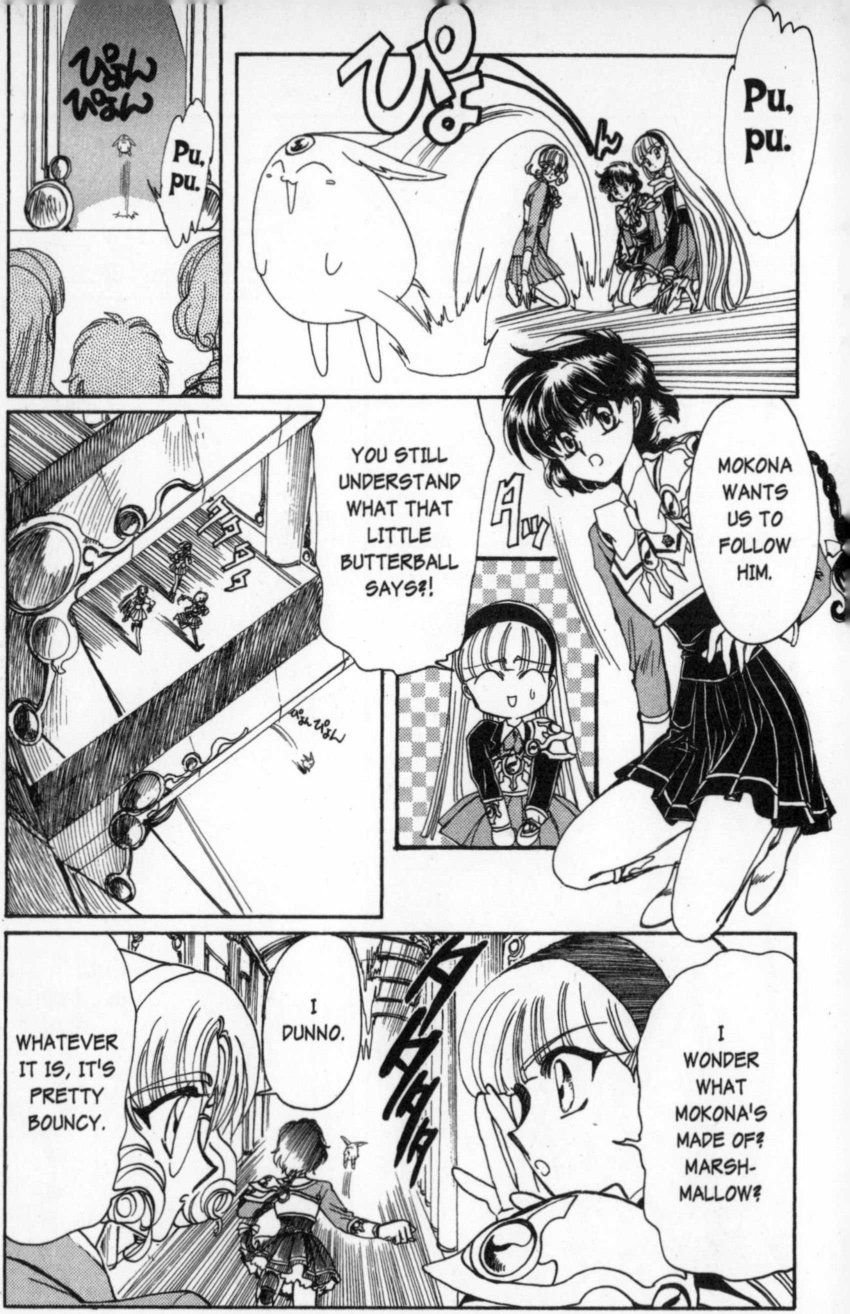
ぴょん
Pu, pu.
ぴょんぴょん
Pu, pu.
MOKONA WANTS US TO FOLLOW HIM.
YOU STILL UNDERSTAND WHAT THAT LITTLE BUTTERBALL SAYS?!
ぴょんぴょん
I WONDER WHAT MOKONA'S MADE OF? MARSH-MALLOW?
I DUNNO.
WHATEVER IT IS, IT'S PRETTY BOUNCY.

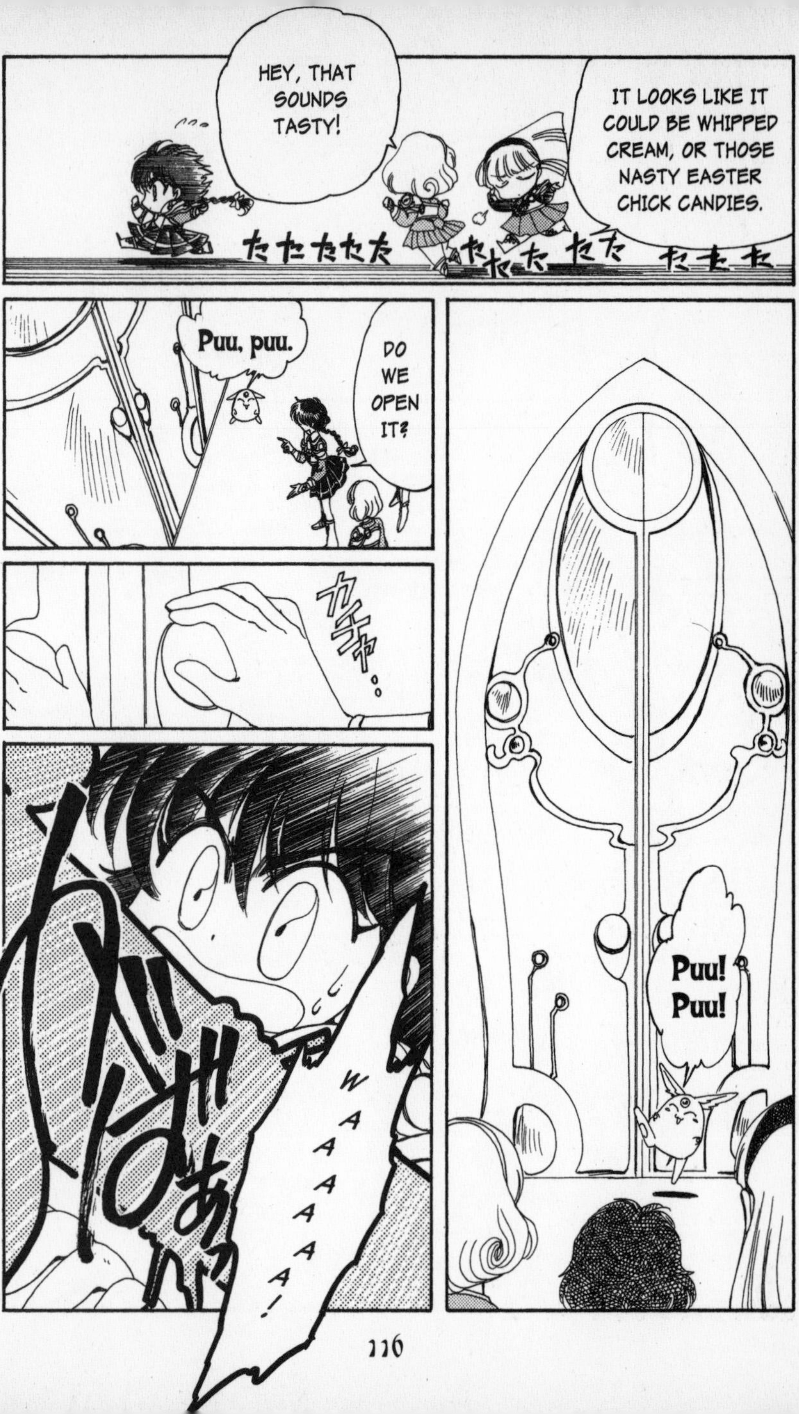
IT LOOKS LIKE IT COULD BE WHIPPED CREAM, OR THOSE NASTY EASTER CHICK CANDIES.
HEY, THAT SOUNDS TASTY!
Puu! Puu!
DO WE OPEN IT?
Puu, puu.
カチャ
WAAAAAAAA!

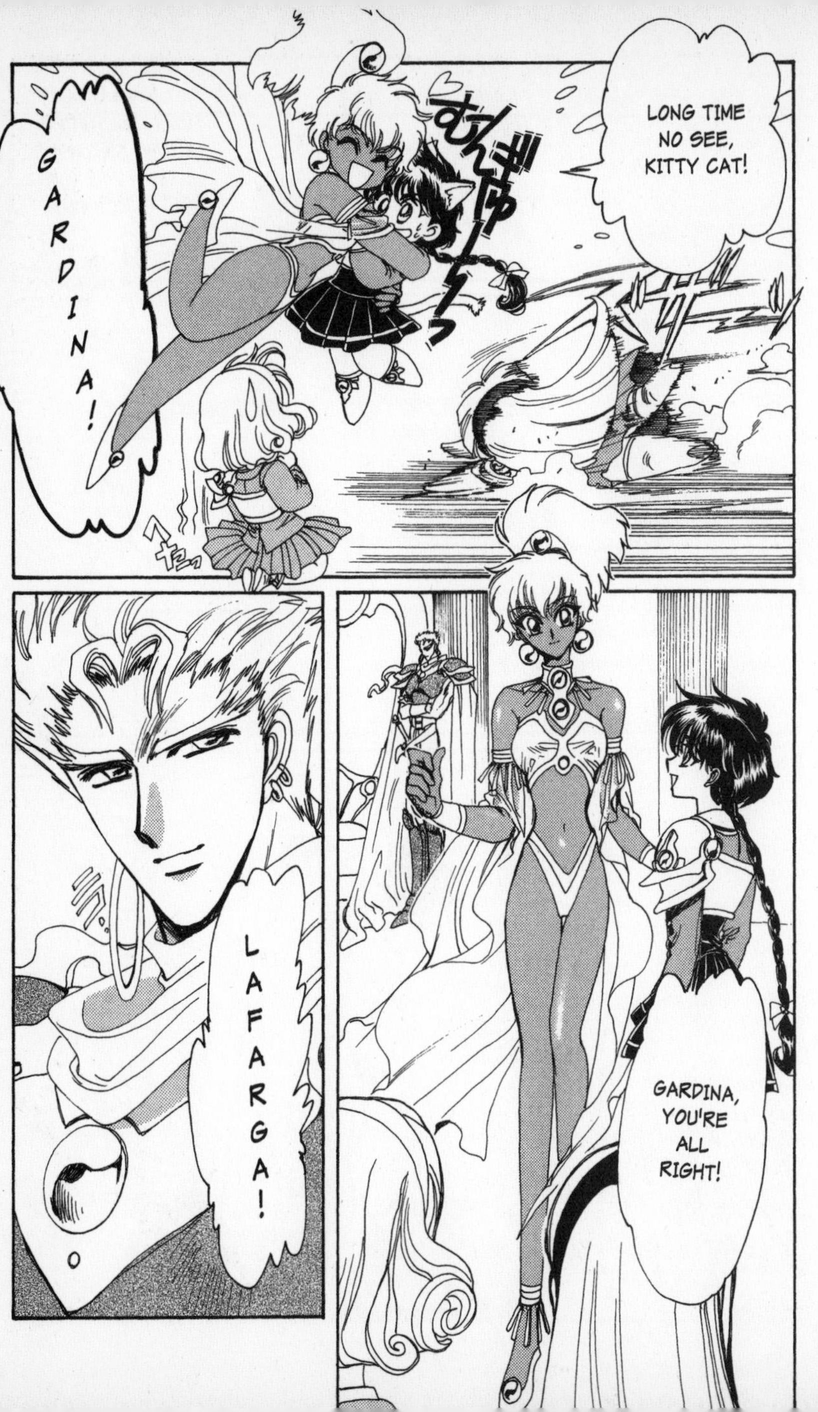
LONG TIME NO SEE, KITTY CAT!
GARDINA!
GARDINA, YOU'RE ALL RIGHT!
LAFARGA!

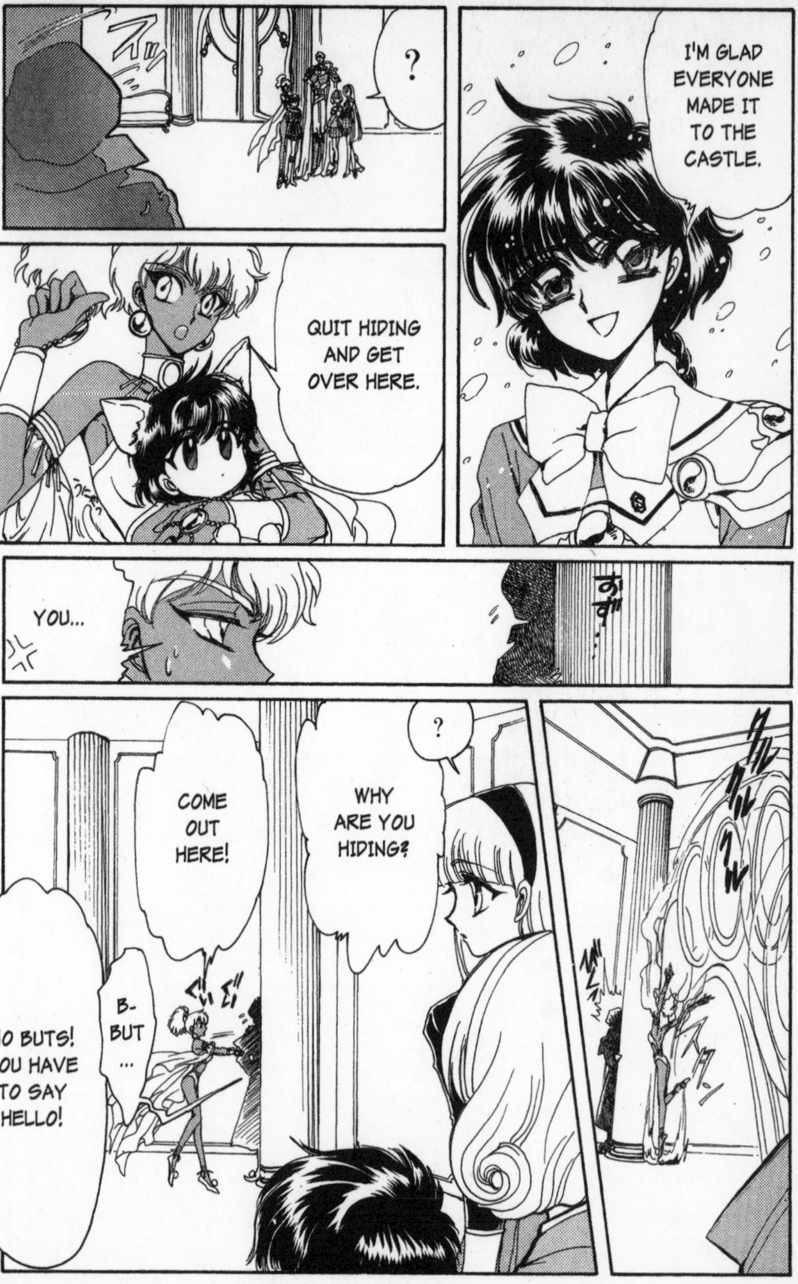
I'M GLAD EVERYONE MADE IT TO THE CASTLE.
?
QUIT HIDING AND GET OVER HERE.
YOU...
?
WHY ARE YOU HIDING?
COME OUT HERE!
B-BUT ...
NO BUTS! YOU HAVE TO SAY HELLO!

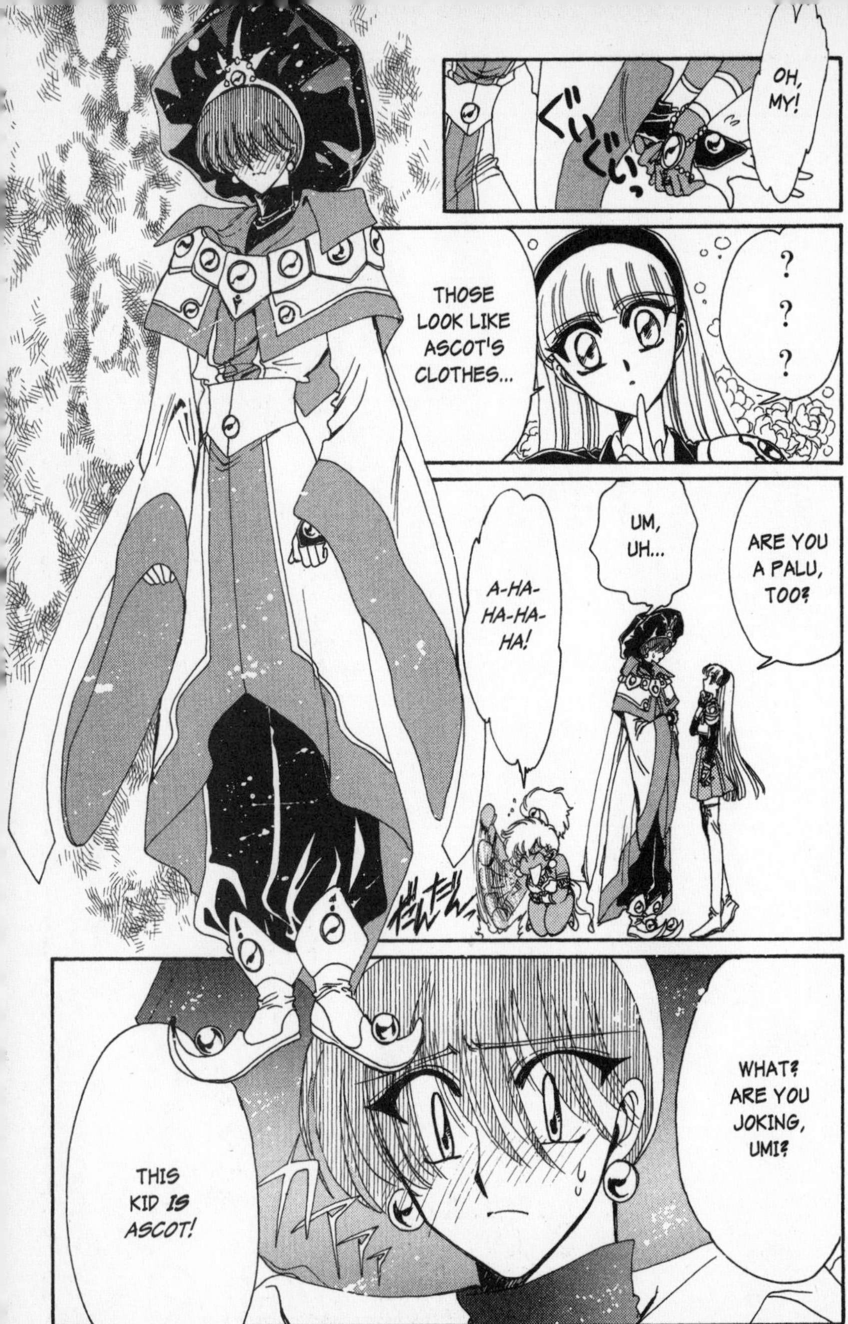
OH, MY!
ぐいぐいっ
???
THOSE LOOK LIKE ASCOT'S CLOTHES...
ARE YOU A PALU, TOO?
UM, UH...
A-HA-HA-HA-HA!
WHAT? ARE YOU JOKING, UMI?
THIS KID *IS* ASCOT!

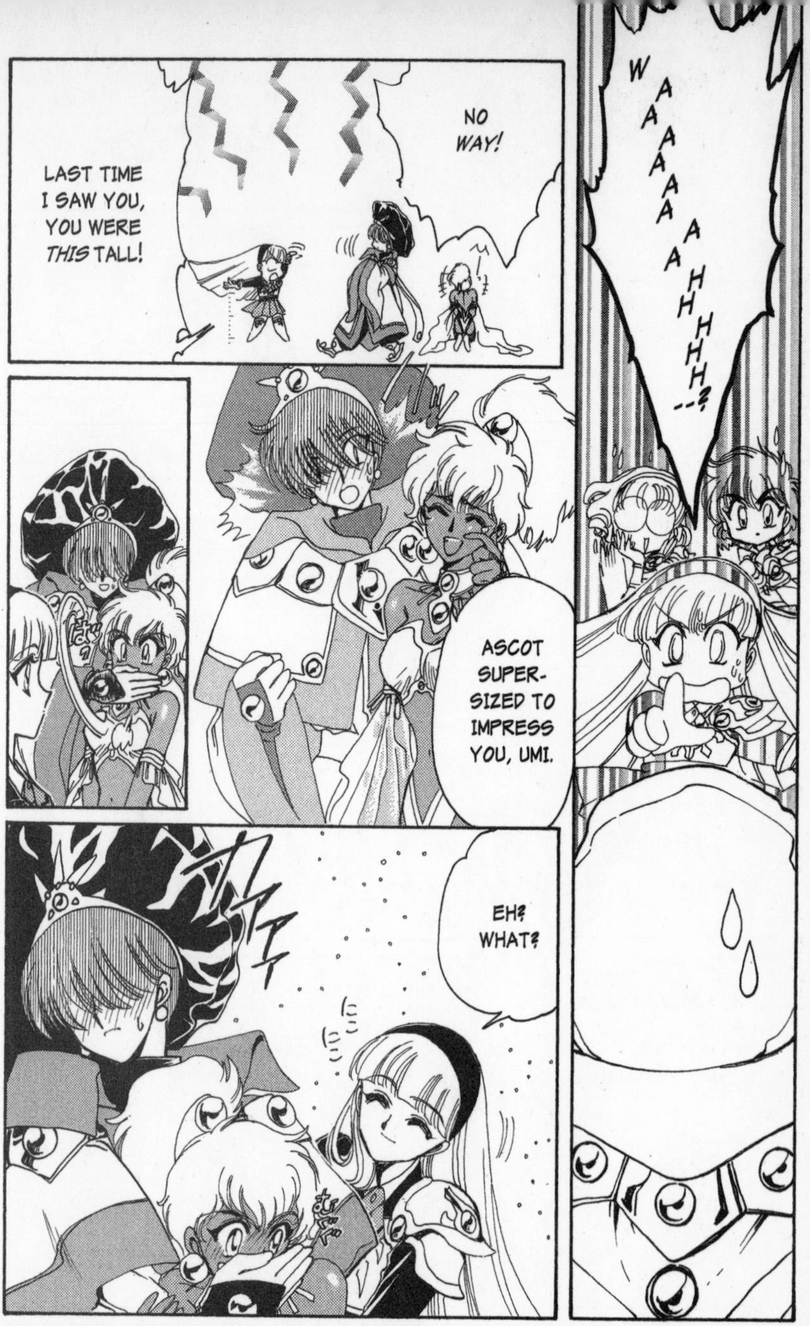
WAAAAAAAAAAHHHHH?
NO WAY!
LAST TIME I SAW YOU, YOU WERE THIS TALL!
ASCOT SUPER-SIZED TO IMPRESS YOU, UMI.
EH? WHAT?

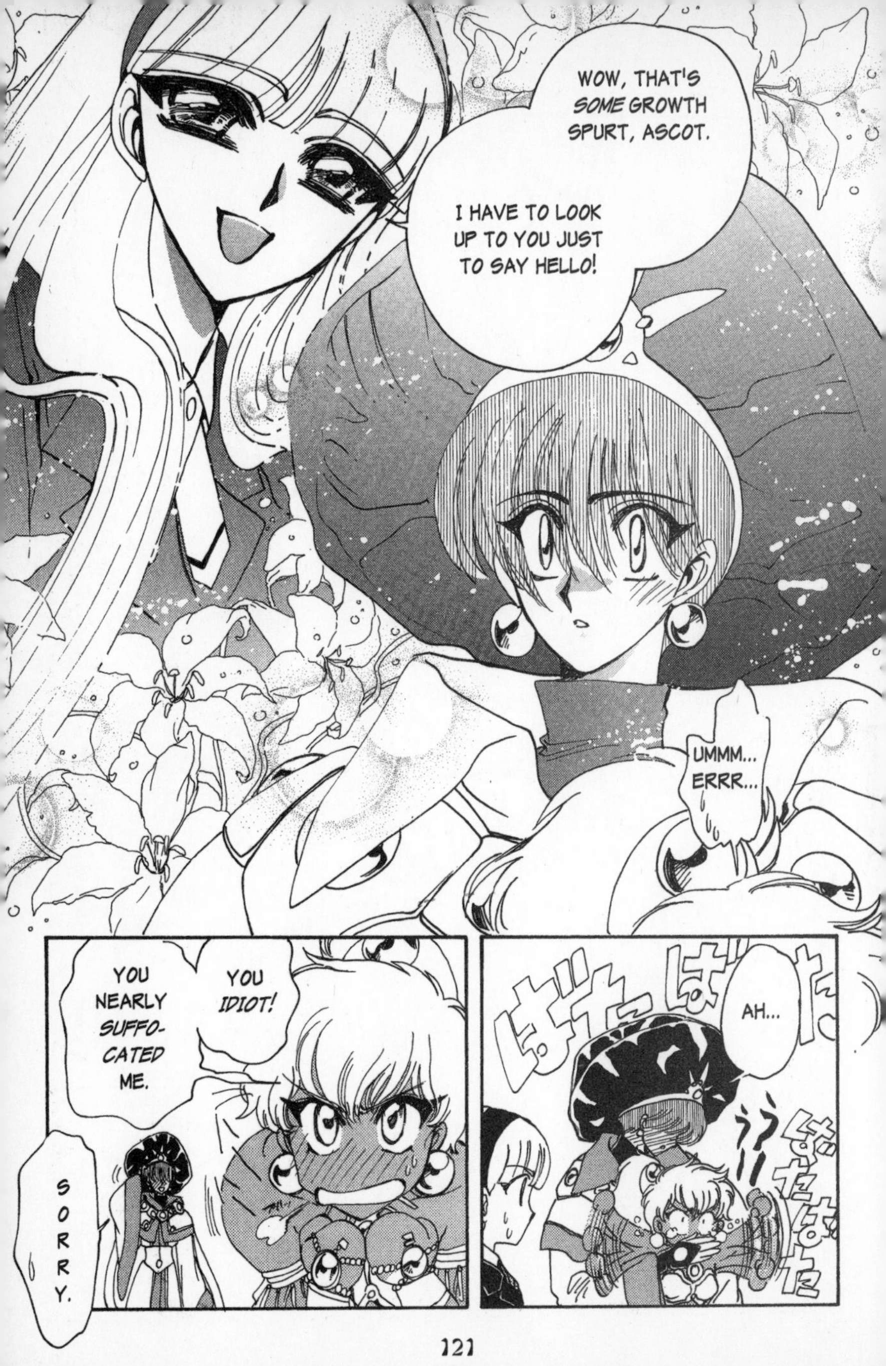

WOW, THAT'S *SOME* GROWTH SPURT, ASCOT.
I HAVE TO LOOK UP TO YOU JUST TO SAY HELLO!
UMMM... ERRR...
AH...
YOU *IDIOT!*
YOU NEARLY *SUFFO-CATED* ME.
SORRY.

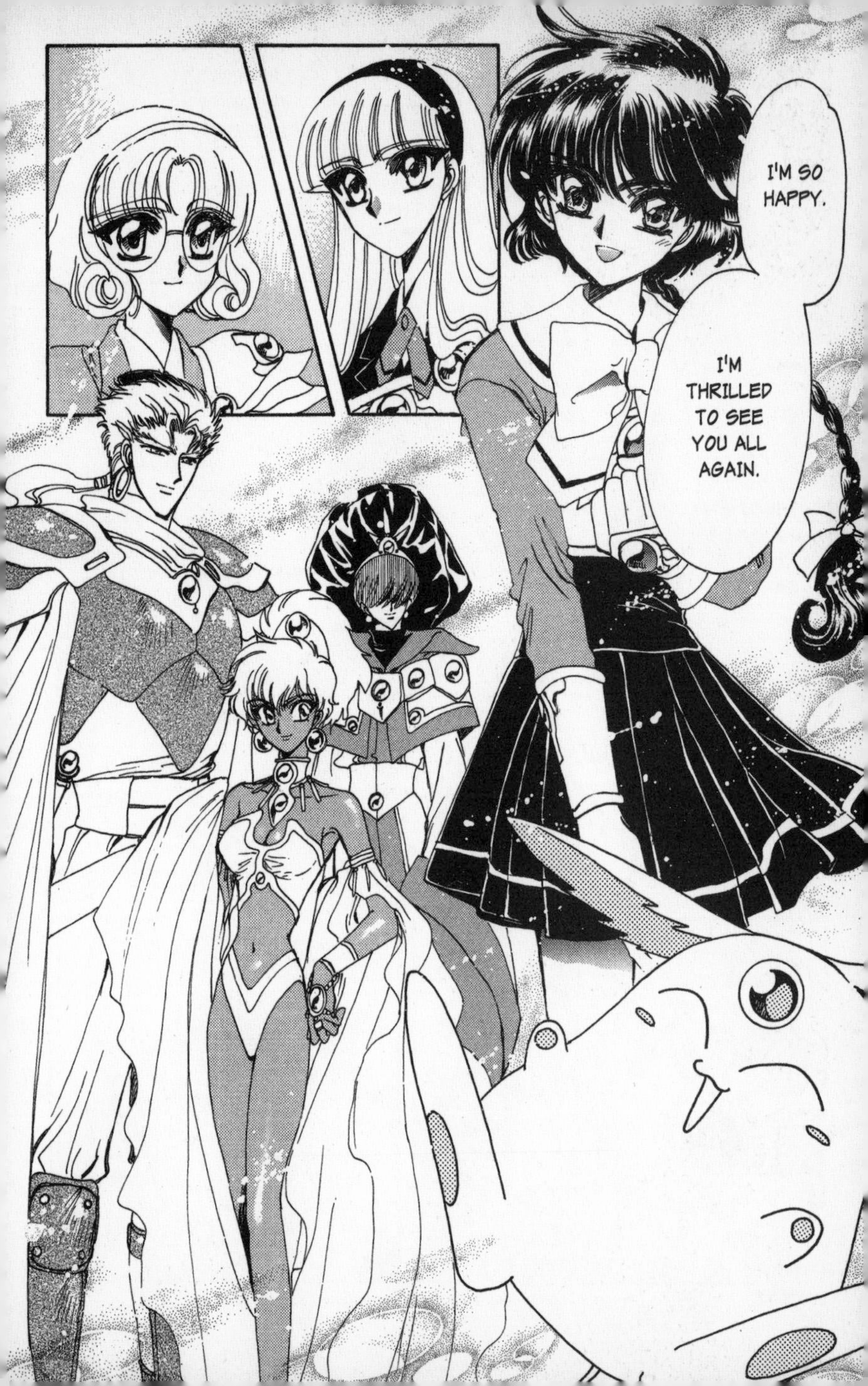
I'M SO HAPPY.
I'M THRILLED TO SEE YOU ALL AGAIN.

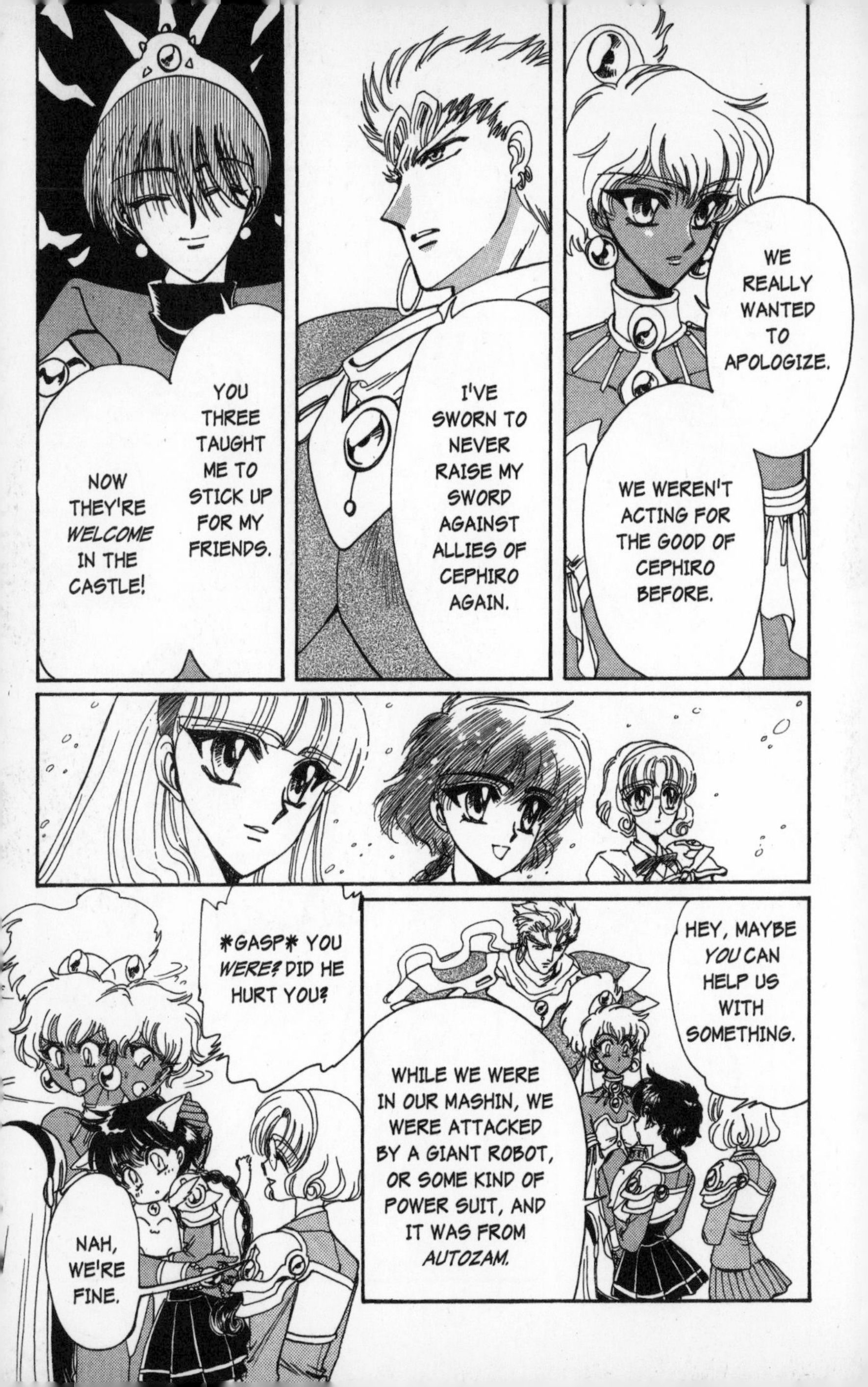
WE REALLY WANTED TO APOLOGIZE.
WE WEREN'T ACTING FOR THE GOOD OF CEPHIRO BEFORE.
I'VE SWORN TO NEVER RAISE MY SWORD AGAINST ALLIES OF CEPHIRO AGAIN.
YOU THREE TAUGHT ME TO STICK UP FOR MY FRIENDS.
NOW THEY'RE *WELCOME* IN THE CASTLE!
HEY, MAYBE *YOU* CAN HELP US WITH SOMETHING.
WHILE WE WERE IN OUR MASHIN, WE WERE ATTACKED BY A GIANT ROBOT, OR SOME KIND OF POWER SUIT, AND IT WAS FROM *AUTOZAM.*
GASP YOU *WERE?* DID HE HURT YOU?
NAH, WE'RE FINE.

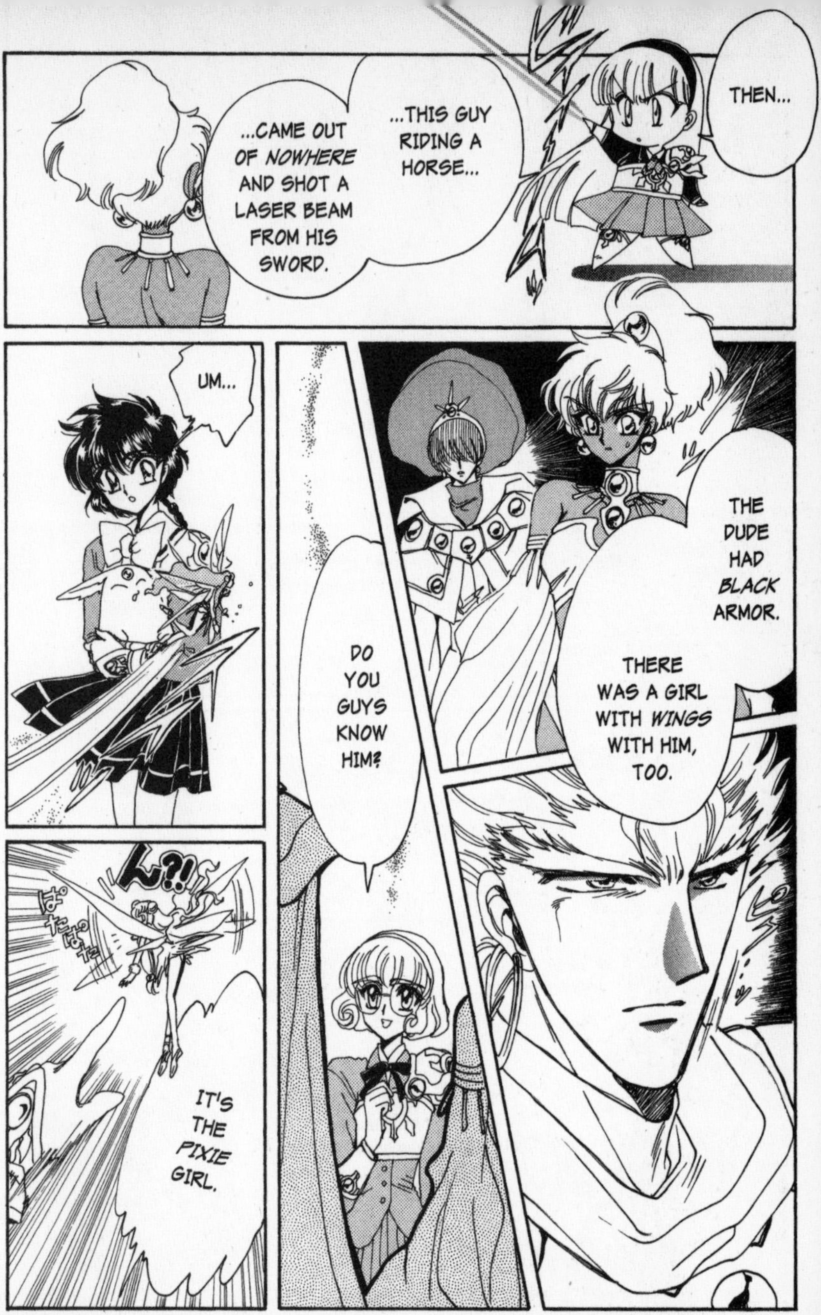
THEN...
...THIS GUY RIDING A HORSE...
...CAME OUT OF *NOWHERE* AND SHOT A LASER BEAM FROM HIS SWORD.
THE DUDE HAD *BLACK* ARMOR.
THERE WAS A GIRL WITH *WINGS* WITH HIM, TOO.
DO YOU GUYS KNOW HIM?
UM...
ん?!
IT'S THE *PIXIE* GIRL.

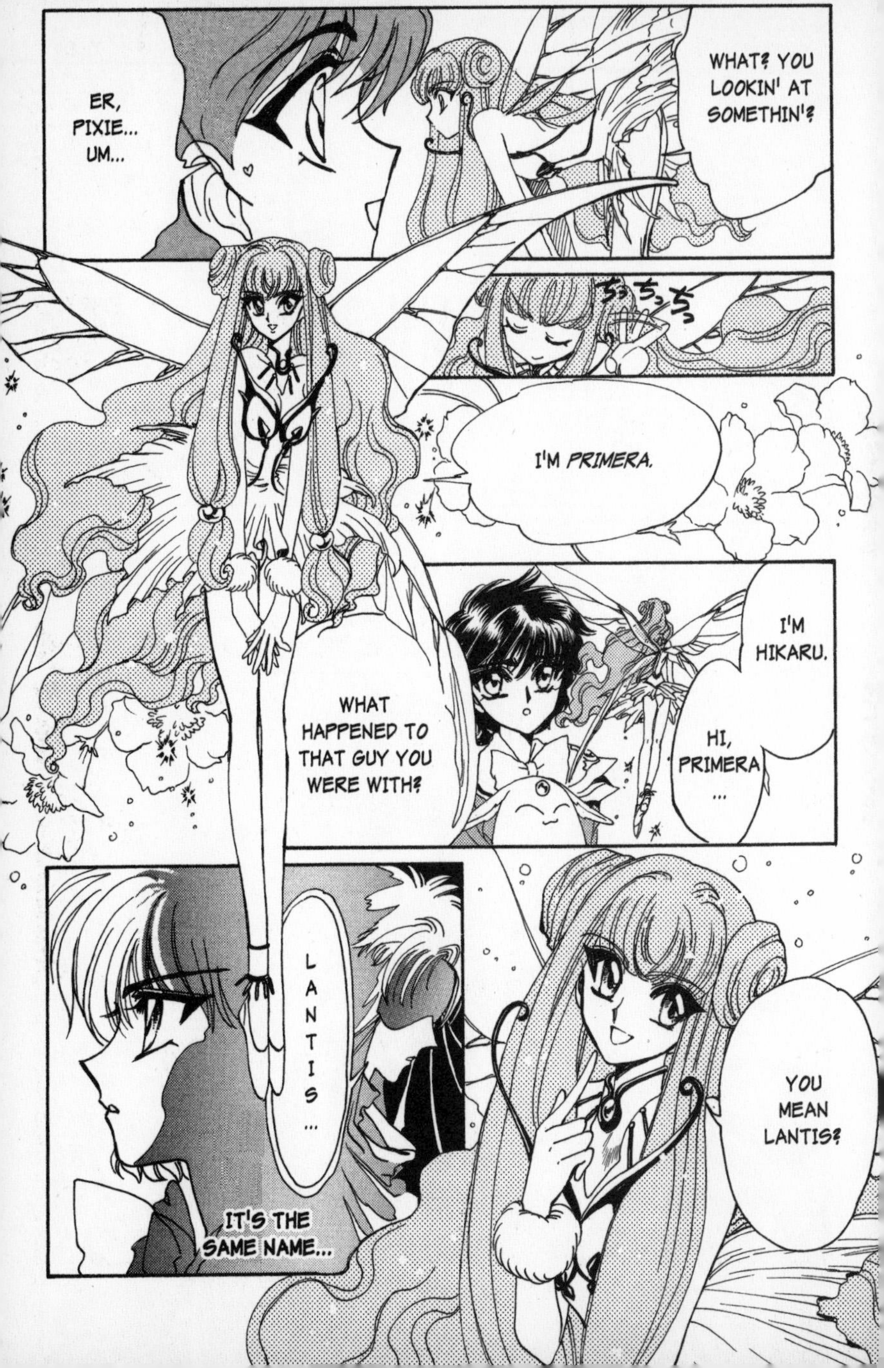
WHAT? YOU LOOKIN' AT SOMETHIN'?
ER, PIXIE... UM...
ちっちっちっ
I'M *PRIMERA*.
I'M HIKARU.
HI, PRIMERA ...
WHAT HAPPENED TO THAT GUY YOU WERE WITH?
YOU MEAN LANTIS?
LANTIS ...
IT'S THE SAME NAME...

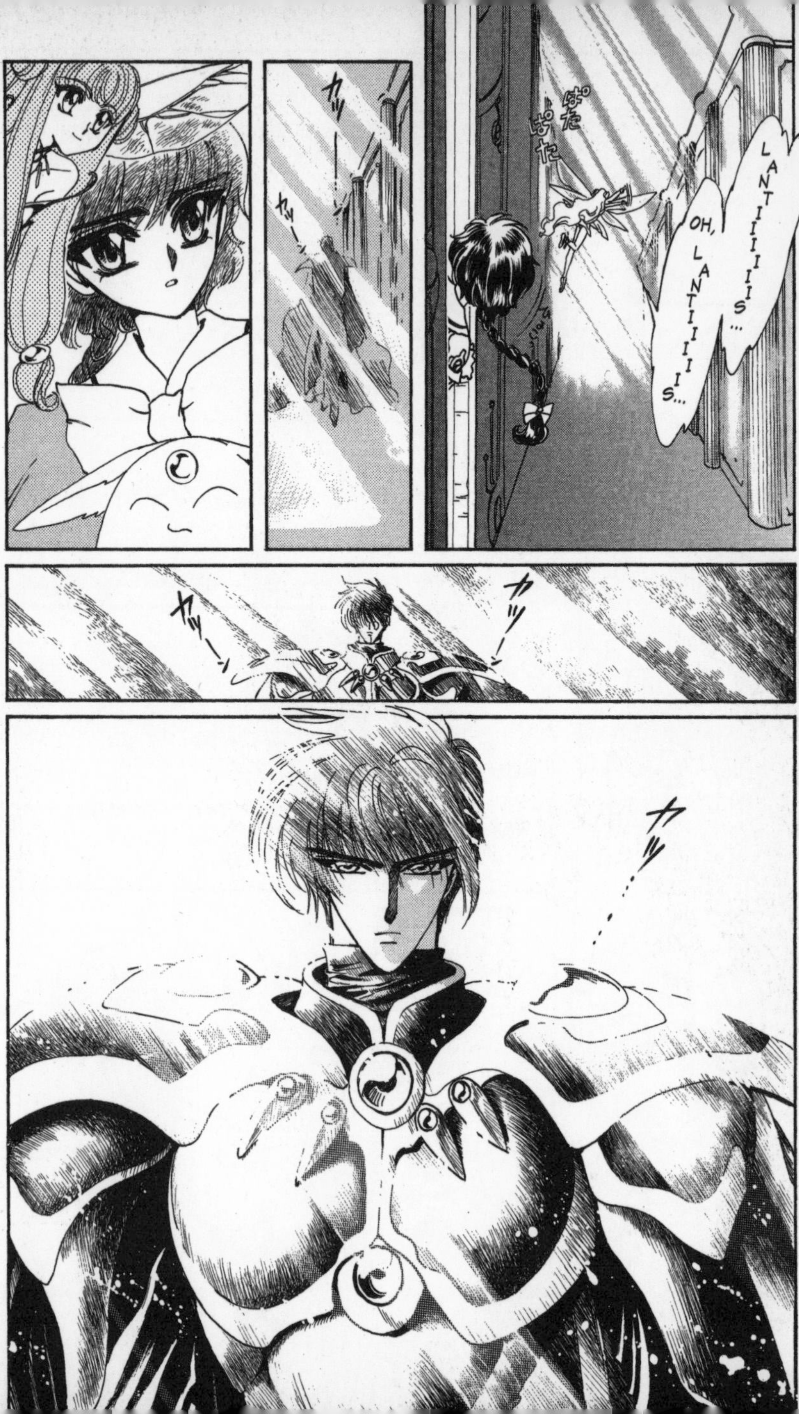
ぱた
ぱた
LANTIIIIIIS...
OH, LANTIIIIIIS...
カッ

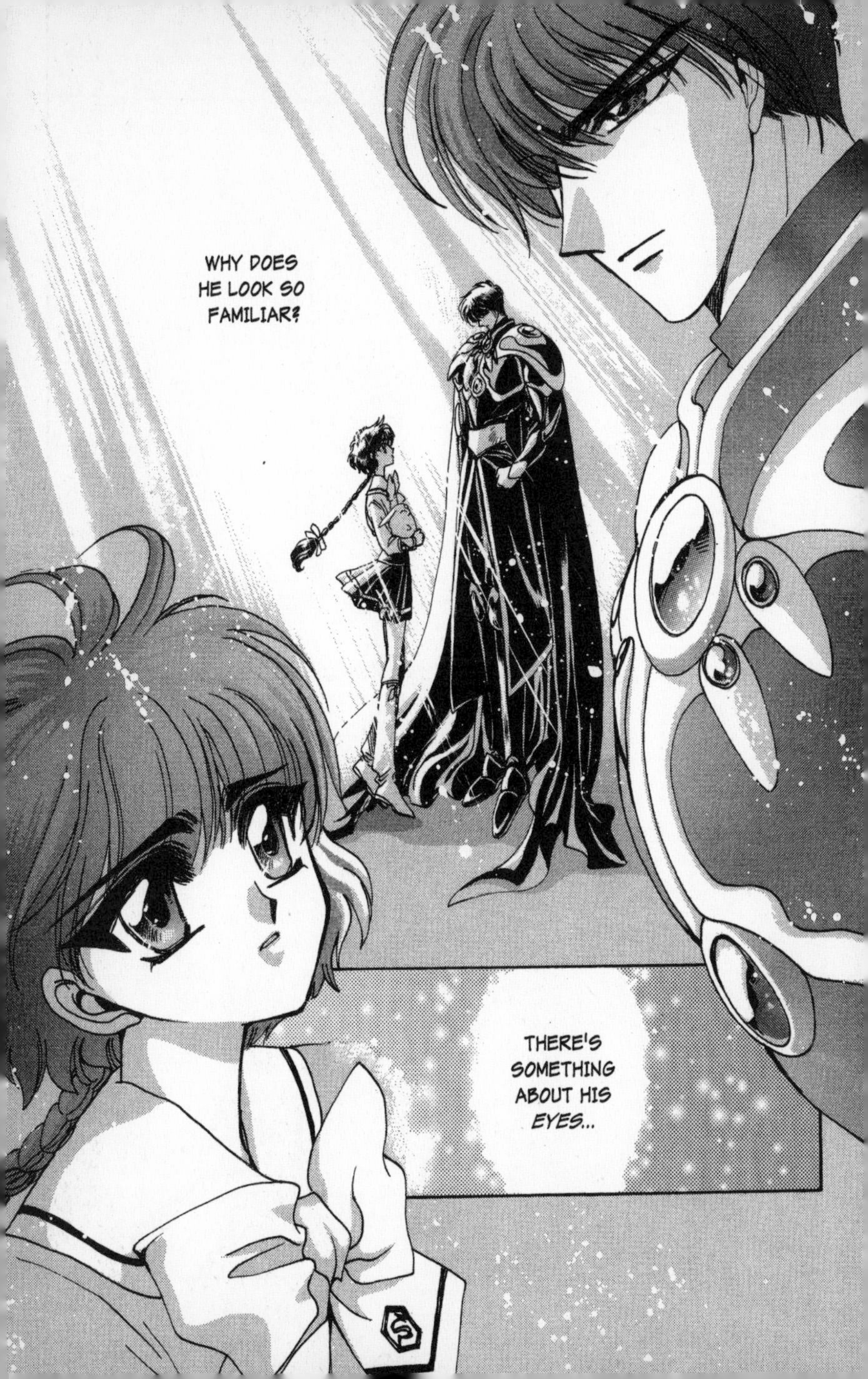
WHY DOES HE LOOK SO FAMILIAR?
THERE'S SOMETHING ABOUT HIS *EYES*...

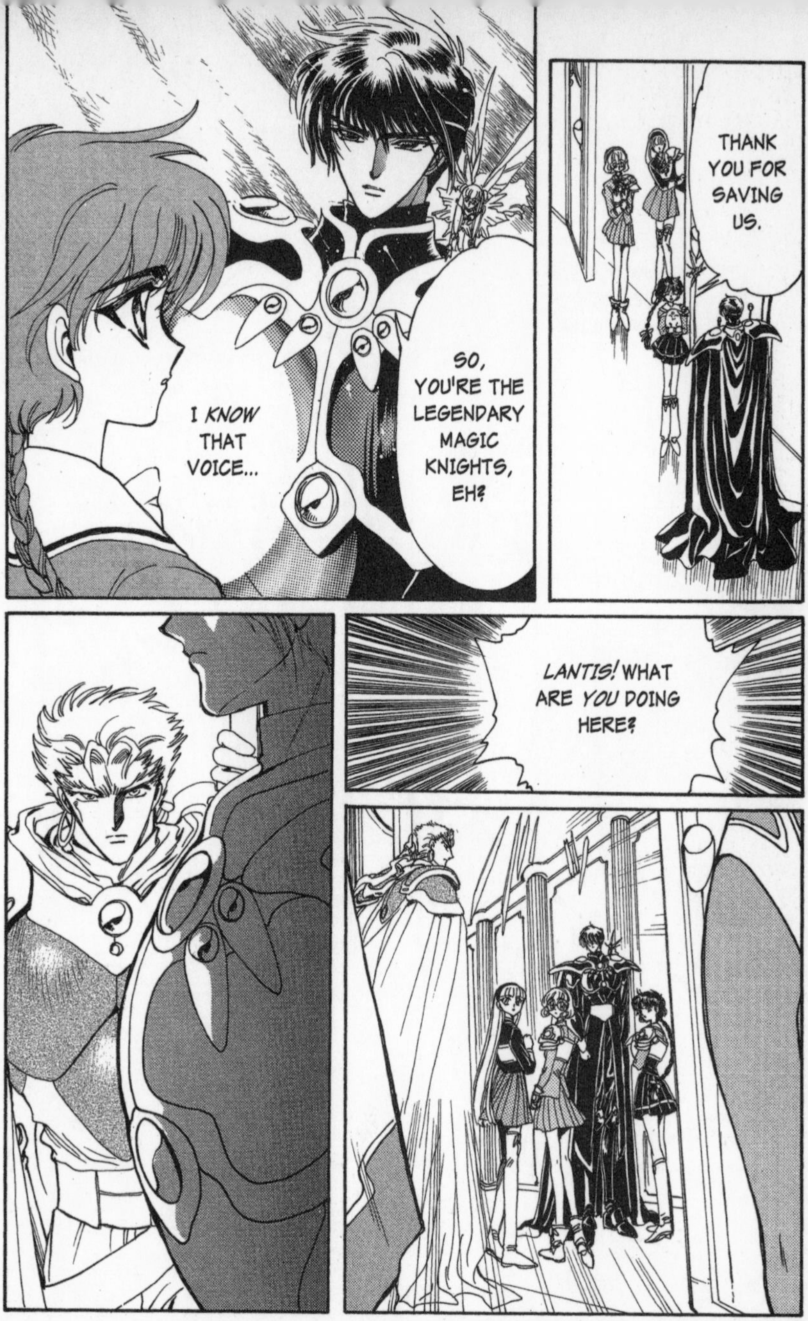
THANK YOU FOR SAVING US.
SO, YOU'RE THE LEGENDARY MAGIC KNIGHTS, EH?
I *KNOW* THAT VOICE...
LANTIS! WHAT ARE *YOU* DOING HERE?

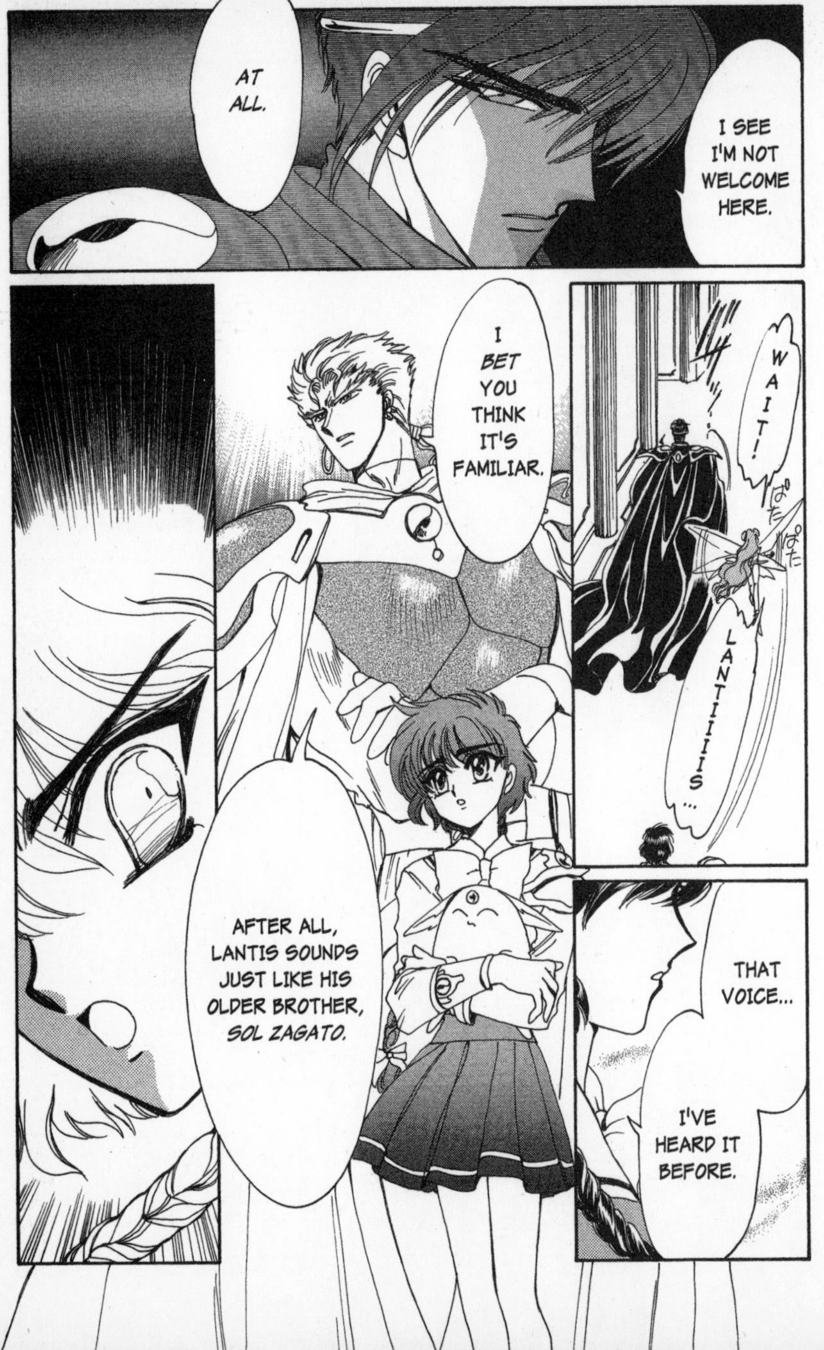
I SEE I'M NOT WELCOME HERE.
AT ALL.
WAIT!
ぱた ぱた
LANTIIIIIS...
THAT VOICE...
I'VE HEARD IT BEFORE.
I BET YOU THINK IT'S FAMILIAR.
AFTER ALL, LANTIS SOUNDS JUST LIKE HIS OLDER BROTHER, SOL ZAGATO.

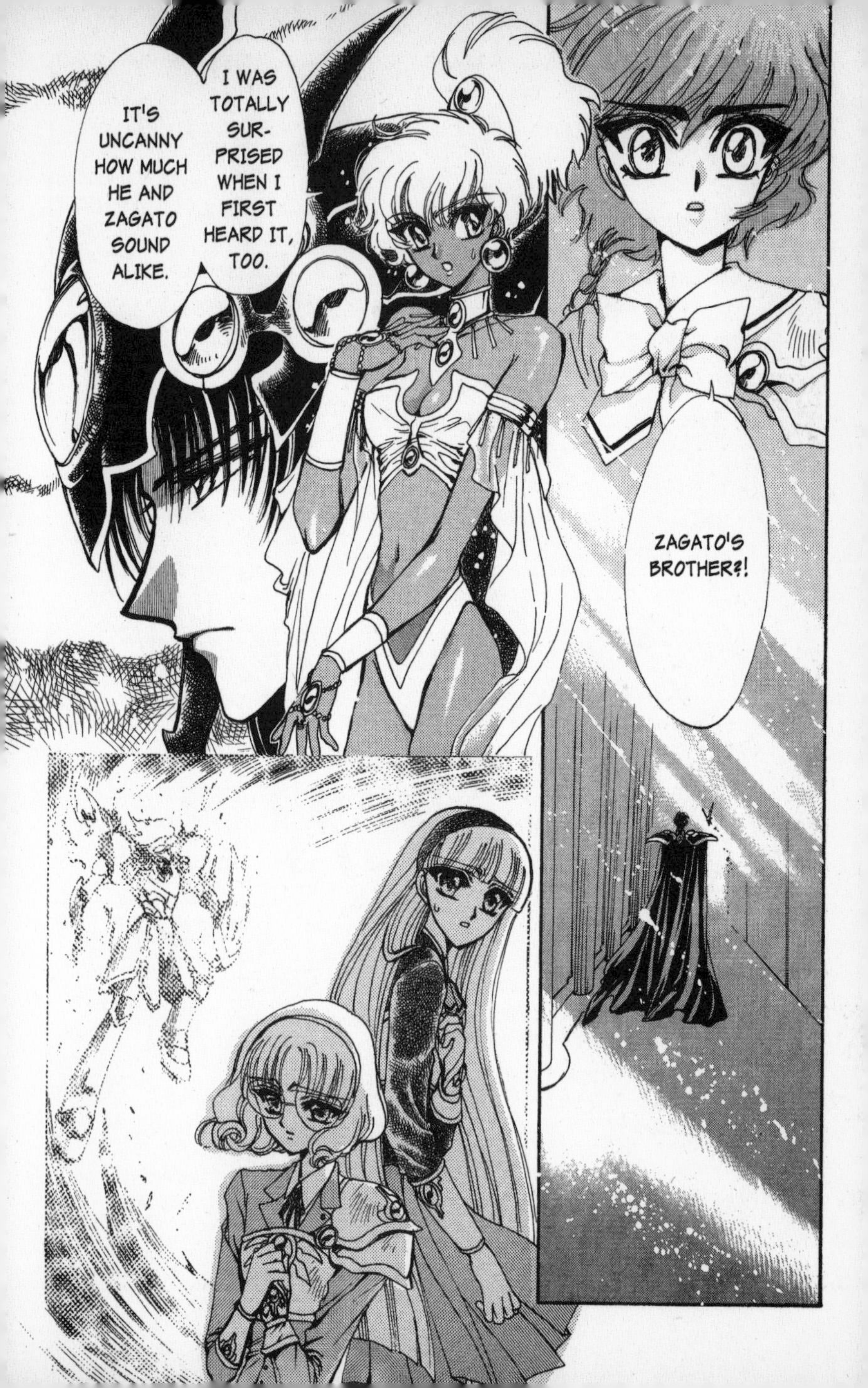
ZAGATO'S BROTHER?!
I WAS TOTALLY SURPRISED WHEN I FIRST HEARD IT, TOO.
IT'S UNCANNY HOW MUCH HE AND ZAGATO SOUND ALIKE.

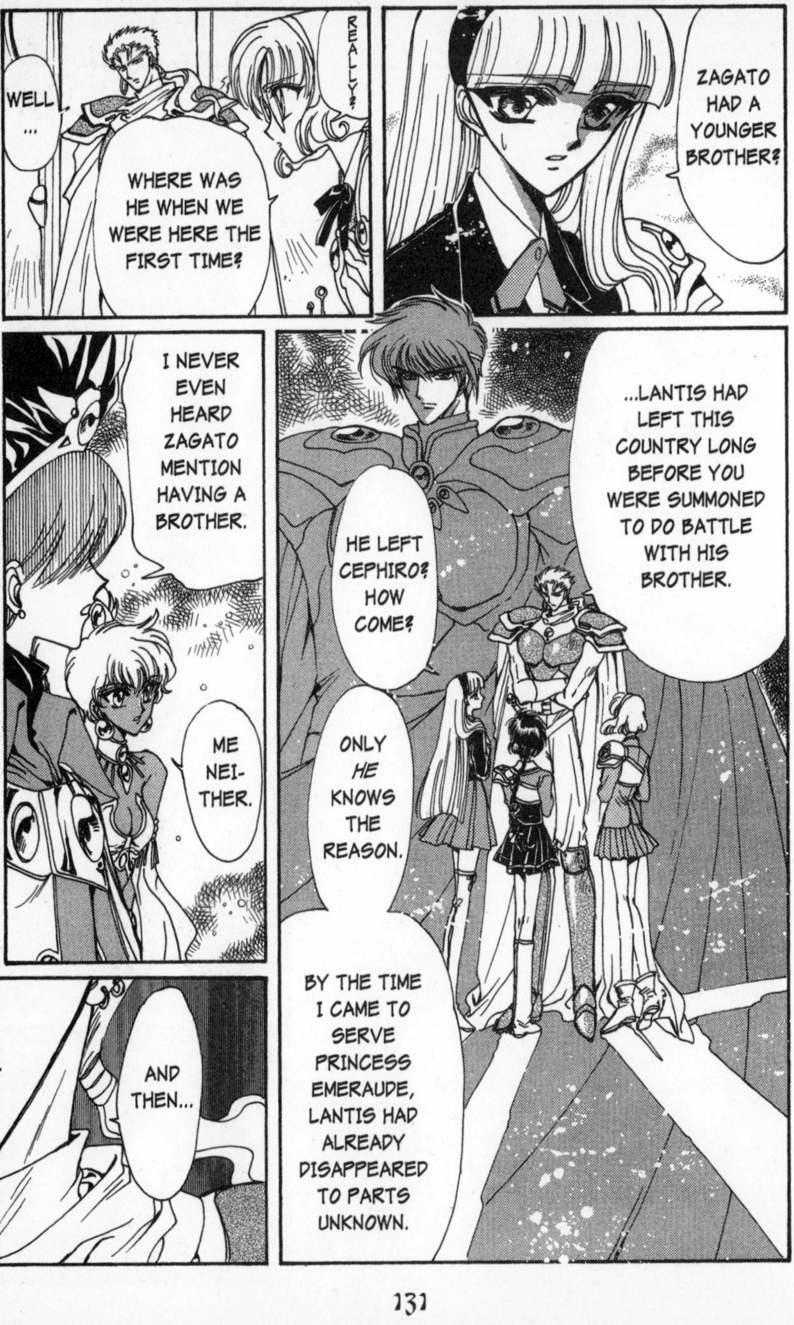
ZAGATO HAD A YOUNGER BROTHER?
REALLY?
WHERE WAS HE WHEN WE WERE HERE THE FIRST TIME?
WELL ...
...LANTIS HAD LEFT THIS COUNTRY LONG BEFORE YOU WERE SUMMONED TO DO BATTLE WITH HIS BROTHER.
HE LEFT CEPHIRO? HOW COME?
ONLY *HE* KNOWS THE REASON.
BY THE TIME I CAME TO SERVE PRINCESS EMERAUDE, LANTIS HAD ALREADY DISAPPEARED TO PARTS UNKNOWN.
I NEVER EVEN HEARD ZAGATO MENTION HAVING A BROTHER.
ME NEI-THER.
AND THEN...

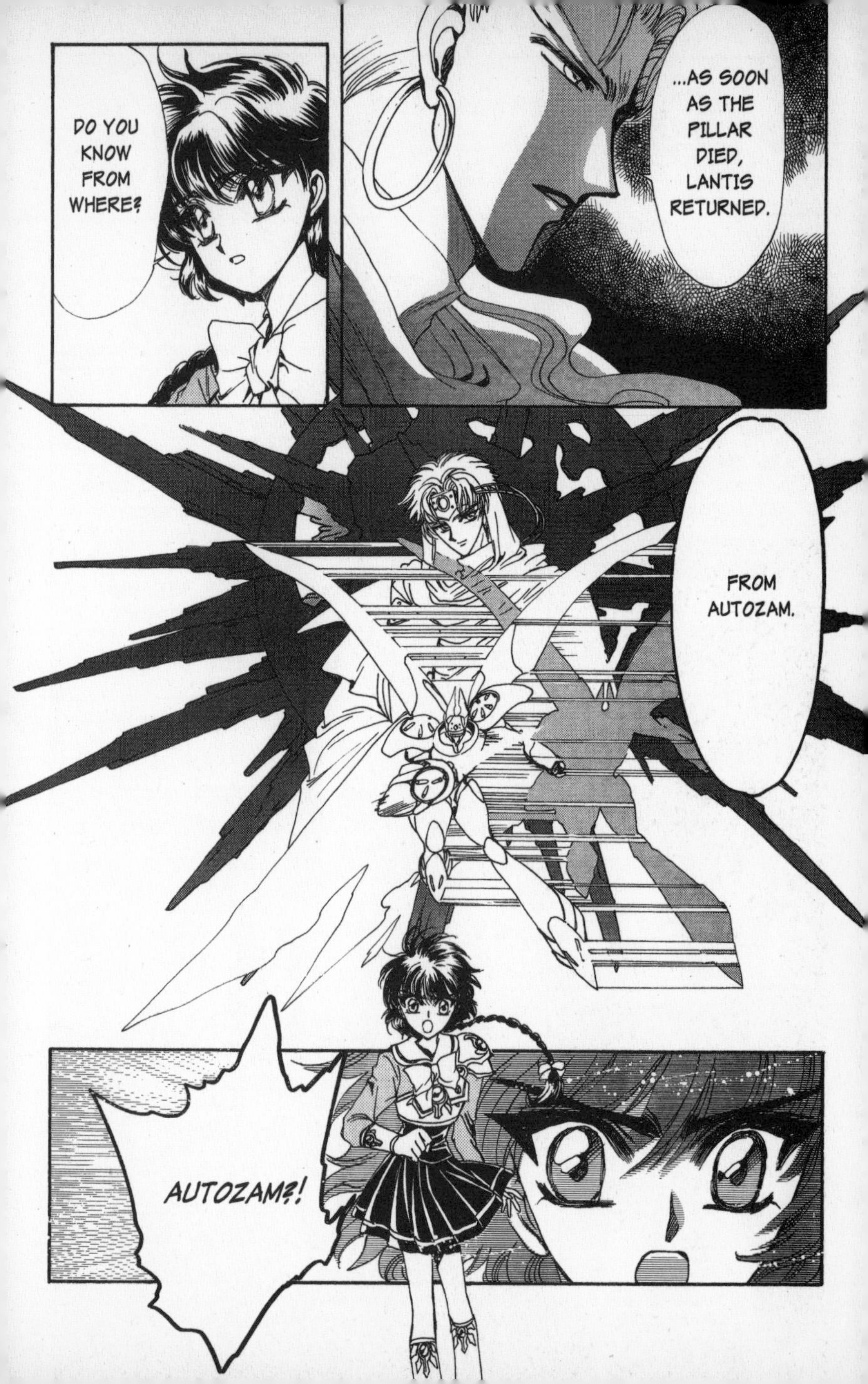
...AS SOON AS THE PILLAR DIED, LANTIS RETURNED.
DO YOU KNOW FROM WHERE?
FROM AUTOZAM.
AUTOZAM?!

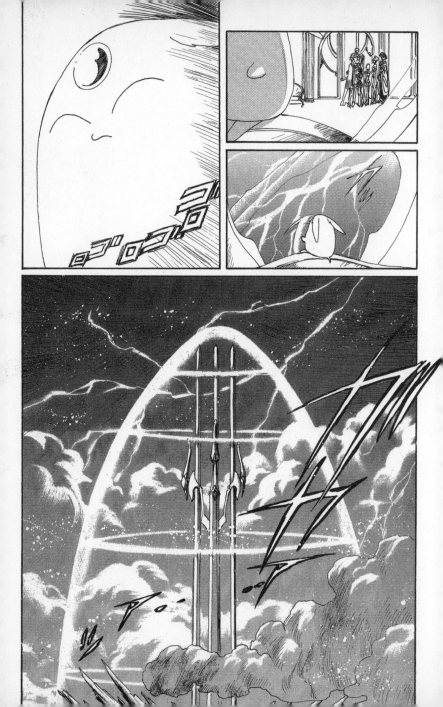

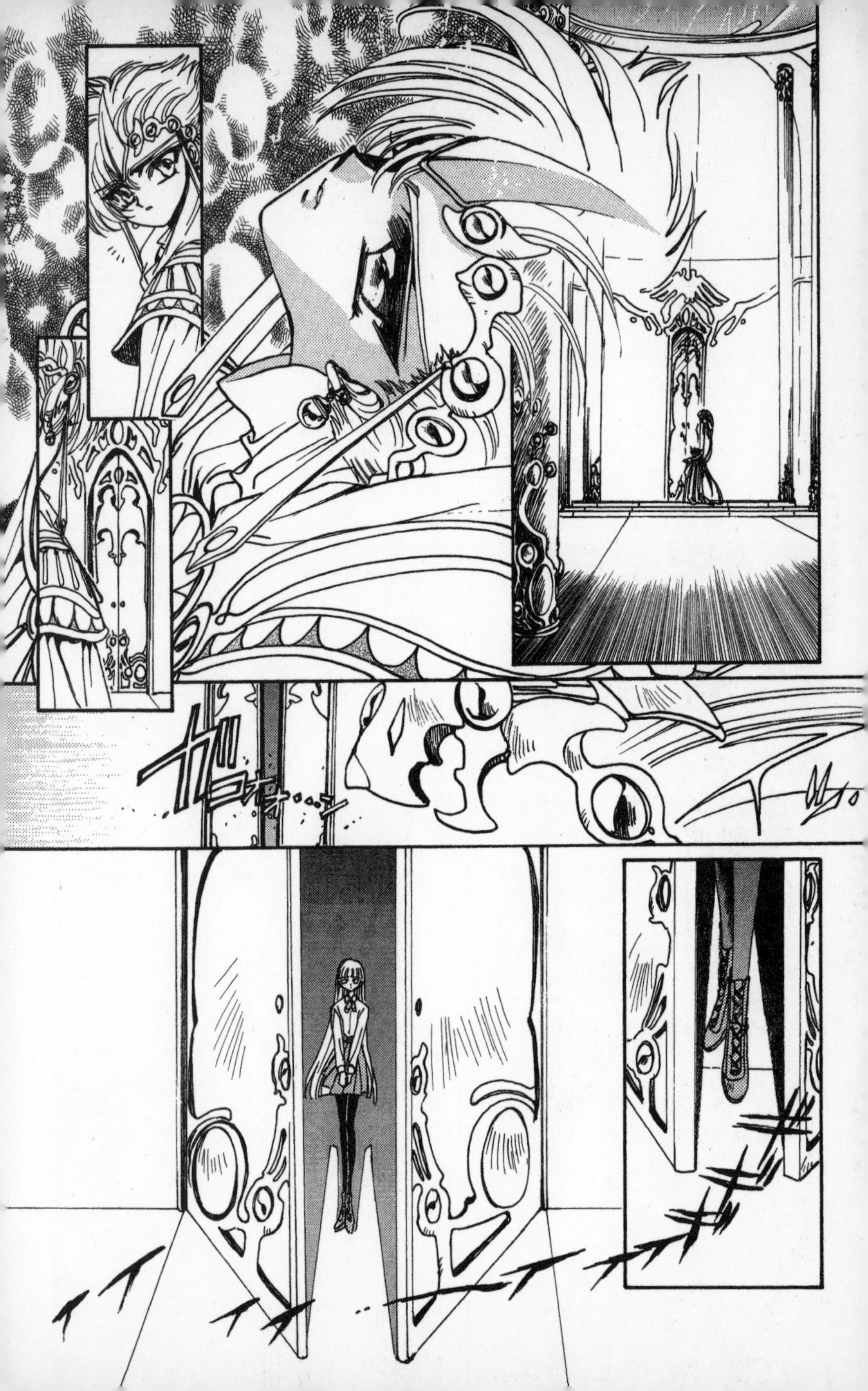
ガコォォ…ン

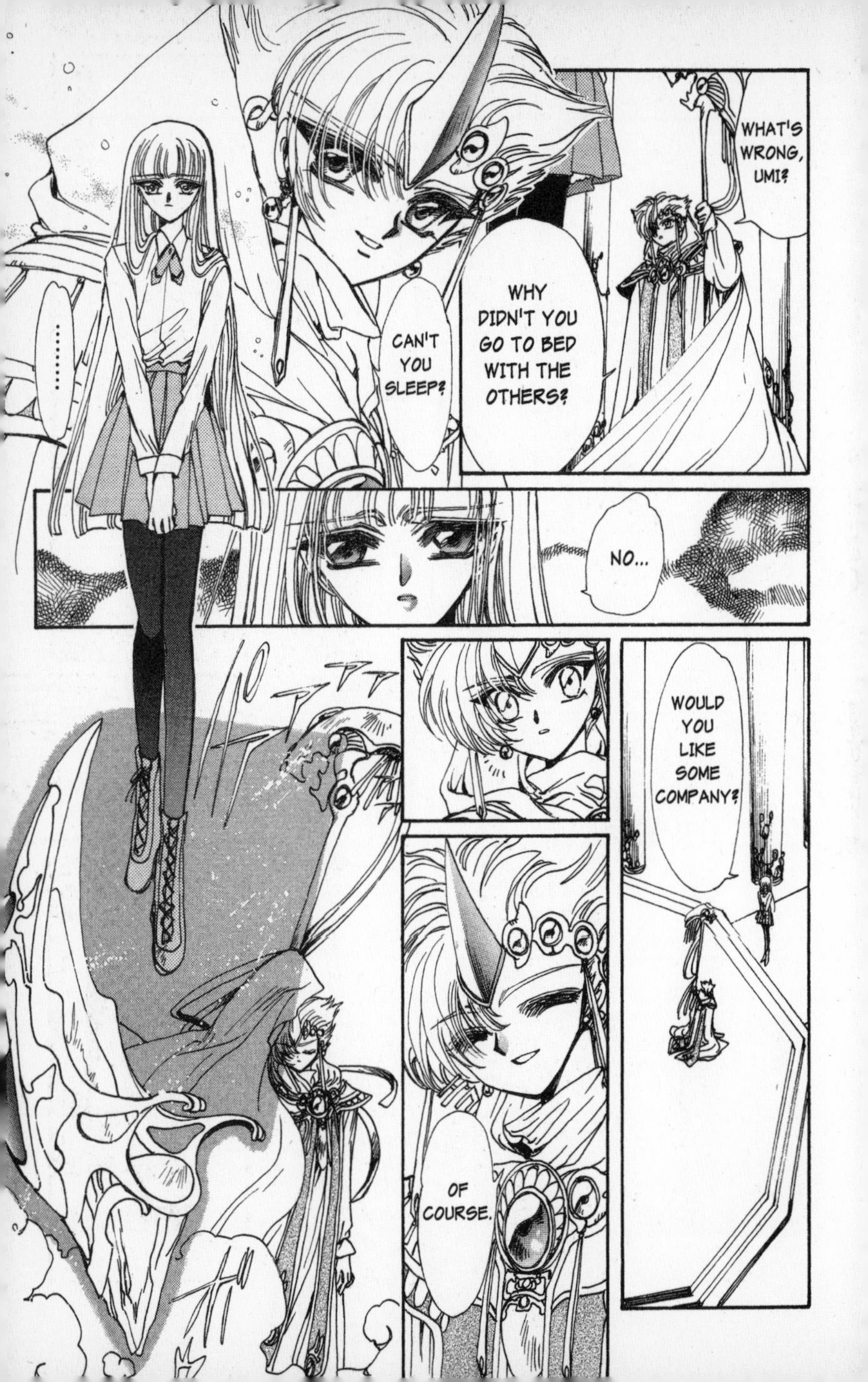

WHAT'S WRONG, UMI?
WHY DIDN'T YOU GO TO BED WITH THE OTHERS?
CAN'T YOU SLEEP?
......
NO...
WOULD YOU LIKE SOME COMPANY?
OF COURSE.

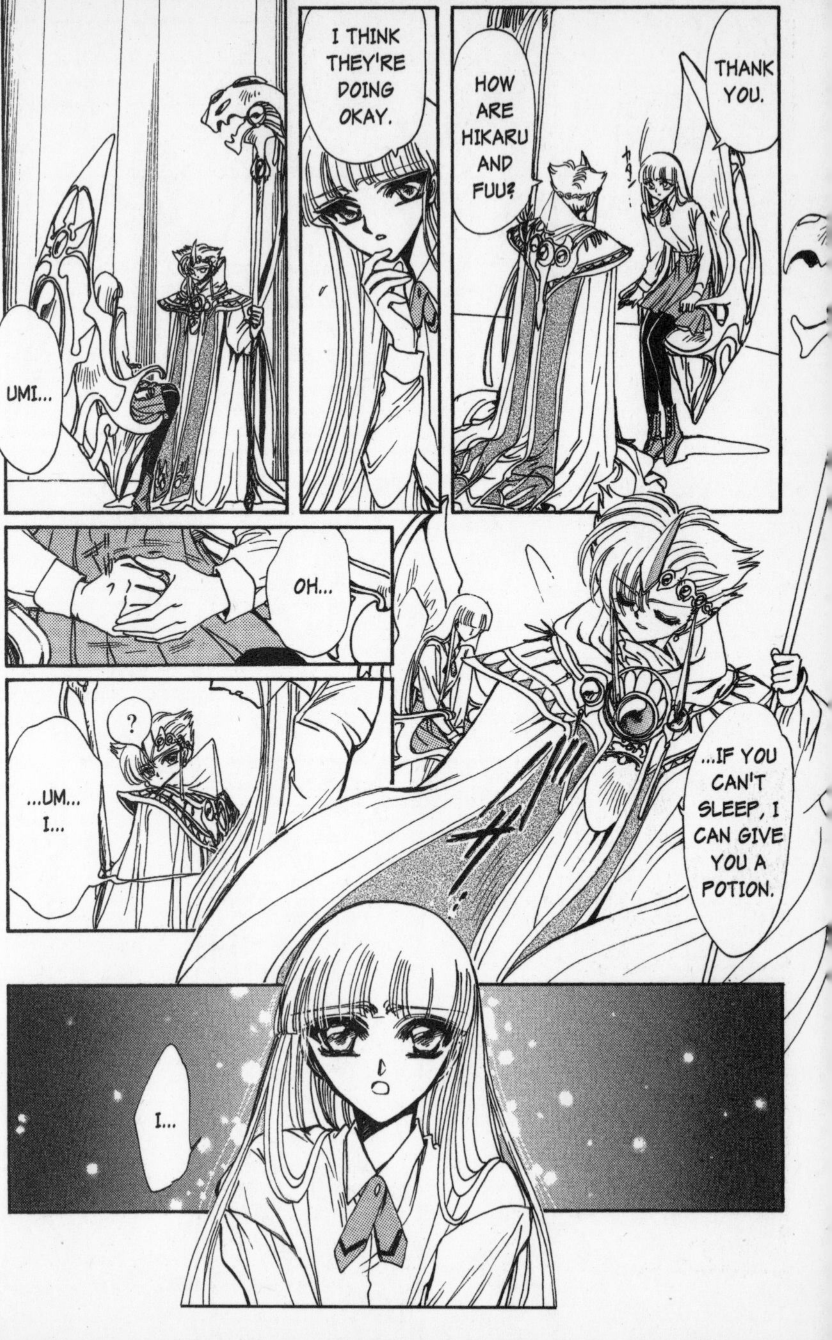
THANK YOU.
カタン
HOW ARE HIKARU AND FUU?
I THINK THEY'RE DOING OKAY.
UMI...
...IF YOU CAN'T SLEEP, I CAN GIVE YOU A POTION.
OH...
?
...UM... I...
I...

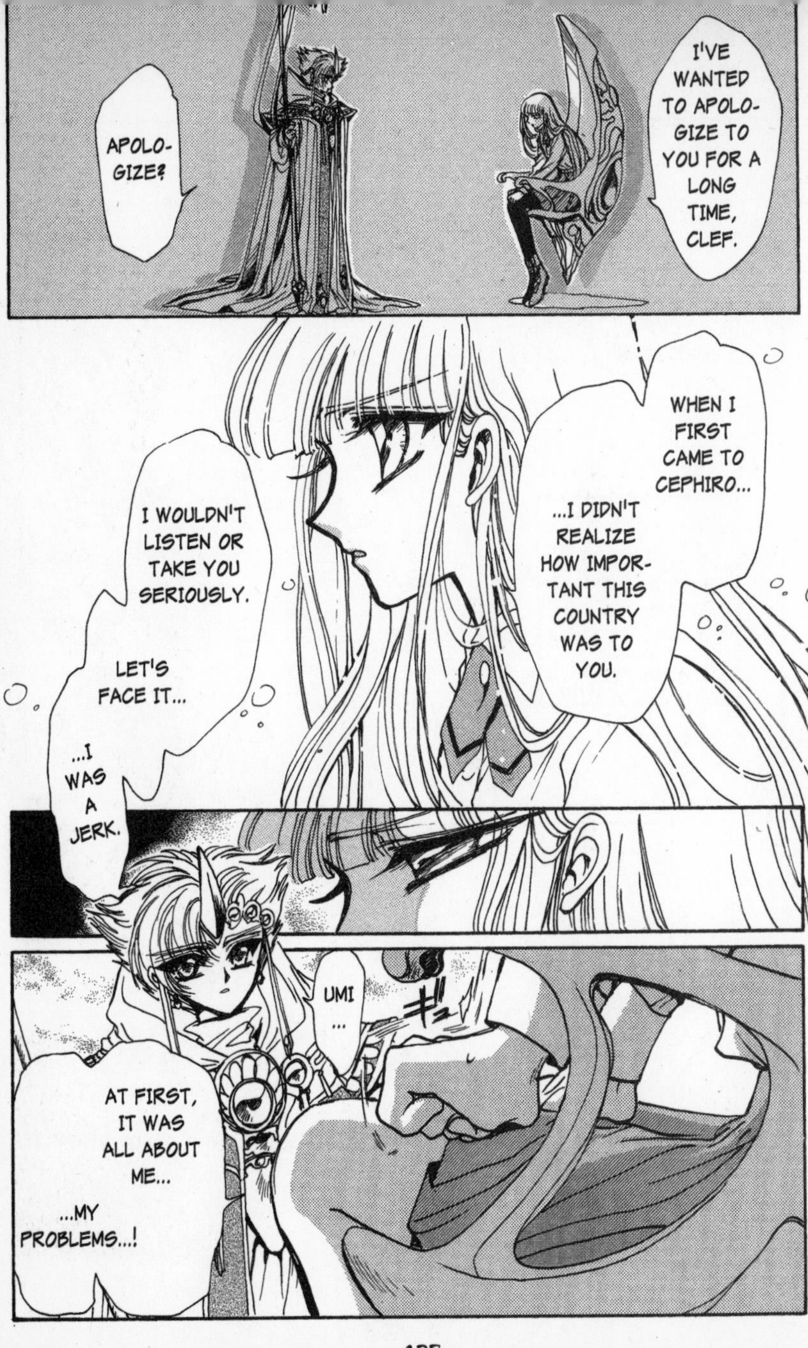
I'VE WANTED TO APOLOGIZE TO YOU FOR A LONG TIME, CLEF.
APOLOGIZE?
WHEN I FIRST CAME TO CEPHIRO...
...I DIDN'T REALIZE HOW IMPORTANT THIS COUNTRY WAS TO YOU.
I WOULDN'T LISTEN OR TAKE YOU SERIOUSLY.
LET'S FACE IT...
...I WAS A JERK.
UMI...
AT FIRST, IT WAS ALL ABOUT ME...
...MY PROBLEMS...!

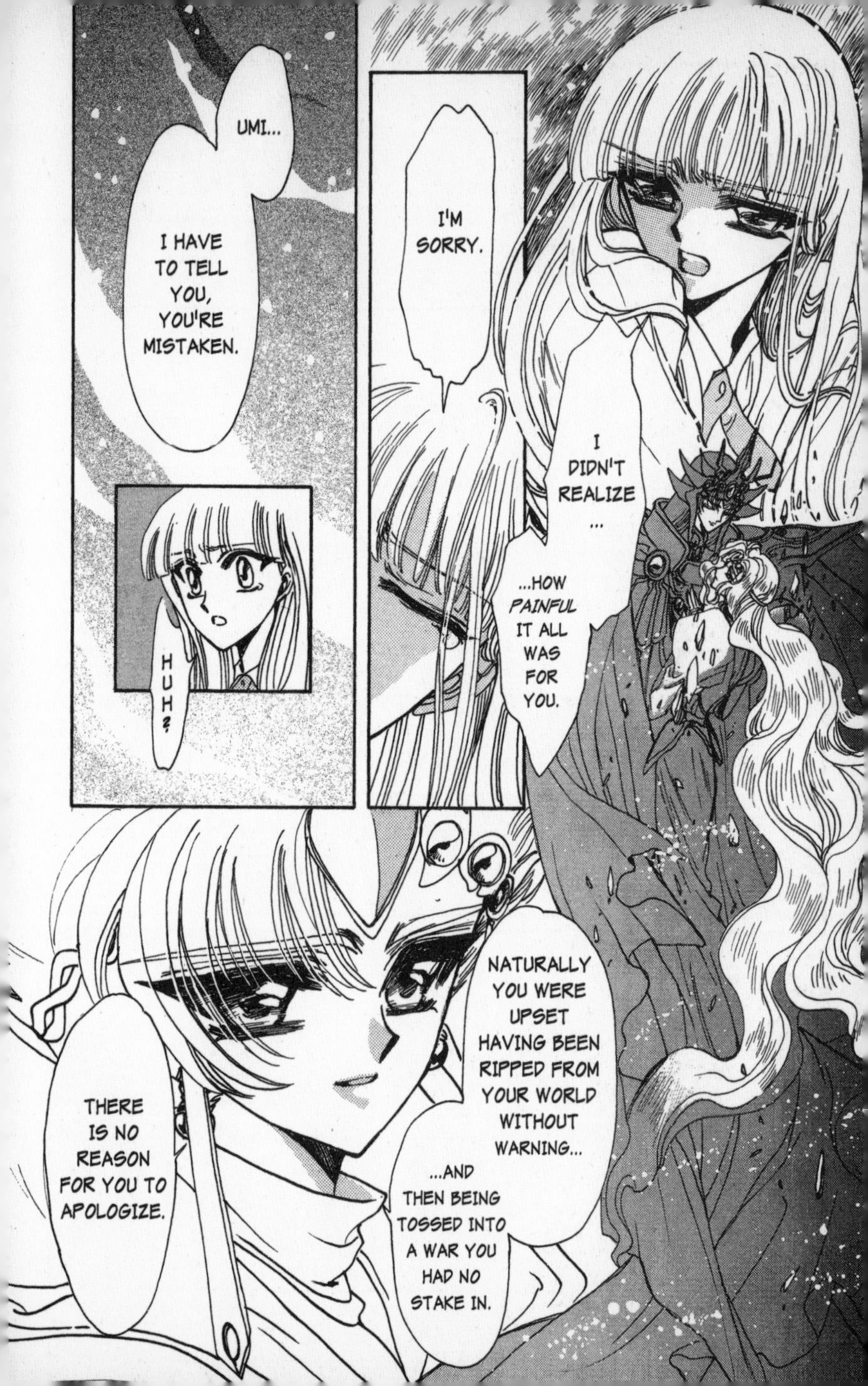
I'M SORRY.
I DIDN'T REALIZE ...
...HOW *PAINFUL* IT ALL WAS FOR YOU.
UMI...
I HAVE TO TELL YOU, YOU'RE MISTAKEN.
HUH?
NATURALLY YOU WERE UPSET HAVING BEEN RIPPED FROM YOUR WORLD WITHOUT WARNING...
...AND THEN BEING TOSSED INTO A WAR YOU HAD NO STAKE IN.
THERE IS NO REASON FOR YOU TO APOLOGIZE.

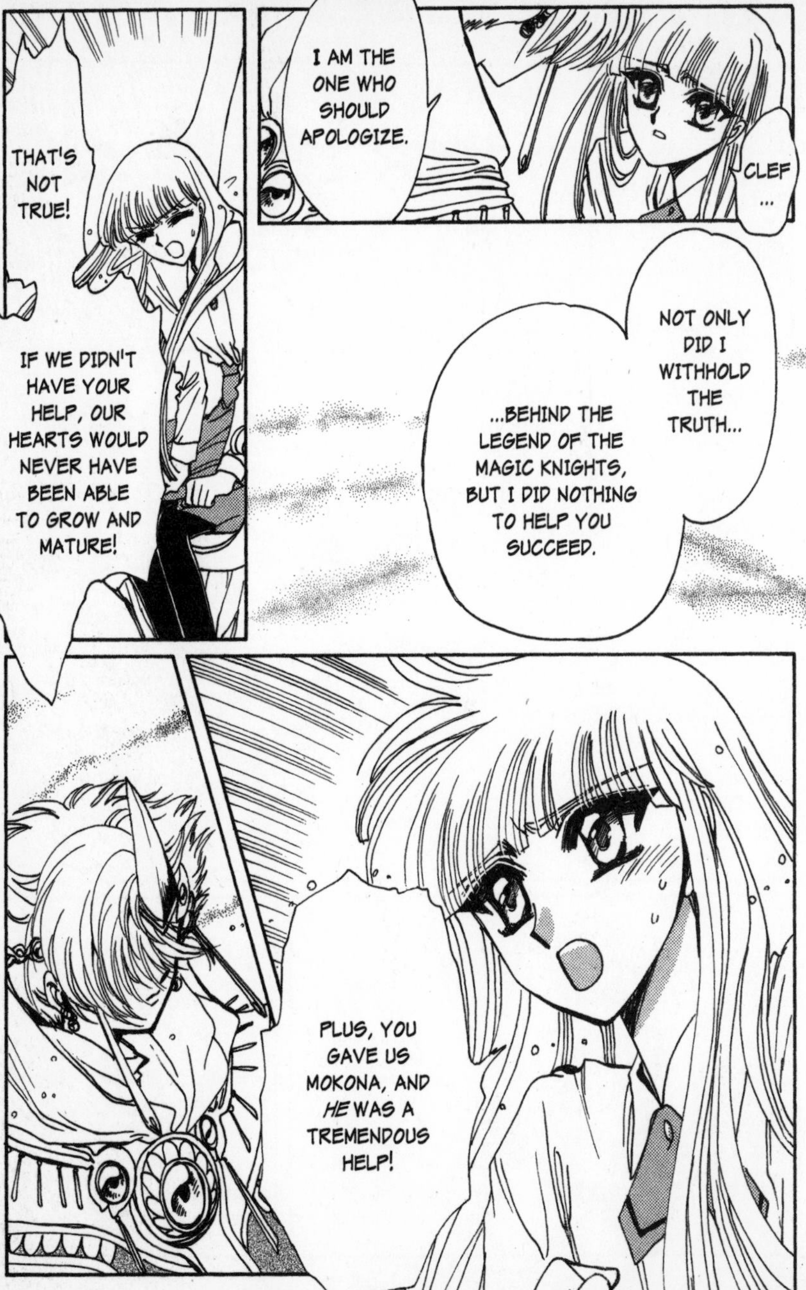

CLEF...
I AM THE ONE WHO SHOULD APOLOGIZE.
NOT ONLY DID I WITHHOLD THE TRUTH...
...BEHIND THE LEGEND OF THE MAGIC KNIGHTS, BUT I DID NOTHING TO HELP YOU SUCCEED.
THAT'S NOT TRUE!
IF WE DIDN'T HAVE YOUR HELP, OUR HEARTS WOULD NEVER HAVE BEEN ABLE TO GROW AND MATURE!
PLUS, YOU GAVE US MOKONA, AND *HE* WAS A TREMENDOUS HELP!

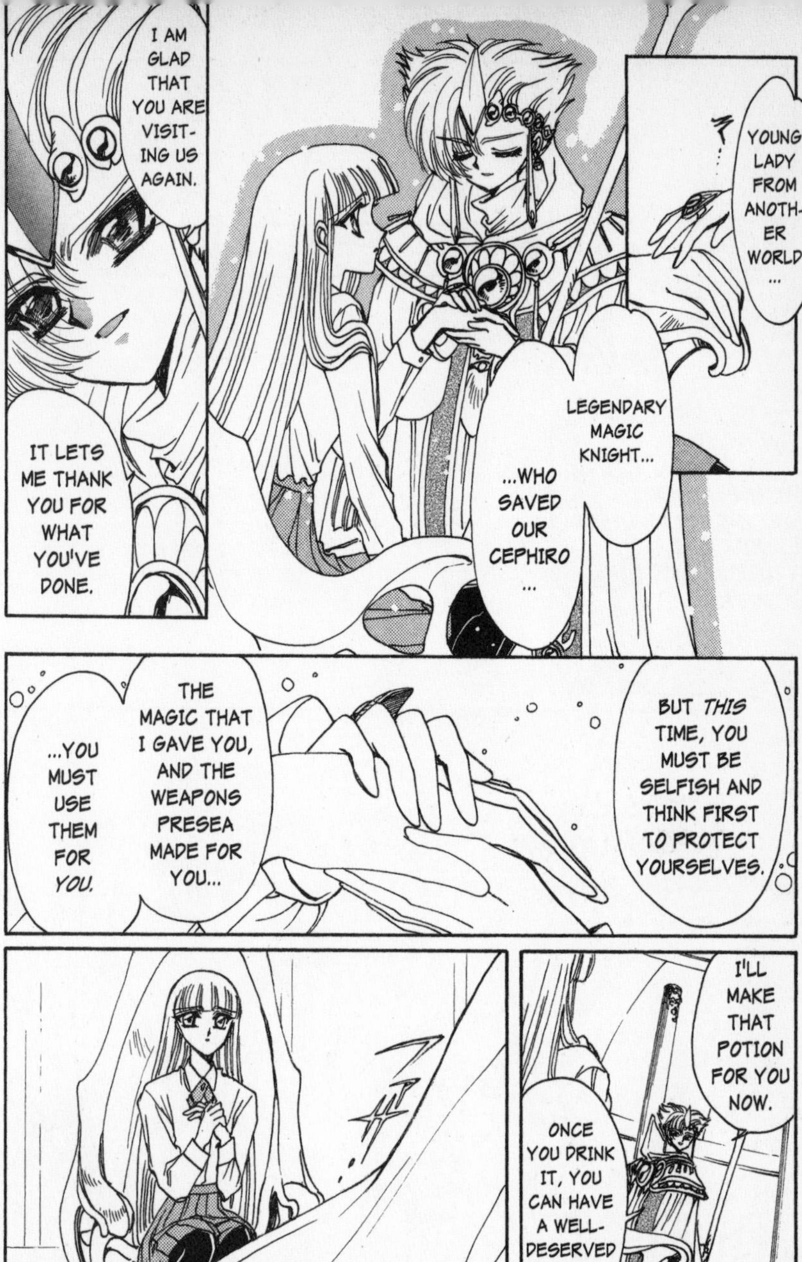
YOUNG LADY FROM ANOTHER-ER WORLD...
LEGENDARY MAGIC KNIGHT...
...WHO SAVED OUR CEPHIRO...
I AM GLAD THAT YOU ARE VISITING US AGAIN.
IT LETS ME THANK YOU FOR WHAT YOU'VE DONE.
BUT *THIS* TIME, YOU MUST BE SELFISH AND THINK FIRST TO PROTECT YOURSELVES.
THE MAGIC THAT I GAVE YOU, AND THE WEAPONS PRESEA MADE FOR YOU...
...YOU MUST USE THEM FOR *YOU.*
I'LL MAKE THAT POTION FOR YOU NOW.
ONCE YOU DRINK IT, YOU CAN HAVE A WELL-DESERVED REST.

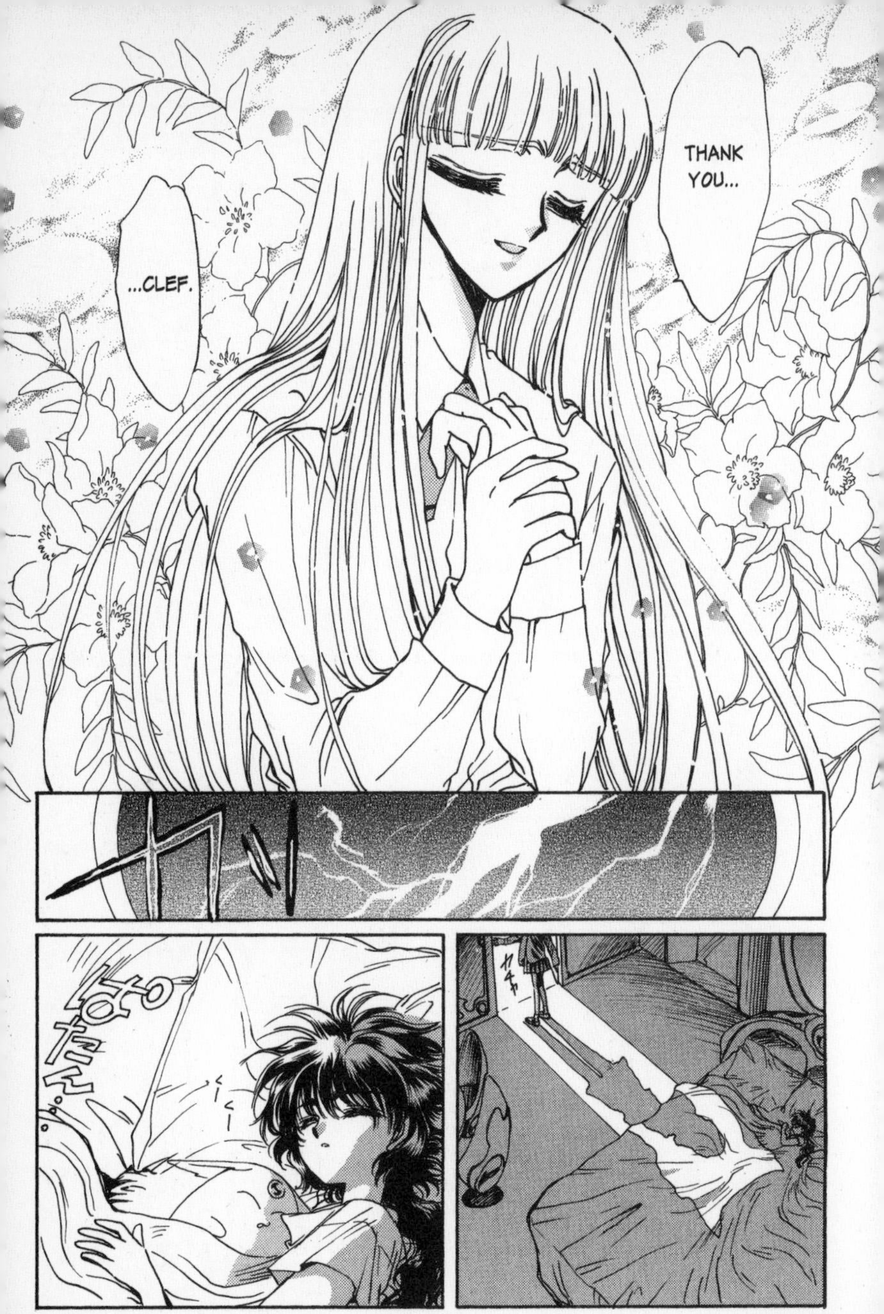
THANK YOU...
...CLEF.

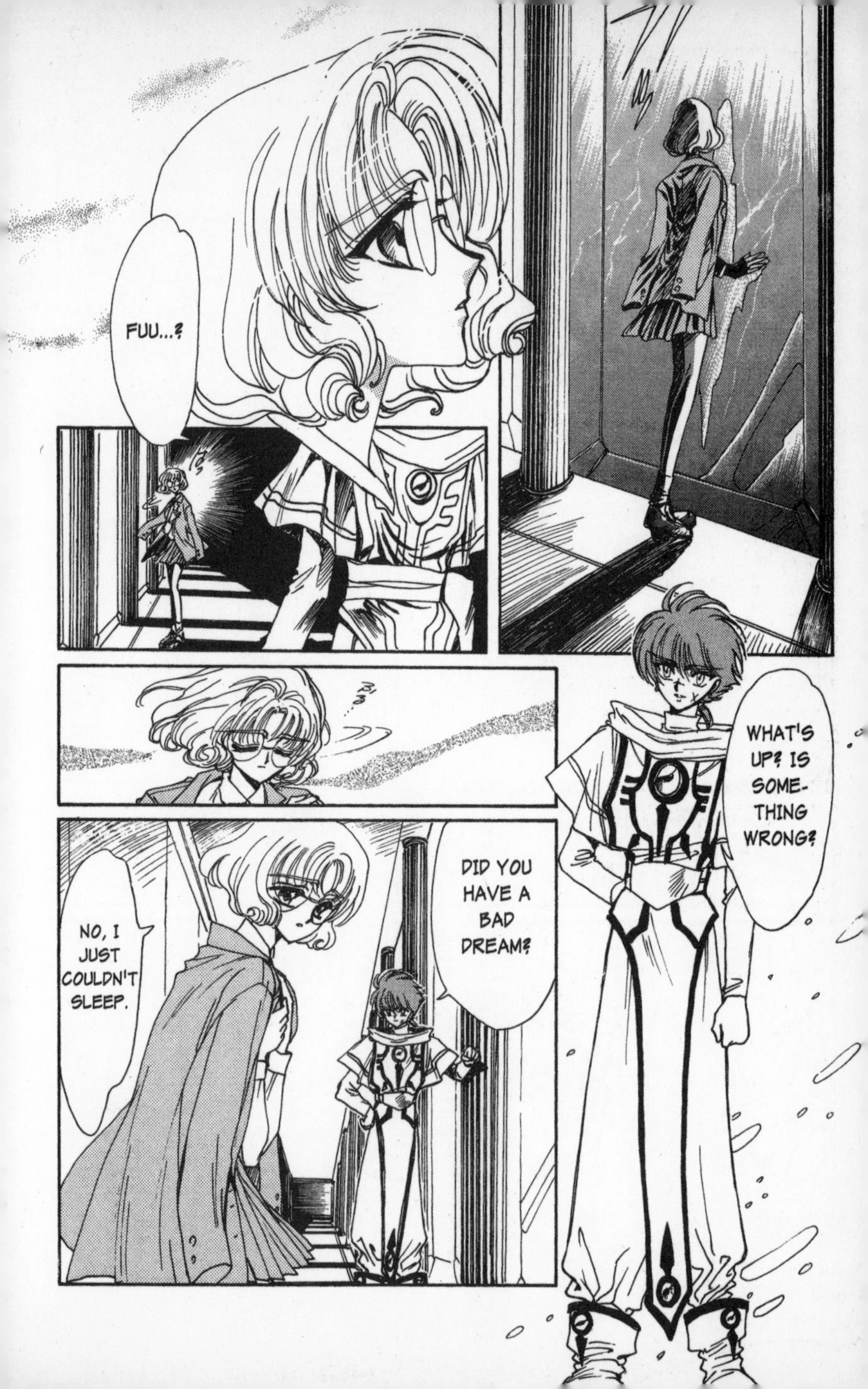

FUU...?
WHAT'S UP? IS SOME- THING WRONG?
DID YOU HAVE A BAD DREAM?
NO, I JUST COULDN'T SLEEP.

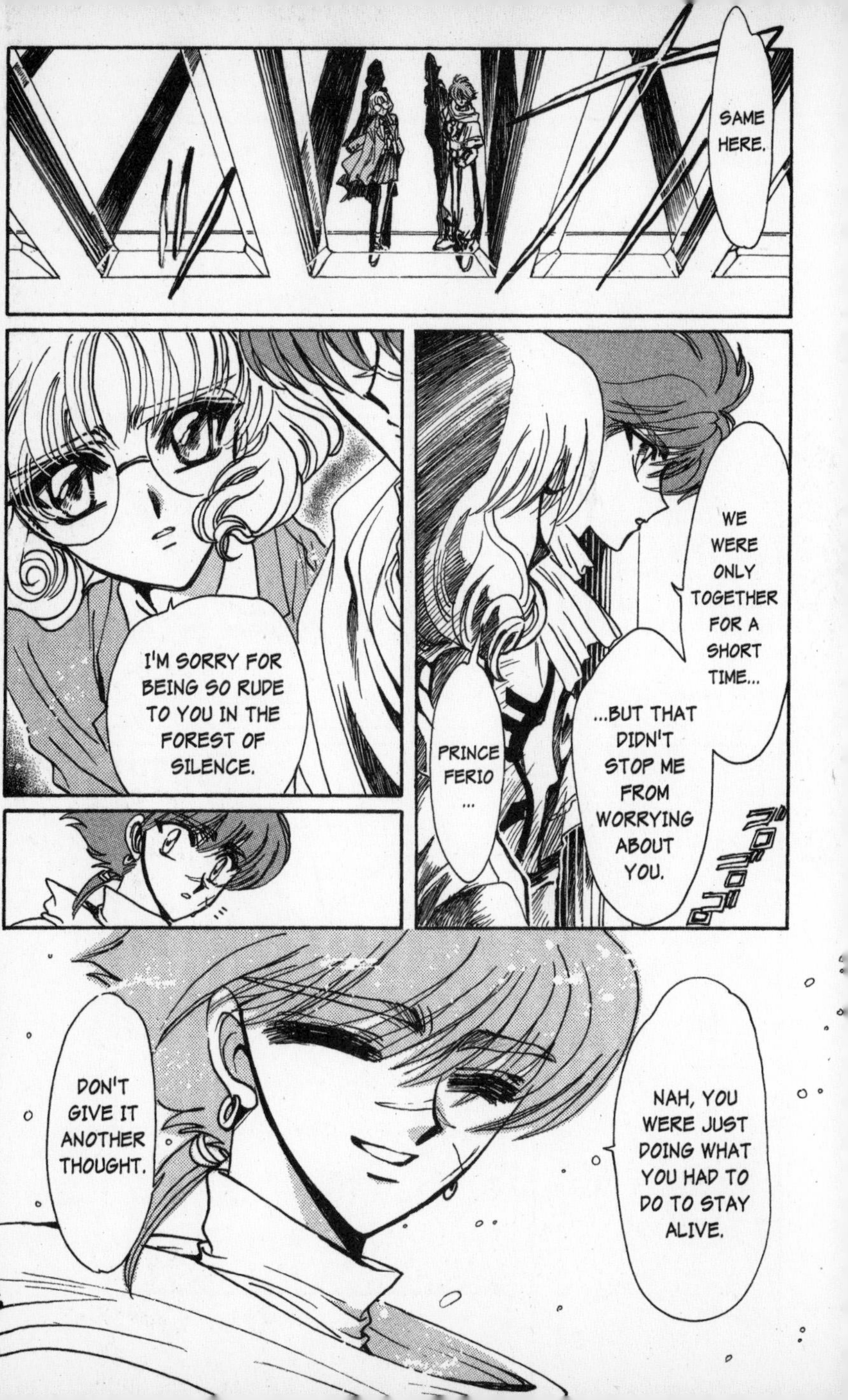
SAME HERE.
WE WERE ONLY TOGETHER FOR A SHORT TIME...
...BUT THAT DIDN'T STOP ME FROM WORRYING ABOUT YOU.
PRINCE FERIO ...
I'M SORRY FOR BEING SO RUDE TO YOU IN THE FOREST OF SILENCE.
NAH, YOU WERE JUST DOING WHAT YOU HAD TO DO TO STAY ALIVE.
DON'T GIVE IT ANOTHER THOUGHT.

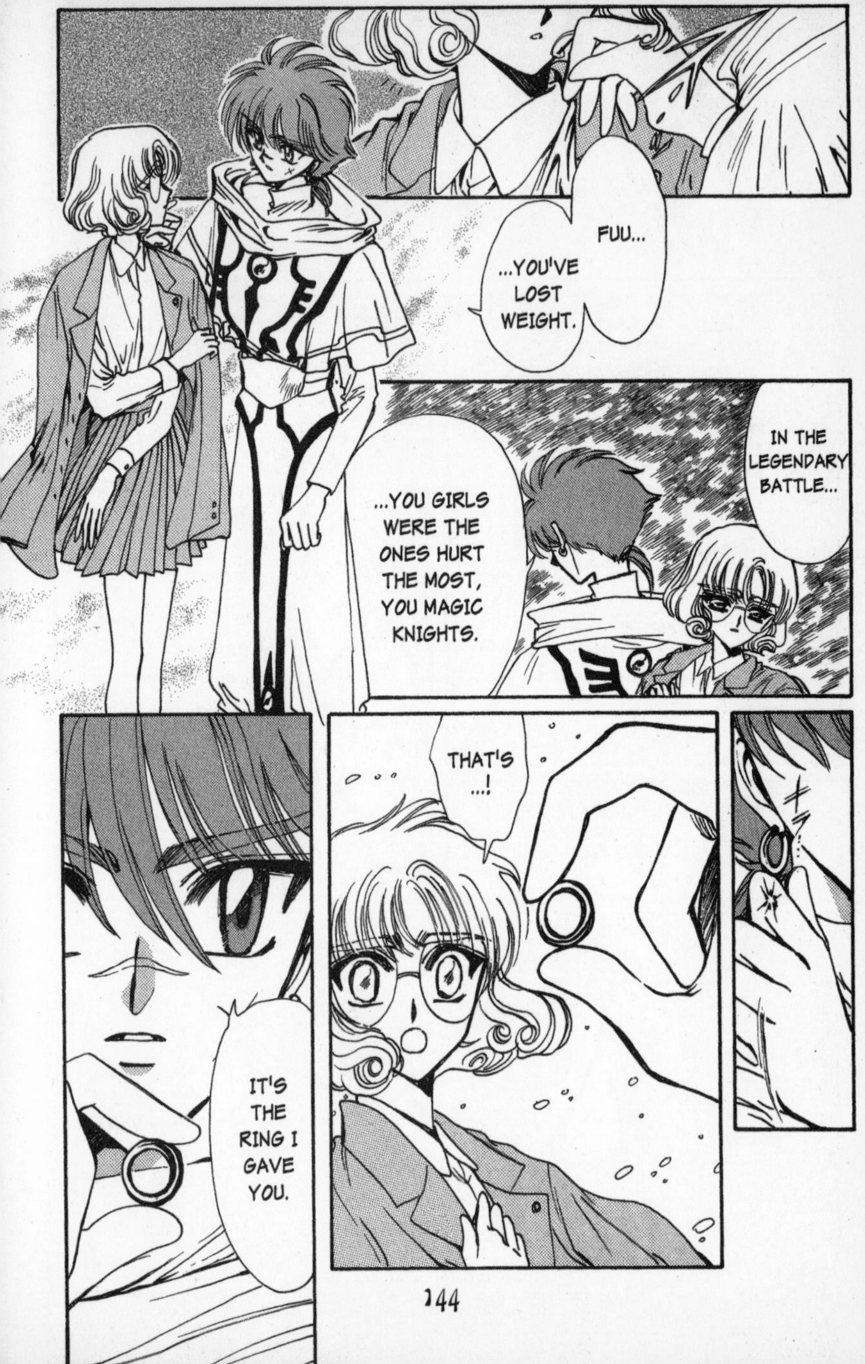
FUU...
...YOU'VE LOST WEIGHT.
IN THE LEGENDARY BATTLE...
...YOU GIRLS WERE THE ONES HURT THE MOST, YOU MAGIC KNIGHTS.
THAT'S ...!
IT'S THE RING I GAVE YOU.

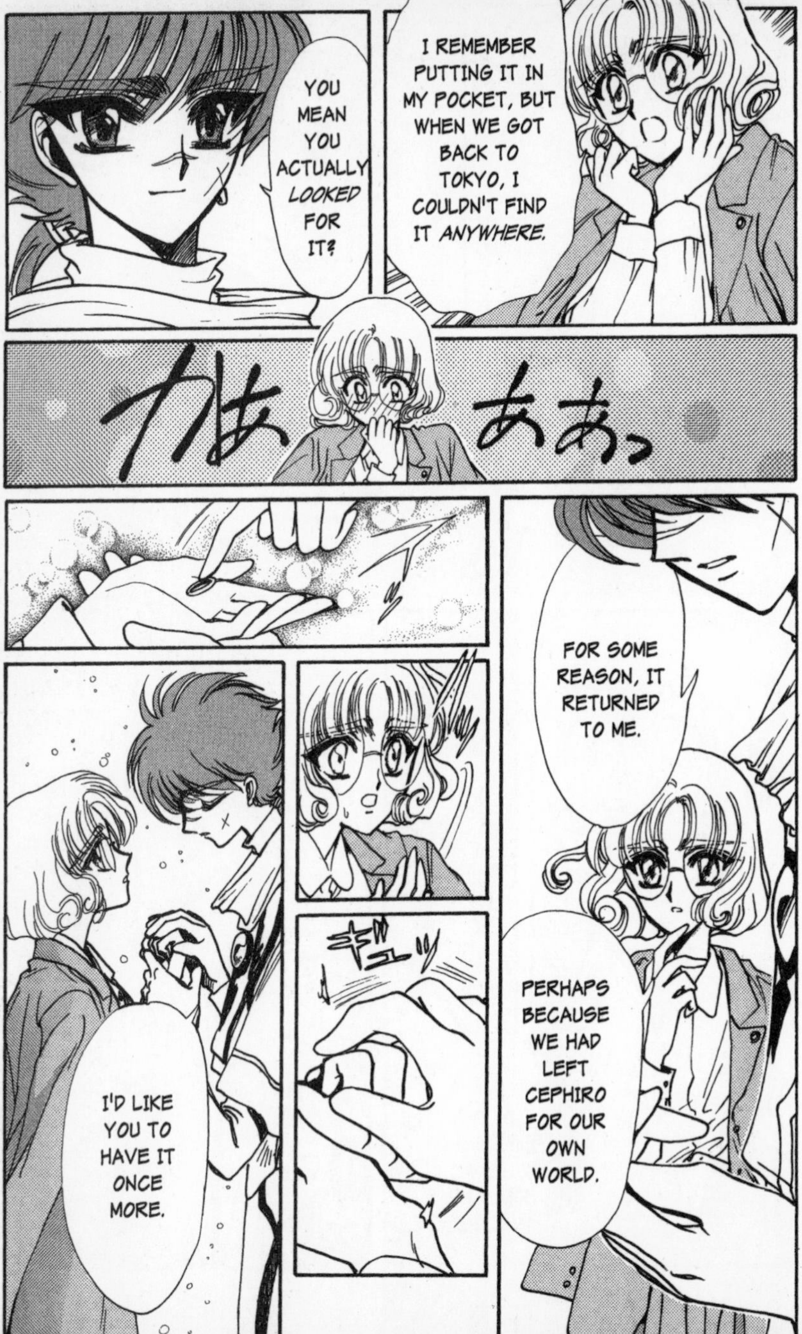
I REMEMBER PUTTING IT IN MY POCKET, BUT WHEN WE GOT BACK TO TOKYO, I COULDN'T FIND IT *ANYWHERE.*
YOU MEAN YOU ACTUALLY *LOOKED* FOR IT?
FOR SOME REASON, IT RETURNED TO ME.
PERHAPS BECAUSE WE HAD LEFT CEPHIRO FOR OUR OWN WORLD.
I'D LIKE YOU TO HAVE IT ONCE MORE.

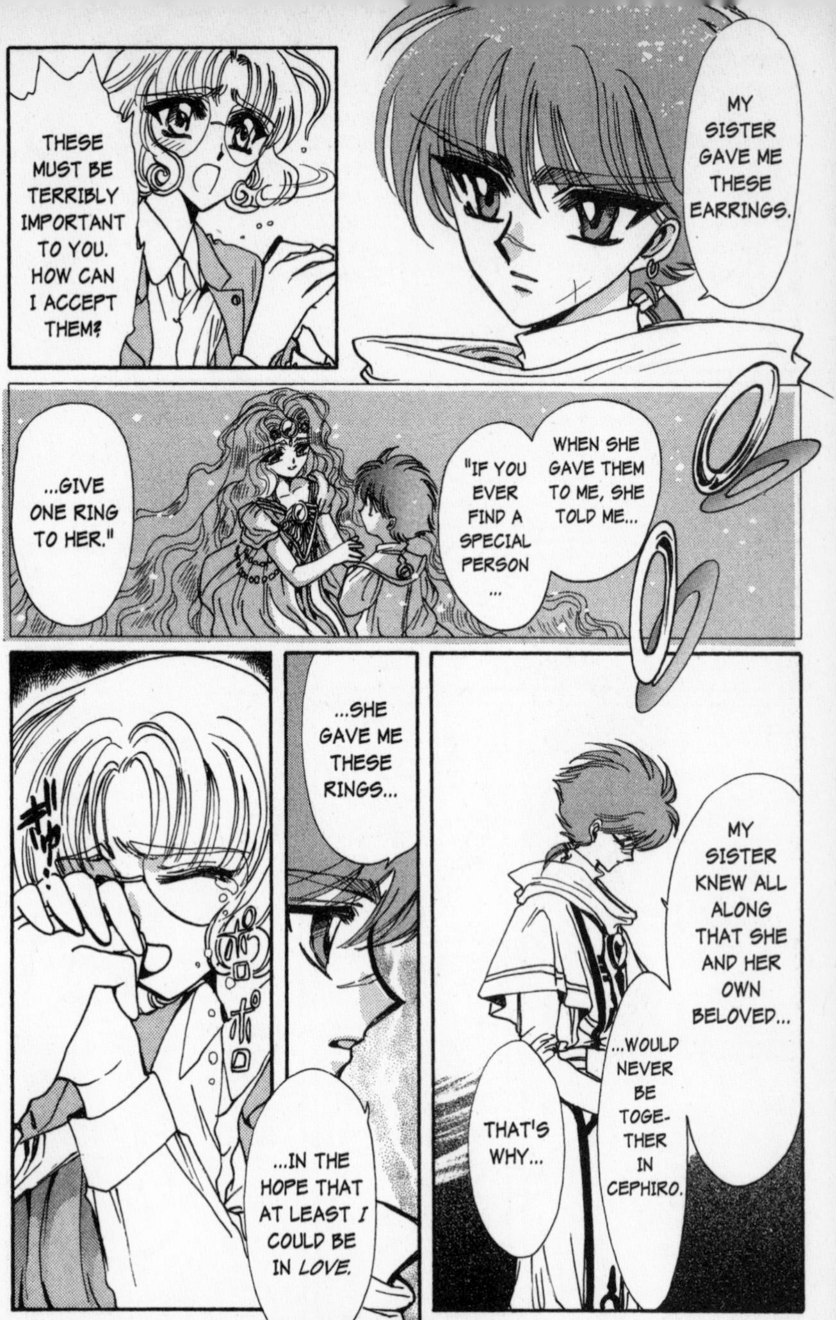
MY SISTER GAVE ME THESE EARRINGS.
THESE MUST BE TERRIBLY IMPORTANT TO YOU. HOW CAN I ACCEPT THEM?
WHEN SHE GAVE THEM TO ME, SHE TOLD ME...
"IF YOU EVER FIND A SPECIAL PERSON ...
...GIVE ONE RING TO HER."
MY SISTER KNEW ALL ALONG THAT SHE AND HER OWN BELOVED...
...WOULD NEVER BE TOGE-THER IN CEPHIRO.
THAT'S WHY...
...SHE GAVE ME THESE RINGS...
...IN THE HOPE THAT AT LEAST *I* COULD BE IN *LOVE.*
ギュ…
ポロ
ポロ

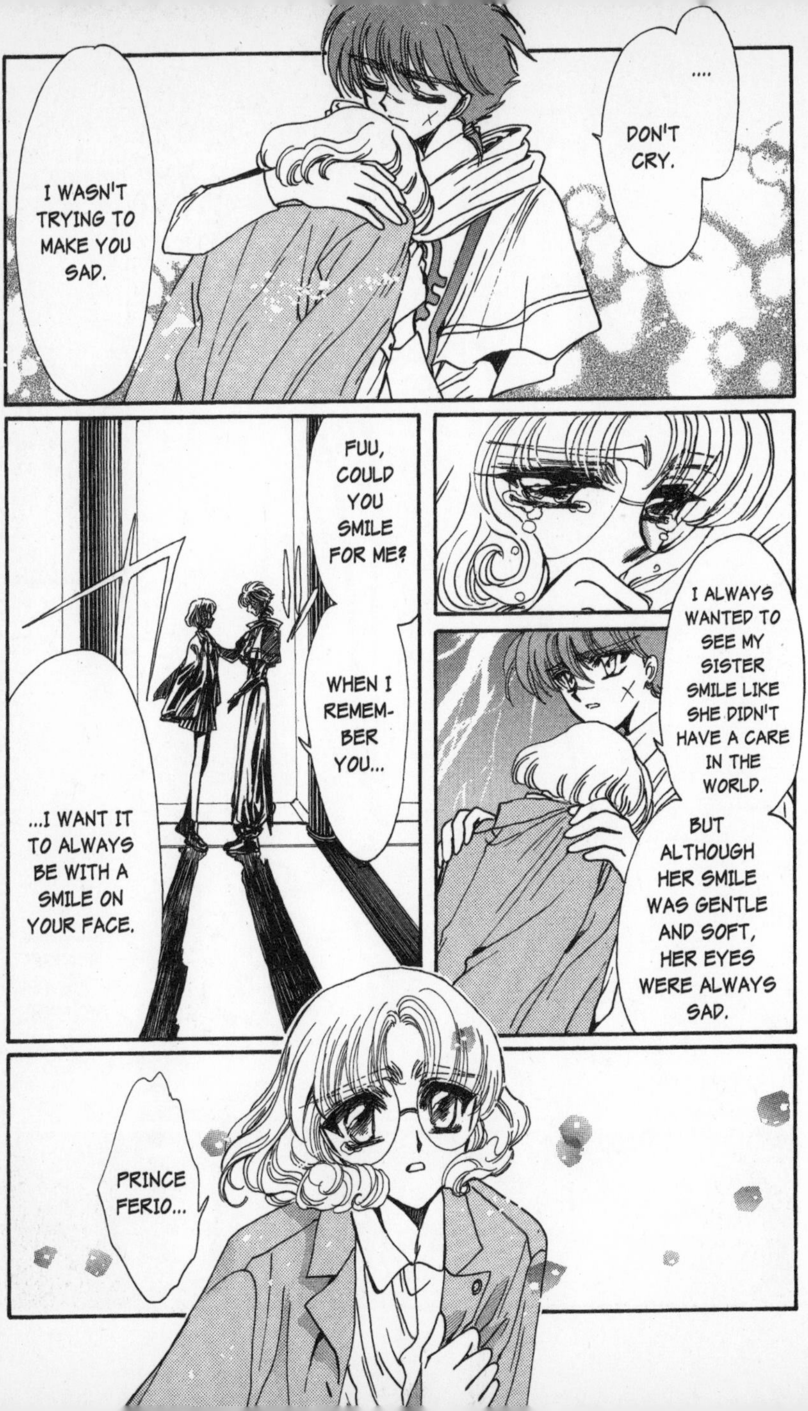
....
DON'T CRY.
I WASN'T TRYING TO MAKE YOU SAD.
I ALWAYS WANTED TO SEE MY SISTER SMILE LIKE SHE DIDN'T HAVE A CARE IN THE WORLD.
BUT ALTHOUGH HER SMILE WAS GENTLE AND SOFT, HER EYES WERE ALWAYS SAD.
FUU, COULD YOU SMILE FOR ME?
WHEN I REMEM-BER YOU...
...I WANT IT TO ALWAYS BE WITH A SMILE ON YOUR FACE.
PRINCE FERIO...

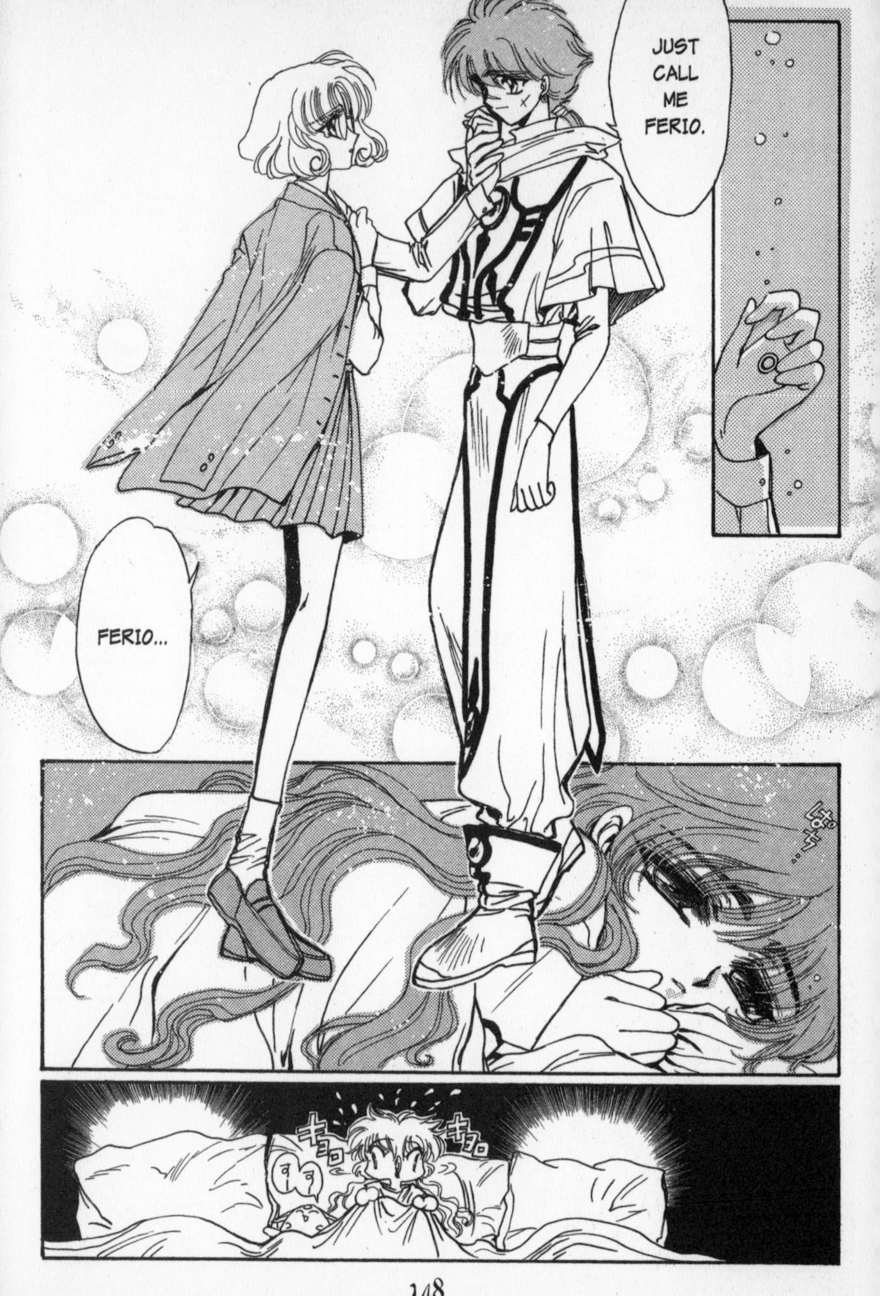
JUST CALL ME FERIO.
FERIO...
キョロ
キョロ

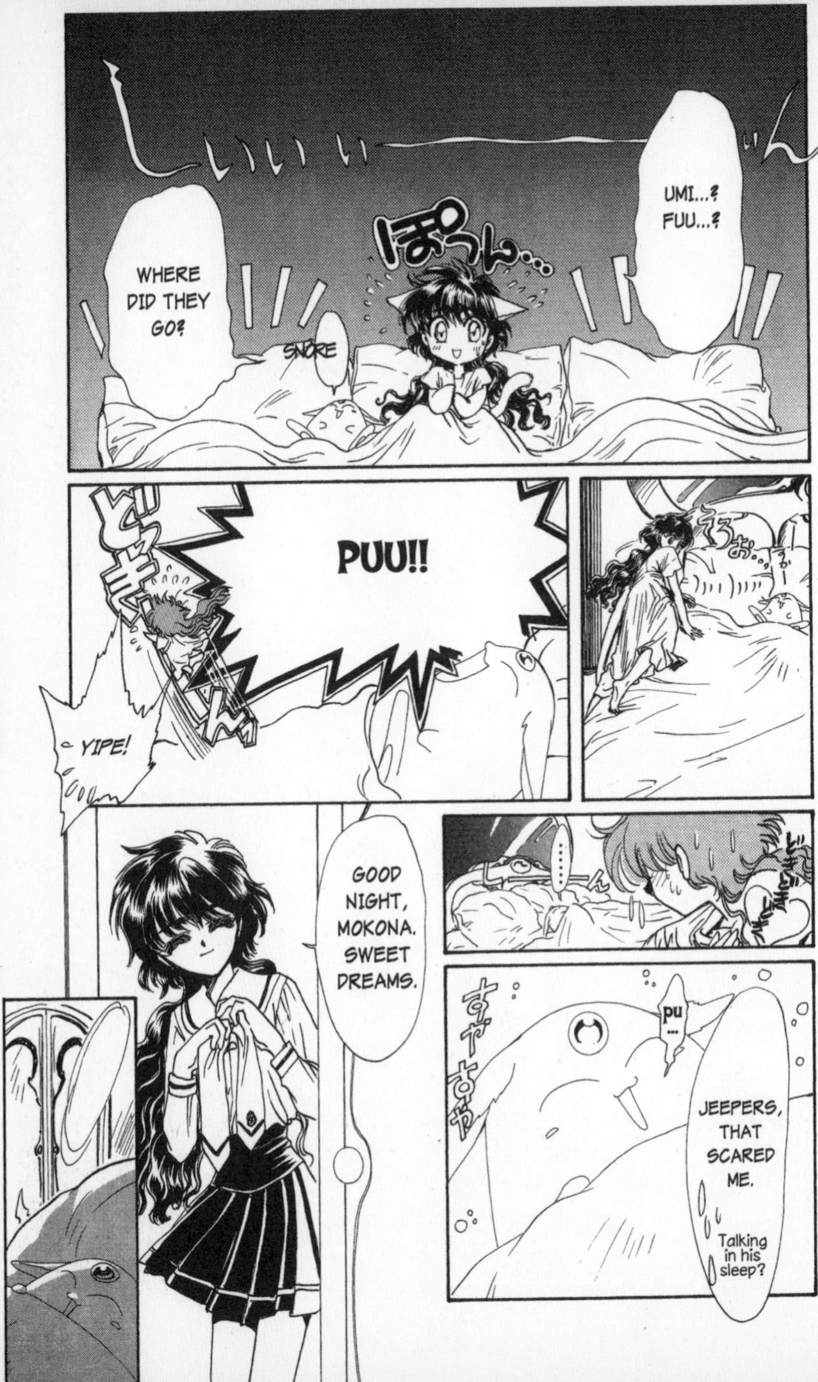
UMI...? FUU...?
WHERE DID THEY GO?
SNORE
PUU!!
YIPE!
....
pu ...
JEEPERS, THAT SCARED ME.
Talking in his sleep?
GOOD NIGHT, MOKONA. SWEET DREAMS.

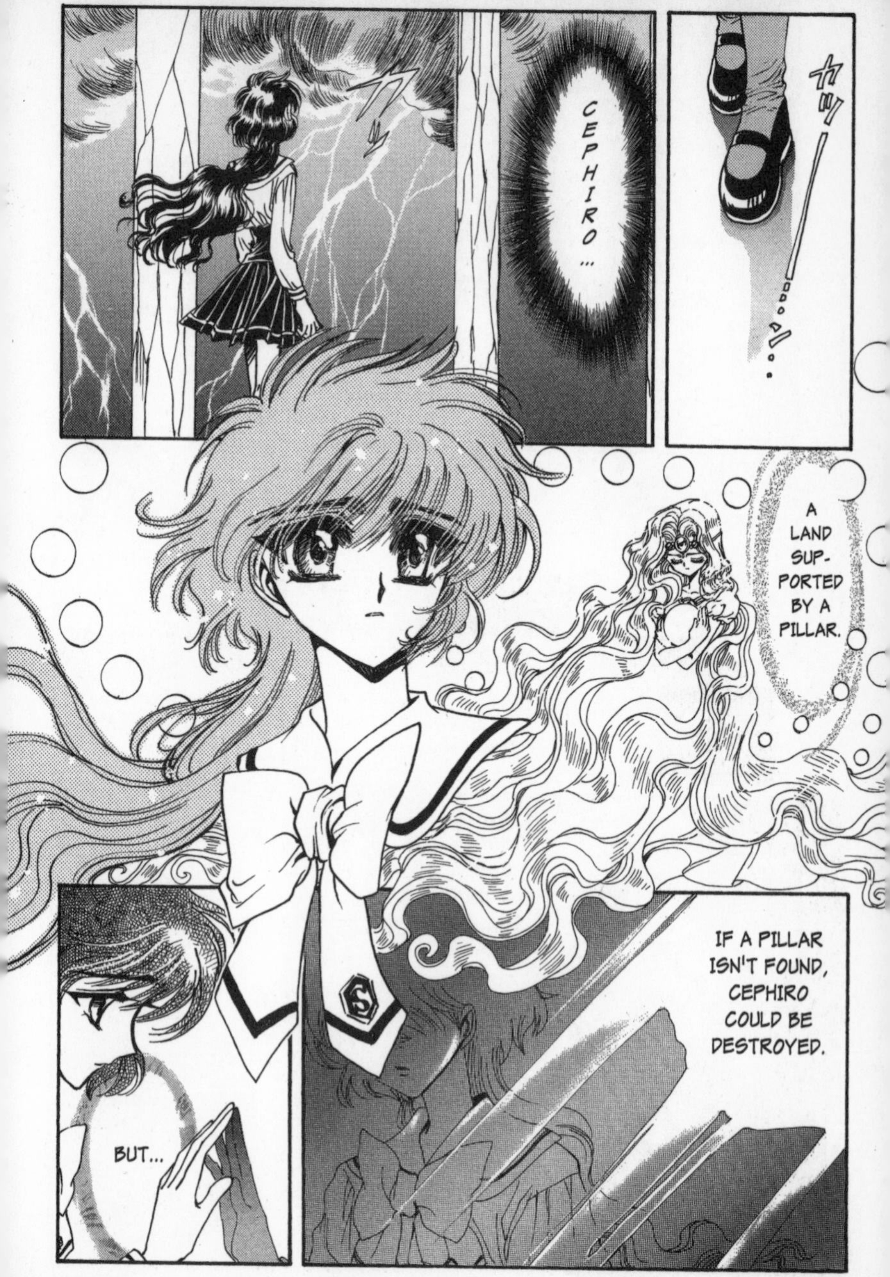
CEPHIRO...
A LAND SUP-PORTED BY A PILLAR.
IF A PILLAR ISN'T FOUND, CEPHIRO COULD BE DESTROYED.
BUT...

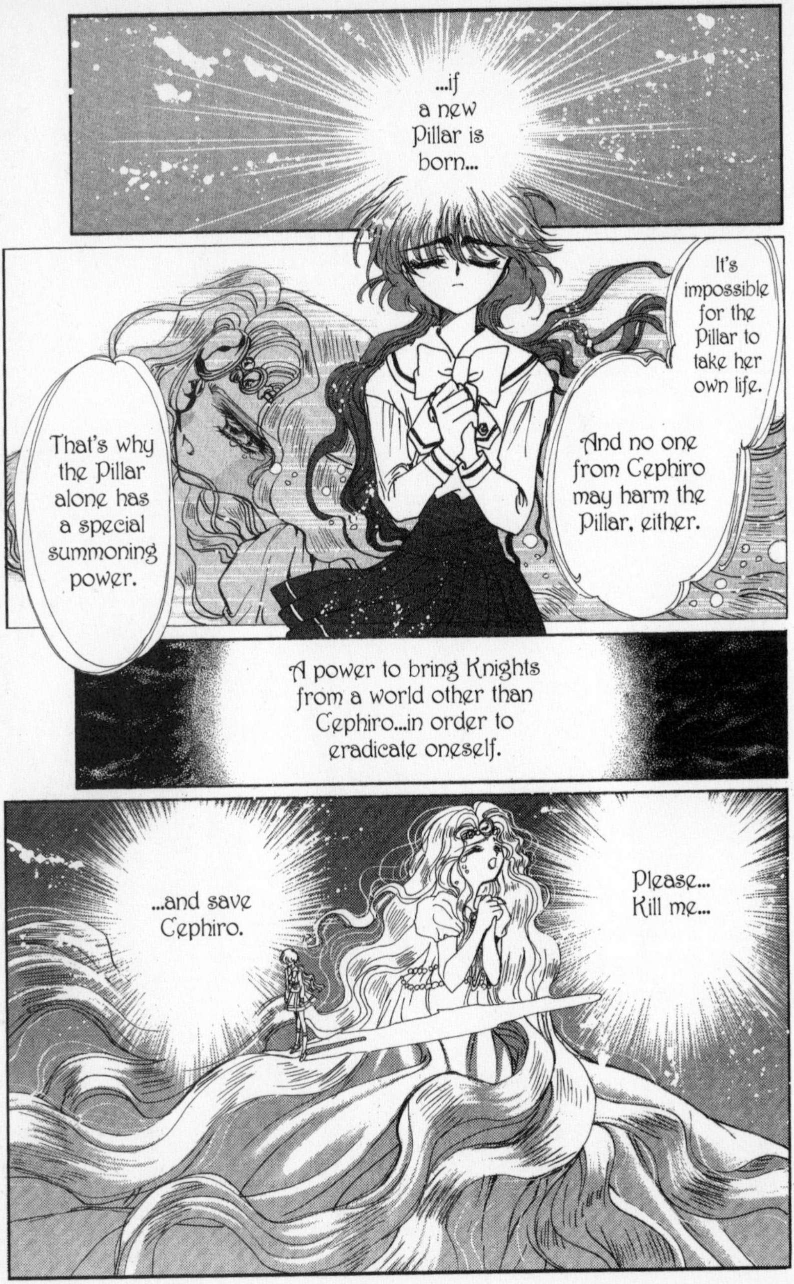
...if a new Pillar is born...
It's impossible for the Pillar to take her own life.
And no one from Cephiro may harm the Pillar, either.
That's why the Pillar alone has a special summoning power.
A power to bring Knights from a world other than Cephiro...in order to eradicate oneself.
Please... Kill me...
...and save Cephiro.

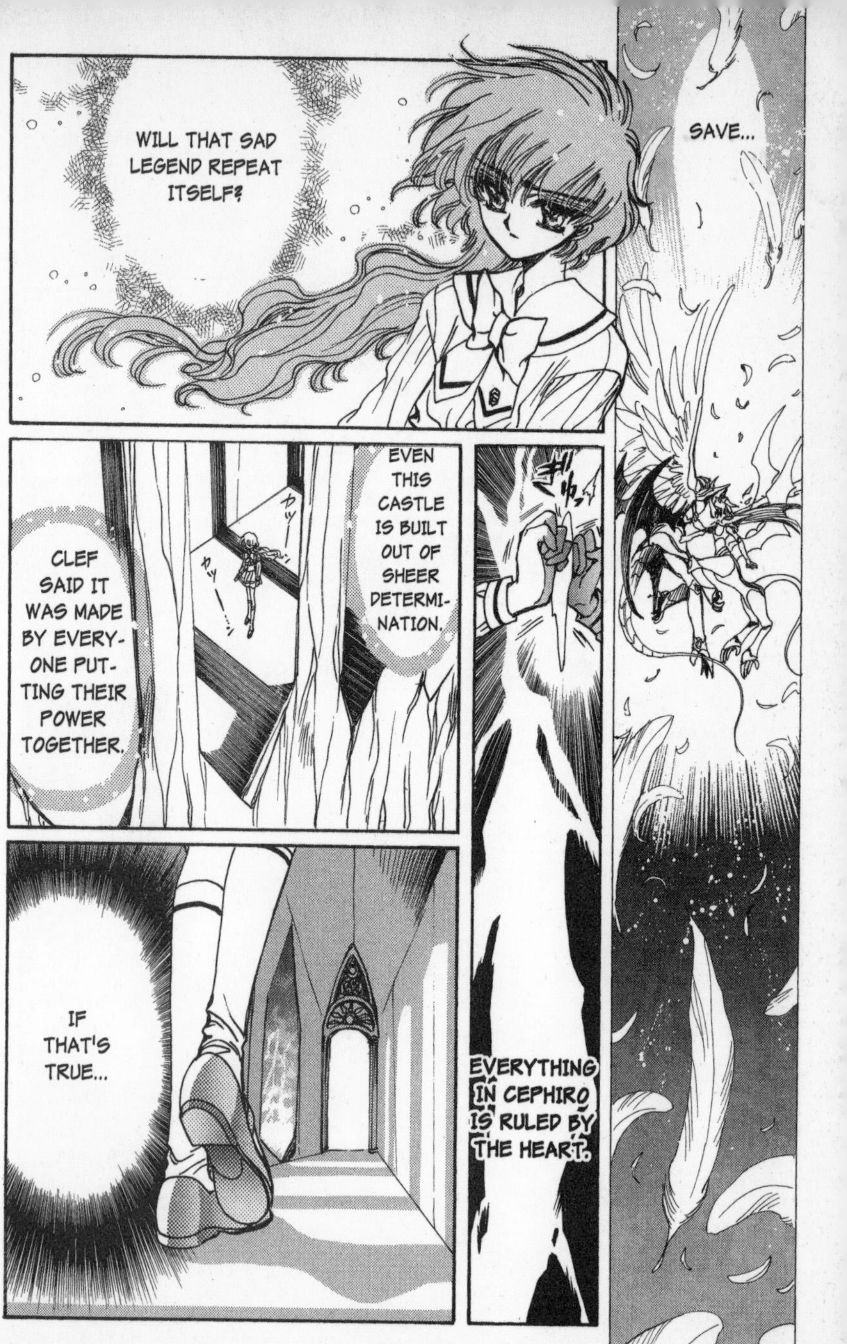
SAVE...
WILL THAT SAD LEGEND REPEAT ITSELF?
EVERYTHING IN CEPHIRO IS RULED BY THE HEART.
EVEN THIS CASTLE IS BUILT OUT OF SHEER DETERMINATION.
CLEF SAID IT WAS MADE BY EVERYONE PUTTING THEIR POWER TOGETHER.
IF THAT'S TRUE...

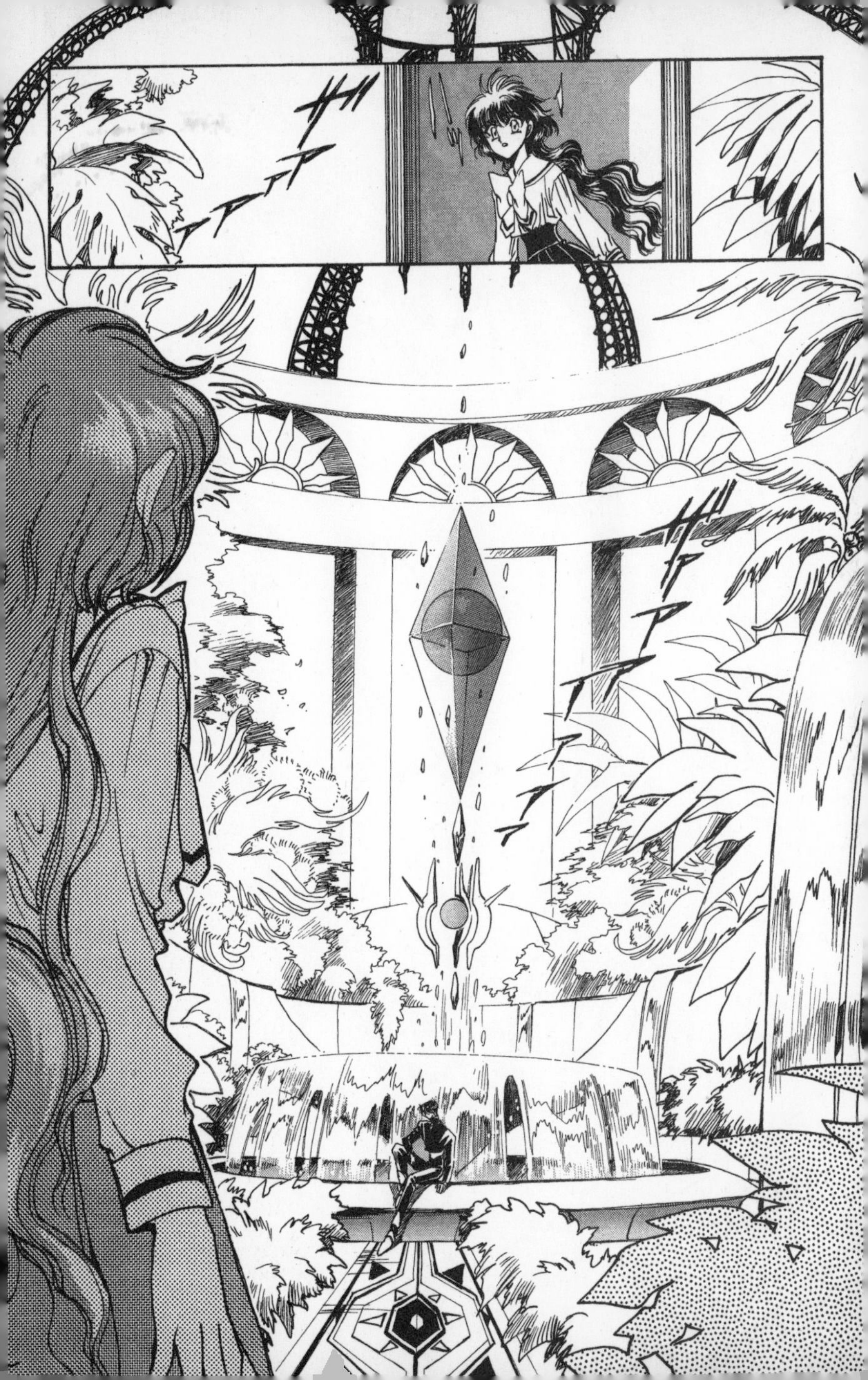
ザァァァァァ
ザァァァァァァァ

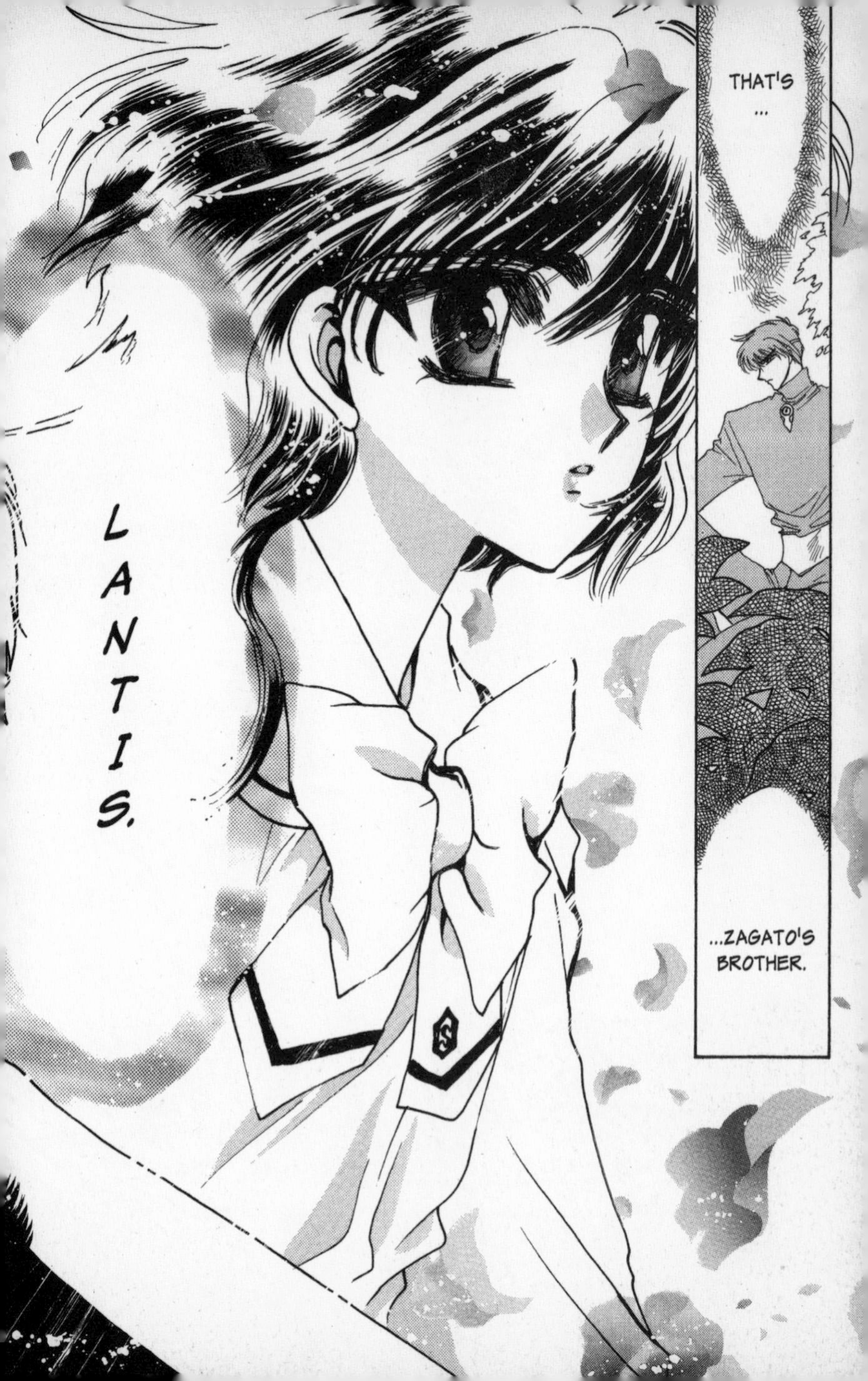
THAT'S ...
...ZAGATO'S BROTHER.
LANTIS.

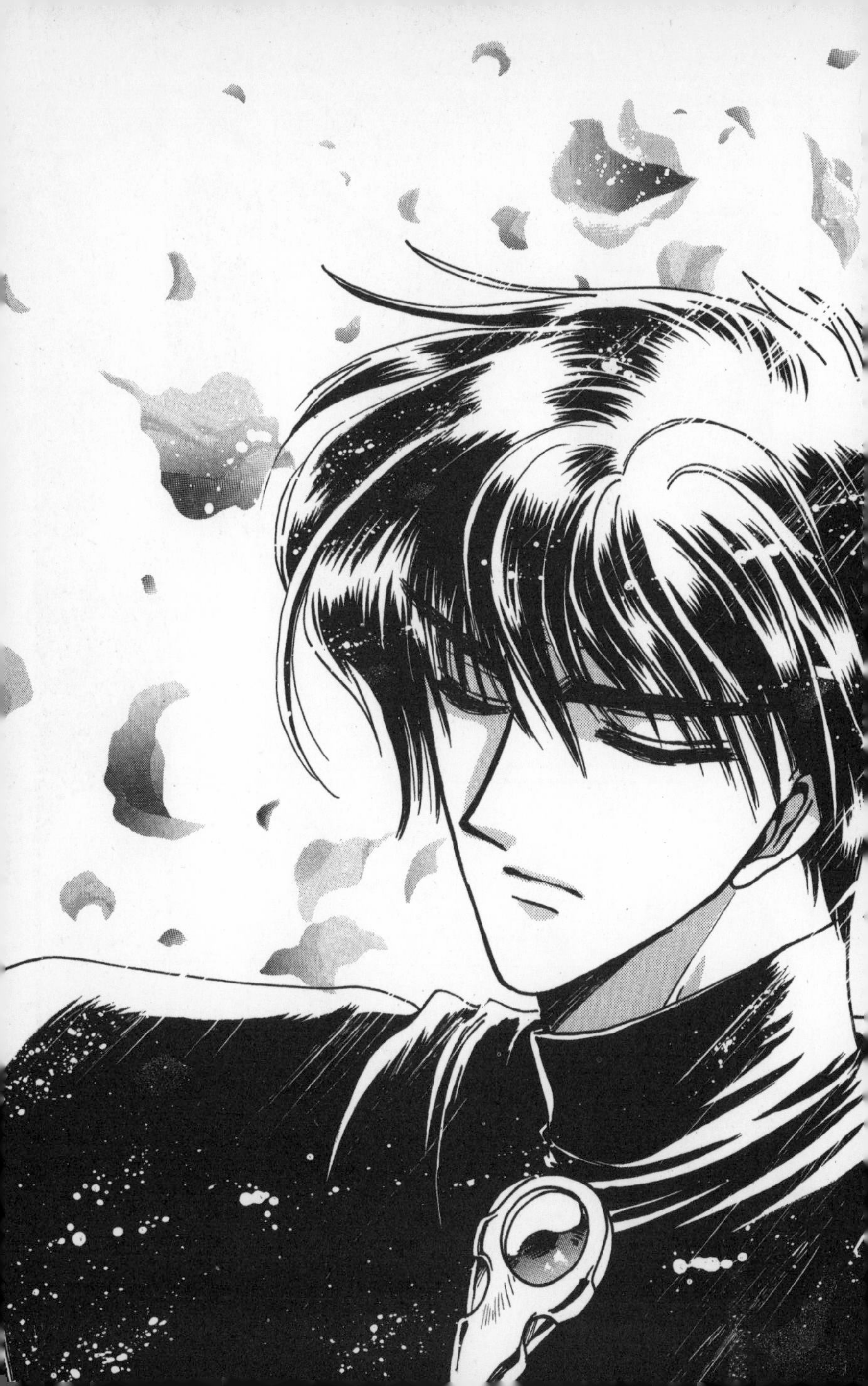

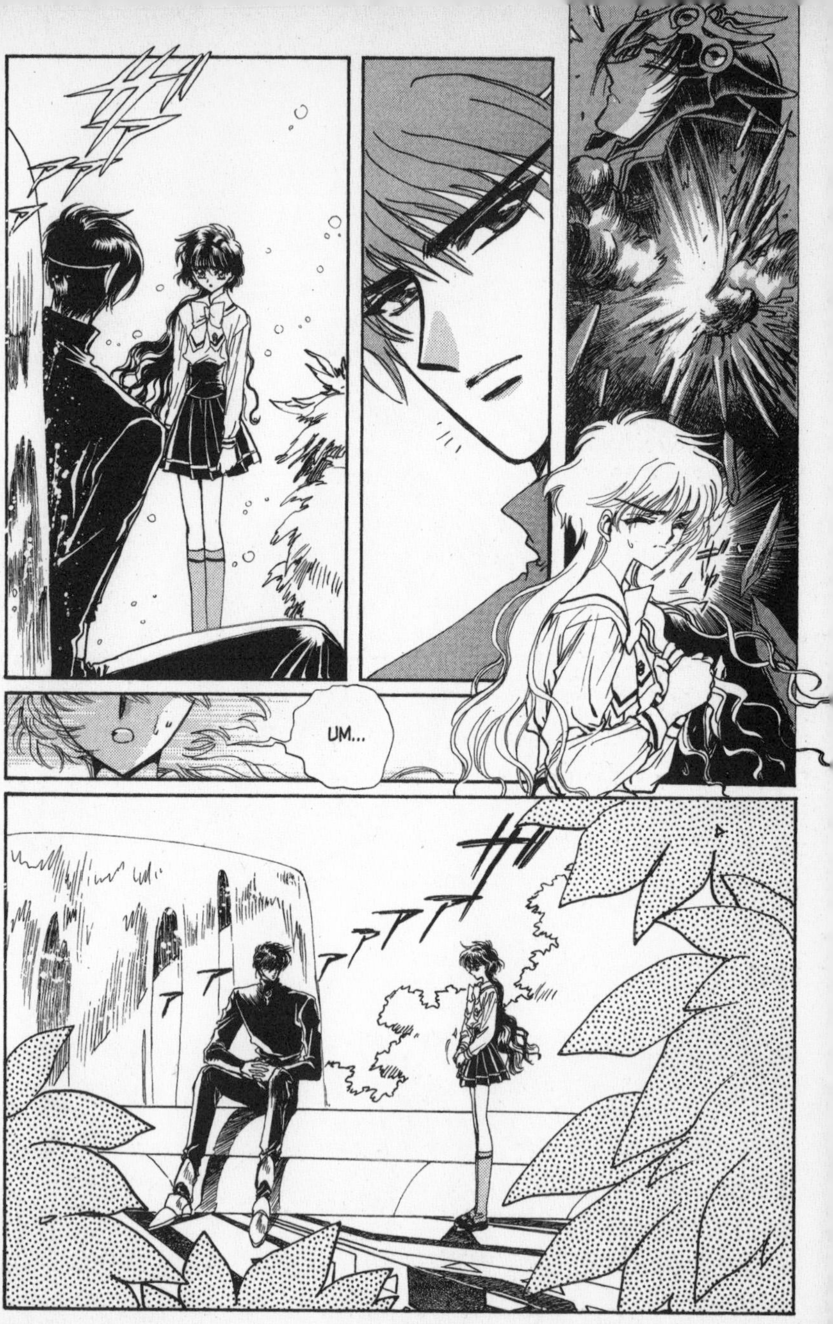
UM...

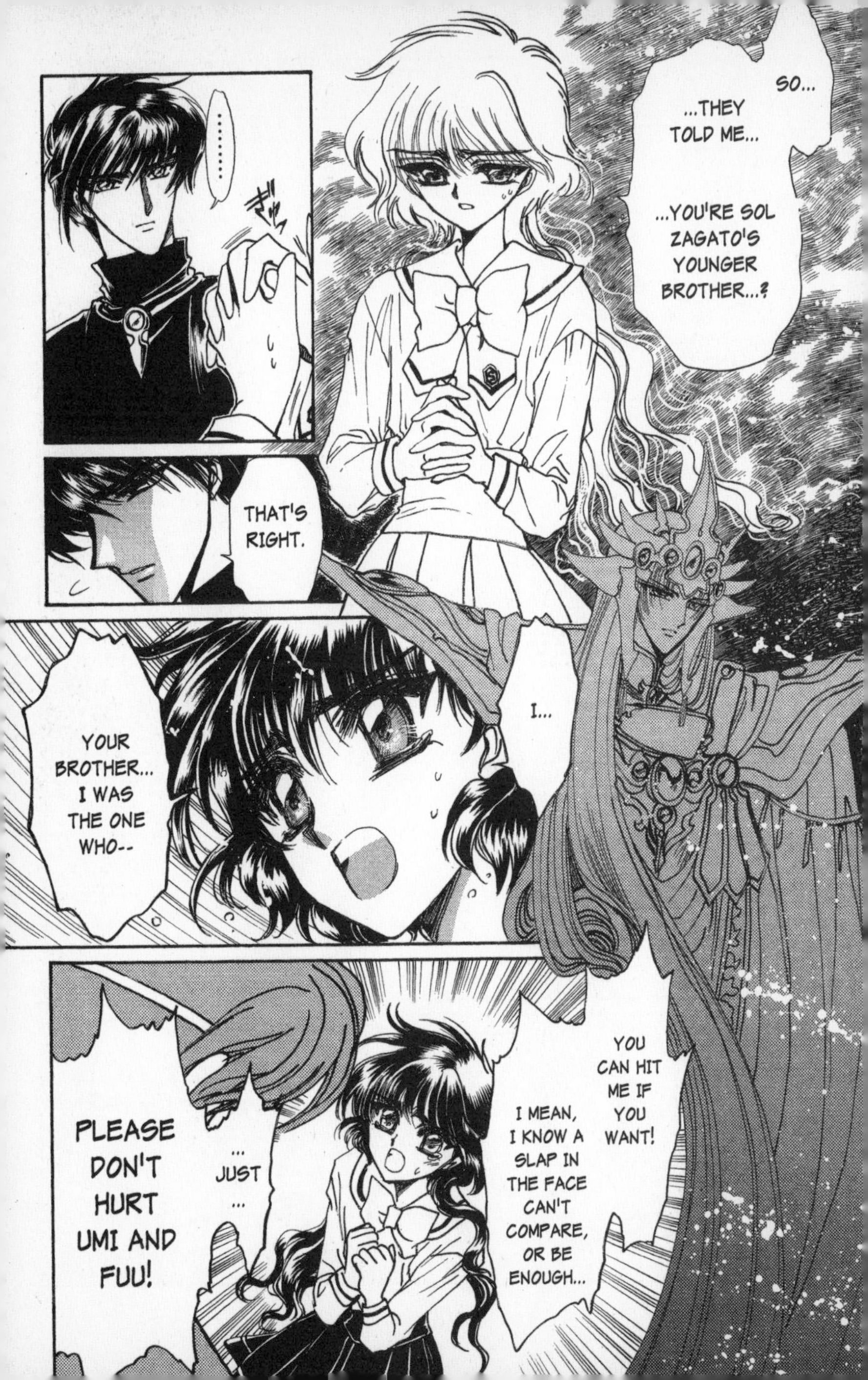
SO...
...THEY TOLD ME...
...YOU'RE SOL ZAGATO'S YOUNGER BROTHER...?
......
THAT'S RIGHT.
I...
YOUR BROTHER... I WAS THE ONE WHO--
YOU CAN HIT ME IF YOU WANT!
I MEAN, I KNOW A SLAP IN THE FACE CAN'T COMPARE, OR BE ENOUGH...
... JUST ...
PLEASE DON'T HURT UMI AND FUU!

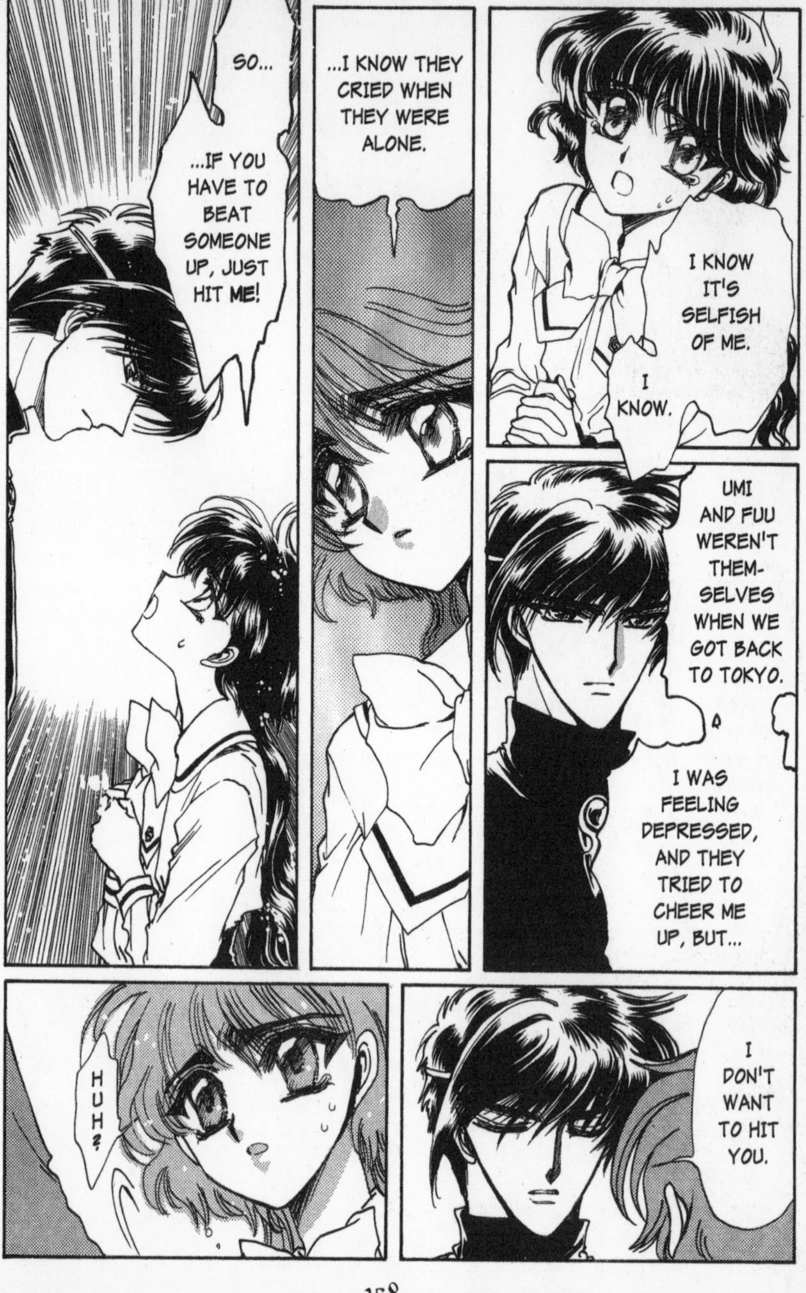
I KNOW IT'S SELFISH OF ME.
I KNOW.
UMI AND FUU WEREN'T THEM-SELVES WHEN WE GOT BACK TO TOKYO.
I WAS FEELING DEPRESSED, AND THEY TRIED TO CHEER ME UP, BUT...
...I KNOW THEY CRIED WHEN THEY WERE ALONE.
SO...
...IF YOU HAVE TO BEAT SOMEONE UP, JUST HIT ME!
I DON'T WANT TO HIT YOU.
HUH?

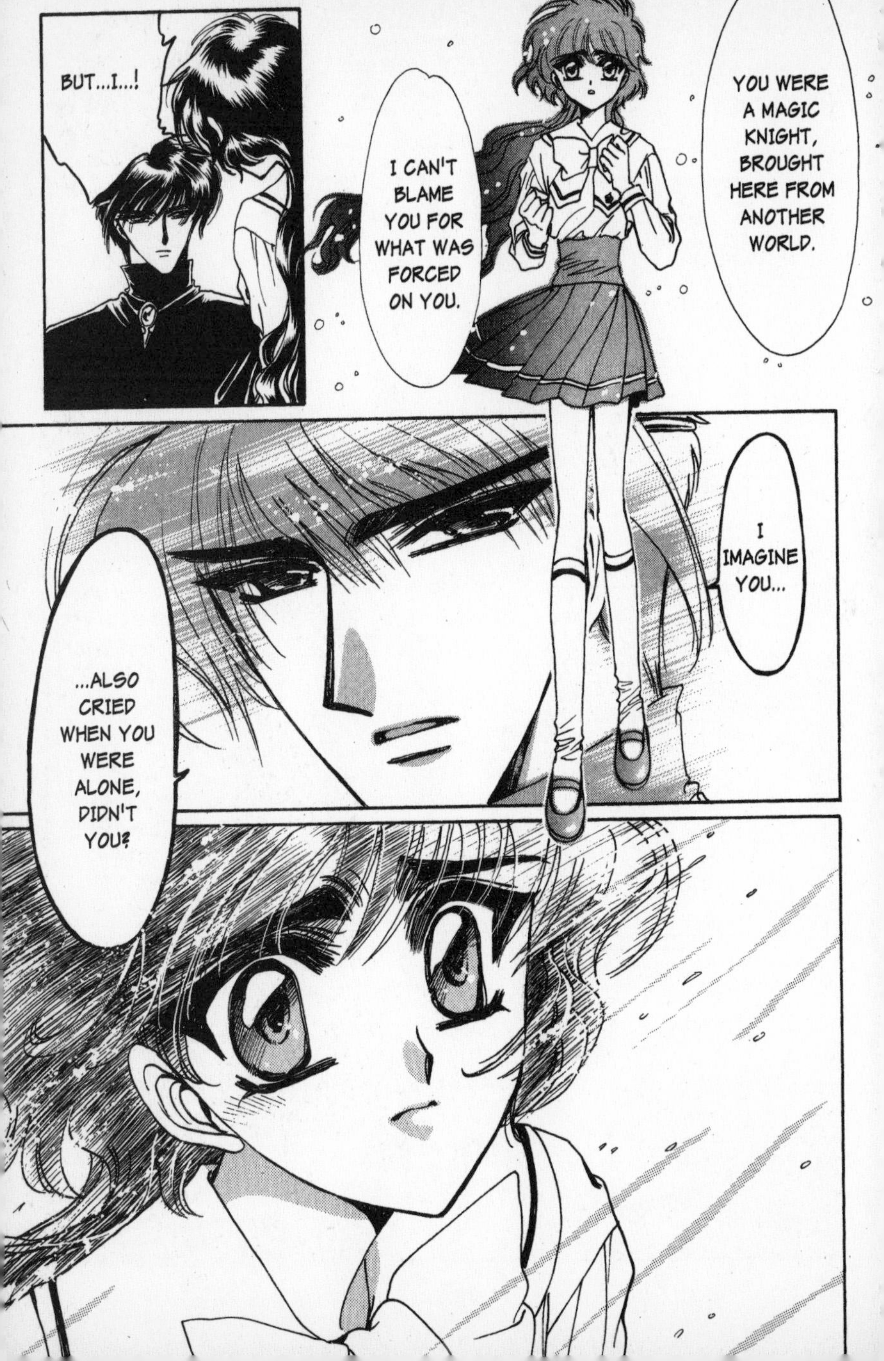
YOU WERE A MAGIC KNIGHT, BROUGHT HERE FROM ANOTHER WORLD.
I CAN'T BLAME YOU FOR WHAT WAS FORCED ON YOU.
BUT...I...!
I IMAGINE YOU...
...ALSO CRIED WHEN YOU WERE ALONE, DIDN'T YOU?

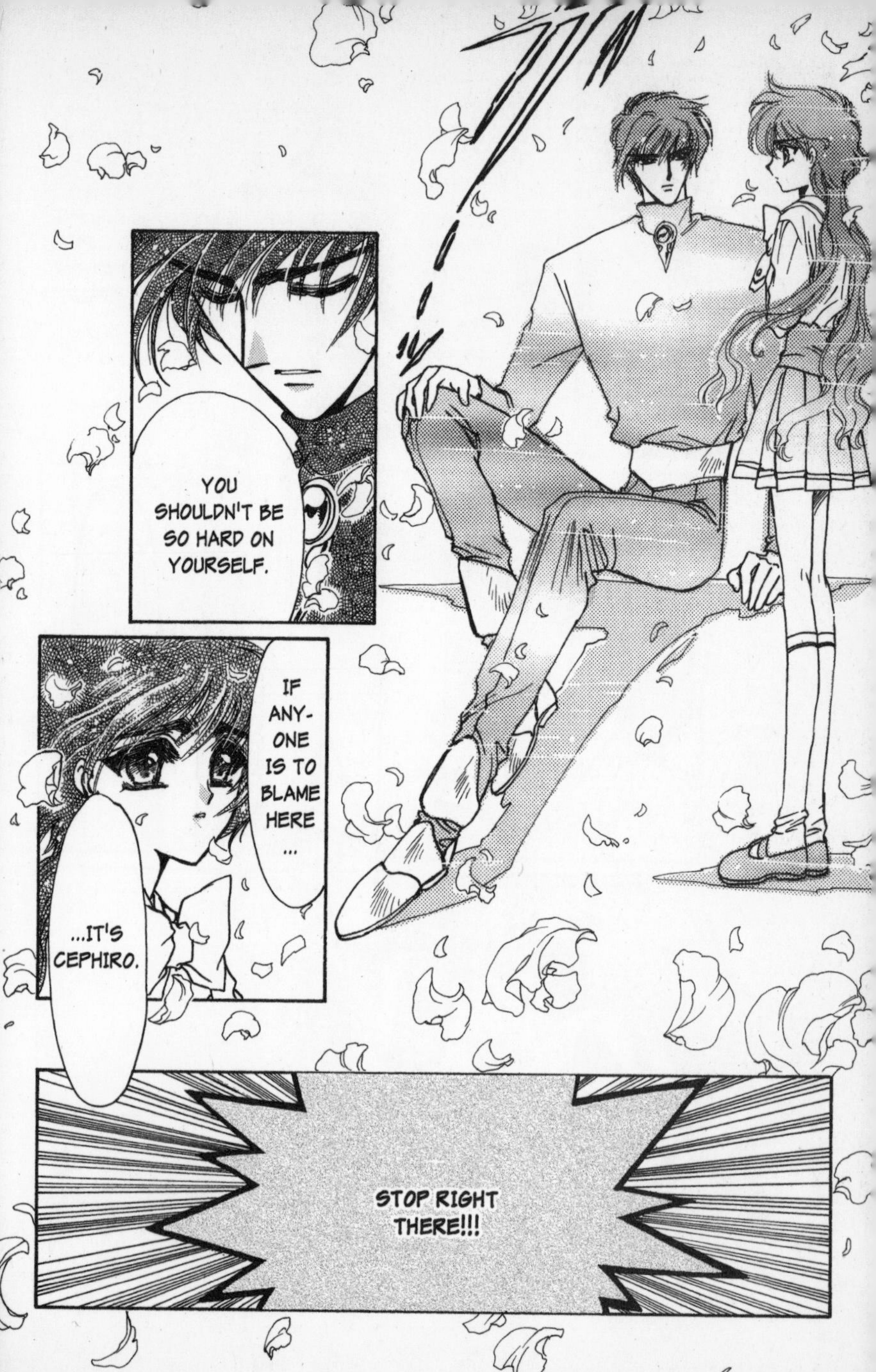
YOU SHOULDN'T BE SO HARD ON YOURSELF.
IF ANY-ONE IS TO BLAME HERE ...
...IT'S CEPHIRO.
STOP RIGHT THERE!!!

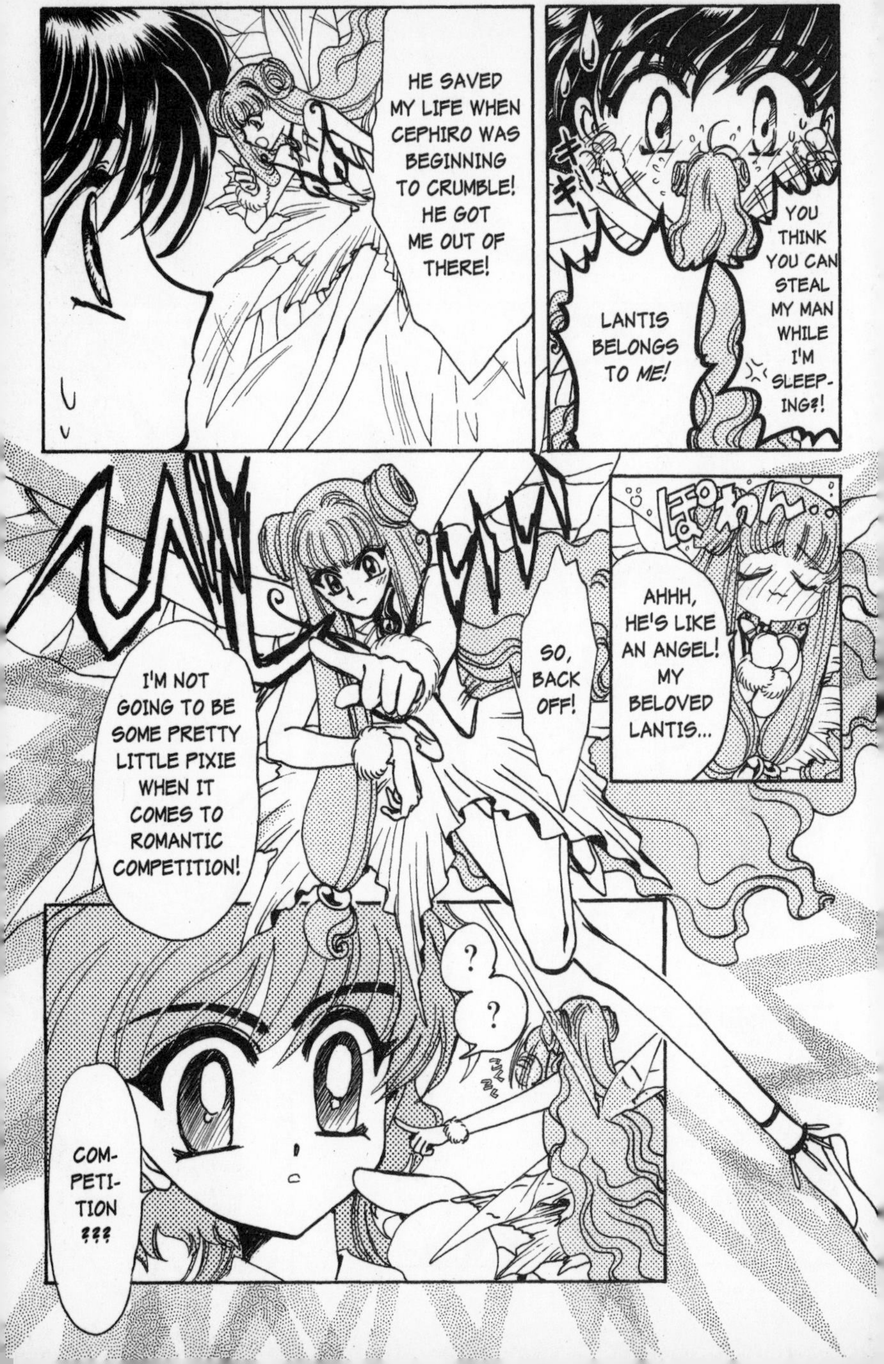

YOU THINK YOU CAN STEAL MY MAN WHILE I'M SLEEPING?!
LANTIS BELONGS TO ME!
HE SAVED MY LIFE WHEN CEPHIRO WAS BEGINNING TO CRUMBLE! HE GOT ME OUT OF THERE!
ぽわん
AHHH, HE'S LIKE AN ANGEL! MY BELOVED LANTIS...
SO, BACK OFF!
I'M NOT GOING TO BE SOME PRETTY LITTLE PIXIE WHEN IT COMES TO ROMANTIC COMPETITION!
??
COMPETITION???

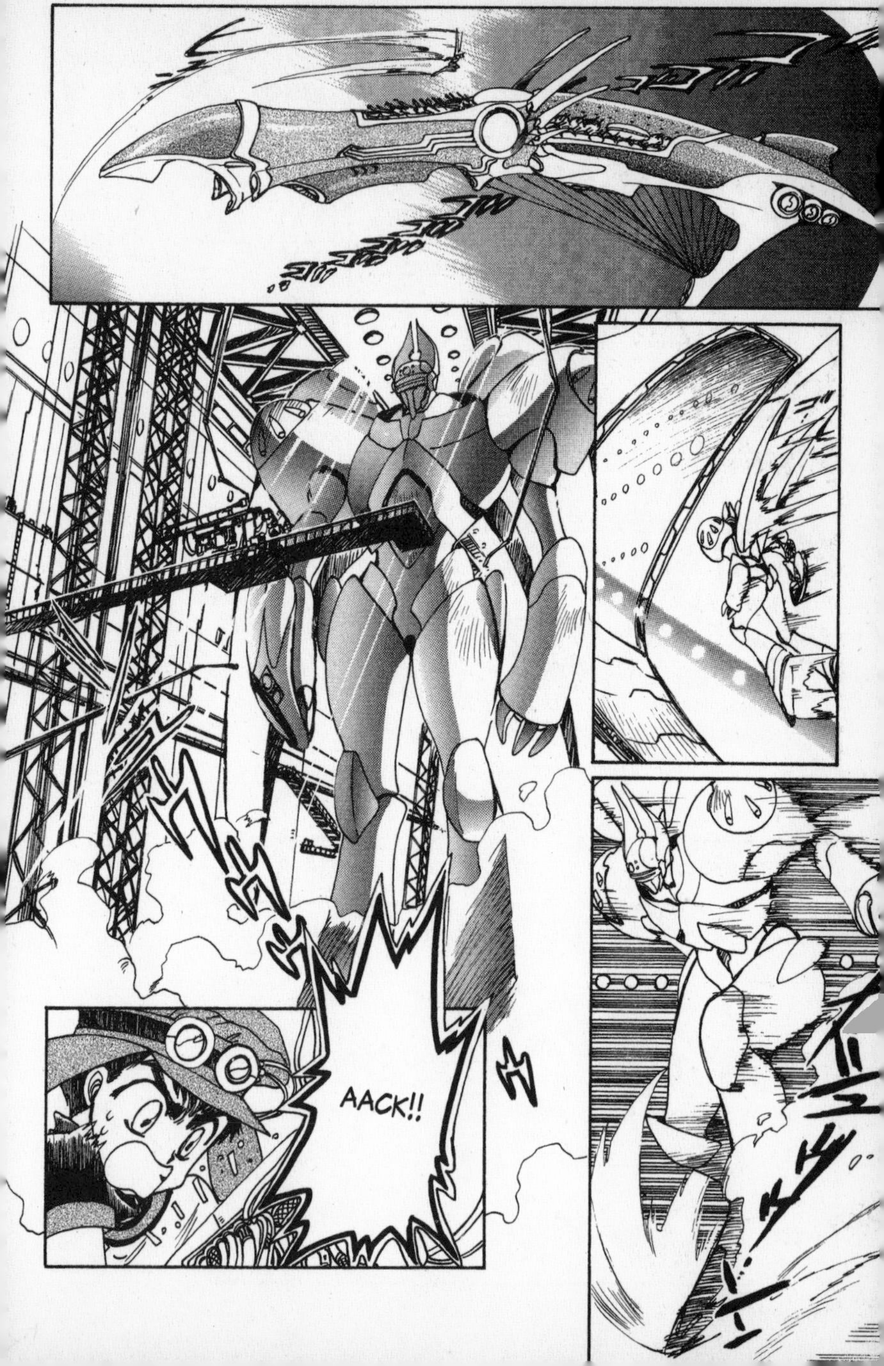
AACK!!

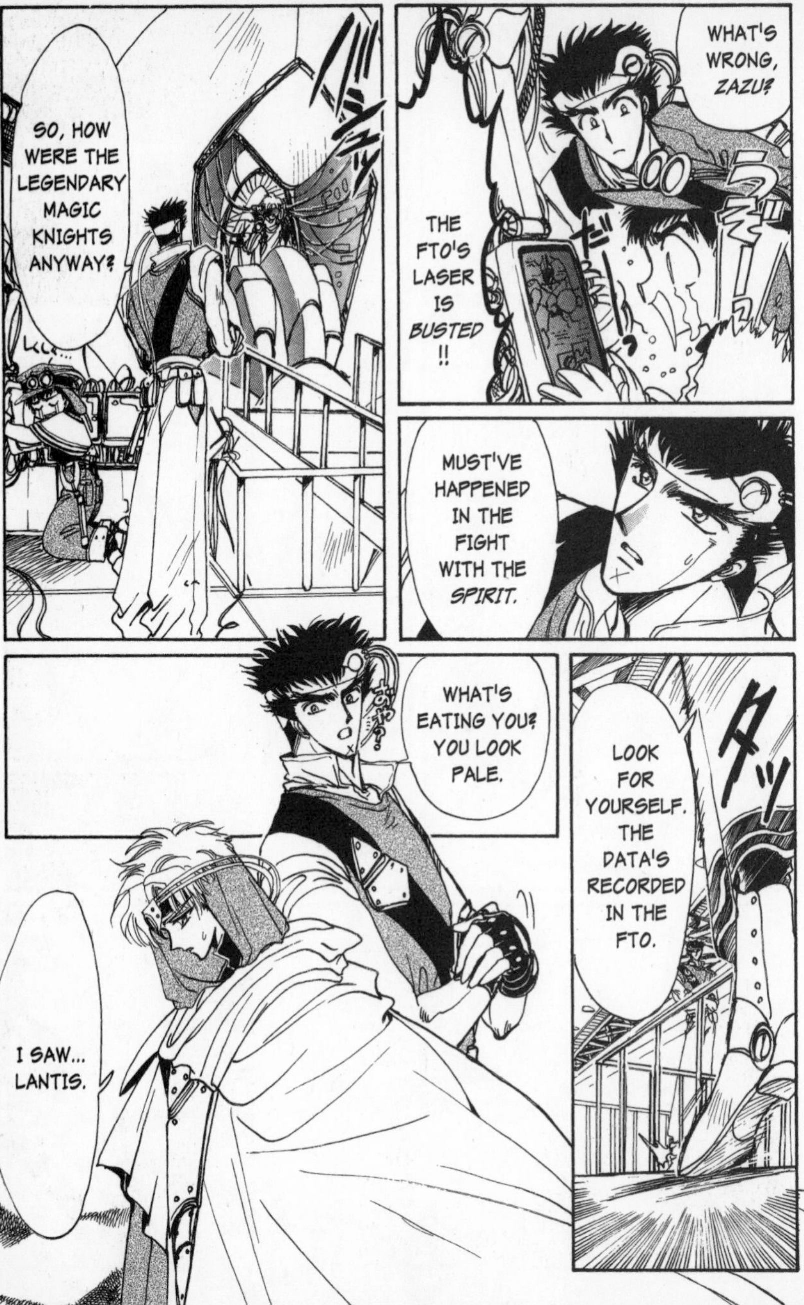
WHAT'S WRONG, ZAZU?
THE FTO'S LASER IS BUSTED!!
MUST'VE HAPPENED IN THE FIGHT WITH THE *SPIRIT*.
SO, HOW WERE THE LEGENDARY MAGIC KNIGHTS ANYWAY?
LOOK FOR YOURSELF. THE DATA'S RECORDED IN THE FTO.
タッ
WHAT'S EATING YOU? YOU LOOK PALE.
I SAW... LANTIS.

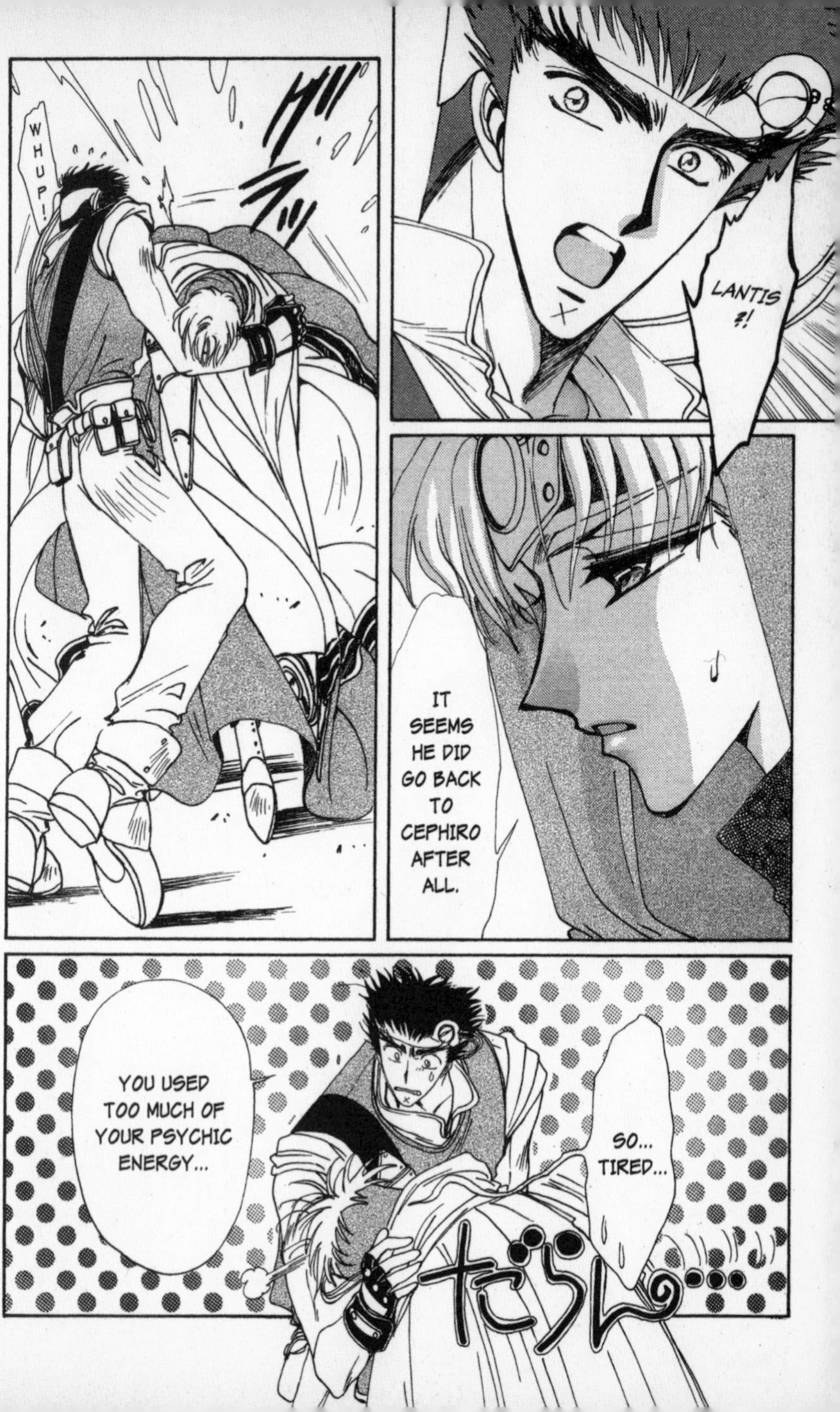
LANTIS ?!
IT SEEMS HE DID GO BACK TO CEPHIRO AFTER ALL.
WHUP!
SO... TIRED...
YOU USED TOO MUCH OF YOUR PSYCHIC ENERGY...

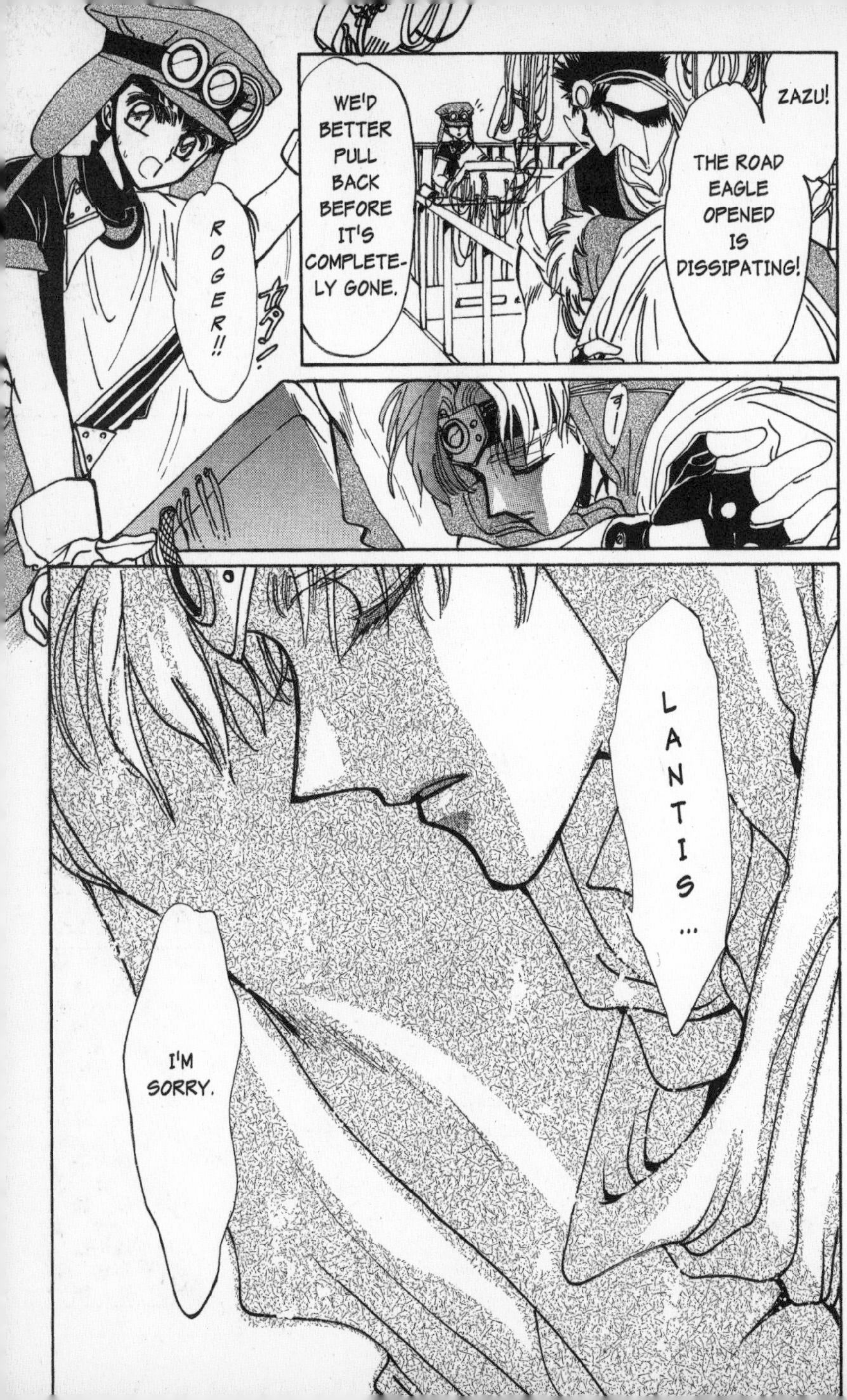
ZAZU!
THE ROAD EAGLE OPENED IS DISSIPATING!
WE'D BETTER PULL BACK BEFORE IT'S COMPLETELY GONE.
ROGER!!
LANTIS...
I'M SORRY.

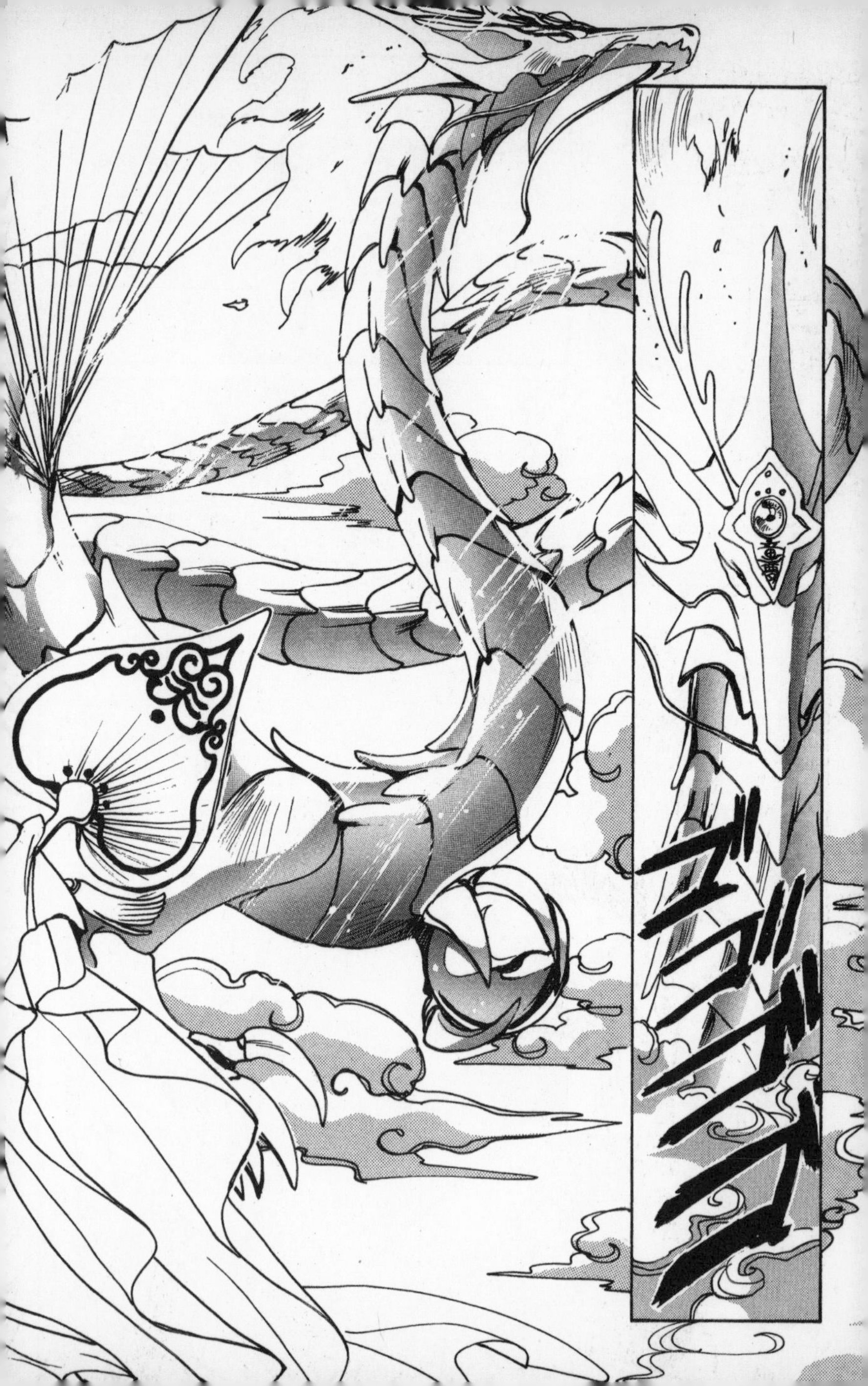

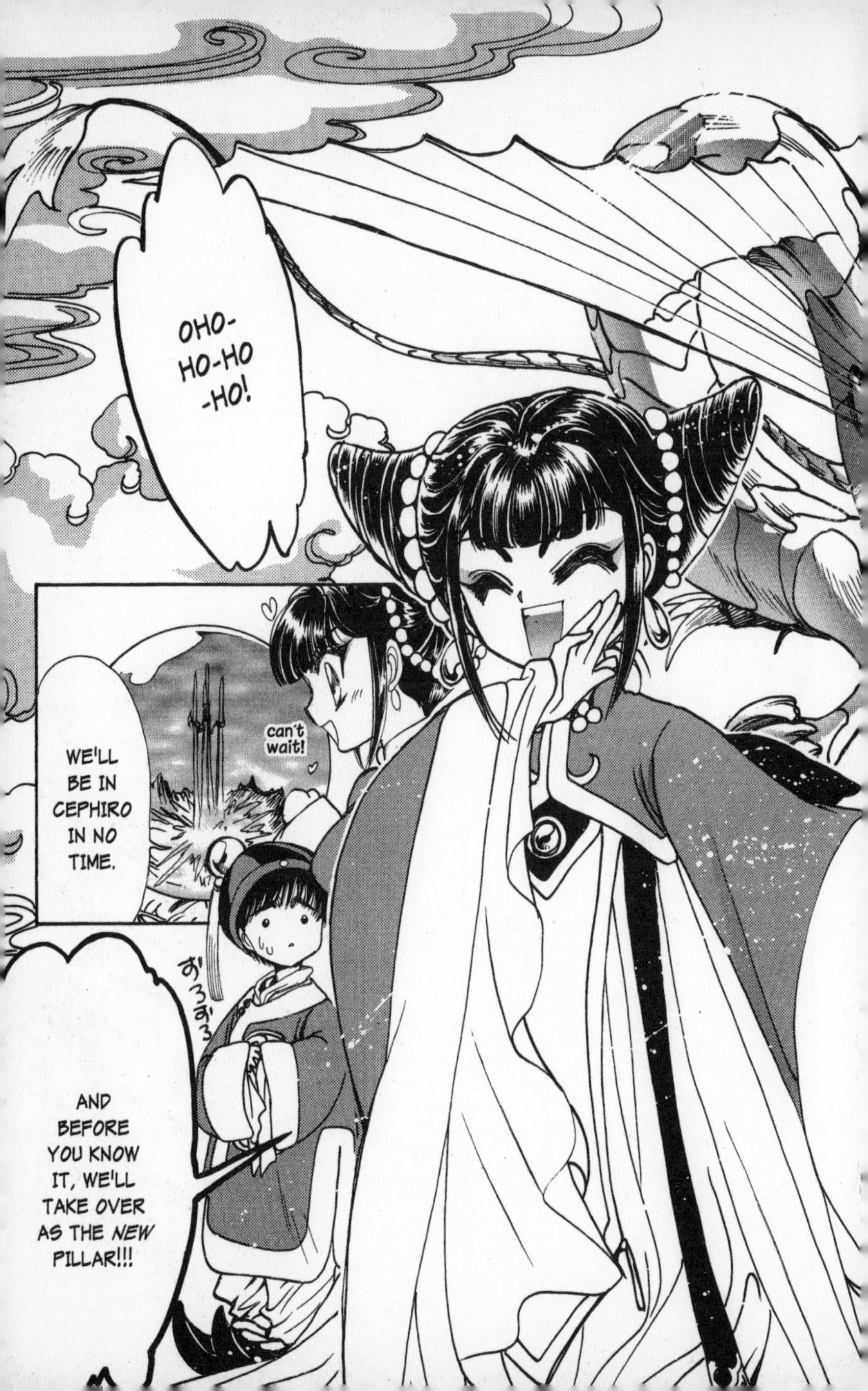
OHO-HO-HO-HO!
WE'LL BE IN CEPHIRO IN NO TIME.
can't wait!
ずるずる
AND BEFORE YOU KNOW IT, WE'LL TAKE OVER AS THE *NEW* PILLAR!!!

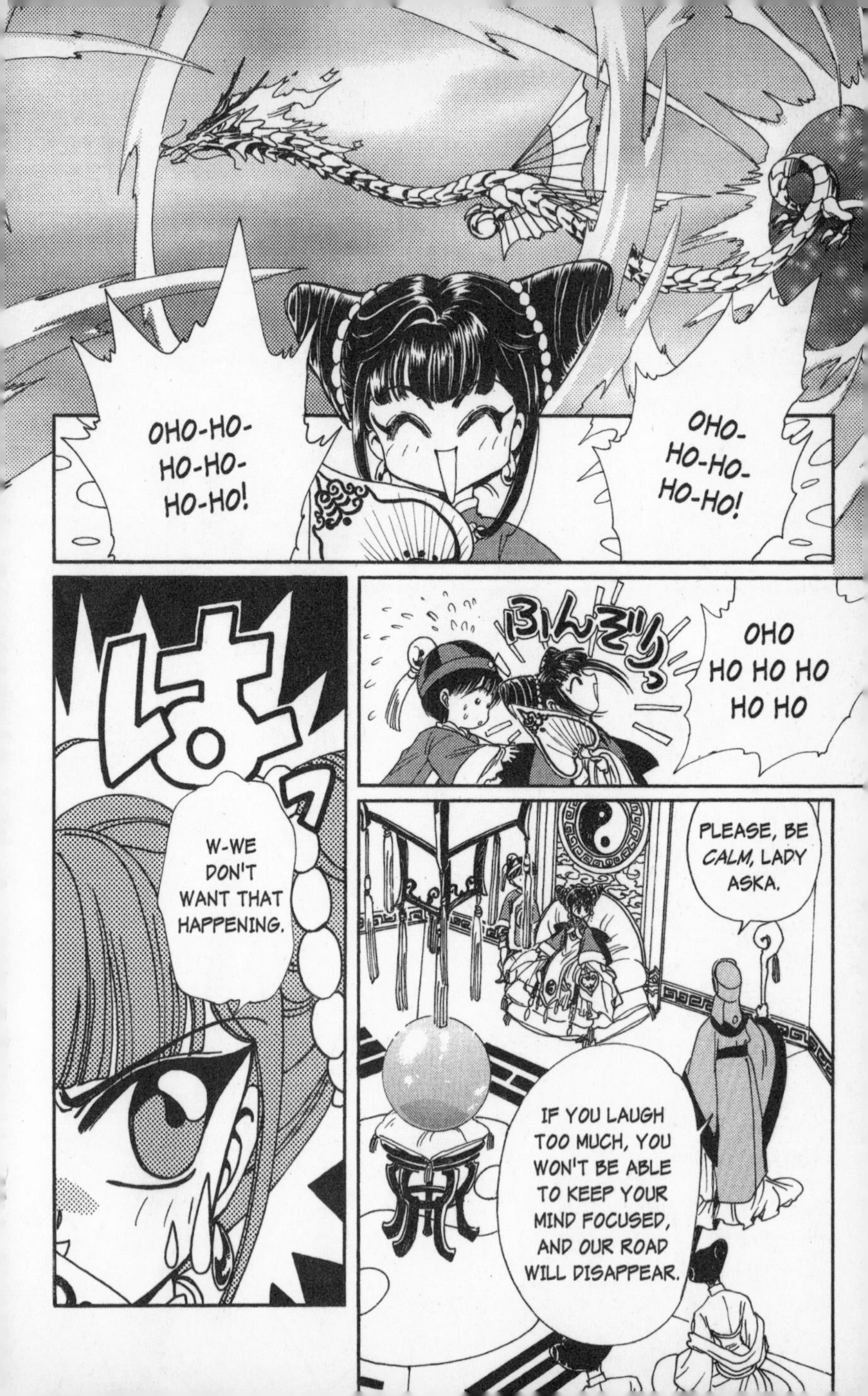
OHO-HO-HO-HO-HO!
OHO-HO-HO-HO-HO-HO!
ふんぞり
OHO HO HO HO HO HO
PLEASE, BE CALM, LADY ASKA.
IF YOU LAUGH TOO MUCH, YOU WON'T BE ABLE TO KEEP YOUR MIND FOCUSED, AND OUR ROAD WILL DISAPPEAR.
はっ
W-WE DON'T WANT THAT HAPPENING.

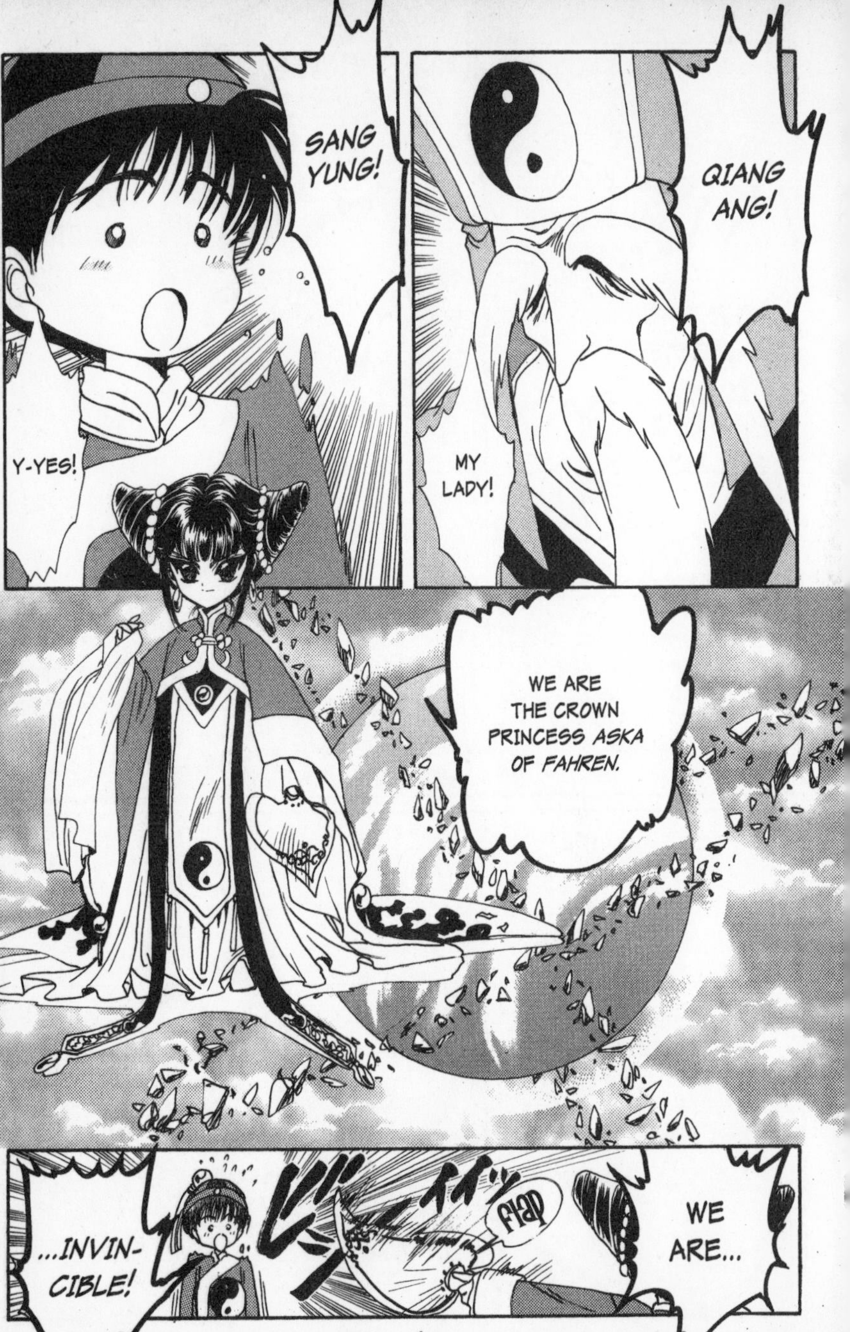
QIANG ANG!
MY LADY!
SANG YUNG!
Y-YES!
WE ARE THE CROWN PRINCESS ASKA OF FAHREN.
WE ARE...
flap
...INVIN- CIBLE!

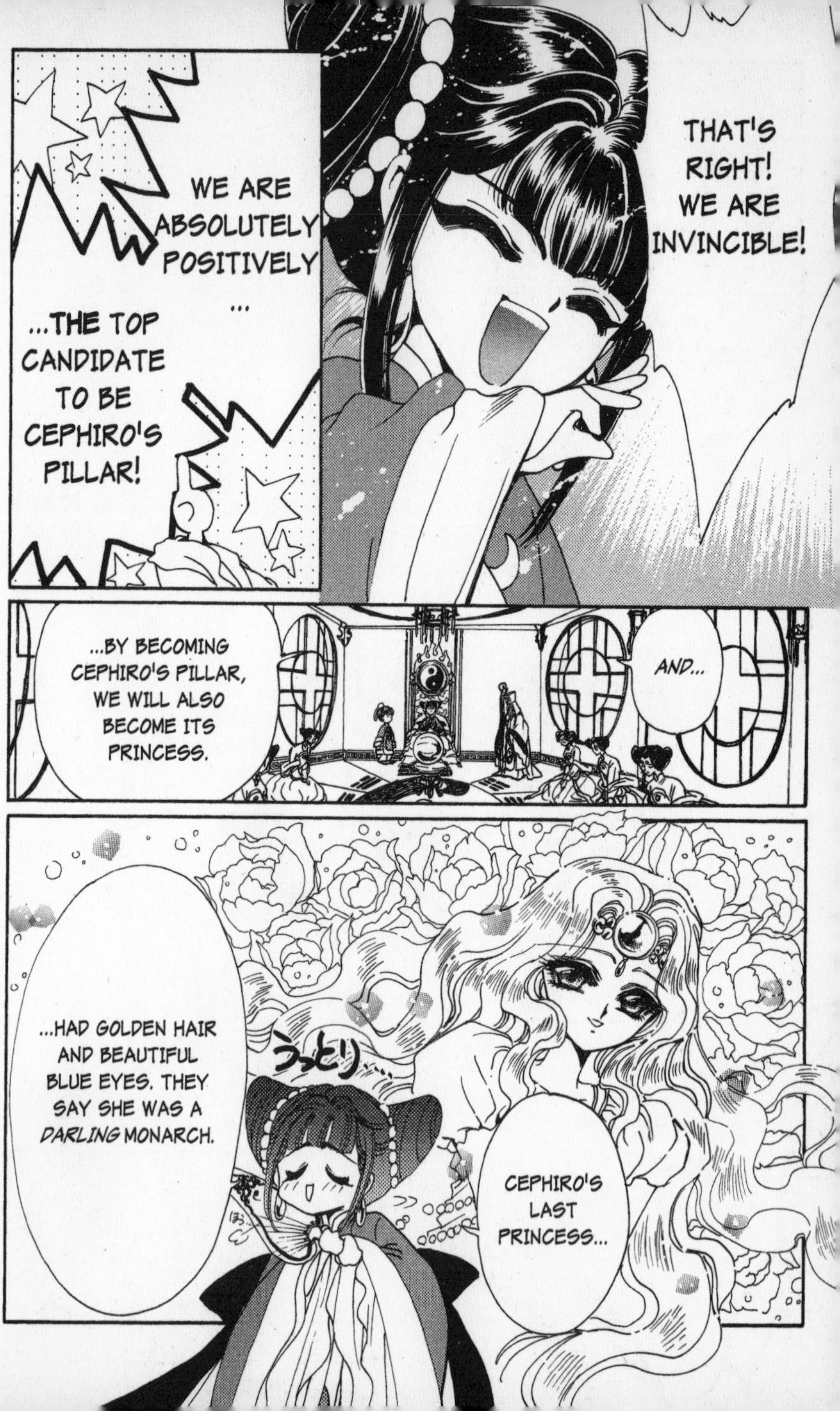
THAT'S RIGHT! WE ARE INVINCIBLE!
WE ARE ABSOLUTELY POSITIVELY ...
...THE TOP CANDIDATE TO BE CEPHIRO'S PILLAR!
AND...
...BY BECOMING CEPHIRO'S PILLAR, WE WILL ALSO BECOME ITS PRINCESS.
CEPHIRO'S LAST PRINCESS...
うっとり…
...HAD GOLDEN HAIR AND BEAUTIFUL BLUE EYES. THEY SAY SHE WAS A *DARLING* MONARCH.

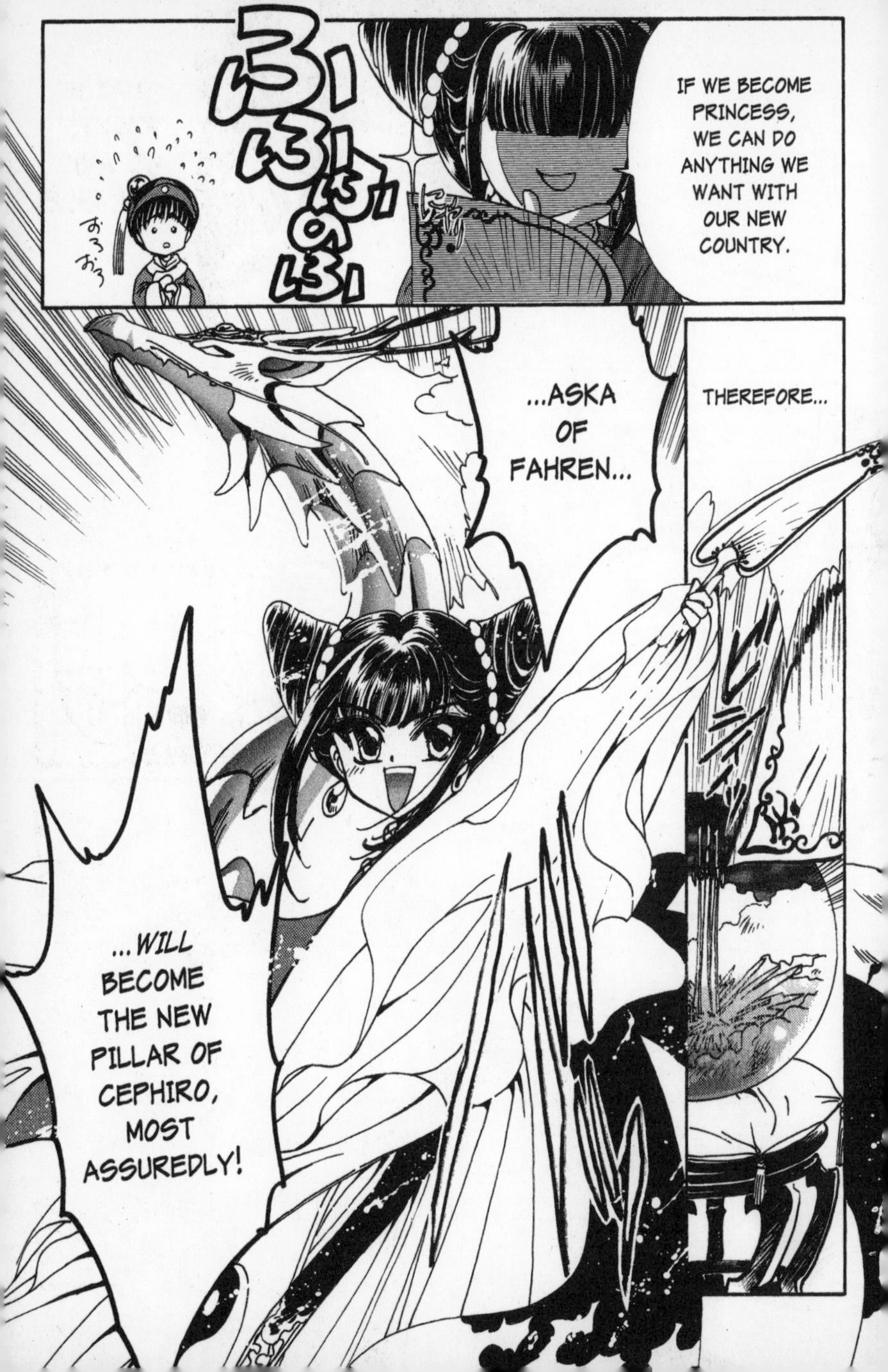
IF WE BECOME PRINCESS, WE CAN DO ANYTHING WE WANT WITH OUR NEW COUNTRY.
ふふふのふ
おろおろ
THEREFORE...
...ASKA OF FAHREN...
...WILL BECOME THE NEW PILLAR OF CEPHIRO, MOST ASSUREDLY!

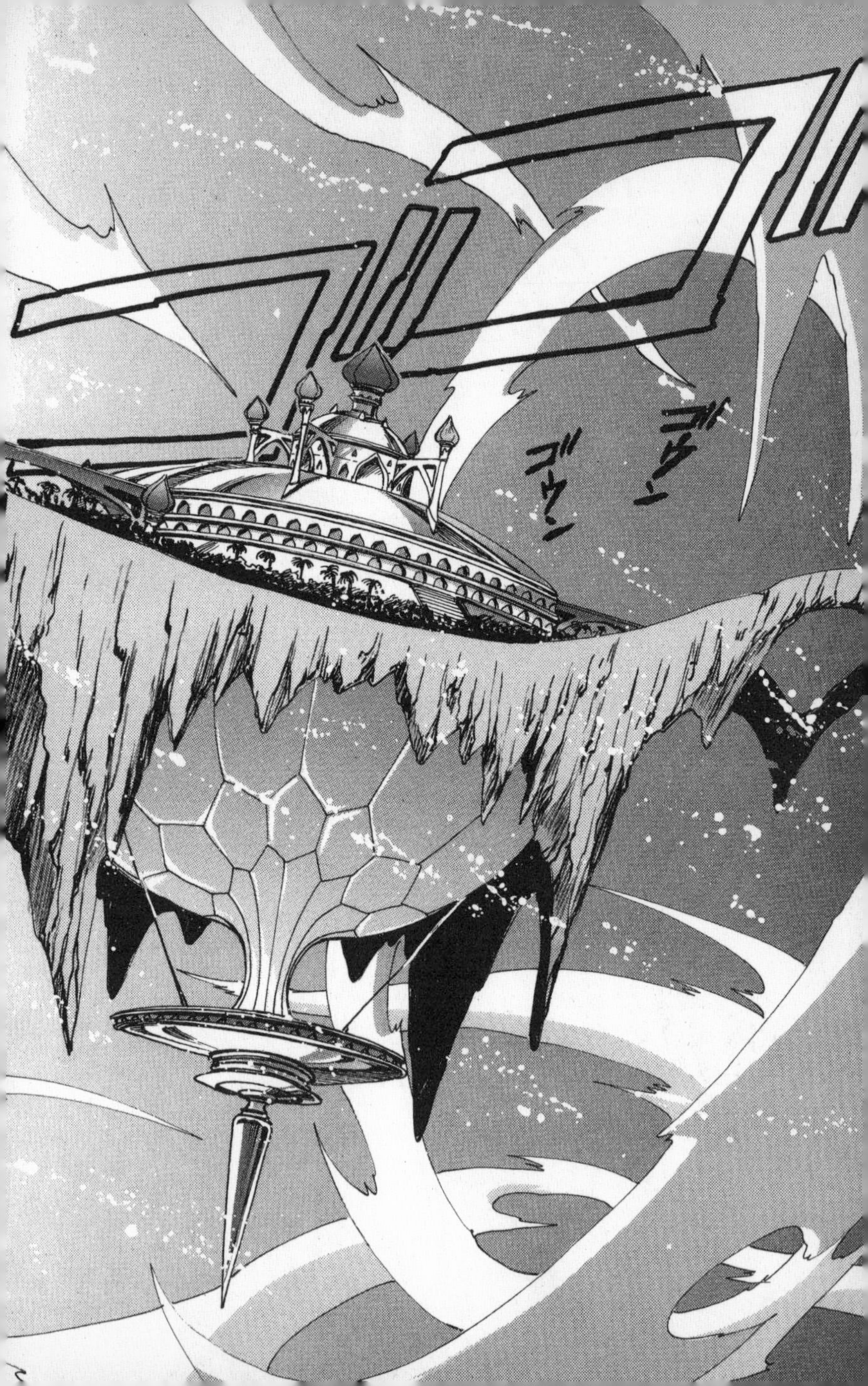
ゴウン
ゴウン

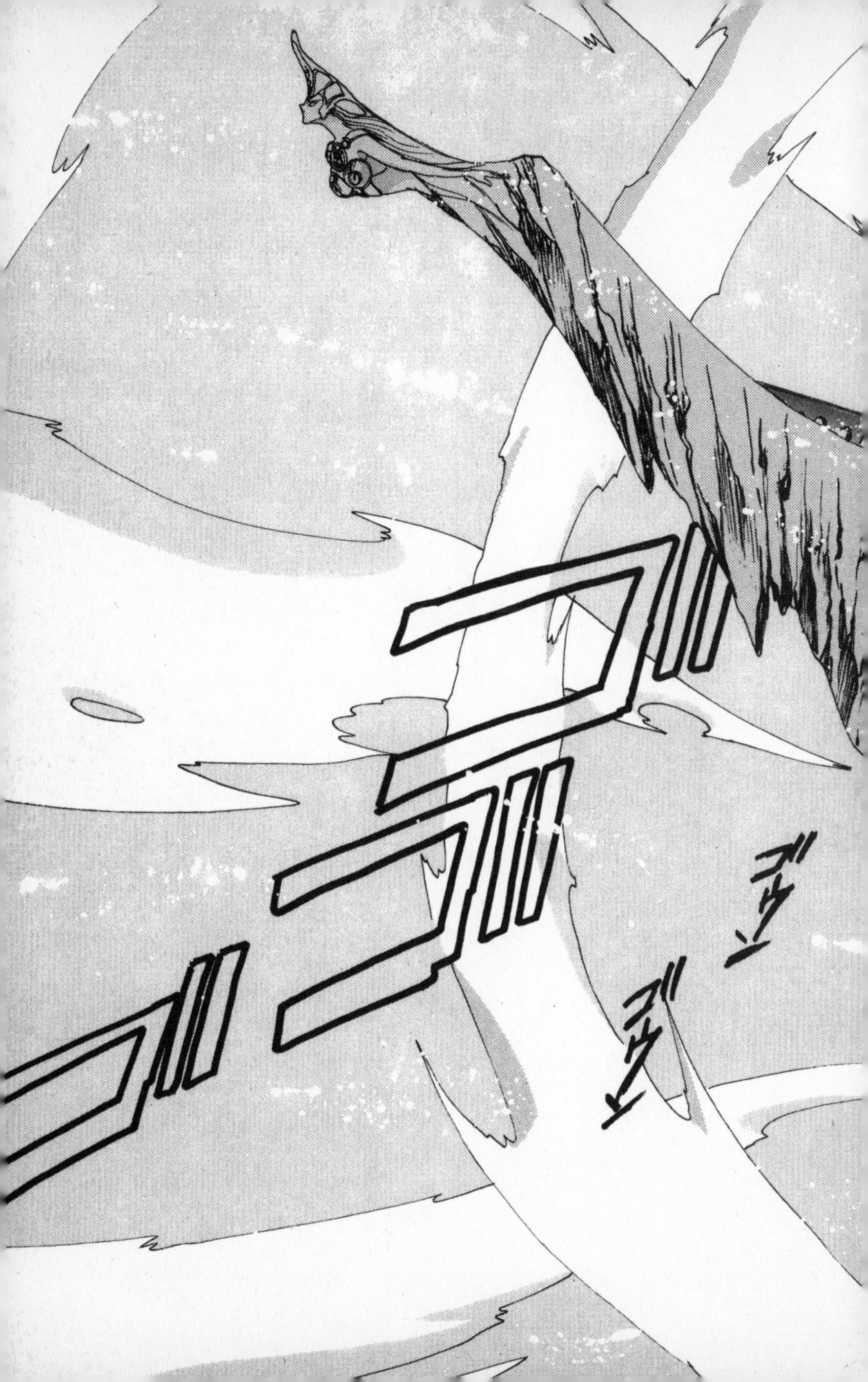
ゴゴゴ
ズゥン
ズゥン

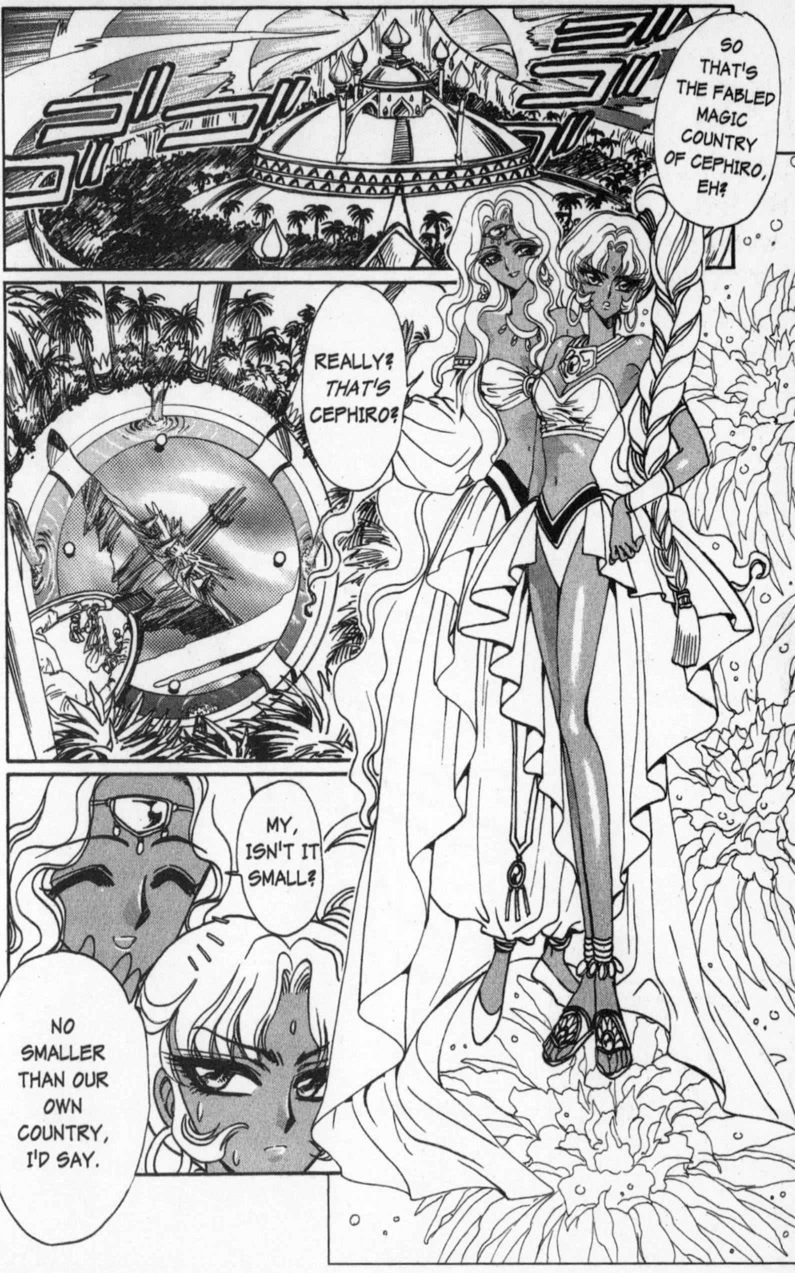
SO THAT'S THE FABLED MAGIC COUNTRY OF CEPHIRO, EH?
REALLY? *THAT'S* CEPHIRO?
MY, ISN'T IT SMALL?
NO SMALLER THAN OUR OWN COUNTRY, I'D SAY.

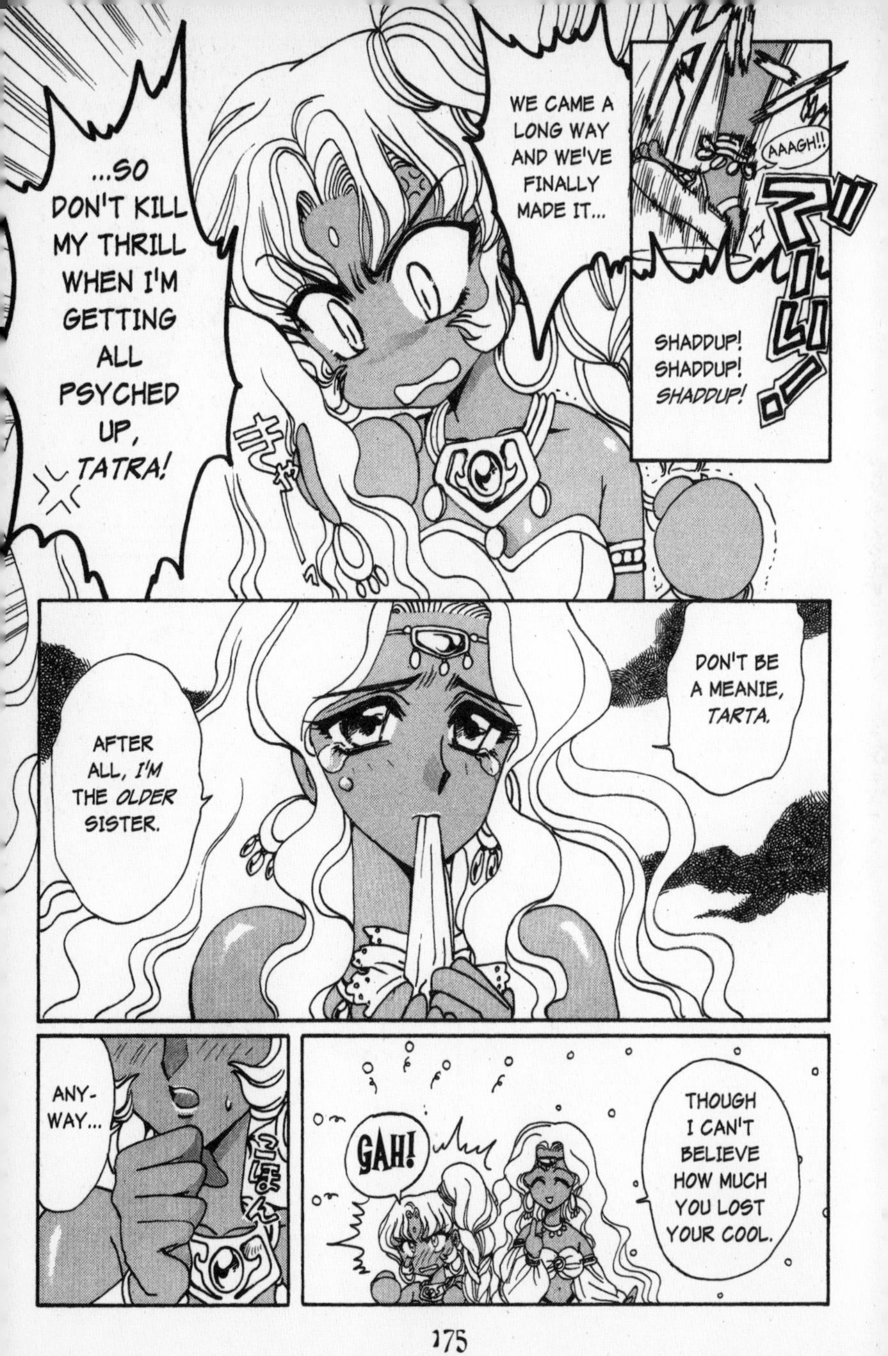
AAAGH!!
SHADDUP! SHADDUP! SHADDUP!
WE CAME A LONG WAY AND WE'VE FINALLY MADE IT...
...SO DON'T KILL MY THRILL WHEN I'M GETTING ALL PSYCHED UP, TATRA!
DON'T BE A MEANIE, TARTA.
AFTER ALL, I'M THE OLDER SISTER.
THOUGH I CAN'T BELIEVE HOW MUCH YOU LOST YOUR COOL.
GAH!
ANY-WAY...

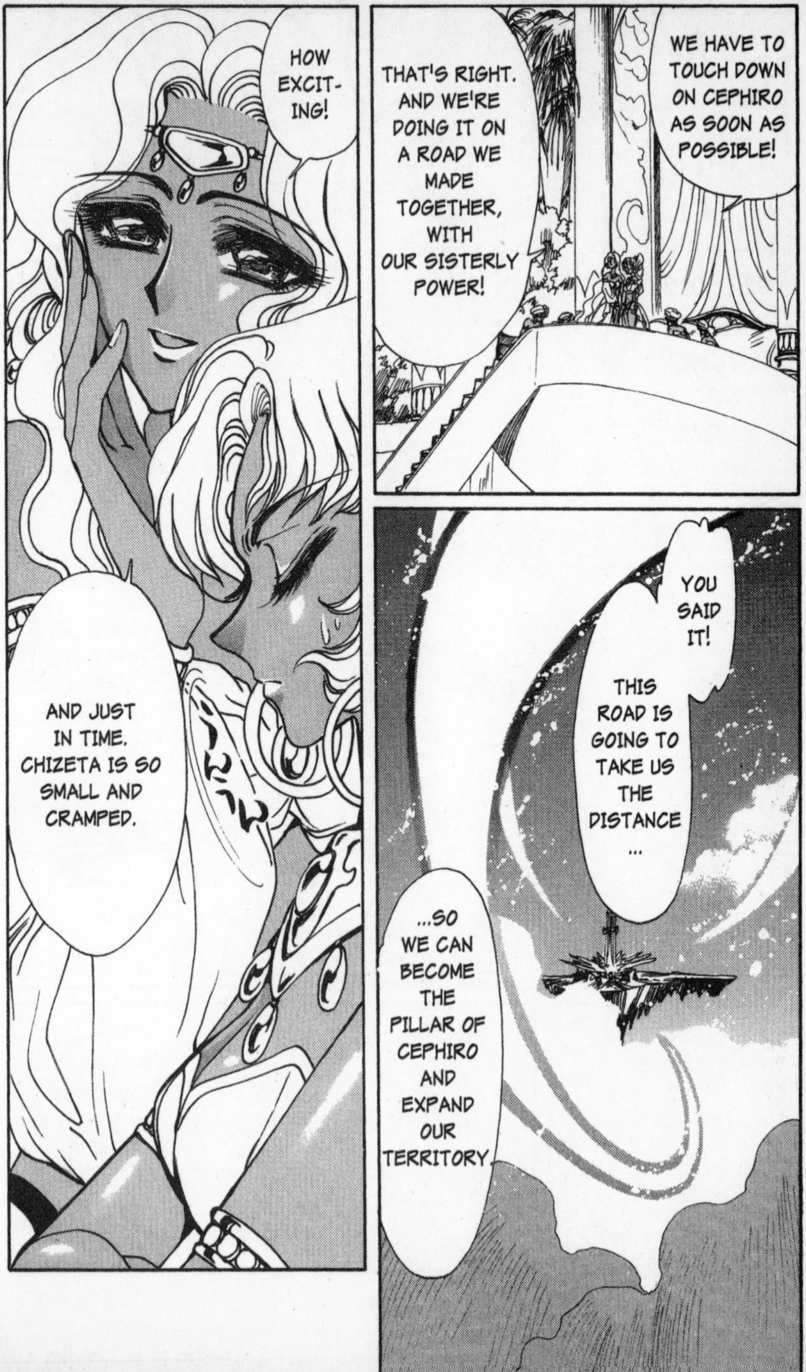
WE HAVE TO TOUCH DOWN ON CEPHIRO AS SOON AS POSSIBLE!
THAT'S RIGHT. AND WE'RE DOING IT ON A ROAD WE MADE TOGETHER, WITH OUR SISTERLY POWER!
YOU SAID IT!
THIS ROAD IS GOING TO TAKE US THE DISTANCE ...
...SO WE CAN BECOME THE PILLAR OF CEPHIRO AND EXPAND OUR TERRITORY.
HOW EXCIT-ING!
AND JUST IN TIME. CHIZETA IS SO SMALL AND CRAMPED.

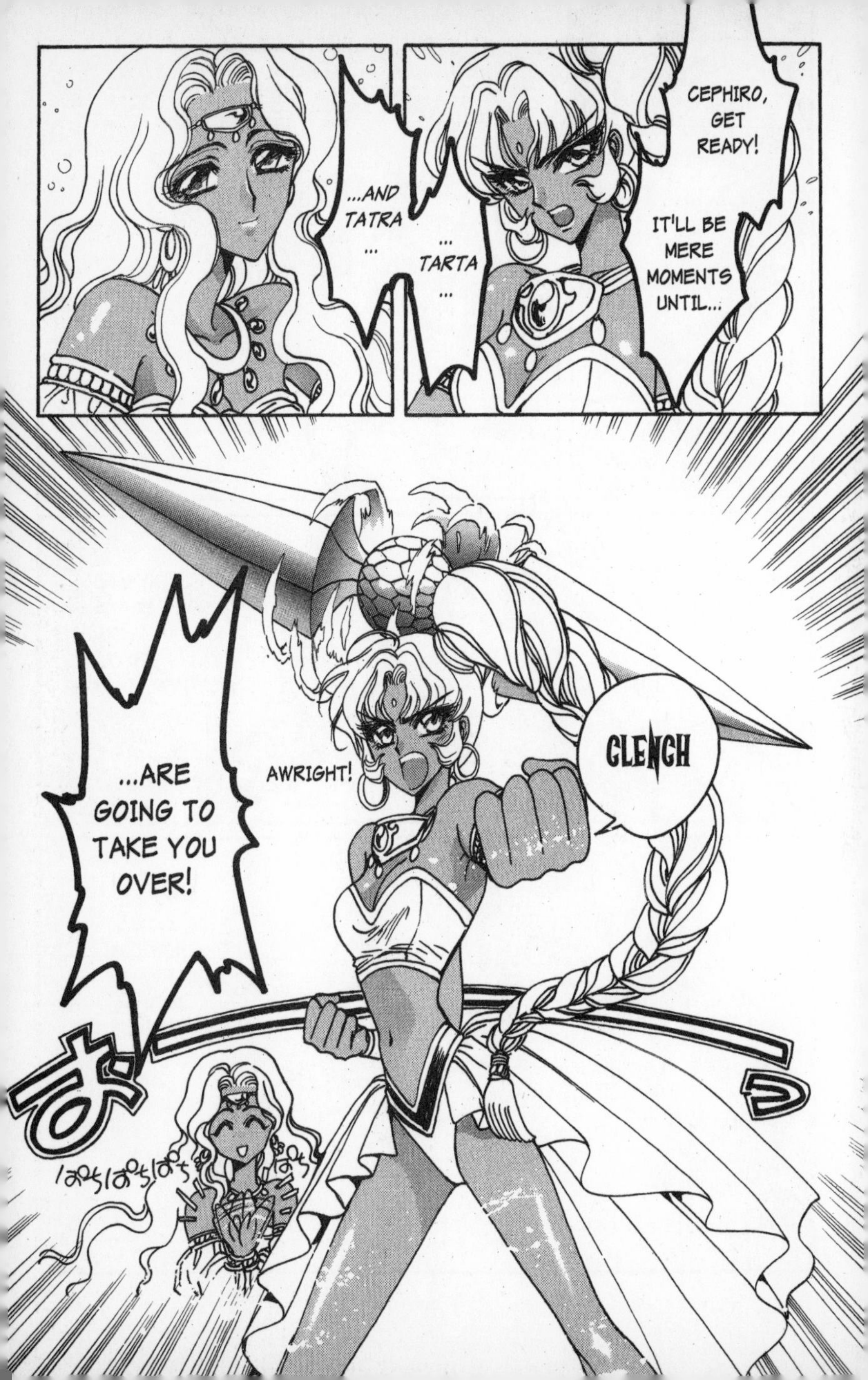
CEPHIRO, GET READY!
IT'LL BE MERE MOMENTS UNTIL...
...AND TATRA ...
... TARTA ...
...ARE GOING TO TAKE YOU OVER!
AWRIGHT!
CLENCH
ぱっ
ぱちぱちぱち ぱち

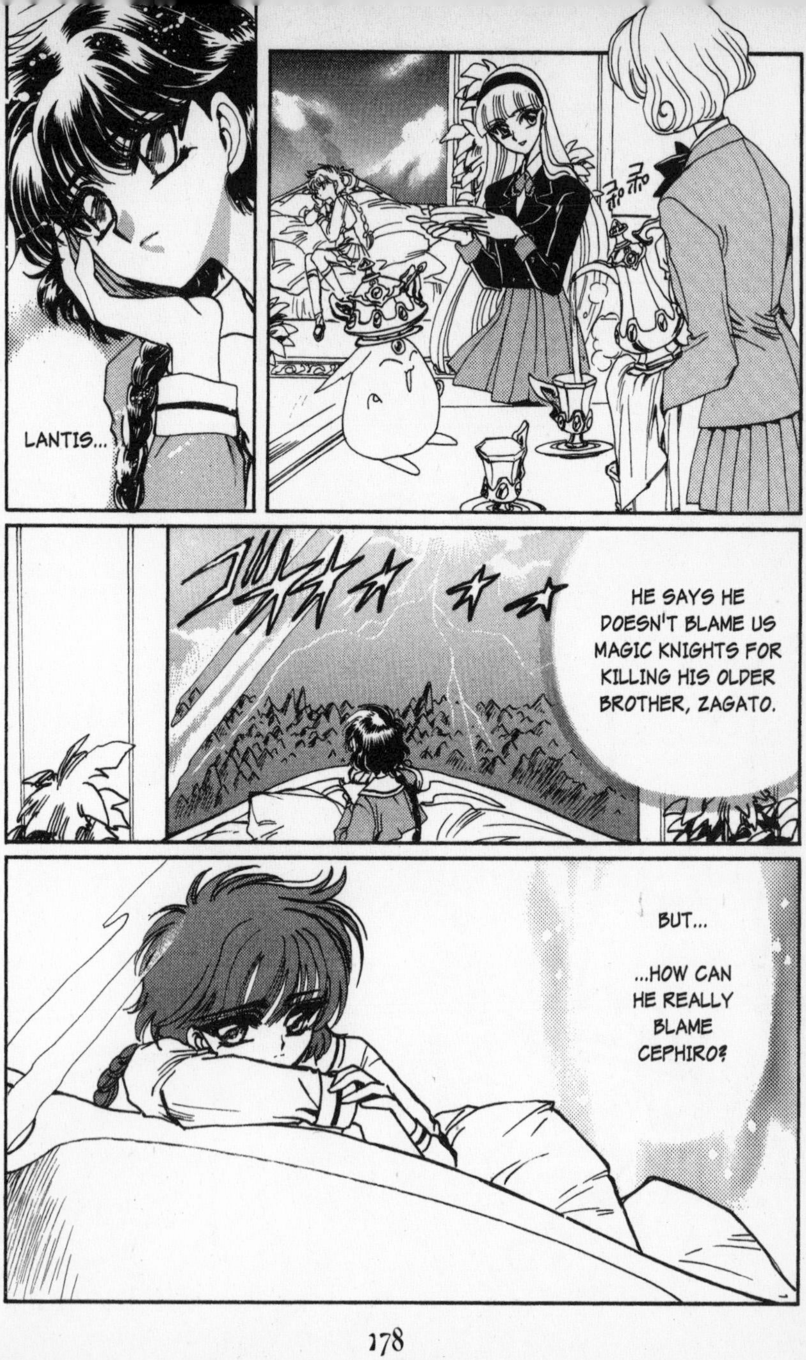
LANTIS...
HE SAYS HE DOESN'T BLAME US MAGIC KNIGHTS FOR KILLING HIS OLDER BROTHER, ZAGATO.
BUT...
...HOW CAN HE REALLY BLAME CEPHIRO?

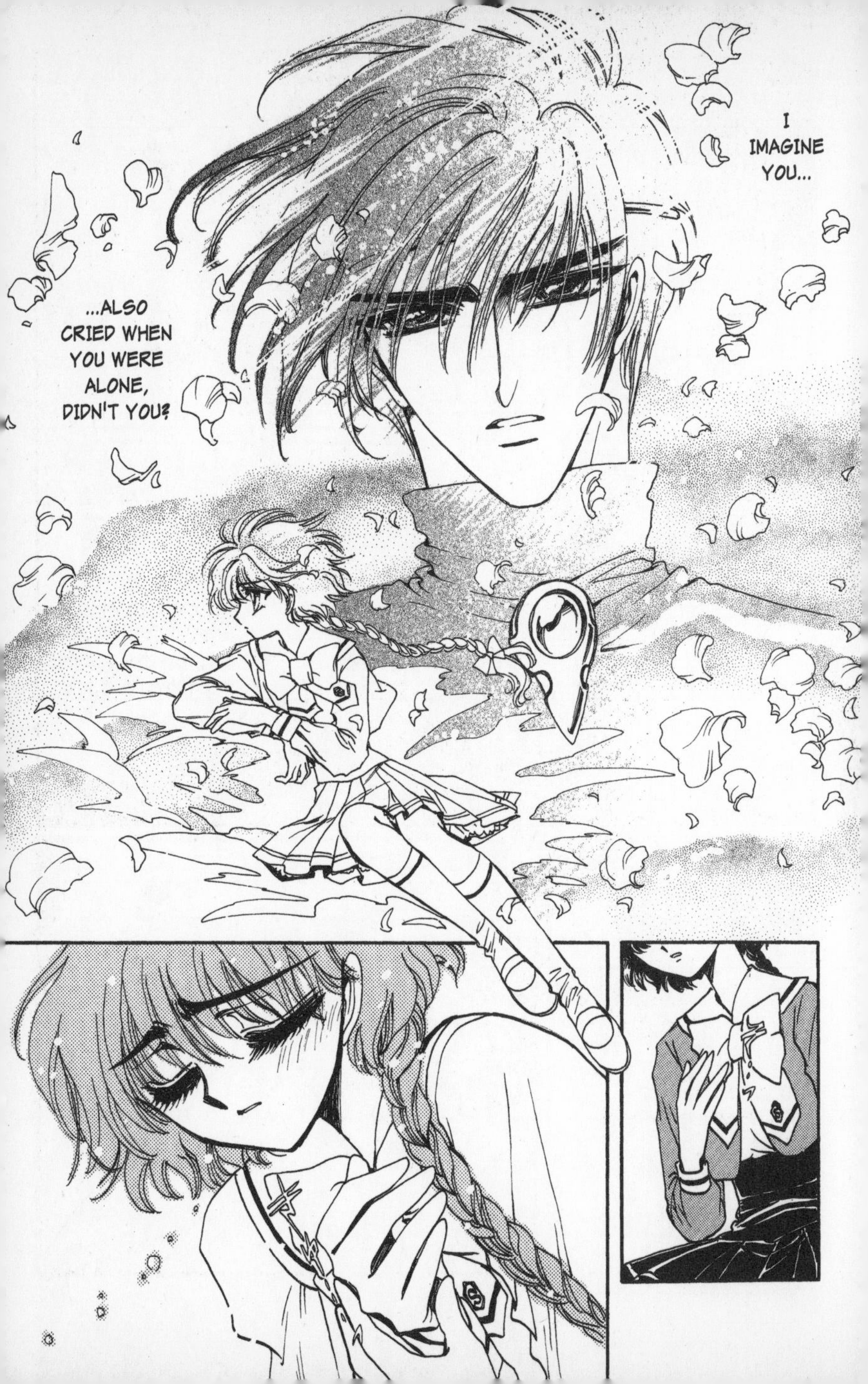
I IMAGINE YOU...
...ALSO CRIED WHEN YOU WERE ALONE, DIDN'T YOU?

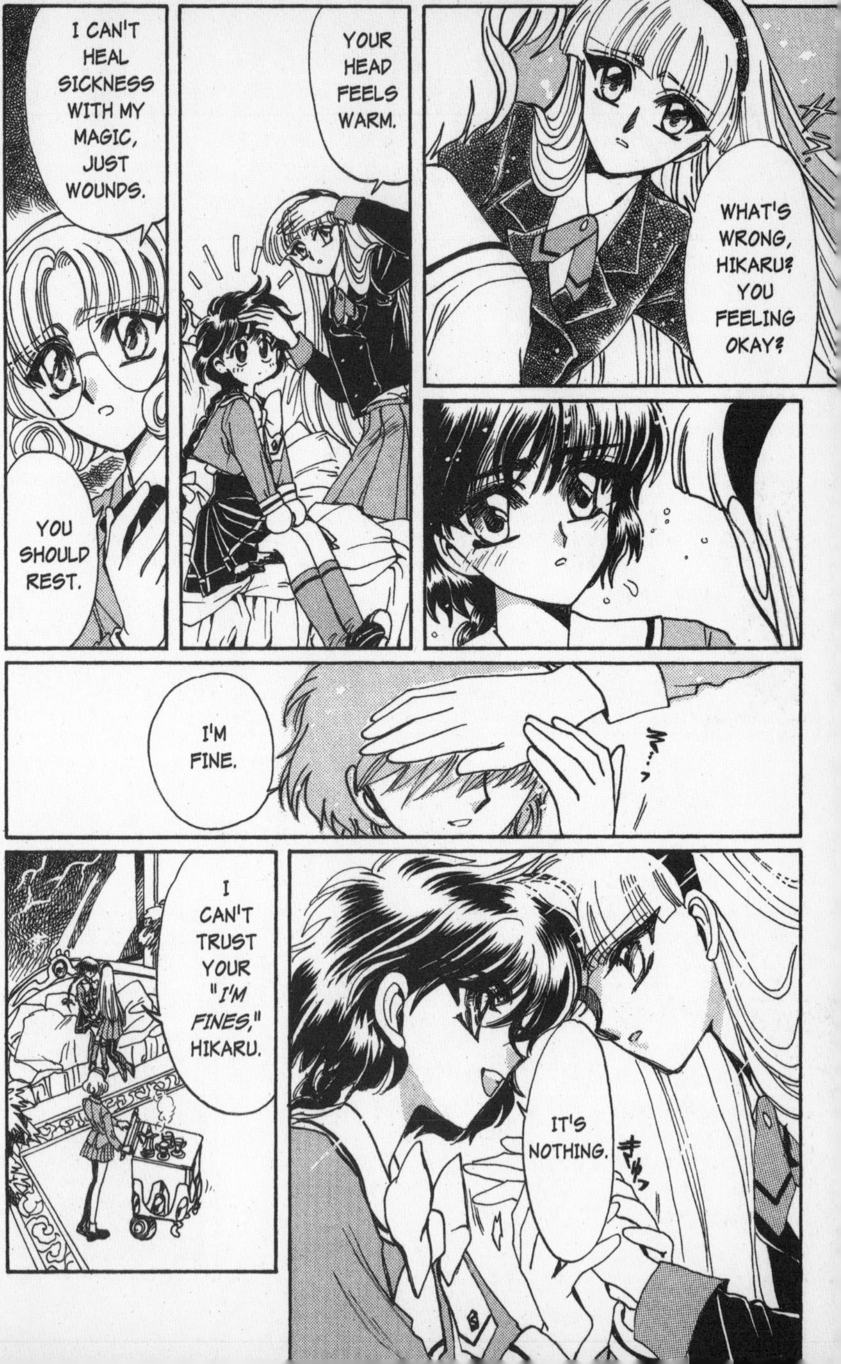
WHAT'S WRONG, HIKARU? YOU FEELING OKAY?
YOUR HEAD FEELS WARM.
I CAN'T HEAL SICKNESS WITH MY MAGIC, JUST WOUNDS.
YOU SHOULD REST.
I'M FINE.
IT'S NOTHING.
I CAN'T TRUST YOUR "*I'M FINES*," HIKARU.

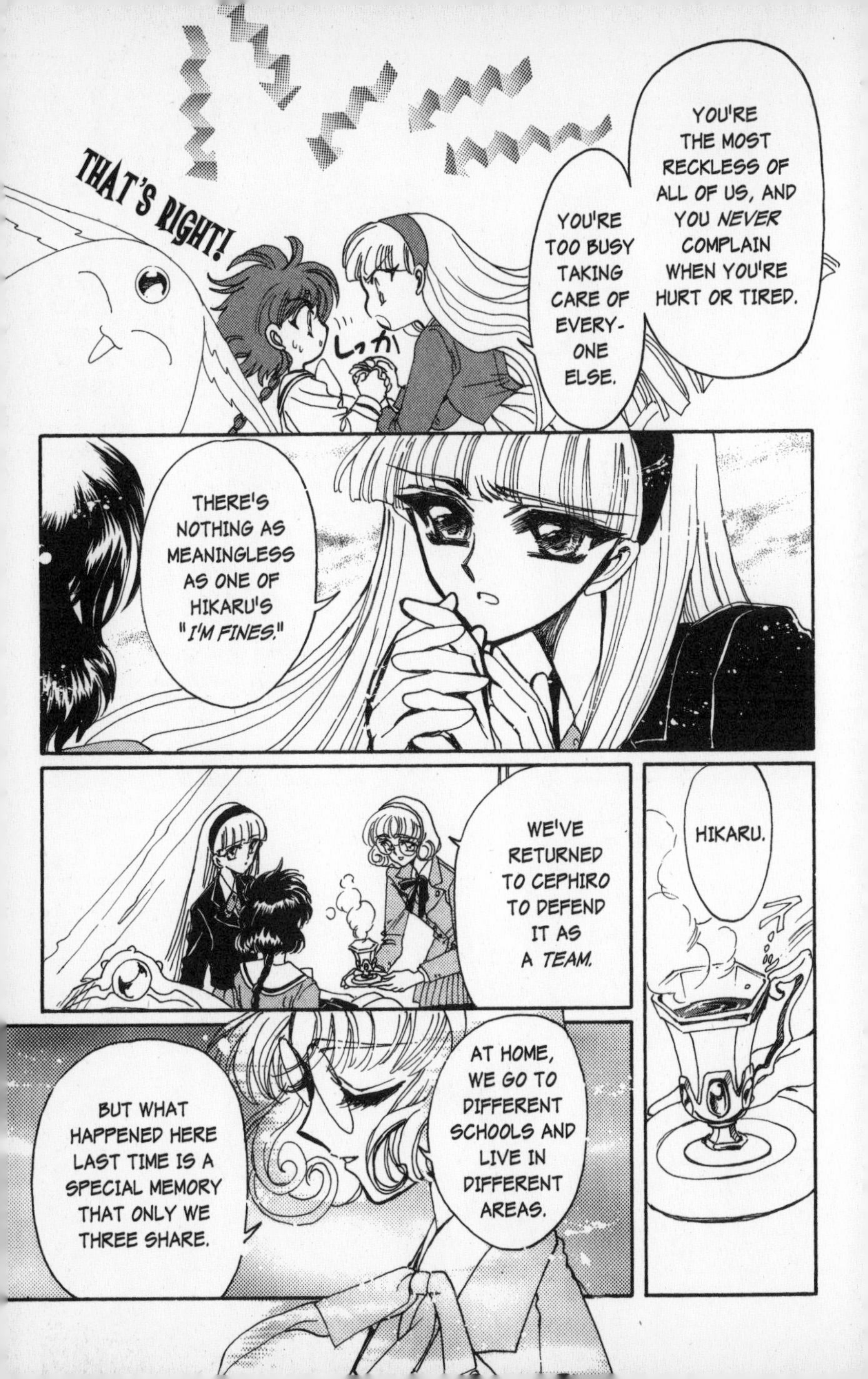
YOU'RE THE MOST RECKLESS OF ALL OF US, AND YOU *NEVER* COMPLAIN WHEN YOU'RE HURT OR TIRED.
YOU'RE TOO BUSY TAKING CARE OF EVERY-ONE ELSE.
THAT'S RIGHT!
しっか
THERE'S NOTHING AS MEANINGLESS AS ONE OF HIKARU'S "*I'M FINES.*"
HIKARU.
WE'VE RETURNED TO CEPHIRO TO DEFEND IT AS A *TEAM.*
AT HOME, WE GO TO DIFFERENT SCHOOLS AND LIVE IN DIFFERENT AREAS.
BUT WHAT HAPPENED HERE LAST TIME IS A SPECIAL MEMORY THAT ONLY WE THREE SHARE.

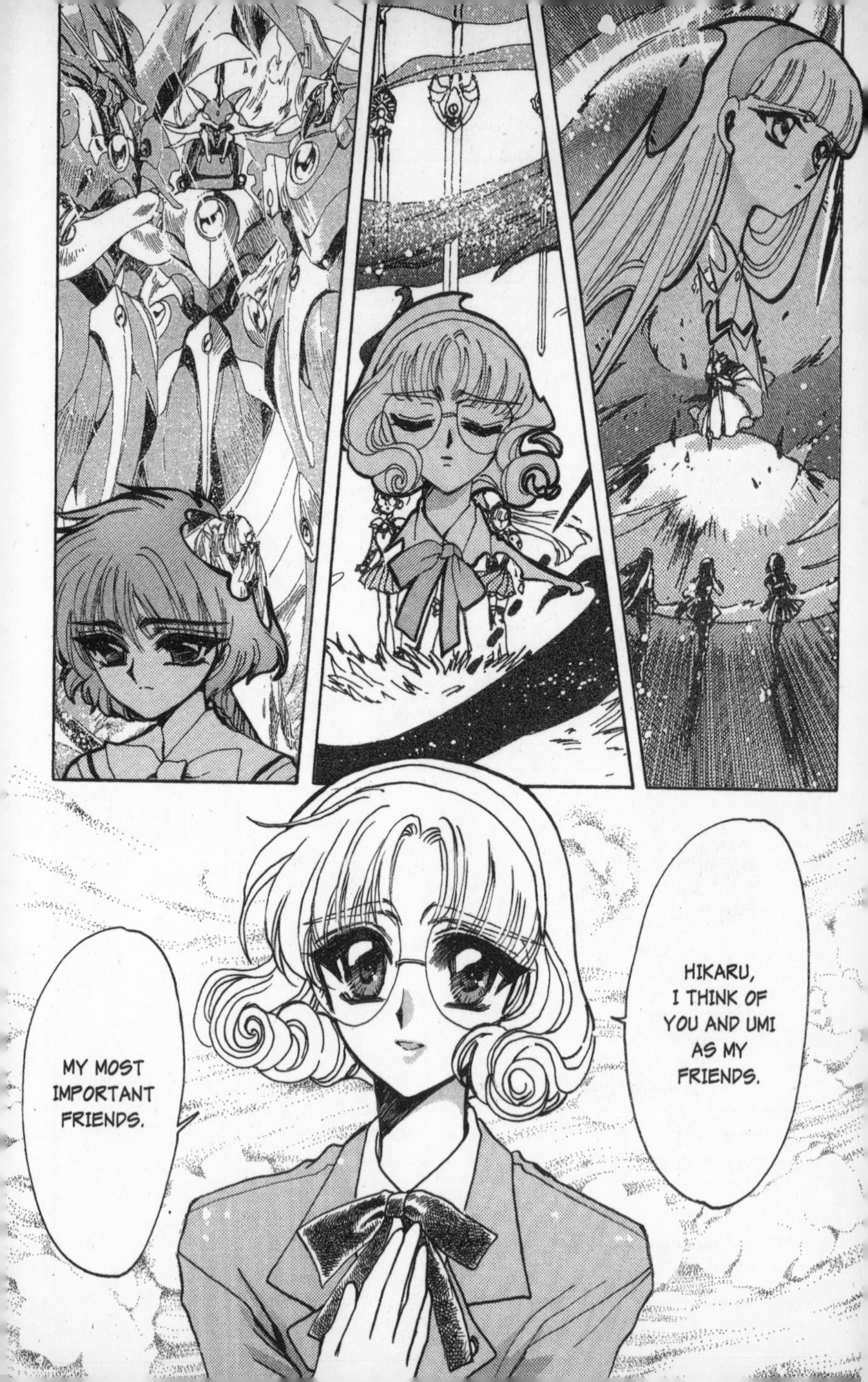
HIKARU, I THINK OF YOU AND UMI AS MY FRIENDS.
MY MOST IMPORTANT FRIENDS.

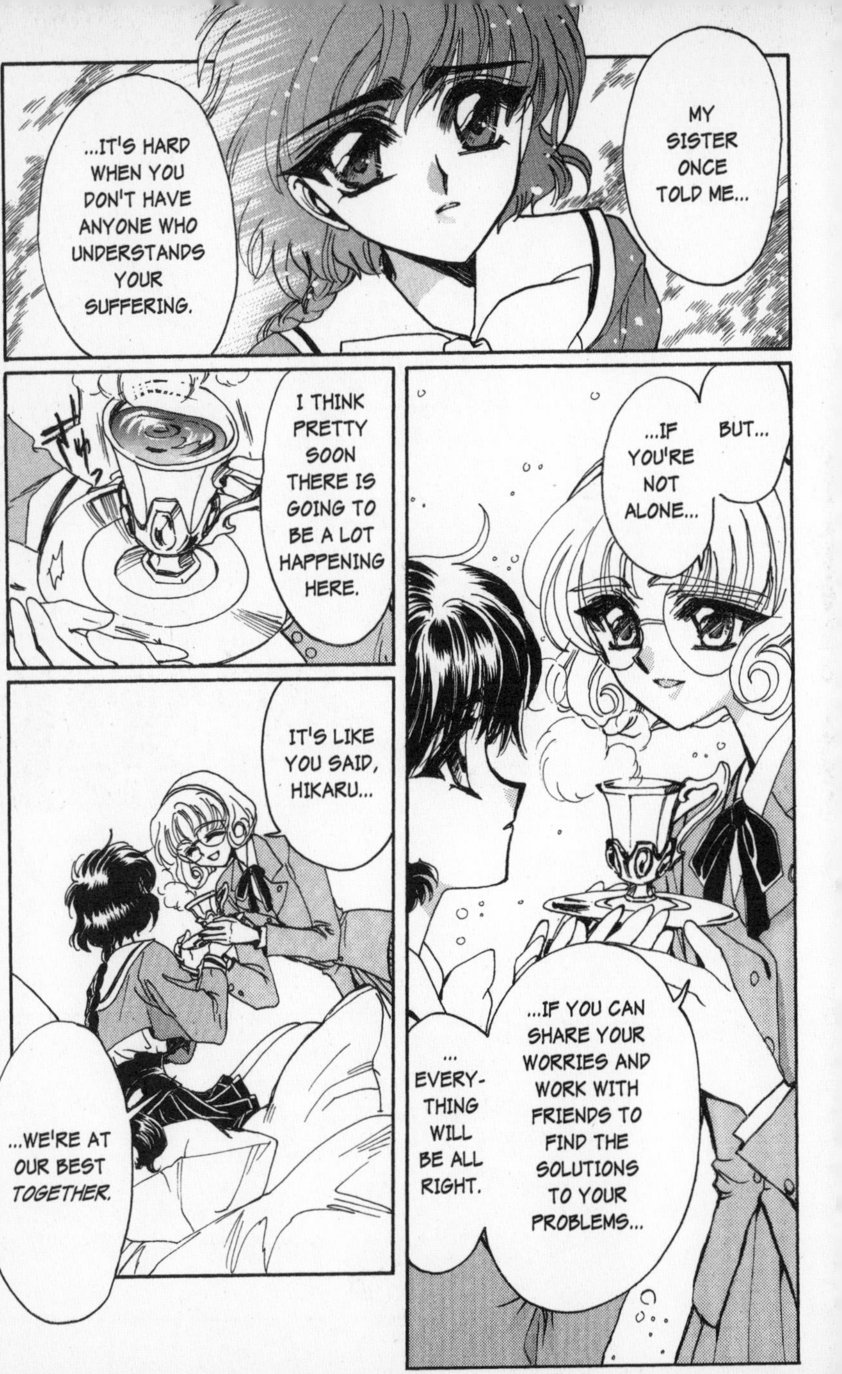
MY SISTER ONCE TOLD ME...
...IT'S HARD WHEN YOU DON'T HAVE ANYONE WHO UNDERSTANDS YOUR SUFFERING.
BUT...
...IF YOU'RE NOT ALONE...
...IF YOU CAN SHARE YOUR WORRIES AND WORK WITH FRIENDS TO FIND THE SOLUTIONS TO YOUR PROBLEMS...
...EVERY-THING WILL BE ALL RIGHT.
I THINK PRETTY SOON THERE IS GOING TO BE A LOT HAPPENING HERE.
IT'S LIKE YOU SAID, HIKARU...
...WE'RE AT OUR BEST *TOGETHER.*

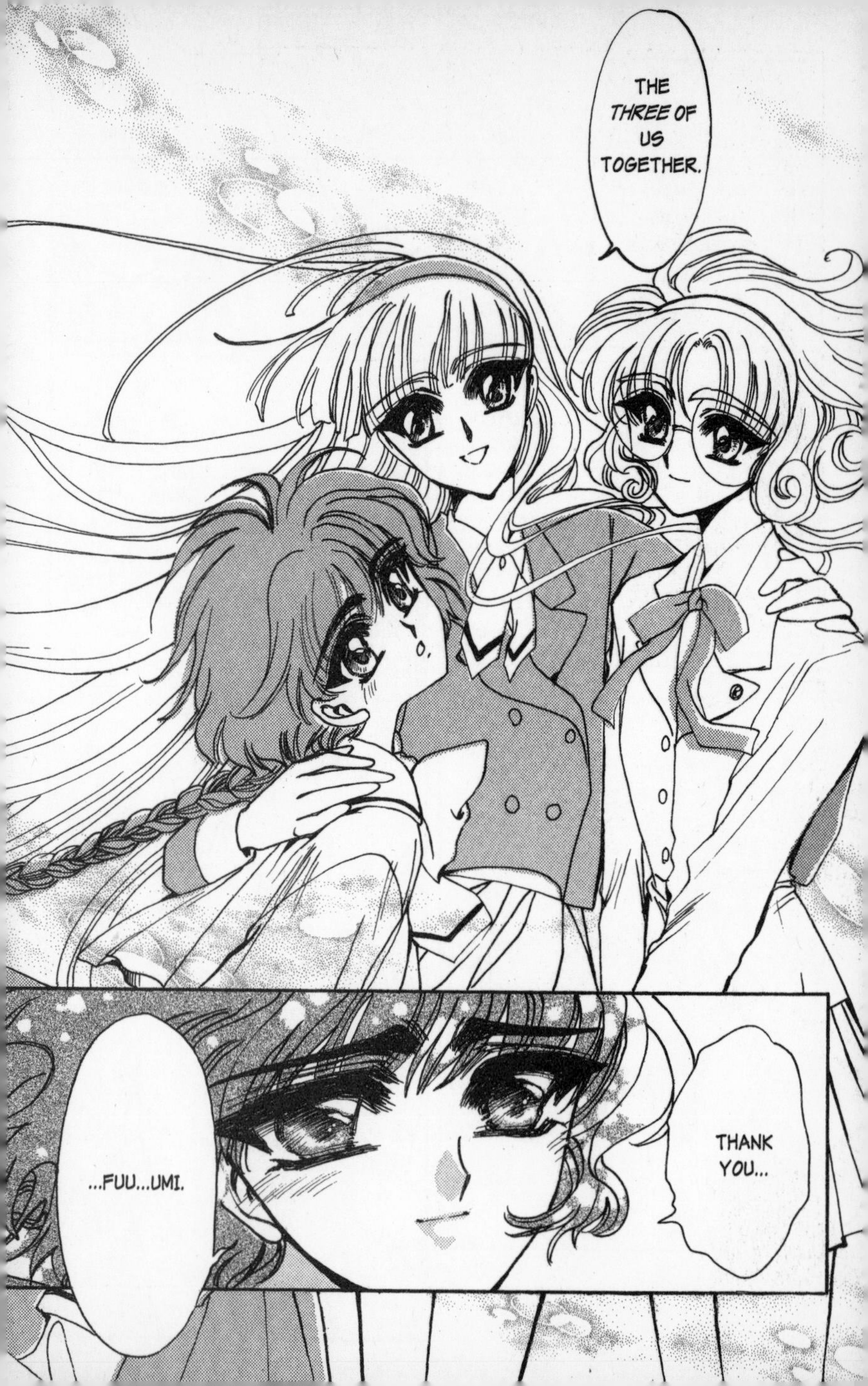
THE THREE OF US TOGETHER.
THANK YOU...
...FUU...UMI.

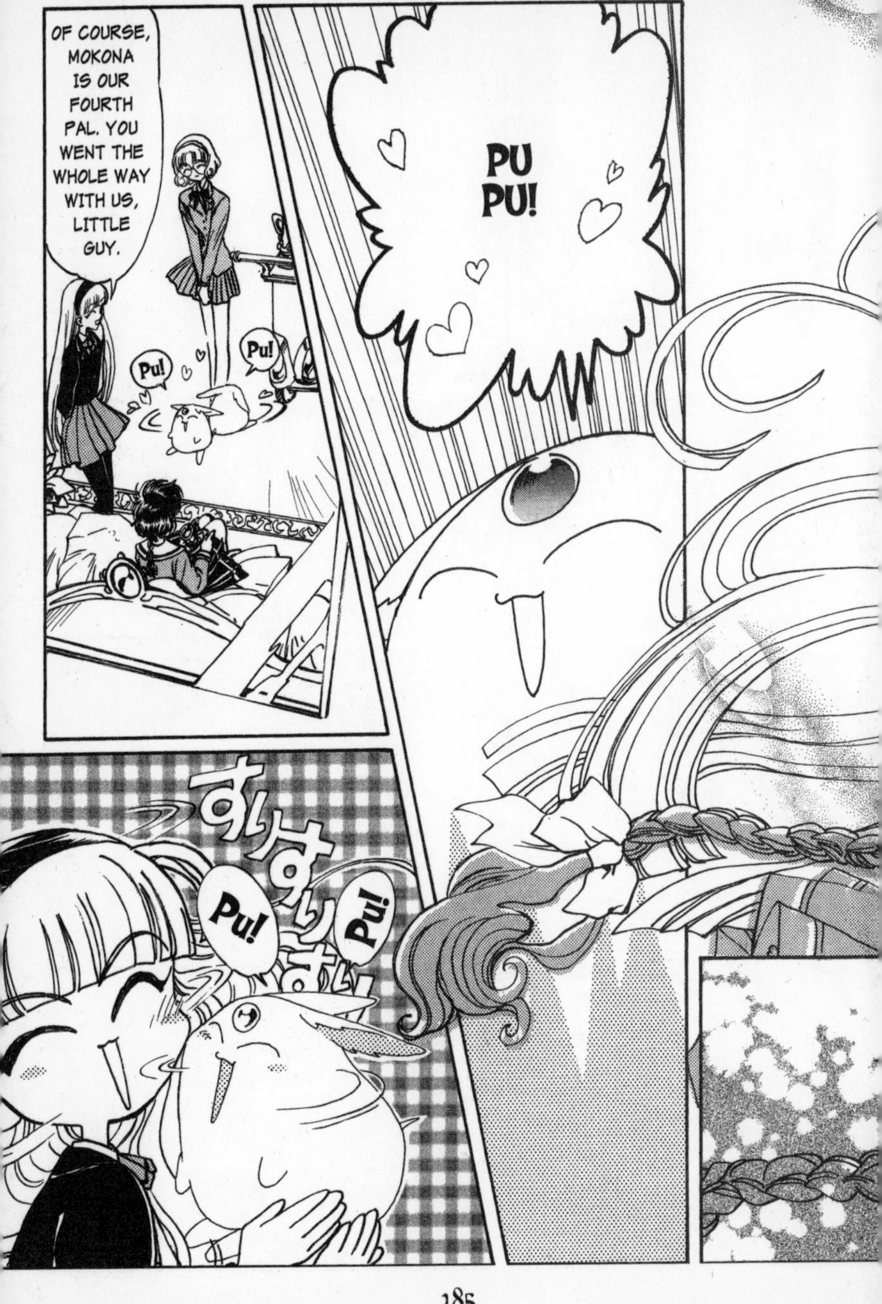
PU PU!
OF COURSE, MOKONA IS OUR FOURTH PAL. YOU WENT THE WHOLE WAY WITH US, LITTLE GUY.
Pu!
Pu!
すりすりすり
Pu!
Pu!

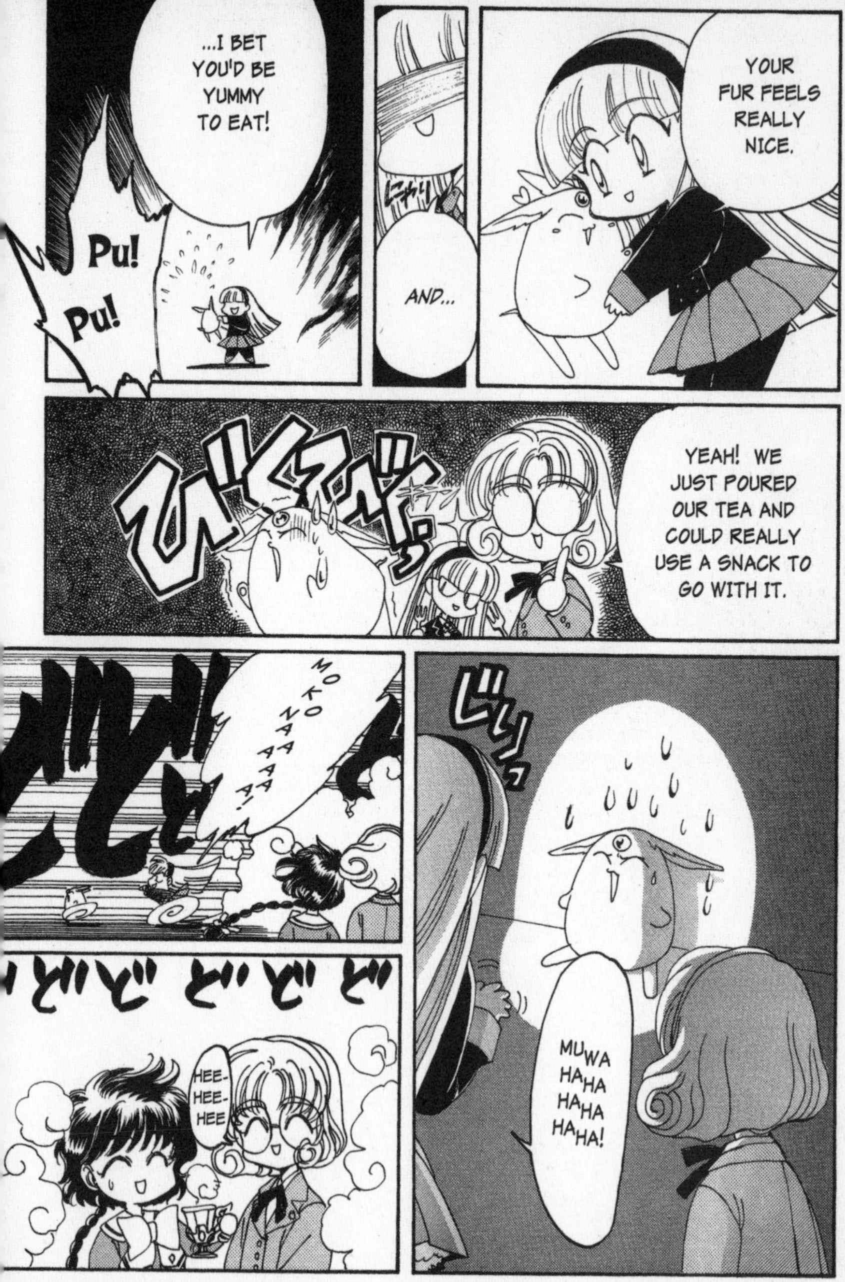
YOUR FUR FEELS REALLY NICE.
AND...
...I BET YOU'D BE YUMMY TO EAT!
Pu!
Pu!
YEAH! WE JUST POURED OUR TEA AND COULD REALLY USE A SNACK TO GO WITH IT.
MUWAHAHAHAHAHAHAHA!
MOKONAAAAAA!
HEE-HEE-HEE

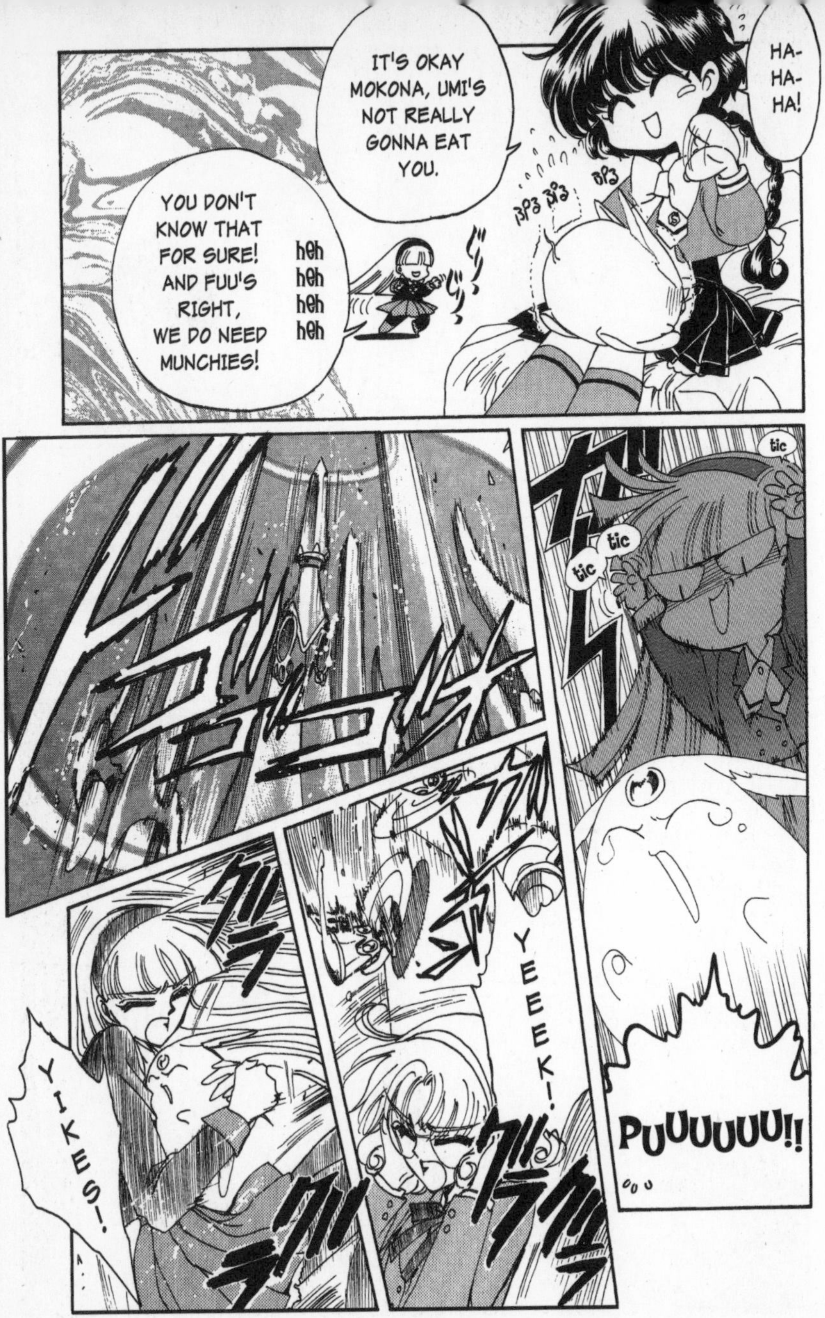
HA-HA-HA!
IT'S OKAY MOKONA, UMI'S NOT REALLY GONNA EAT YOU.
YOU DON'T KNOW THAT FOR SURE! AND FUU'S RIGHT, WE DO NEED MUNCHIES!
heh heh heh heh
tic
tic
tic
PUUUUUU!!
YEEEK!
YIKES!

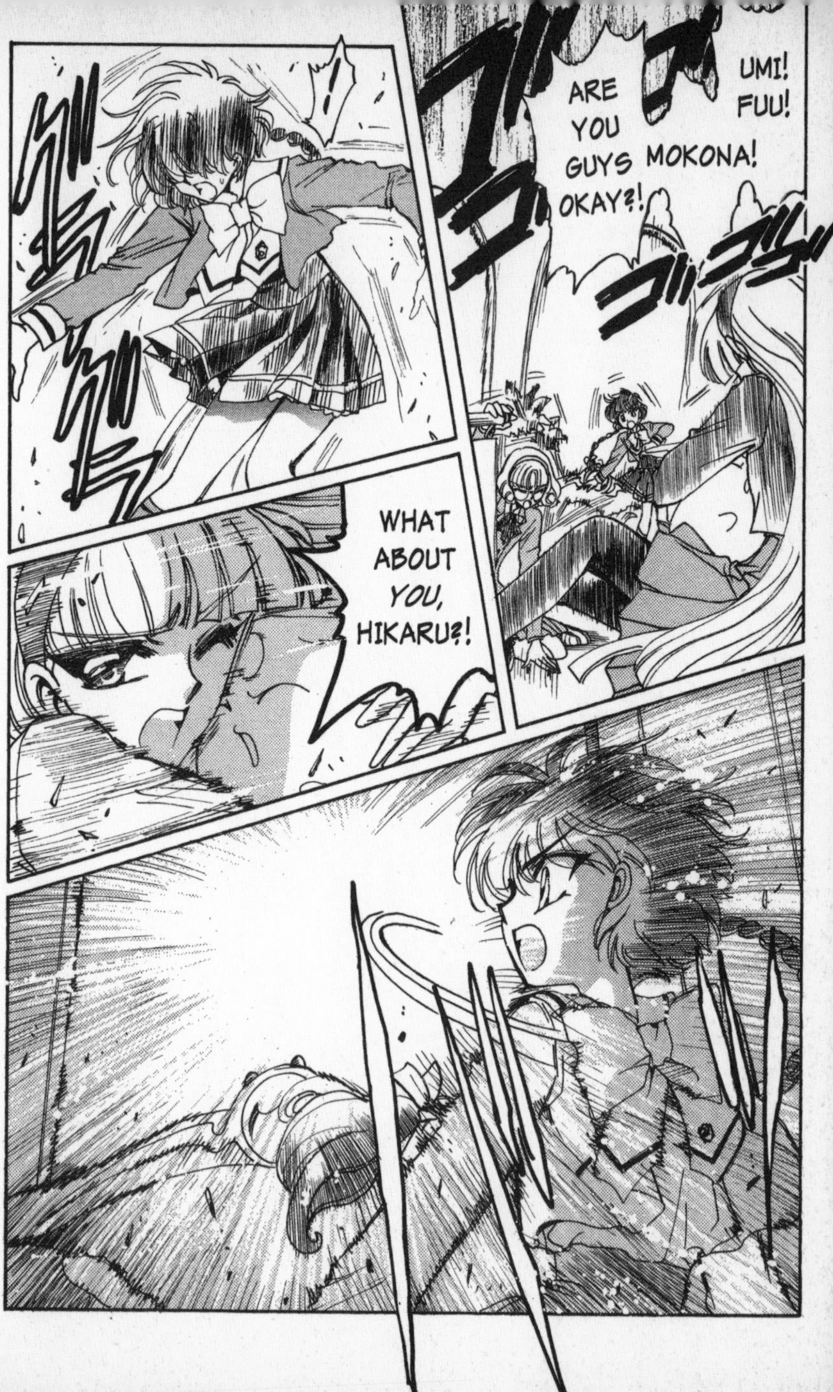
UMI! FUU! MOKONA!
ARE YOU GUYS OKAY?!
WHAT ABOUT *YOU,* HIKARU?!

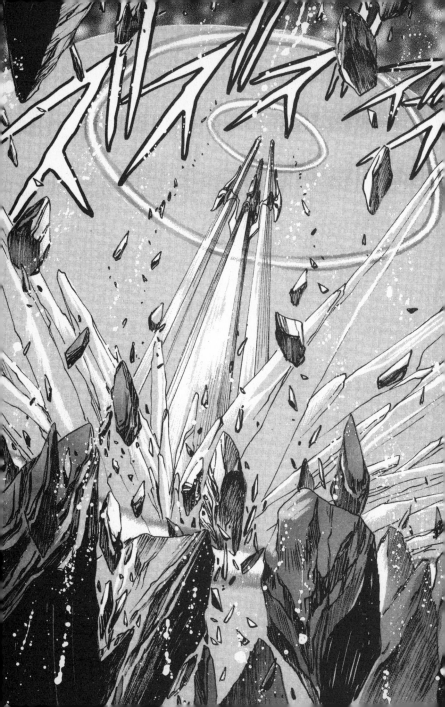

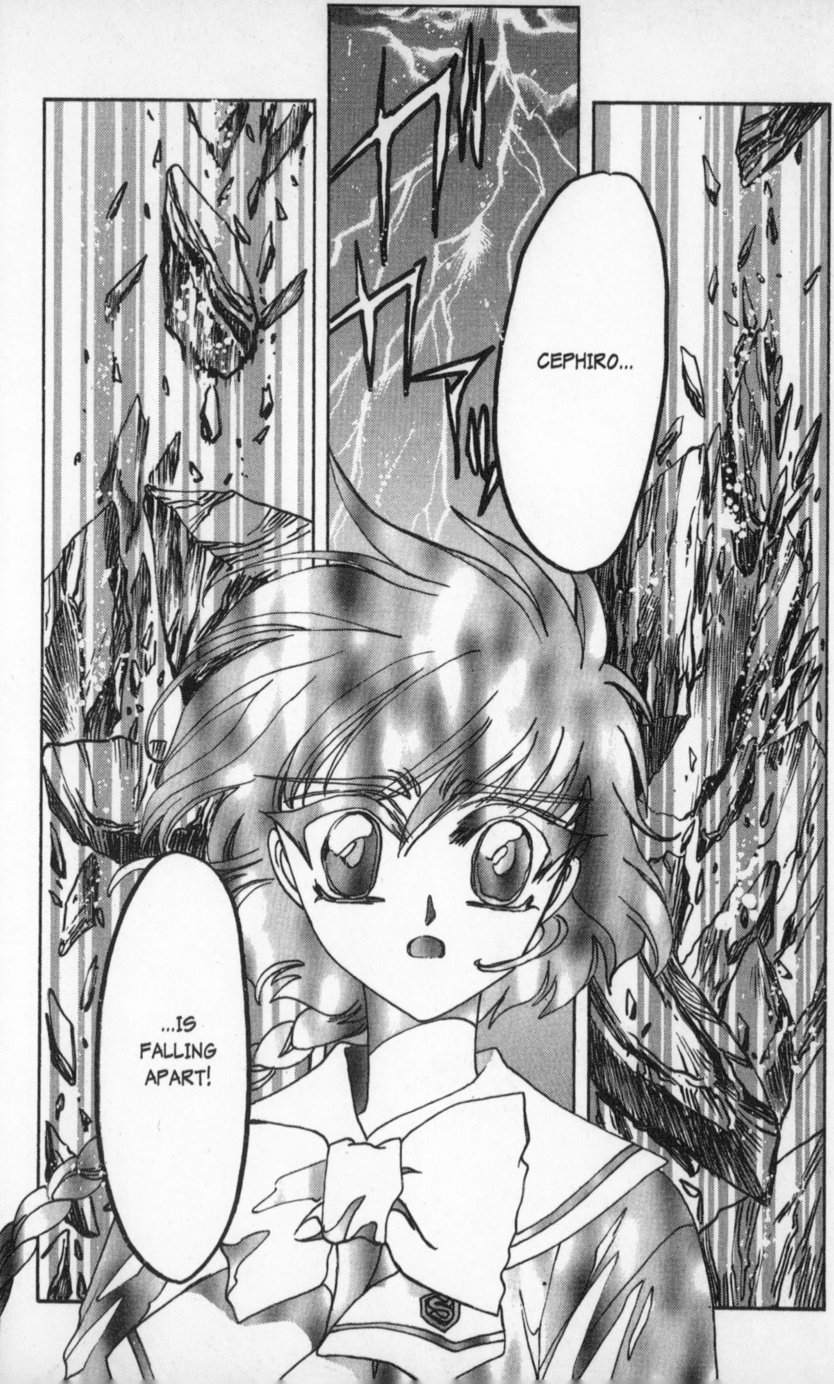
CEPHIRO...
...IS FALLING APART!

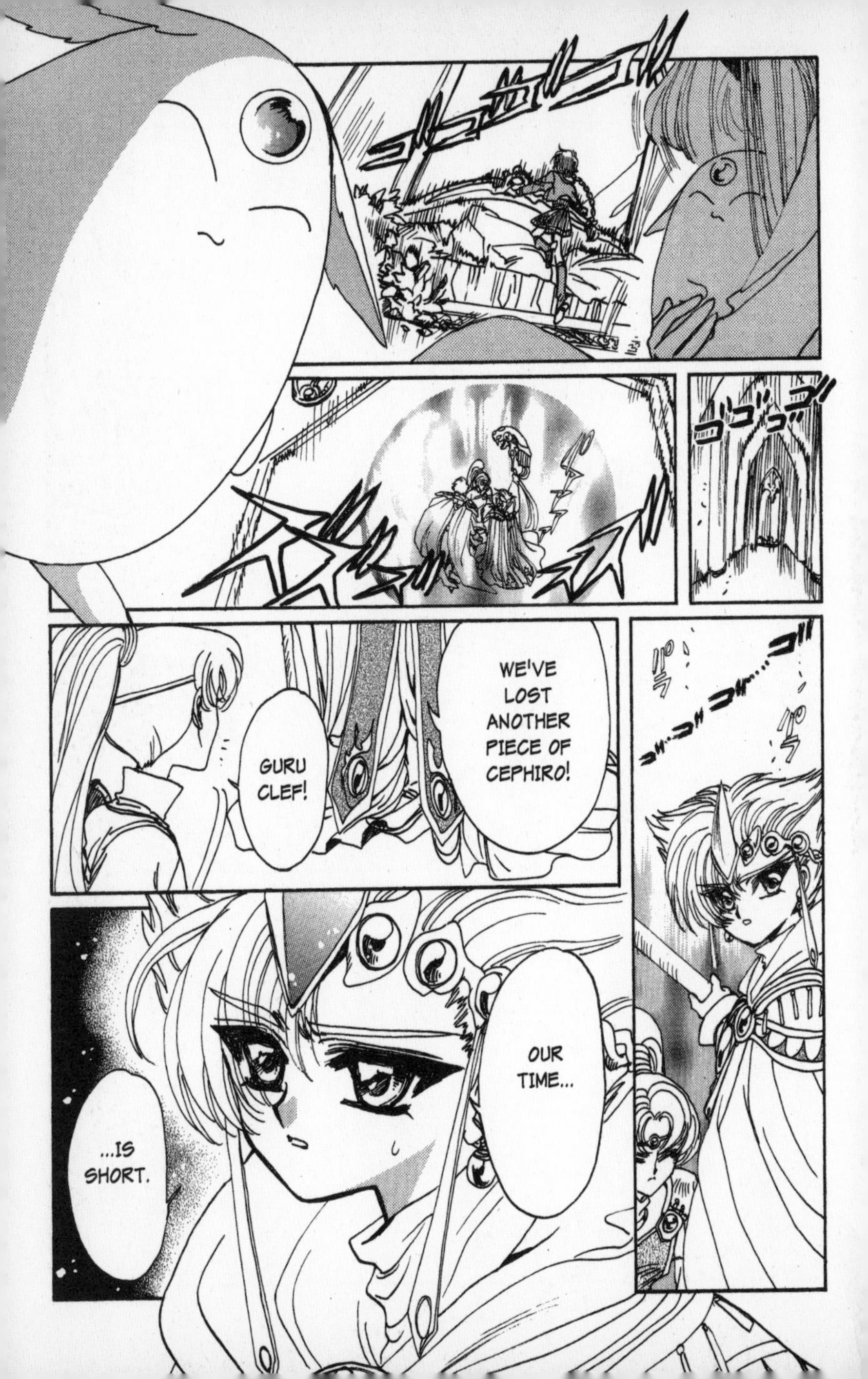
WE'VE LOST ANOTHER PIECE OF CEPHIRO!
GURU CLEF!
OUR TIME...
...IS SHORT.

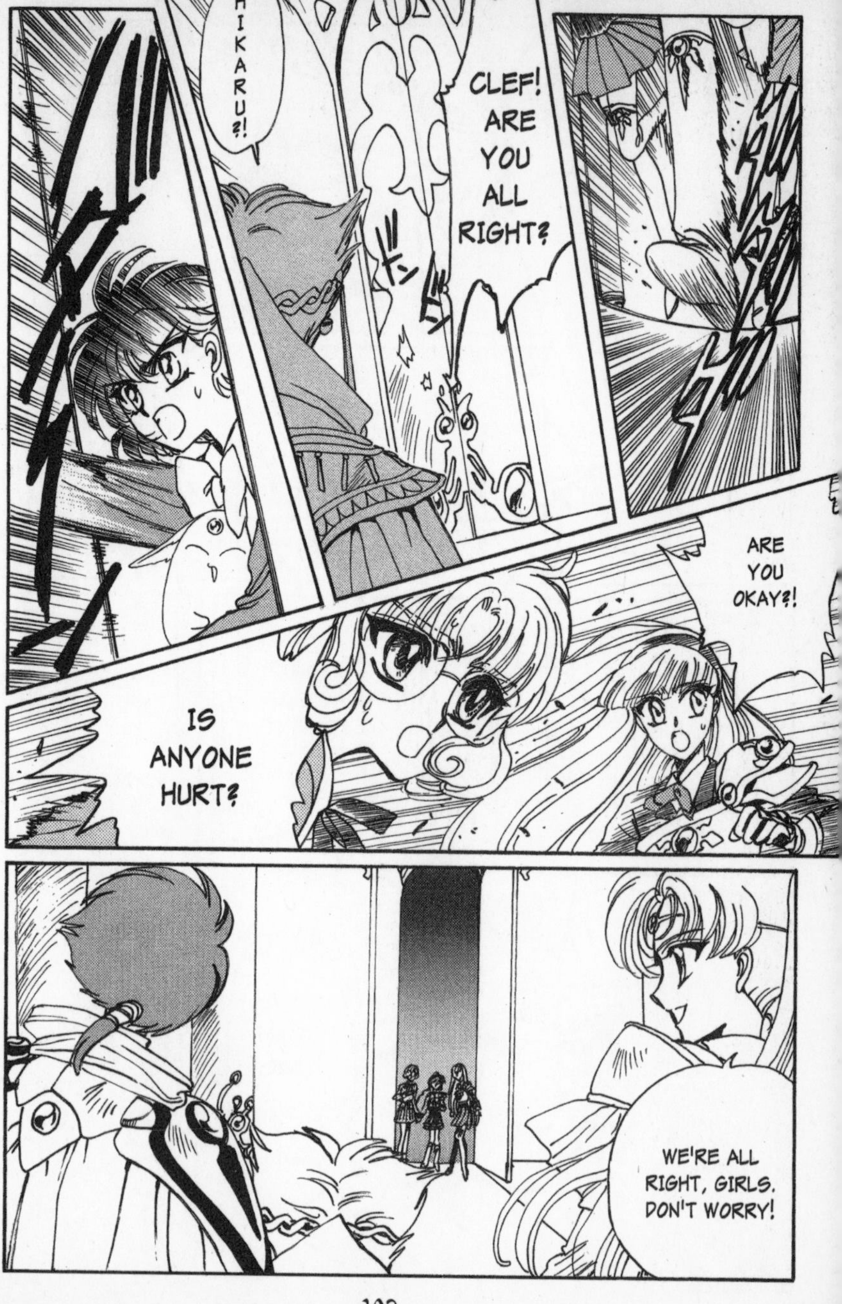
CLEF! ARE YOU ALL RIGHT?
HIKARU?!
ARE YOU OKAY?!
IS ANYONE HURT?
WE'RE ALL RIGHT, GIRLS. DON'T WORRY!

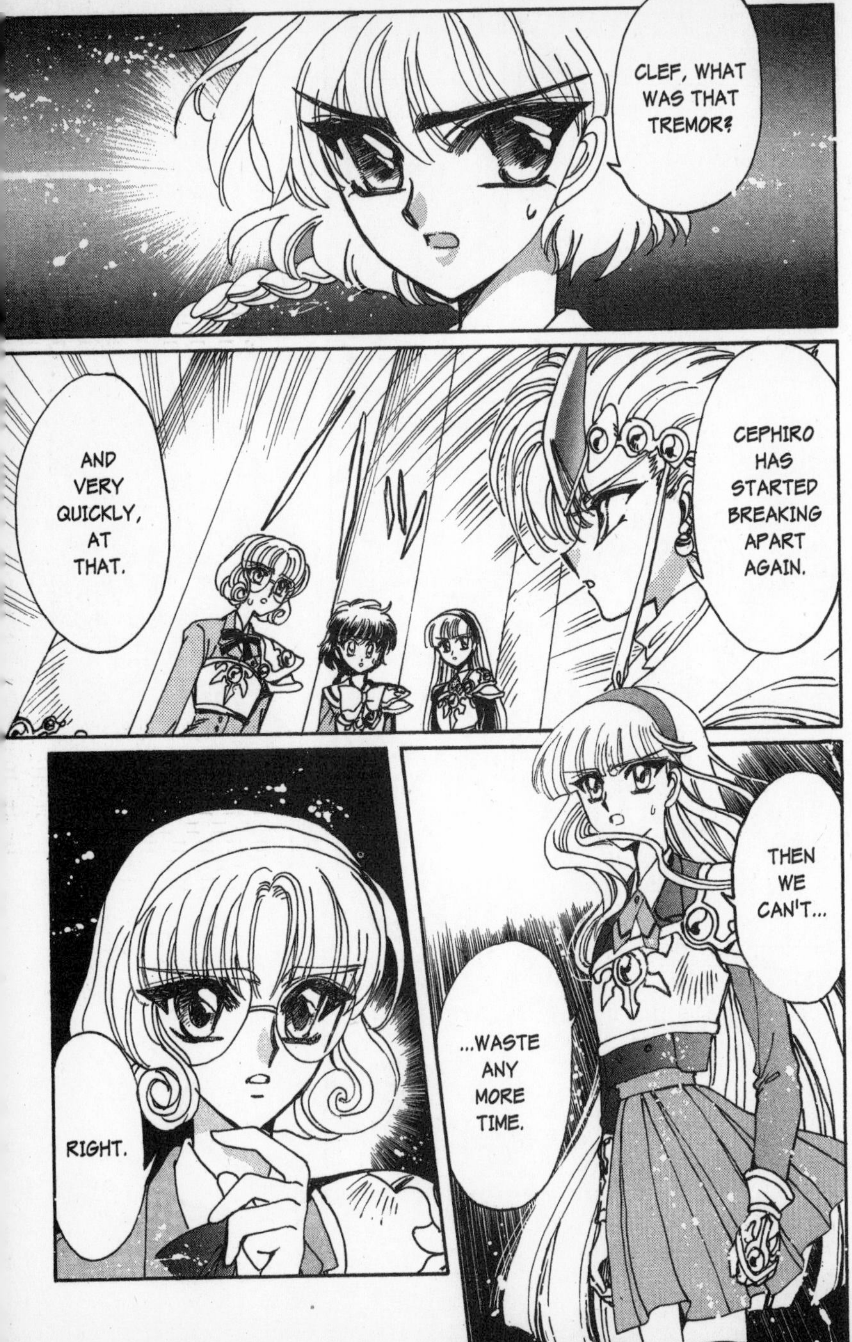
CLEF, WHAT WAS THAT TREMOR?
CEPHIRO HAS STARTED BREAKING APART AGAIN.
AND VERY QUICKLY, AT THAT.
THEN WE CAN'T...
...WASTE ANY MORE TIME.
RIGHT.

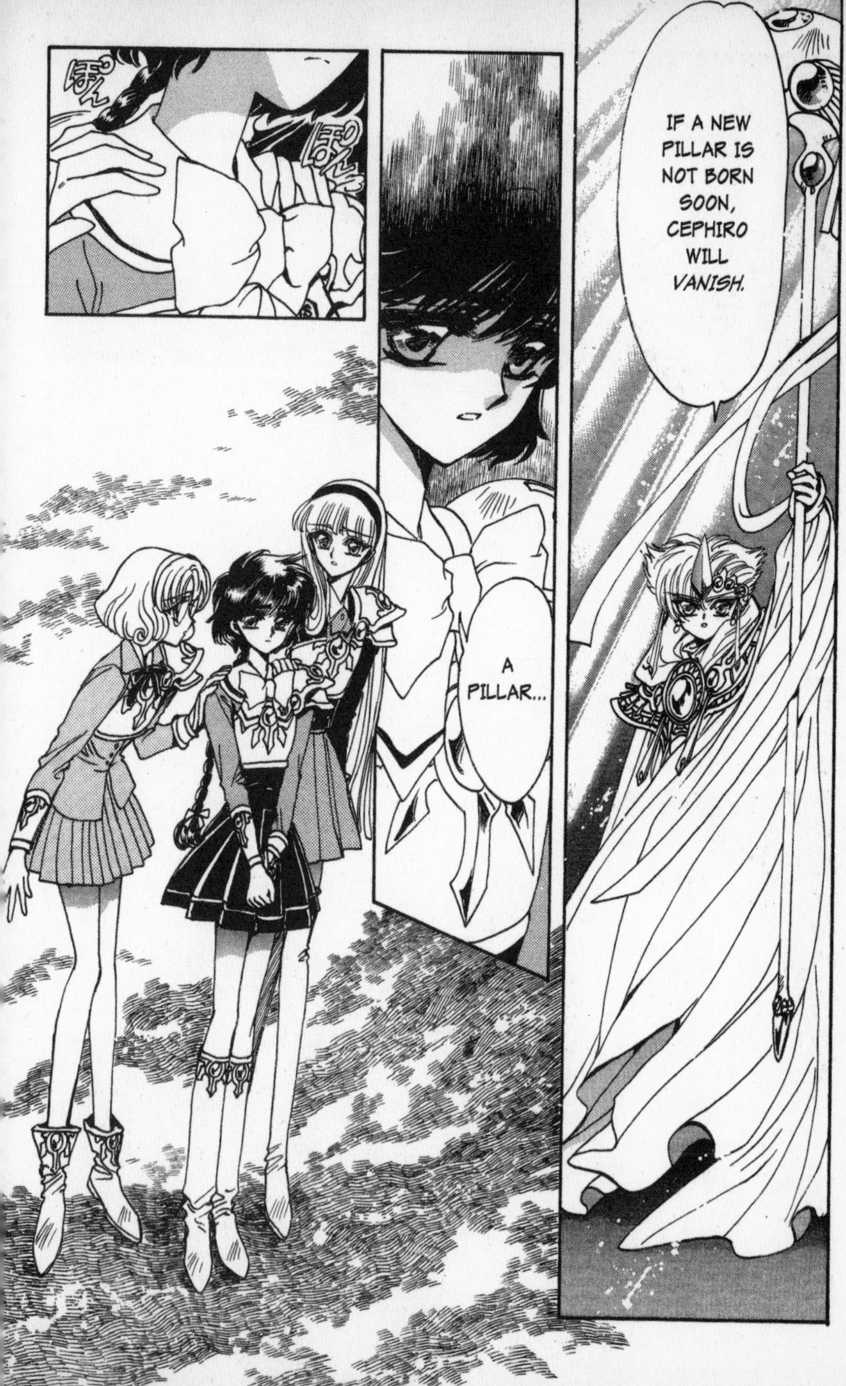
IF A NEW PILLAR IS NOT BORN SOON, CEPHIRO WILL *VANISH.*
A PILLAR...
ぽんっ
ぽん

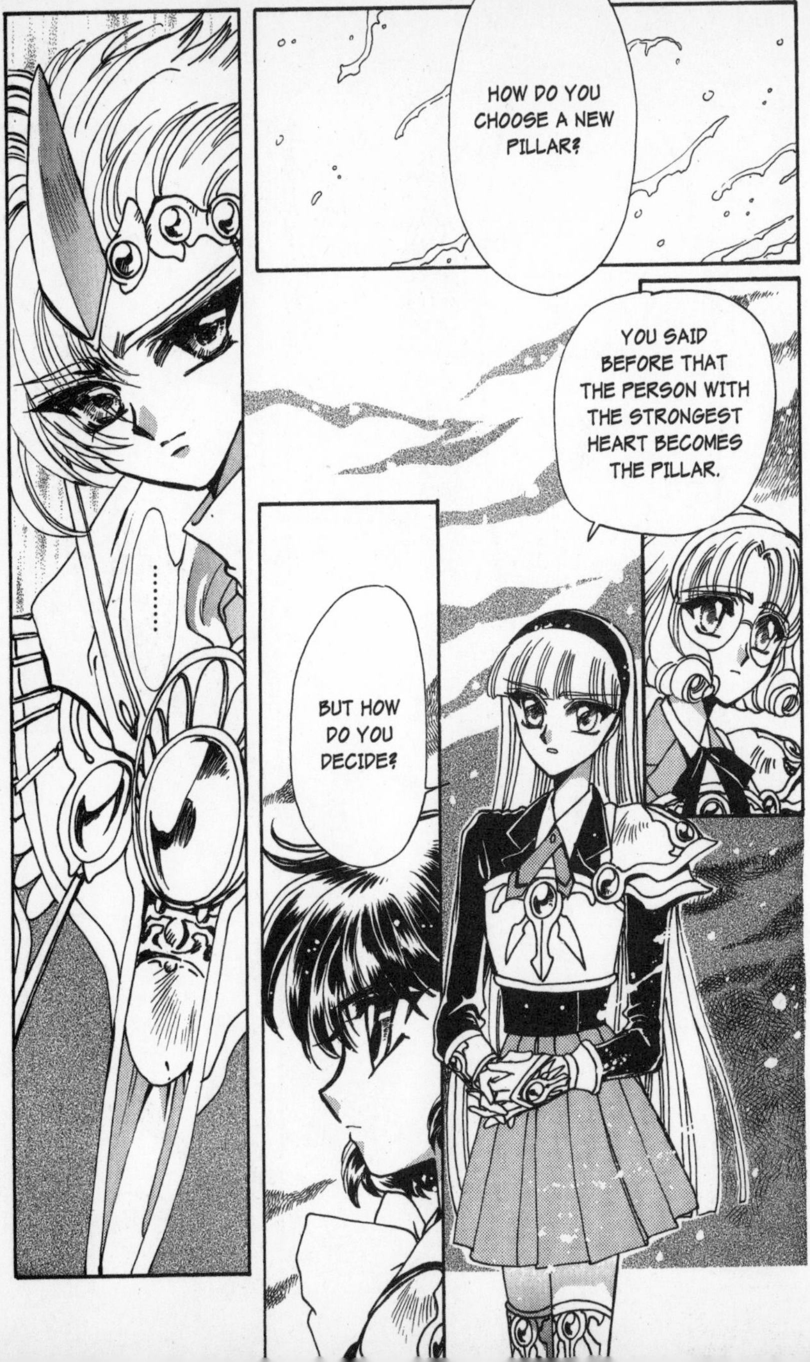
HOW DO YOU CHOOSE A NEW PILLAR?
YOU SAID BEFORE THAT THE PERSON WITH THE STRONGEST HEART BECOMES THE PILLAR.
BUT HOW DO YOU DECIDE?
......

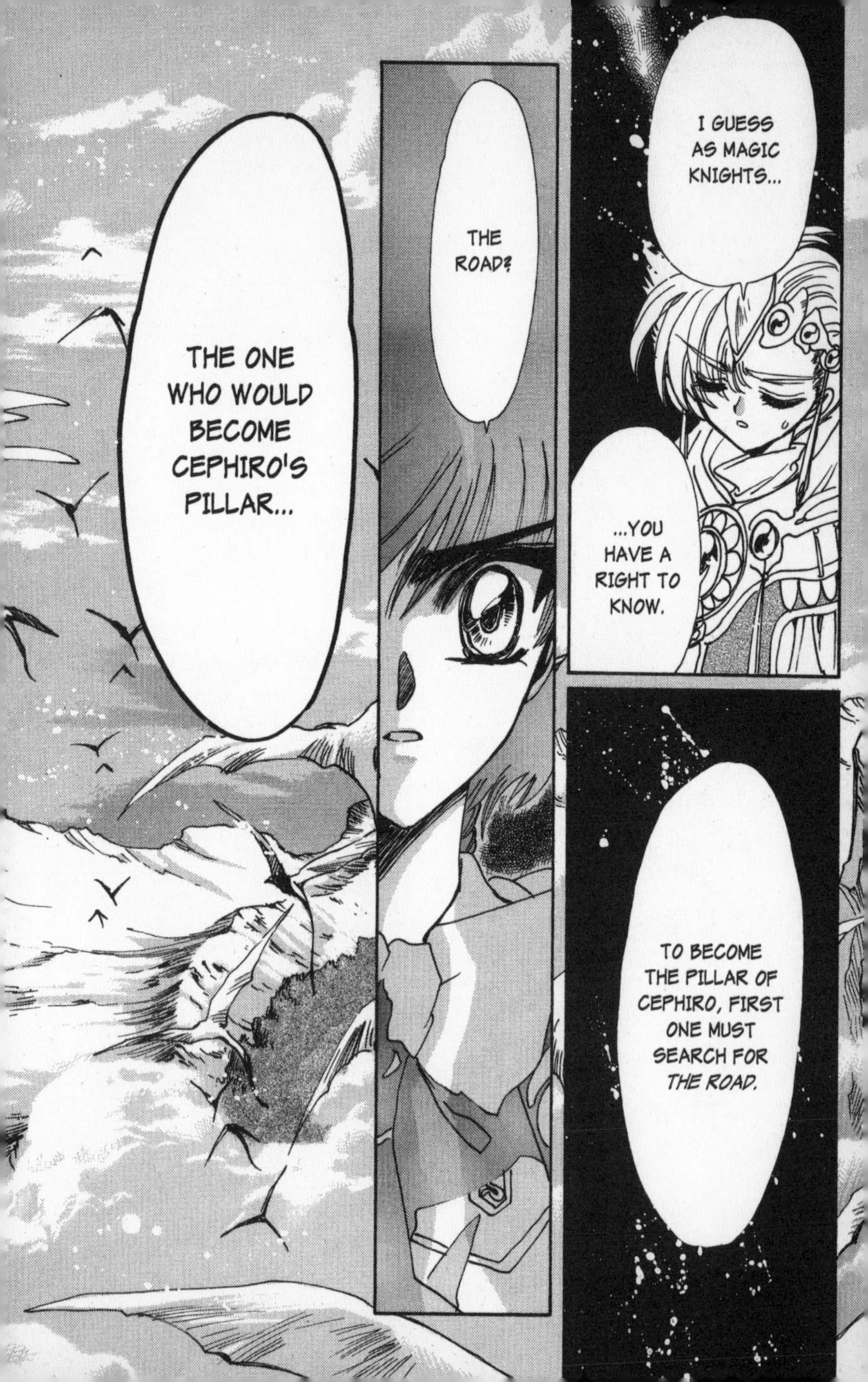
I GUESS AS MAGIC KNIGHTS...
...YOU HAVE A RIGHT TO KNOW.
TO BECOME THE PILLAR OF CEPHIRO, FIRST ONE MUST SEARCH FOR *THE ROAD.*
THE ROAD?
THE ONE WHO WOULD BECOME CEPHIRO'S PILLAR...

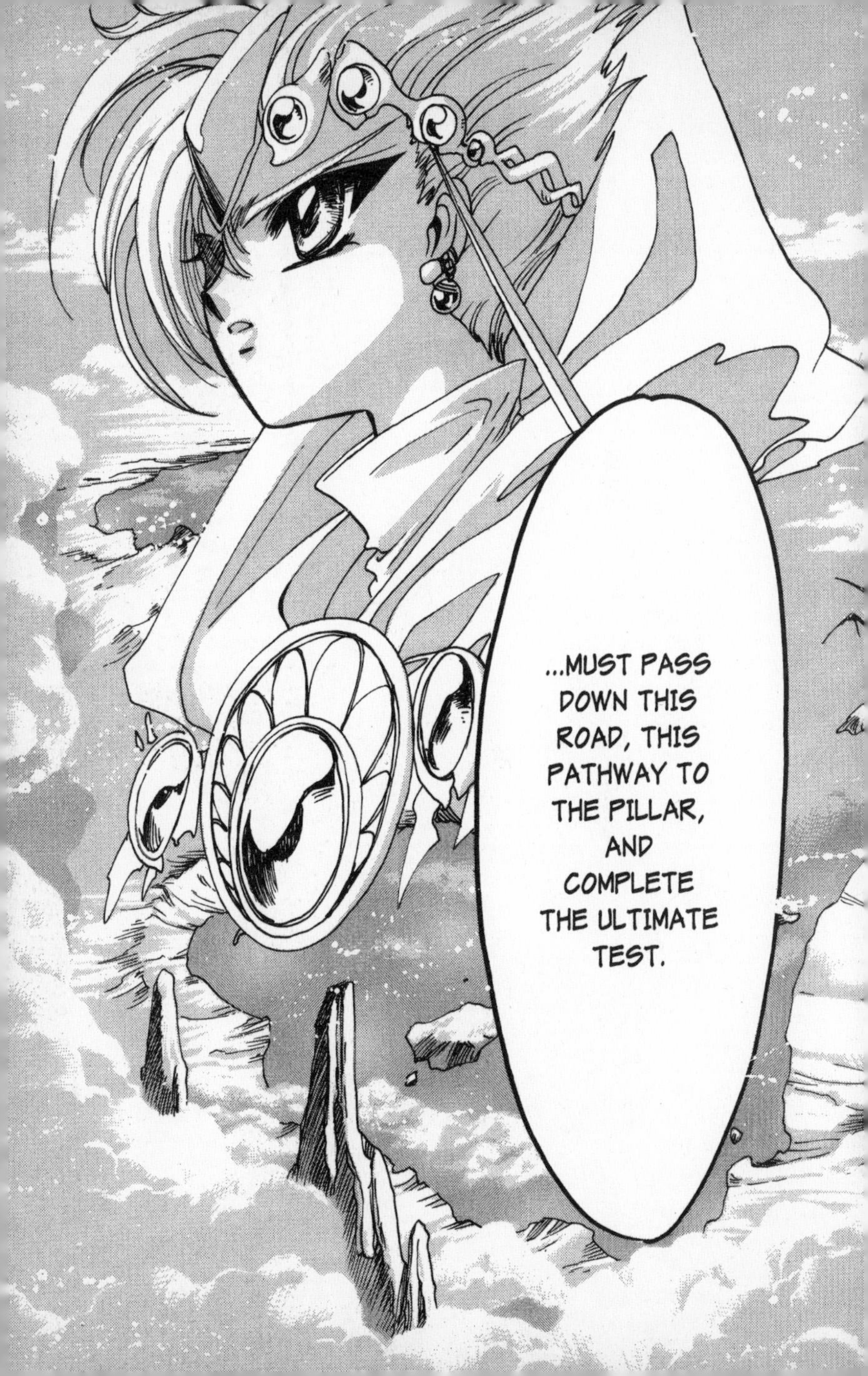
...MUST PASS DOWN THIS ROAD, THIS PATHWAY TO THE PILLAR, AND COMPLETE THE ULTIMATE TEST.

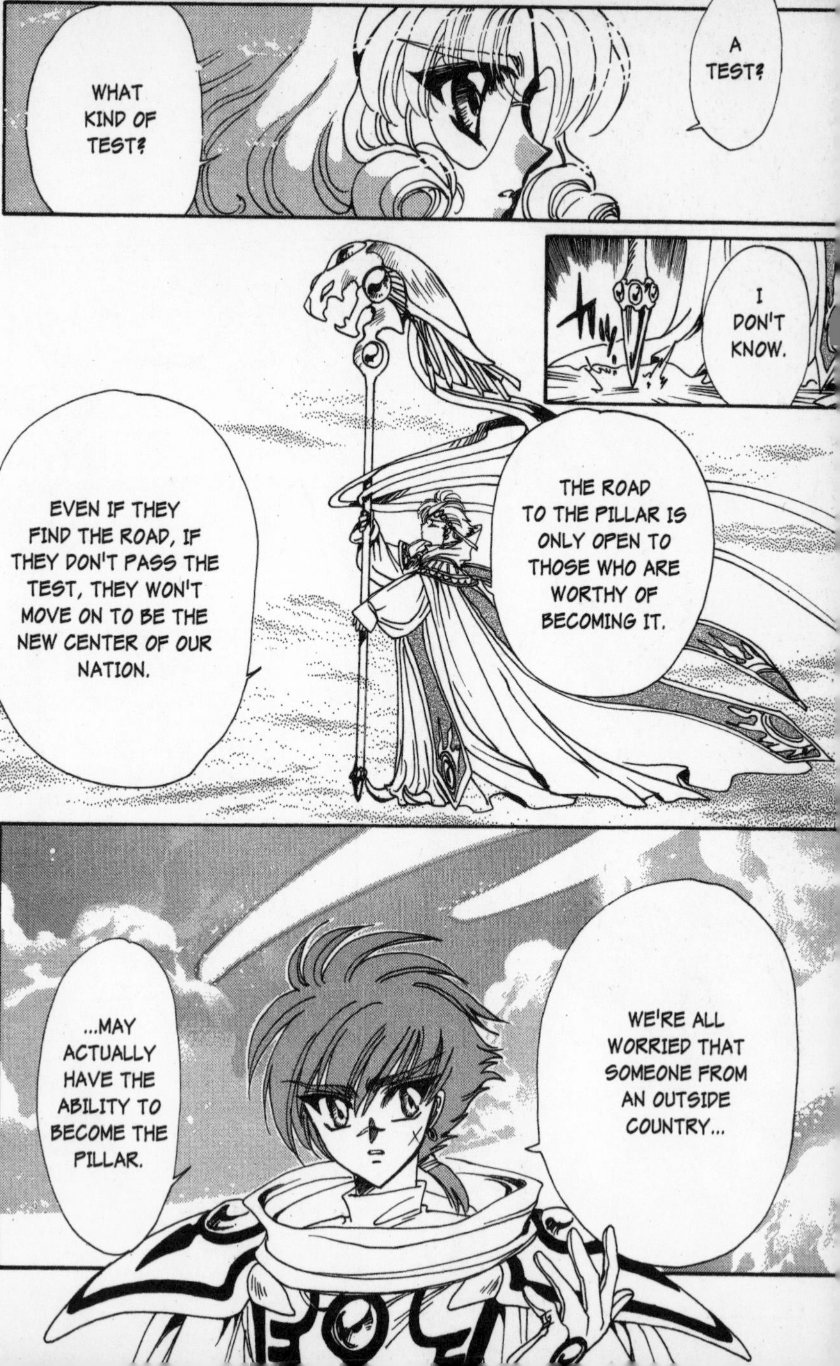
A TEST?
WHAT KIND OF TEST?
I DON'T KNOW.
THE ROAD TO THE PILLAR IS ONLY OPEN TO THOSE WHO ARE WORTHY OF BECOMING IT.
EVEN IF THEY FIND THE ROAD, IF THEY DON'T PASS THE TEST, THEY WON'T MOVE ON TO BE THE NEW CENTER OF OUR NATION.
WE'RE ALL WORRIED THAT SOMEONE FROM AN OUTSIDE COUNTRY...
...MAY ACTUALLY HAVE THE ABILITY TO BECOME THE PILLAR.

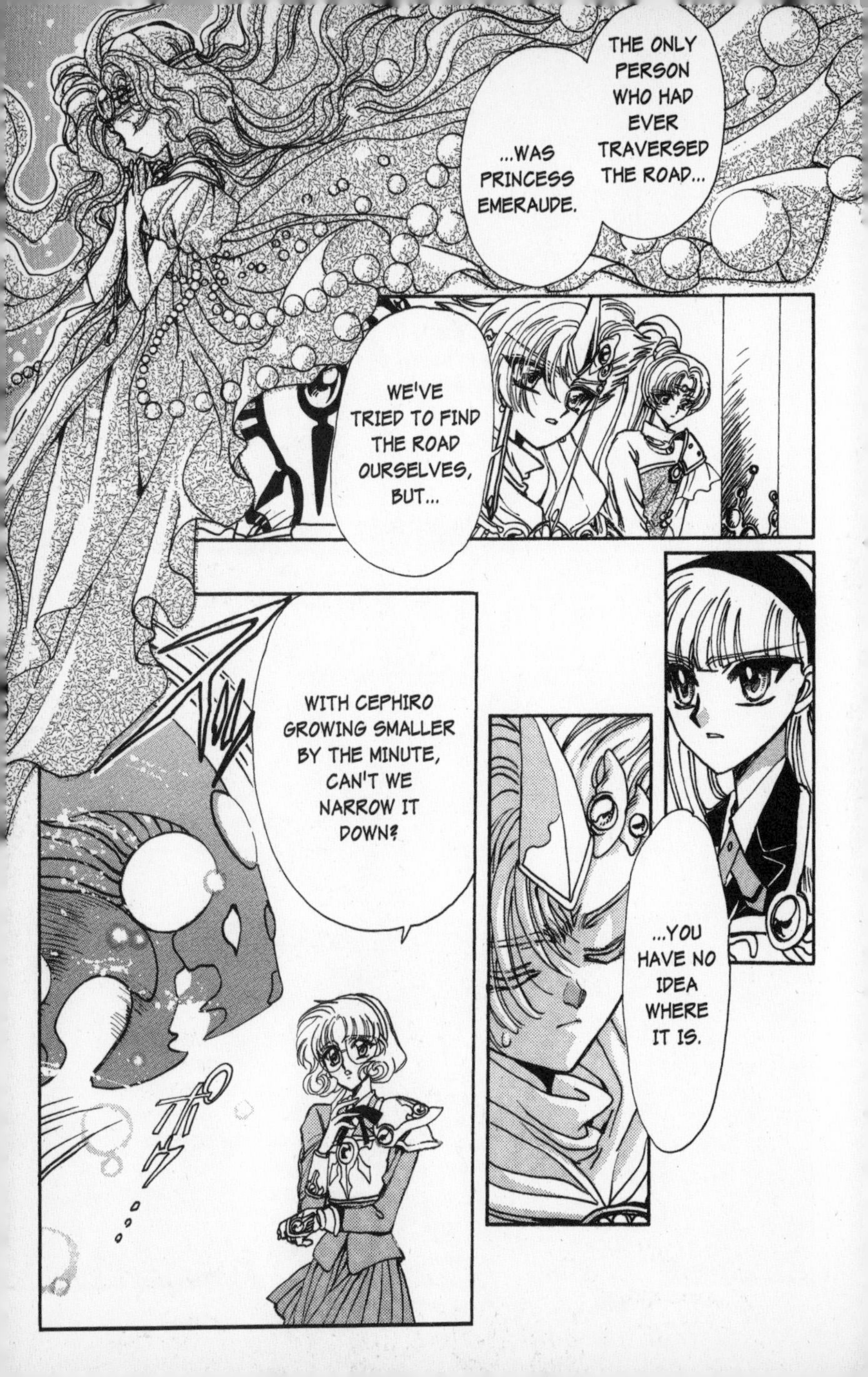
THE ONLY PERSON WHO HAD EVER TRAVERSED THE ROAD...
...WAS PRINCESS EMERAUDE.
WE'VE TRIED TO FIND THE ROAD OURSELVES, BUT...
...YOU HAVE NO IDEA WHERE IT IS.
WITH CEPHIRO GROWING SMALLER BY THE MINUTE, CAN'T WE NARROW IT DOWN?

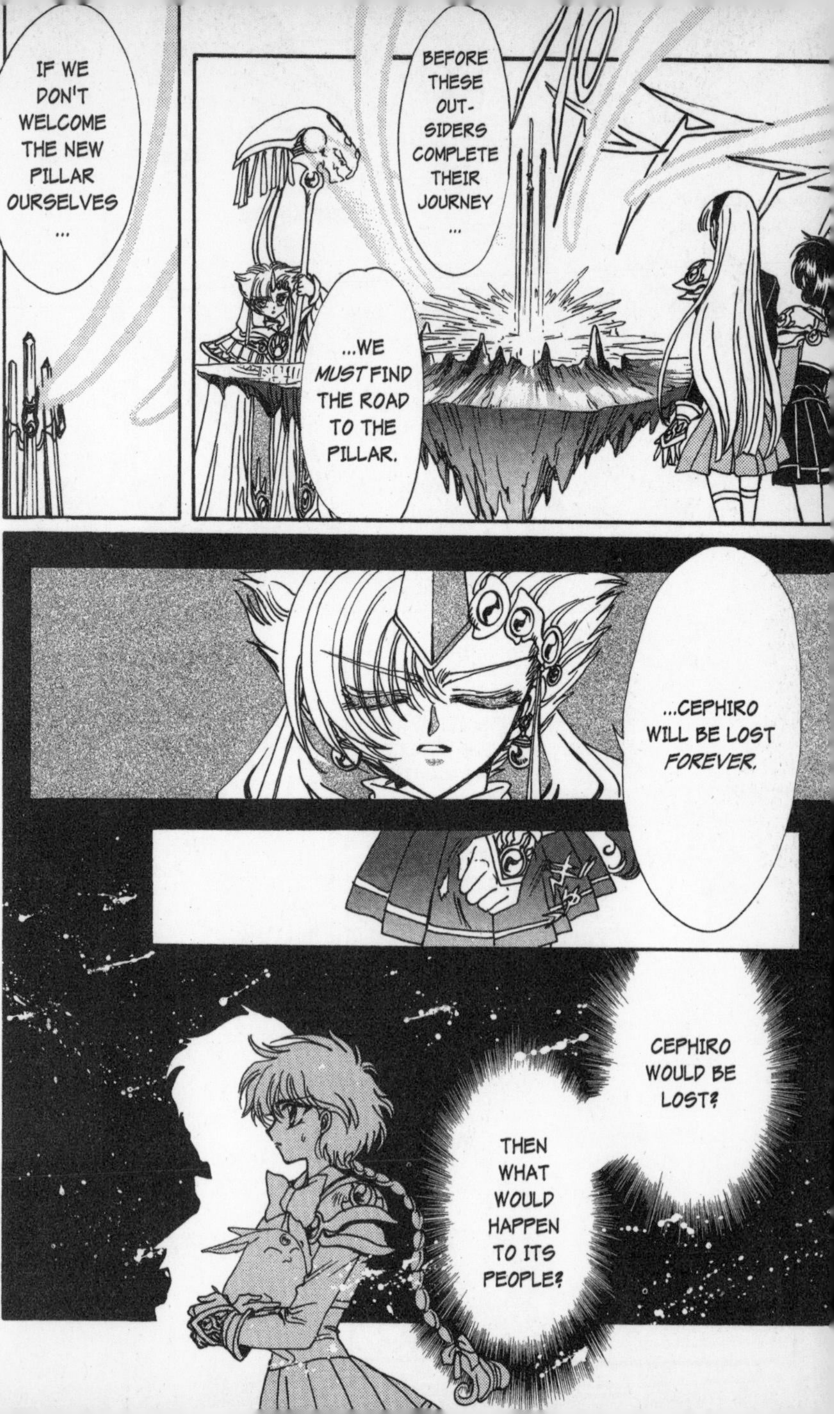
BEFORE THESE OUT-SIDERS COMPLETE THEIR JOURNEY ...
...WE *MUST* FIND THE ROAD TO THE PILLAR.
IF WE DON'T WELCOME THE NEW PILLAR OURSELVES ...
...CEPHIRO WILL BE LOST *FOREVER.*
CEPHIRO WOULD BE LOST?
THEN WHAT WOULD HAPPEN TO ITS PEOPLE?

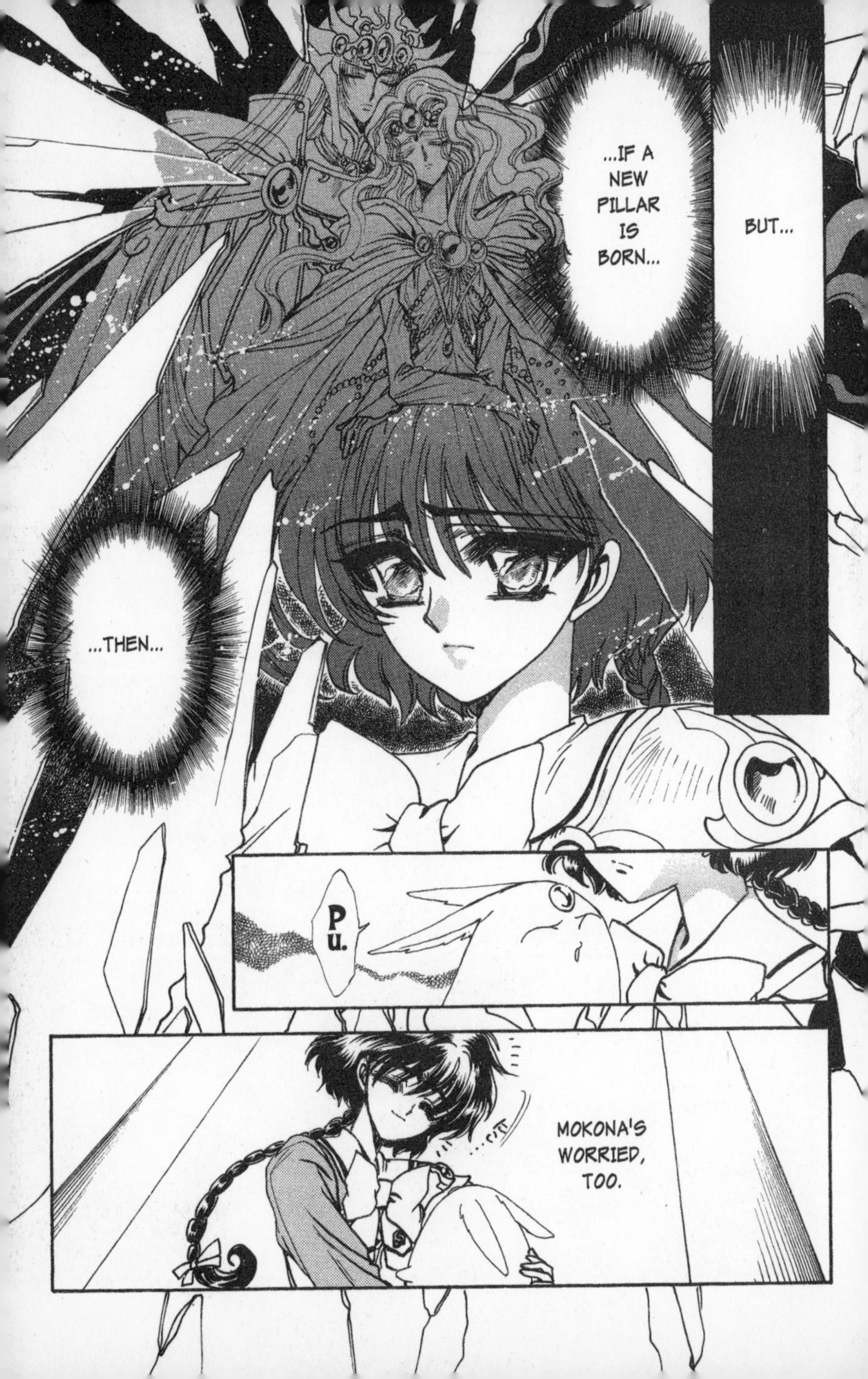
BUT...
...IF A NEW PILLAR IS BORN...
...THEN...
Pu.
MOKONA'S WORRIED, TOO.

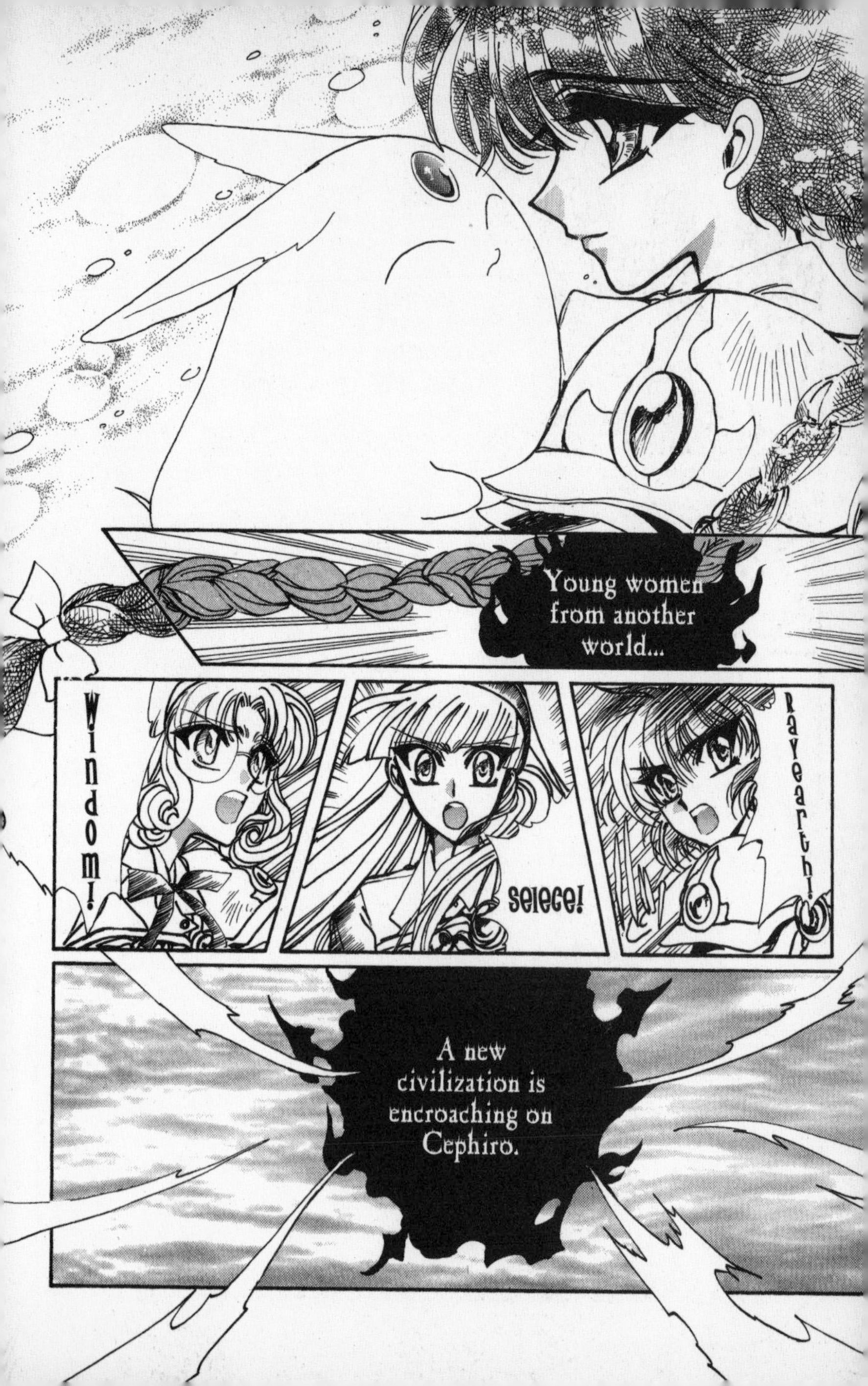
Young women from another world...
Rayearth!
Selece!
Windom!
A new civilization is encroaching on Cephiro.

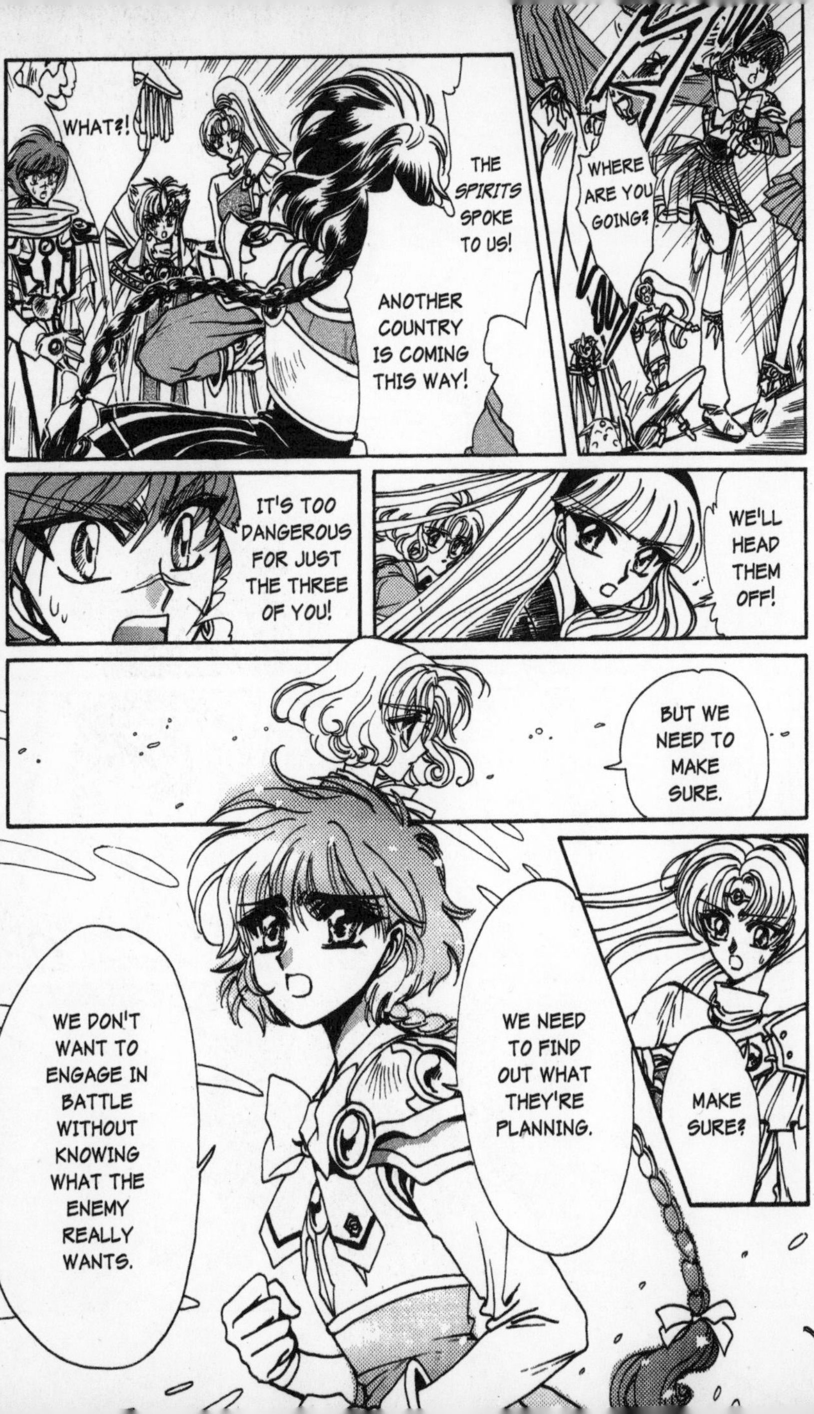
WHERE ARE YOU GOING?
THE SPIRITS SPOKE TO US!
ANOTHER COUNTRY IS COMING THIS WAY!
WHAT?!
WE'LL HEAD THEM OFF!
IT'S TOO DANGEROUS FOR JUST THE THREE OF YOU!
BUT WE NEED TO MAKE SURE.
MAKE SURE?
WE NEED TO FIND OUT WHAT THEY'RE PLANNING.
WE DON'T WANT TO ENGAGE IN BATTLE WITHOUT KNOWING WHAT THE ENEMY REALLY WANTS.

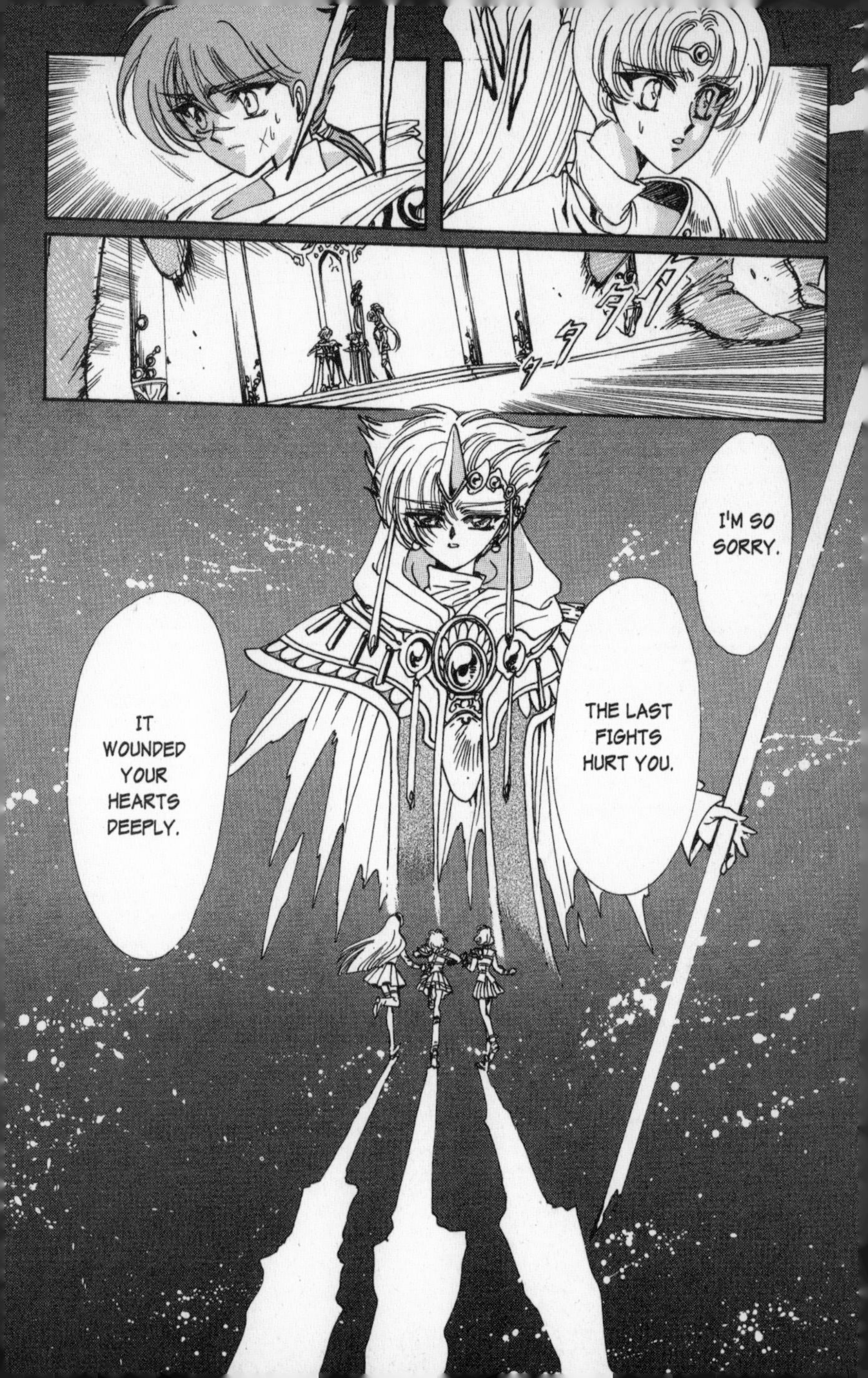
I'M SO SORRY.
THE LAST FIGHTS HURT YOU.
IT WOUNDED YOUR HEARTS DEEPLY.

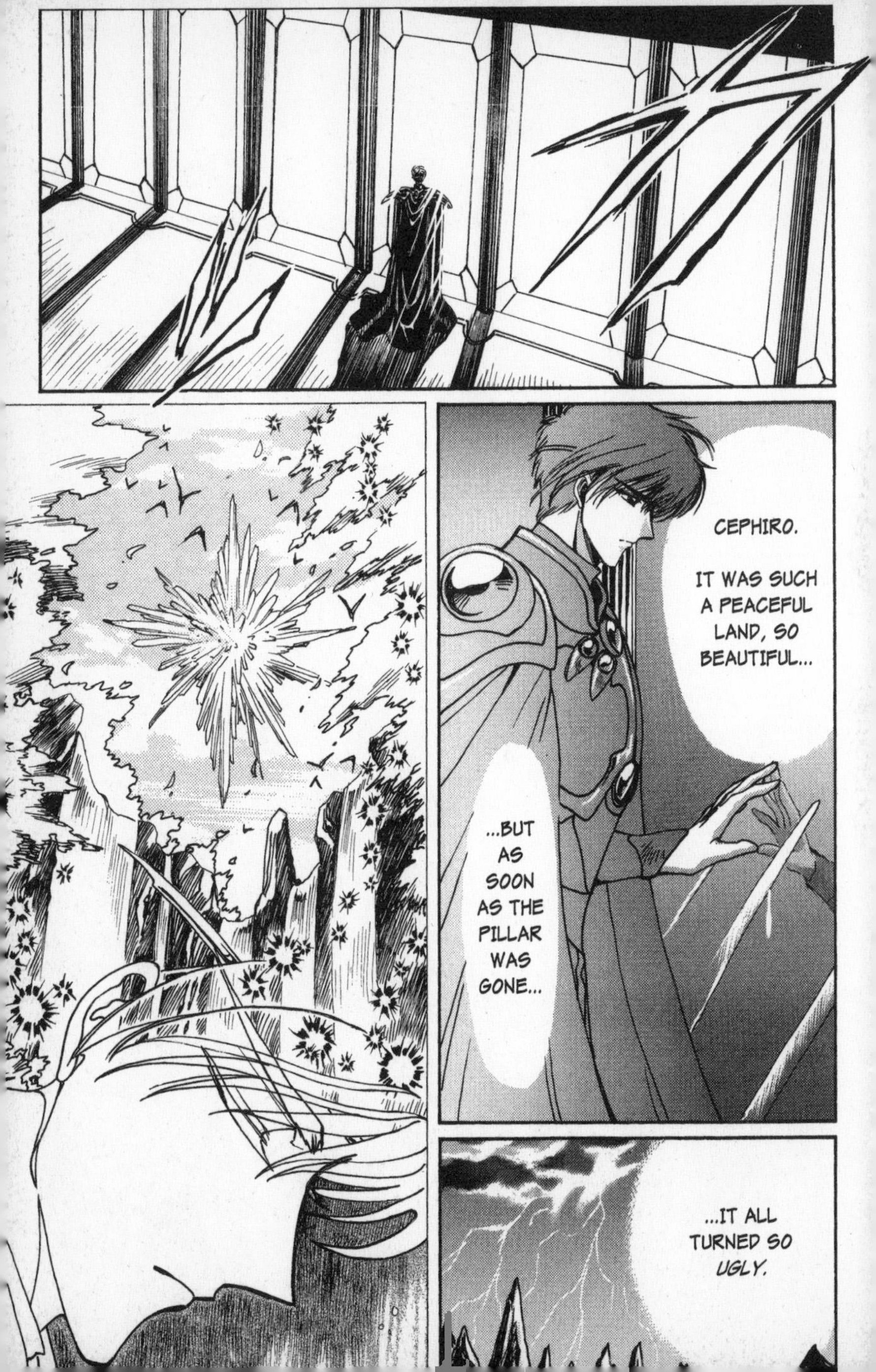
CEPHIRO.
IT WAS SUCH A PEACEFUL LAND, SO BEAUTIFUL...
...BUT AS SOON AS THE PILLAR WAS GONE...
...IT ALL TURNED SO *UGLY.*

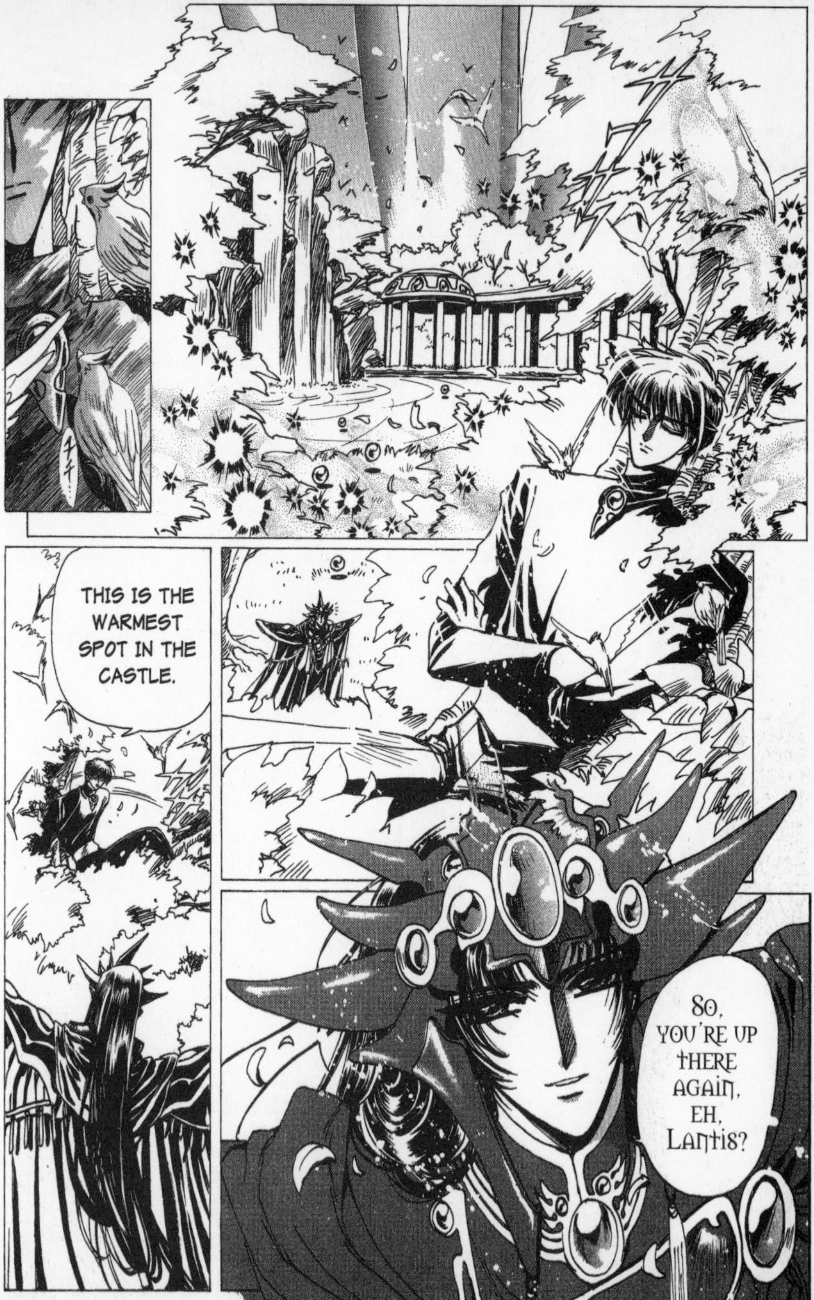
チチ…
SO, YOU'RE UP THERE AGAIN, EH, LANTIS?
THIS IS THE WARMEST SPOT IN THE CASTLE.

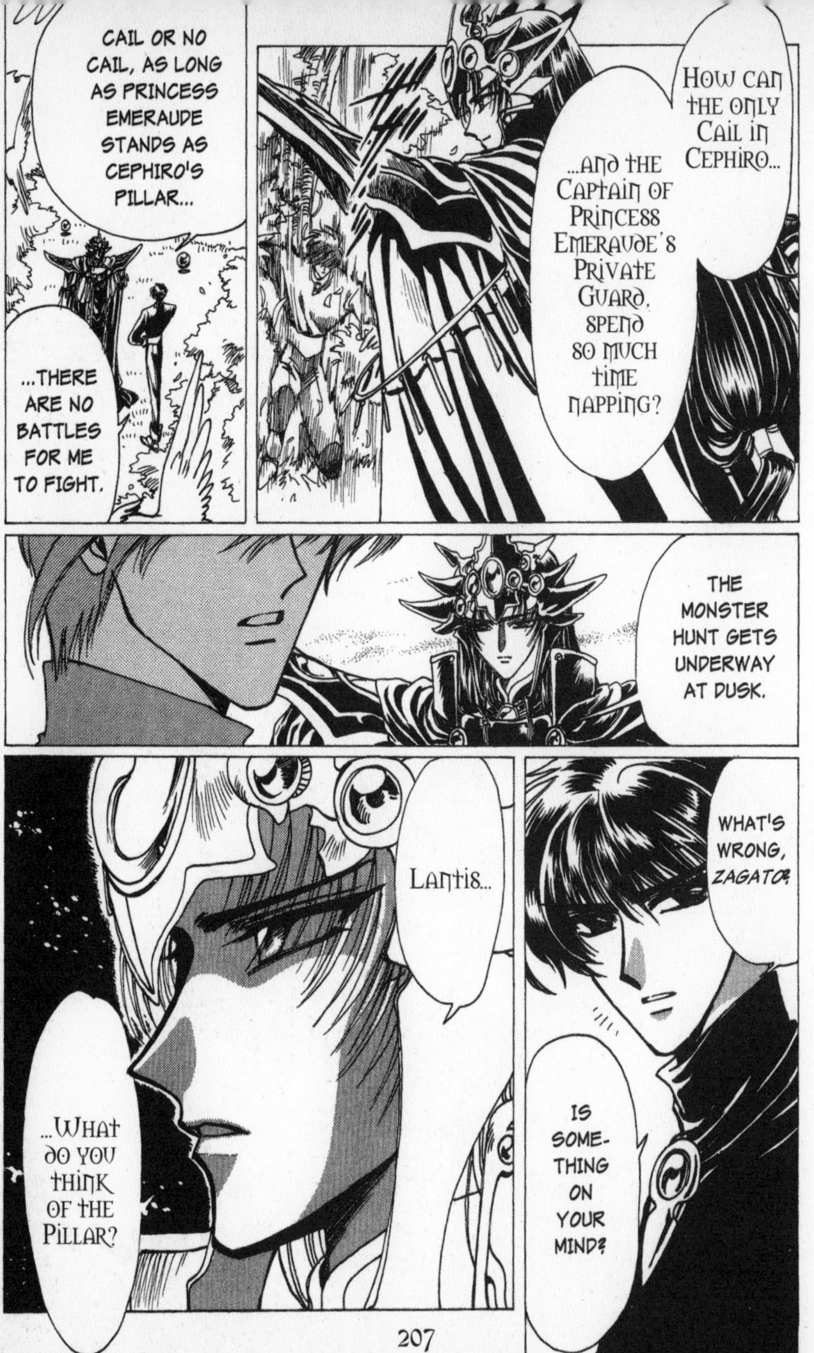
How can the only Cail in Cephiro...
...and the Captain of Princess Emeraude's Private Guard, spend so much time napping?
Cail or no Cail, as long as Princess Emeraude stands as Cephiro's pillar...
...there are no battles for me to fight.
The monster hunt gets underway at dusk.
What's wrong, Zagato?
Is something on your mind?
Lantis...
...What do you think of the Pillar?

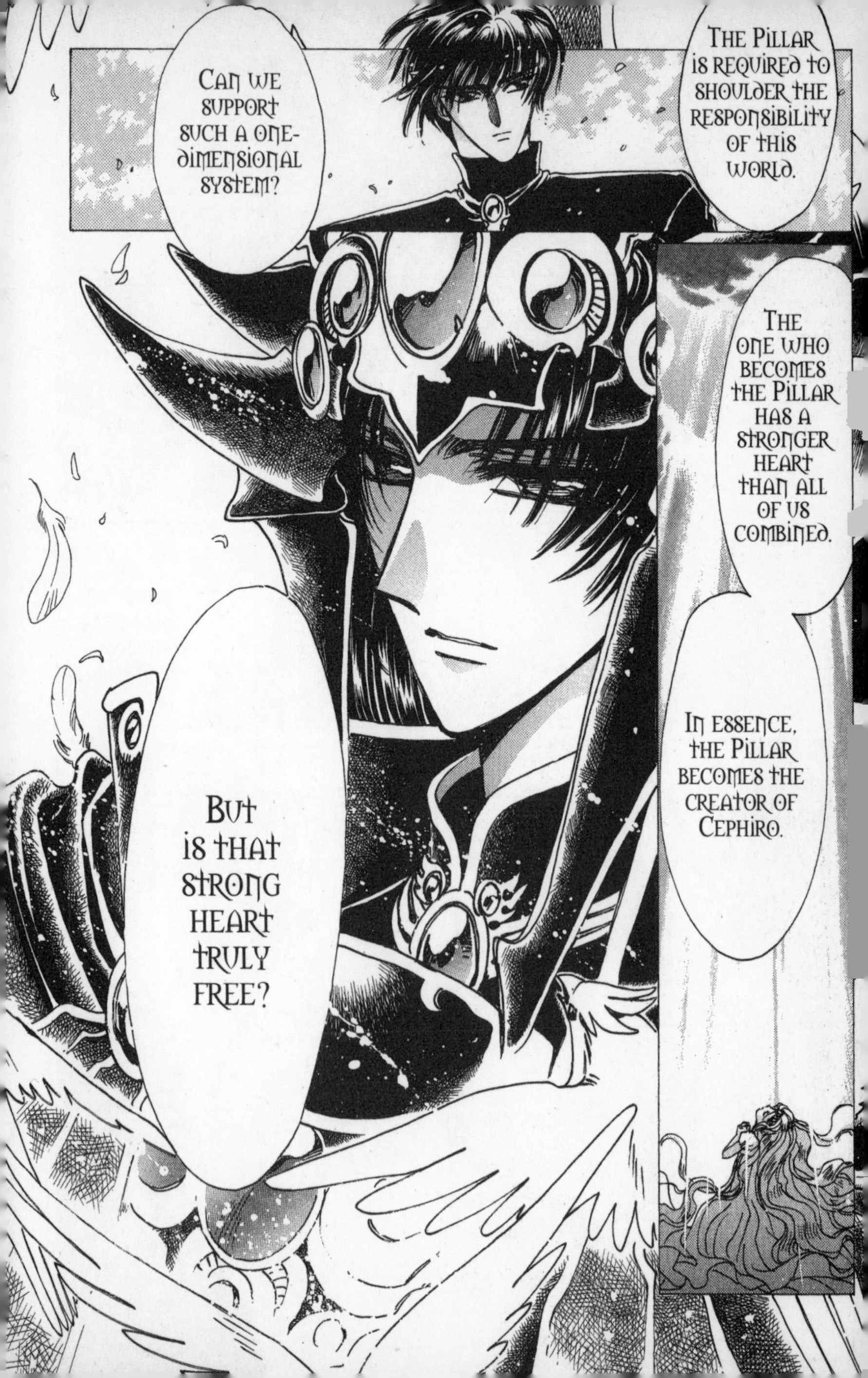
THE PILLAR IS REQUIRED TO SHOULDER THE RESPONSIBILITY OF THIS WORLD.
CAN WE SUPPORT SUCH A ONE-DIMENSIONAL SYSTEM?
THE ONE WHO BECOMES THE PILLAR HAS A STRONGER HEART THAN ALL OF US COMBINED.
IN ESSENCE, THE PILLAR BECOMES THE CREATOR OF CEPHIRO.
BUT IS THAT STRONG HEART TRULY FREE?

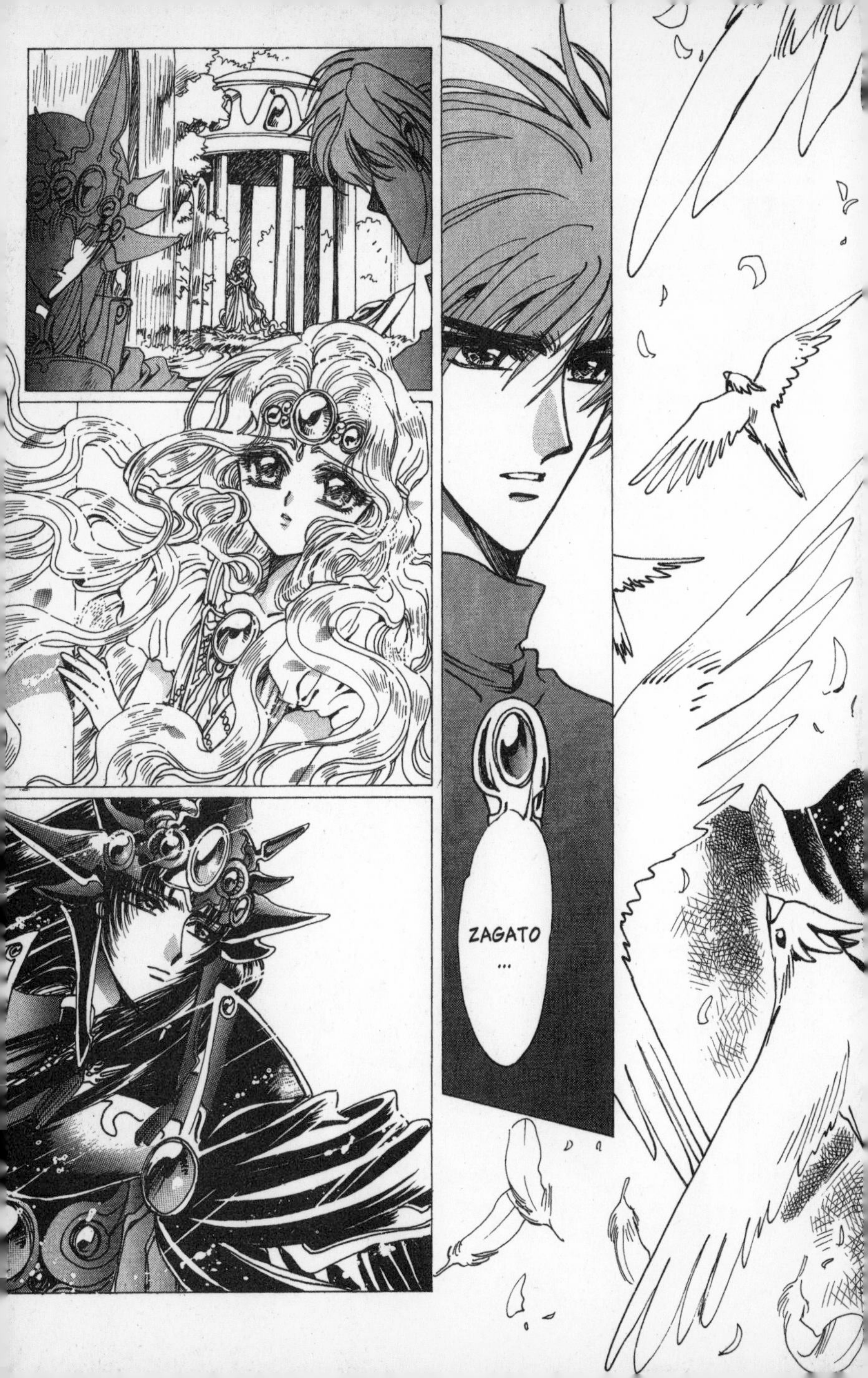
ZAGATO ...

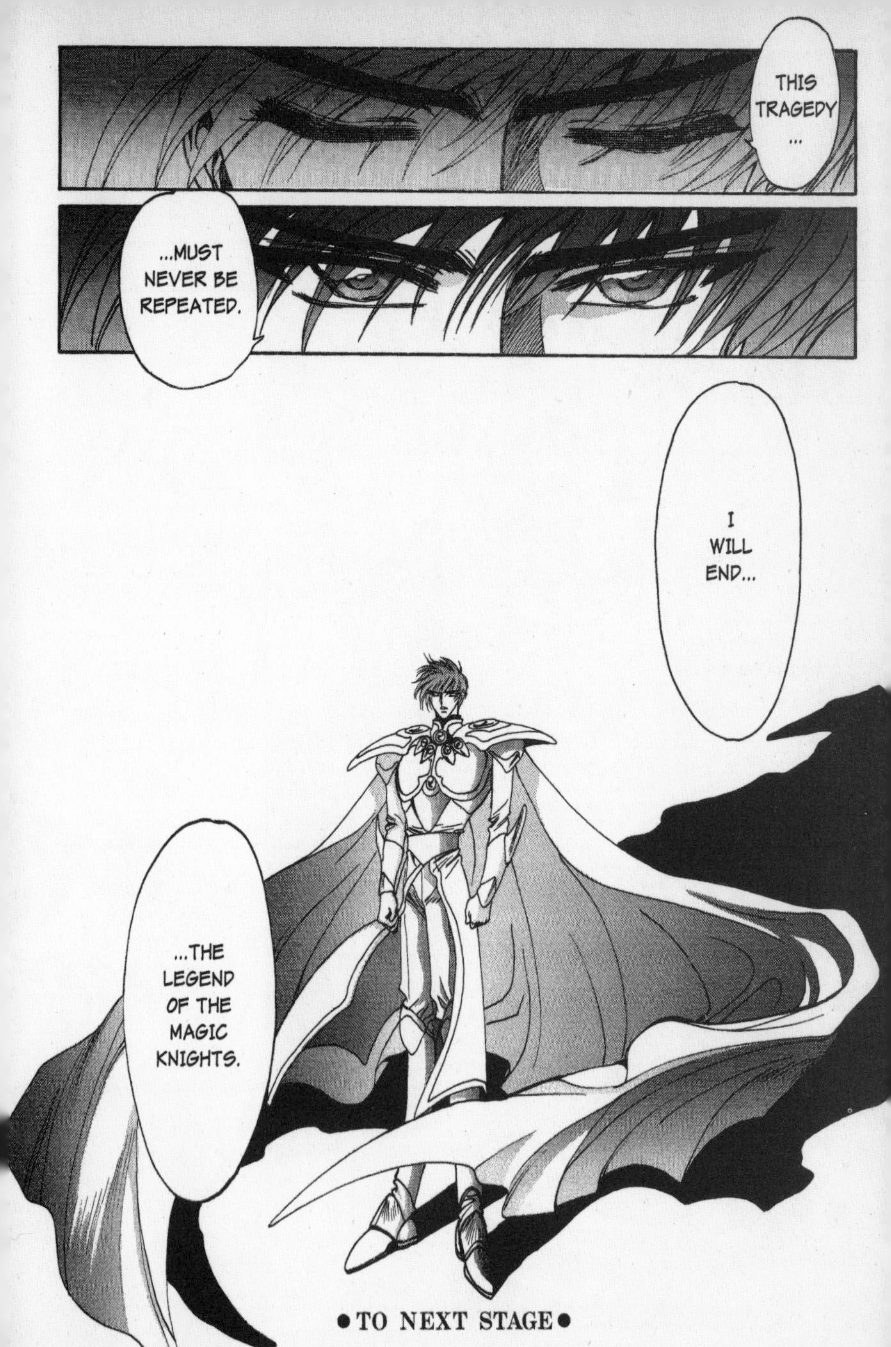
THIS TRAGEDY ...
...MUST NEVER BE REPEATED.
I WILL END...
...THE LEGEND OF THE MAGIC KNIGHTS.

•TO NEXT STAGE•

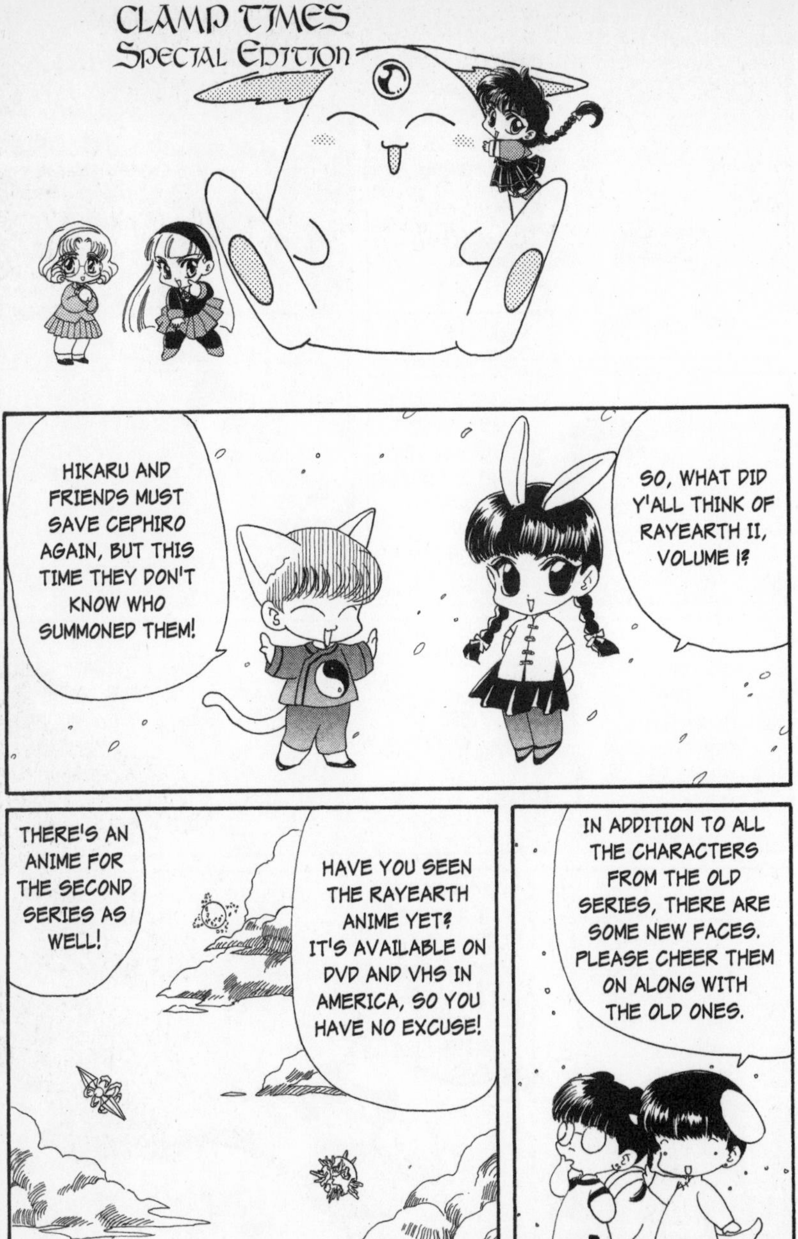
CLAMP TIMES
Special Edition
SO, WHAT DID Y'ALL THINK OF RAYEARTH II, VOLUME 1?
HIKARU AND FRIENDS MUST SAVE CEPHIRO AGAIN, BUT THIS TIME THEY DON'T KNOW WHO SUMMONED THEM!
IN ADDITION TO ALL THE CHARACTERS FROM THE OLD SERIES, THERE ARE SOME NEW FACES. PLEASE CHEER THEM ON ALONG WITH THE OLD ONES.
HAVE YOU SEEN THE RAYEARTH ANIME YET? IT'S AVAILABLE ON DVD AND VHS IN AMERICA, SO YOU HAVE NO EXCUSE!
THERE'S AN ANIME FOR THE SECOND SERIES AS WELL!

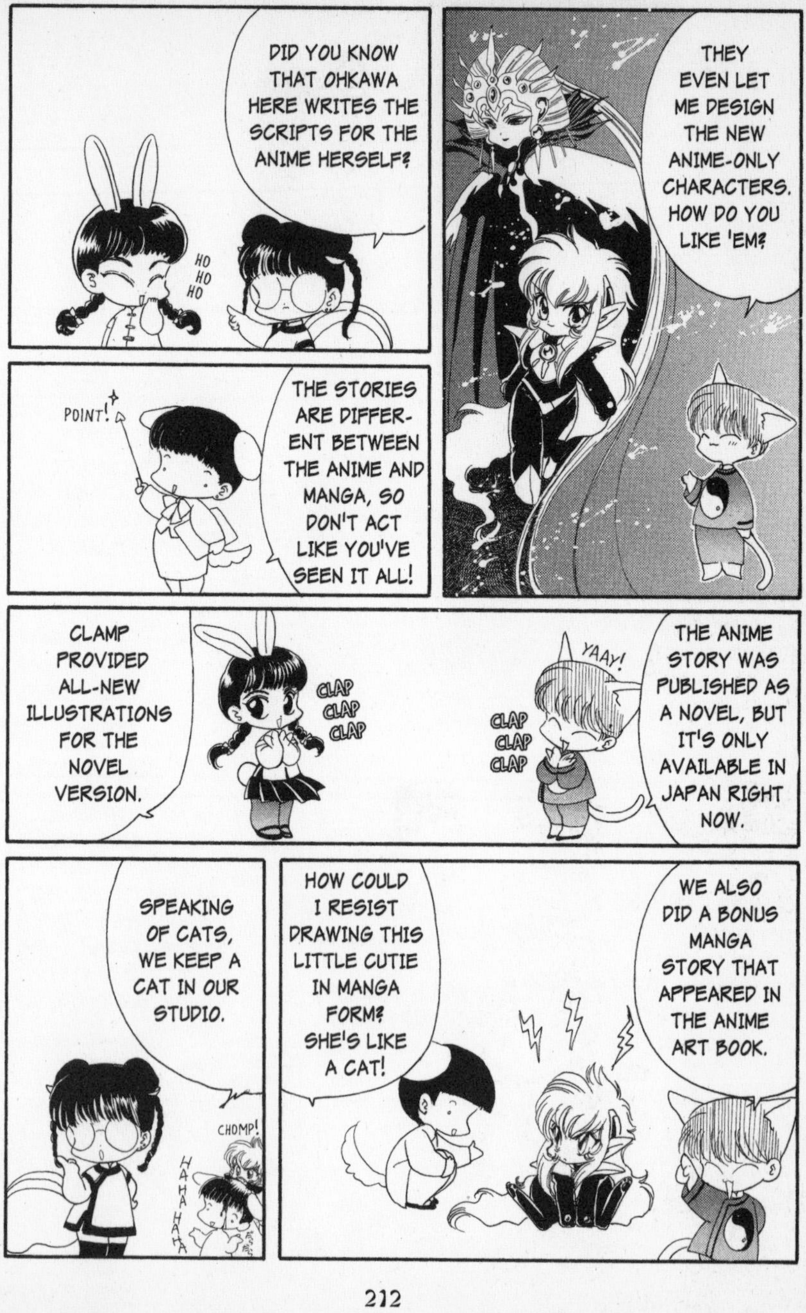
THEY EVEN LET ME DESIGN THE NEW ANIME-ONLY CHARACTERS. HOW DO YOU LIKE 'EM?
DID YOU KNOW THAT OHKAWA HERE WRITES THE SCRIPTS FOR THE ANIME HERSELF?
HO HO HO
THE STORIES ARE DIFFER-ENT BETWEEN THE ANIME AND MANGA, SO DON'T ACT LIKE YOU'VE SEEN IT ALL!
POINT!
THE ANIME STORY WAS PUBLISHED AS A NOVEL, BUT IT'S ONLY AVAILABLE IN JAPAN RIGHT NOW.
YAAY!
CLAP CLAP CLAP
CLAP CLAP CLAP
CLAMP PROVIDED ALL-NEW ILLUSTRATIONS FOR THE NOVEL VERSION.
WE ALSO DID A BONUS MANGA STORY THAT APPEARED IN THE ANIME ART BOOK.
HOW COULD I RESIST DRAWING THIS LITTLE CUTIE IN MANGA FORM? SHE'S LIKE A CAT!
SPEAKING OF CATS, WE KEEP A CAT IN OUR STUDIO.
CHOMP!
HAHAHAHA

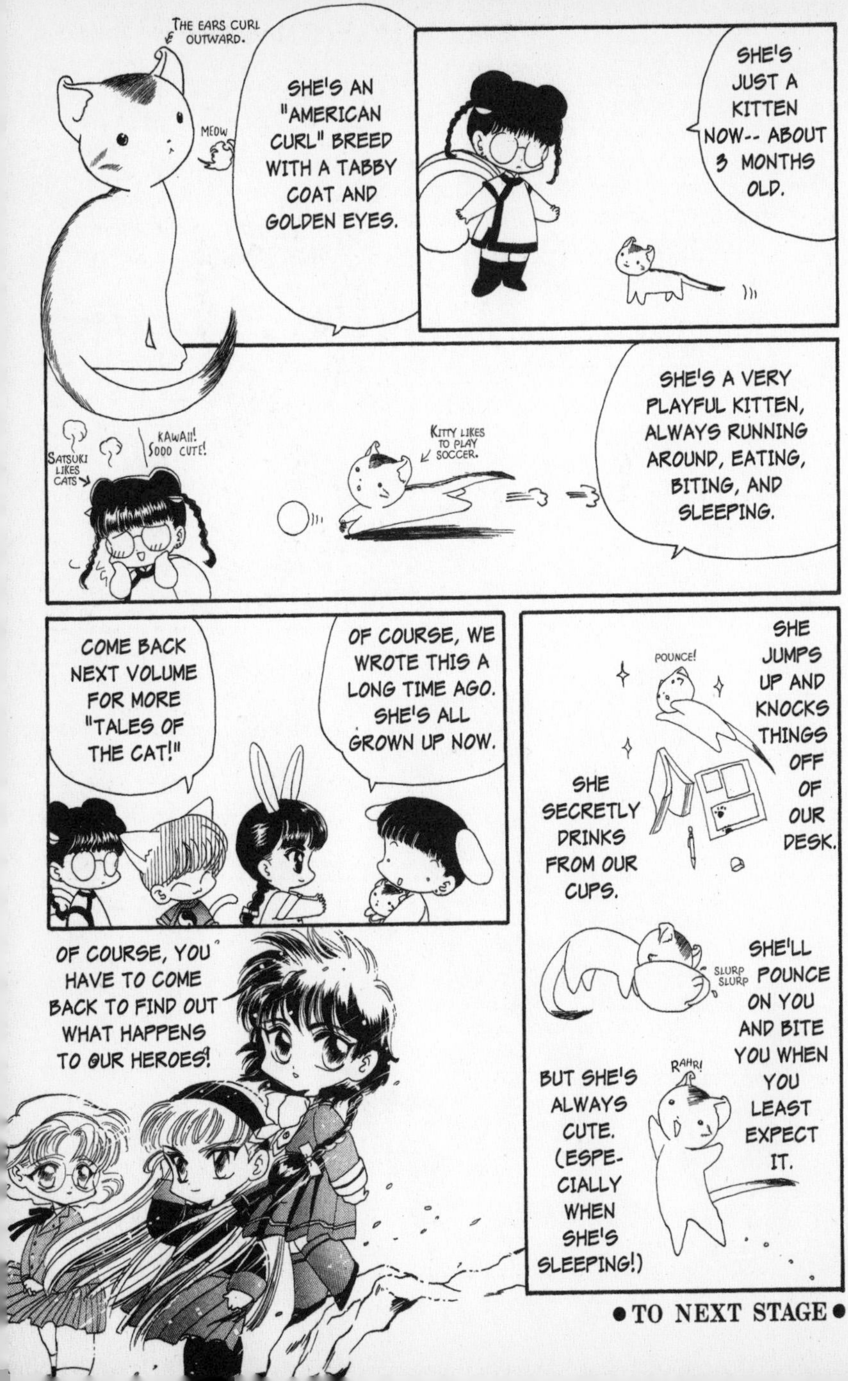
SHE'S JUST A KITTEN NOW-- ABOUT 3 MONTHS OLD.
THE EARS CURL OUTWARD.
MEOW
SHE'S AN "AMERICAN CURL" BREED WITH A TABBY COAT AND GOLDEN EYES.
SHE'S A VERY PLAYFUL KITTEN, ALWAYS RUNNING AROUND, EATING, BITING, AND SLEEPING.
KITTY LIKES TO PLAY SOCCER.
KAWAII! SOOO CUTE!
SATSUKI LIKES CATS
SHE JUMPS UP AND KNOCKS THINGS OFF OF OUR DESK.
POUNCE!
SHE SECRETLY DRINKS FROM OUR CUPS.
SLURP SLURP
SHE'LL POUNCE ON YOU AND BITE YOU WHEN YOU LEAST EXPECT IT.
RAHR!
BUT SHE'S ALWAYS CUTE. (ESPE-CIALLY WHEN SHE'S SLEEPING!)
OF COURSE, WE WROTE THIS A LONG TIME AGO. SHE'S ALL GROWN UP NOW.
COME BACK NEXT VOLUME FOR MORE "TALES OF THE CAT!"
OF COURSE, YOU HAVE TO COME BACK TO FIND OUT WHAT HAPPENS TO OUR HEROES!

●TO NEXT STAGE●

Next time in Magic Knight Rayearth 11...

To control Cephiro means to sacrifice oneself to keep it safe. This is a lesson the Magic Knights know only too well, however, the invading countries are not aware of this and continue the assault with greater force. When powerful Djinns, deadly dragons, and menacing mechs attack the peaceful nation, Hikaru, Umi and Fuu don their sacred armor once more to defend the land as Magic Knights!

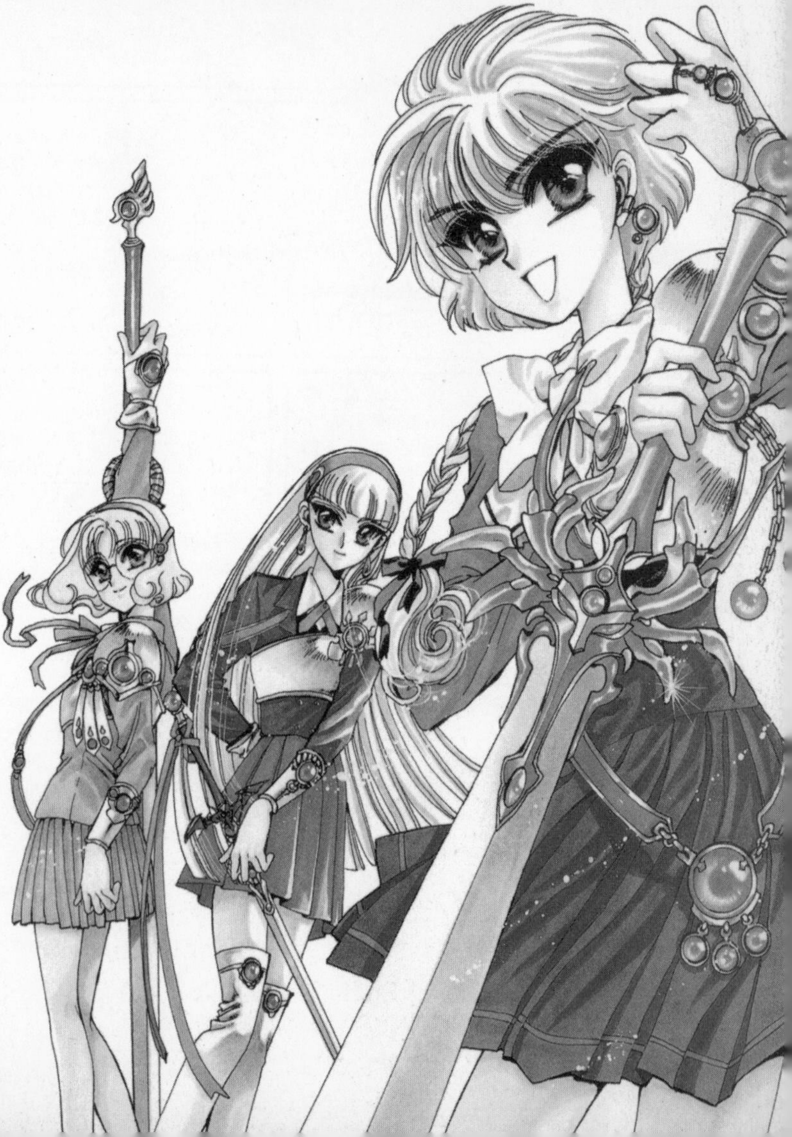

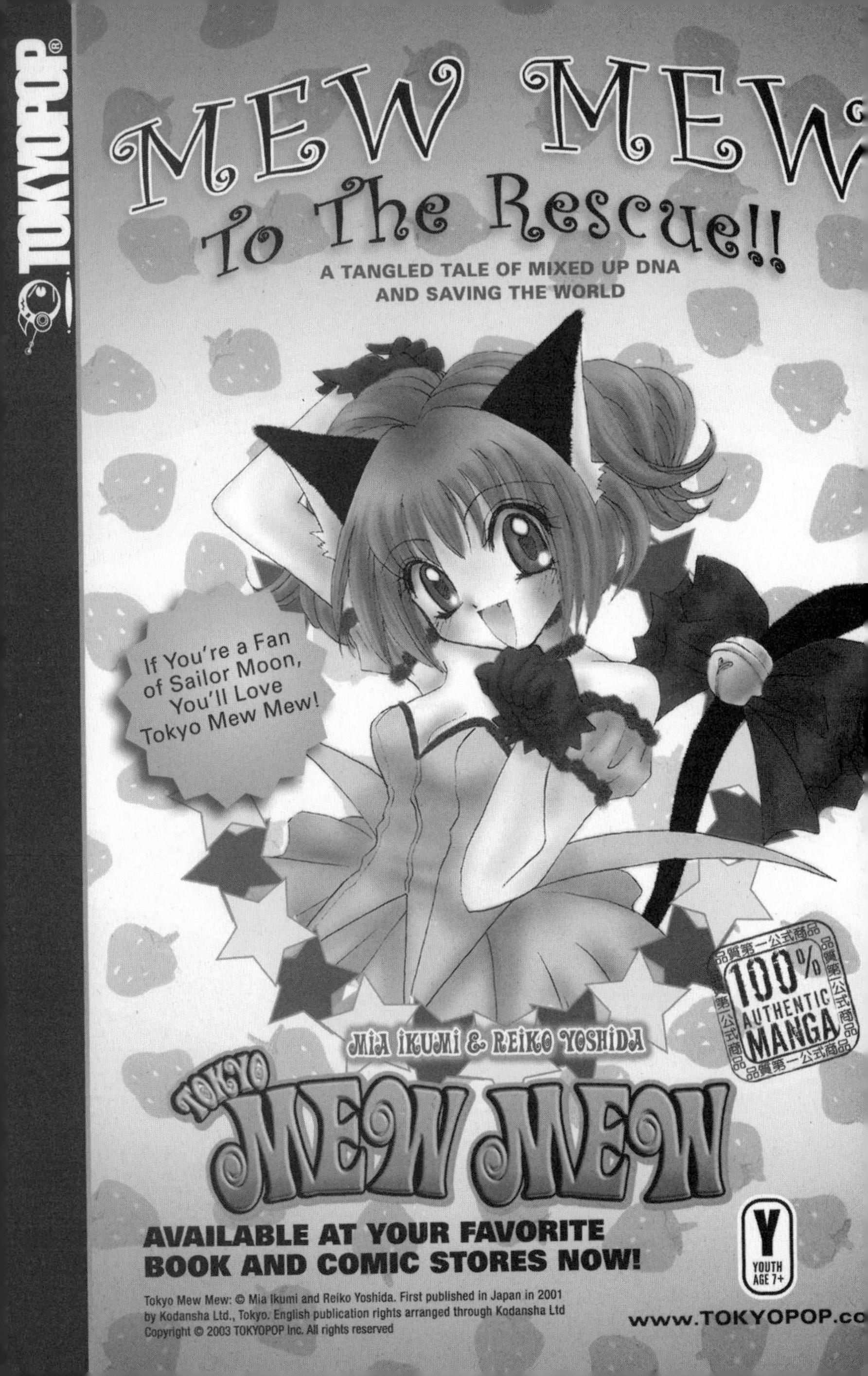
TOKYOPOP®
MEW MEW To The Rescue!!
A TANGLED TALE OF MIXED UP DNA AND SAVING THE WORLD
If You're a Fan of Sailor Moon, You'll Love Tokyo Mew Mew!
100% AUTHENTIC MANGA
品質第一公式商品
MIA IKUMI & REIKO YOSHIDA
TOKYO MEW MEW
AVAILABLE AT YOUR FAVORITE BOOK AND COMIC STORES NOW!
Y YOUTH AGE 7+
Tokyo Mew Mew: © Mia Ikumi and Reiko Yoshida. First published in Japan in 2001 by Kodansha Ltd., Tokyo. English publication rights arranged through Kodansha Ltd
Copyright © 2003 TOKYOPOP Inc. All rights reserved
www.TOKYOPOP.co

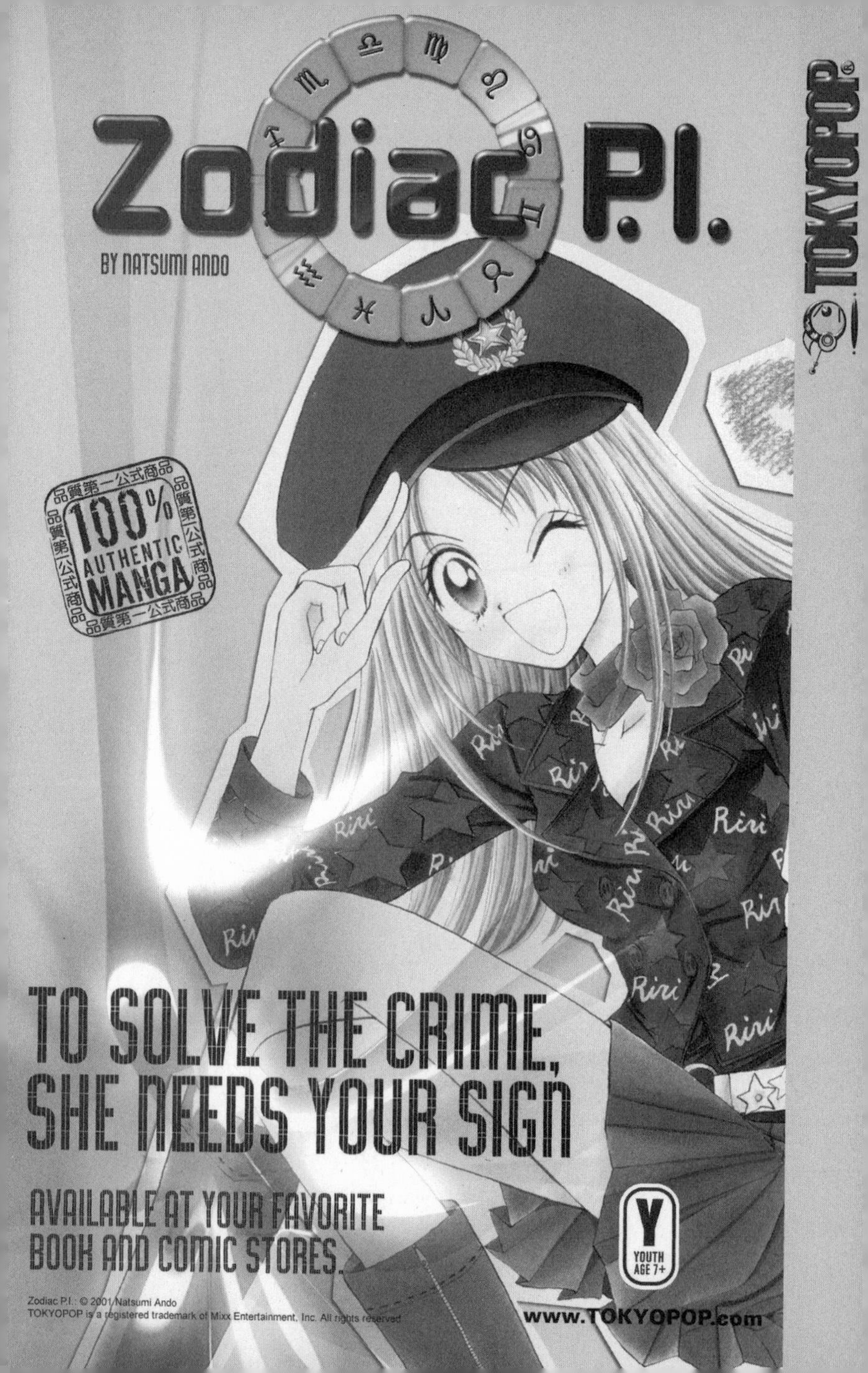

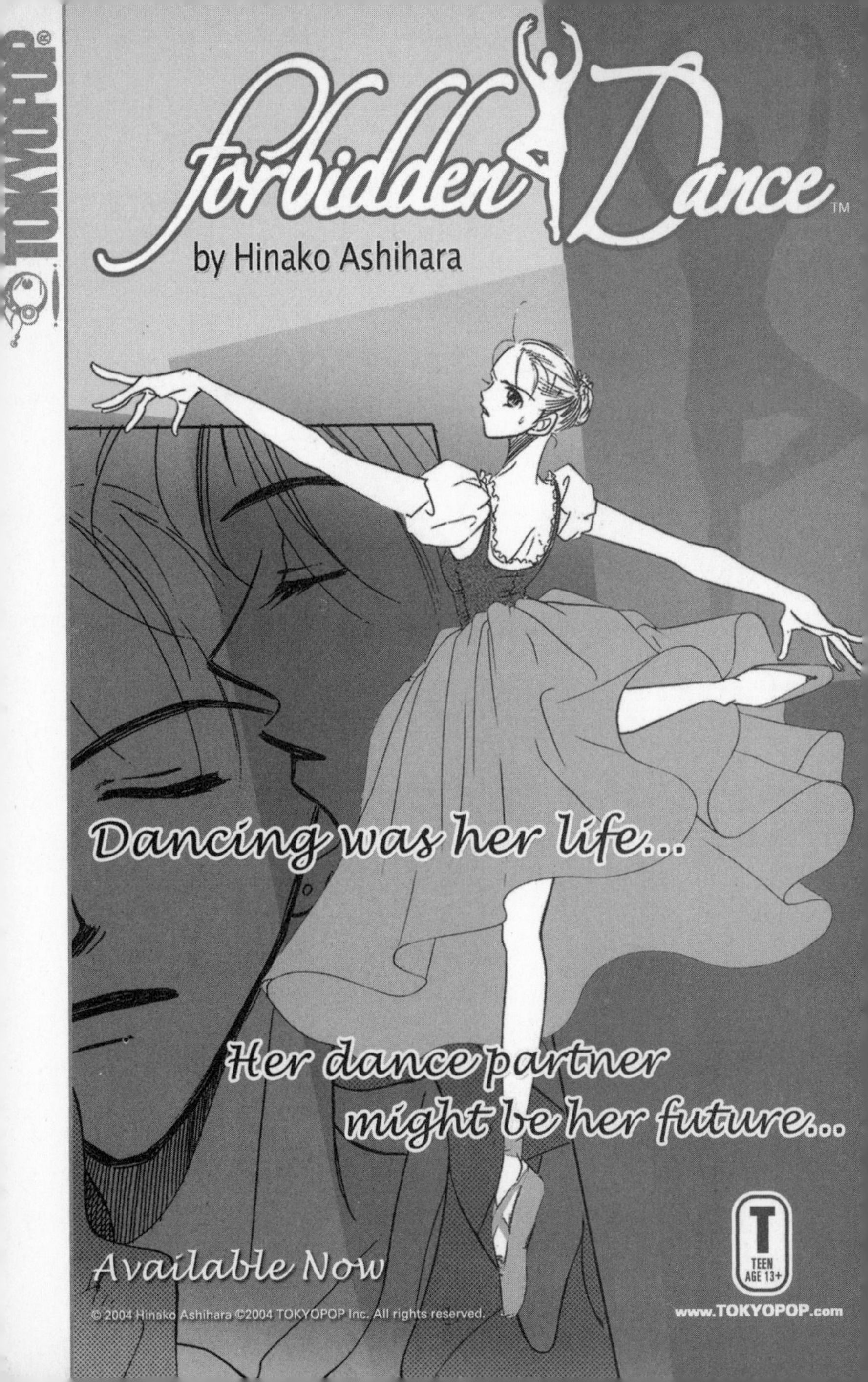
TOKYOPOP®
Forbidden Dance™
by Hinako Ashihara
Dancing was her life...
Her dance partner
might be her future...
Available Now
T
TEEN
AGE 13+
© 2004 Hinako Ashihara ©2004 TOKYOPOP Inc. All rights reserved.
www.TOKYOPOP.com

Fruits Basket™

The most exciting manga release of 2004 is almost here!

TOKYOPOP®

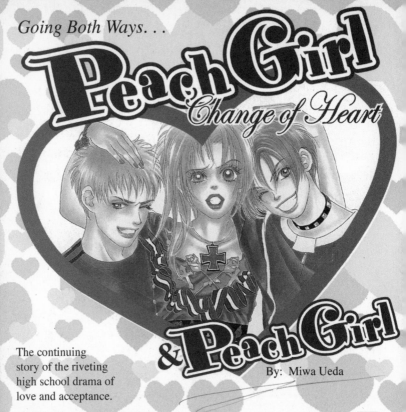

It's time to teach the boys a lesson...

★Girl Got♥Game★

Let the games begin...

Available Now

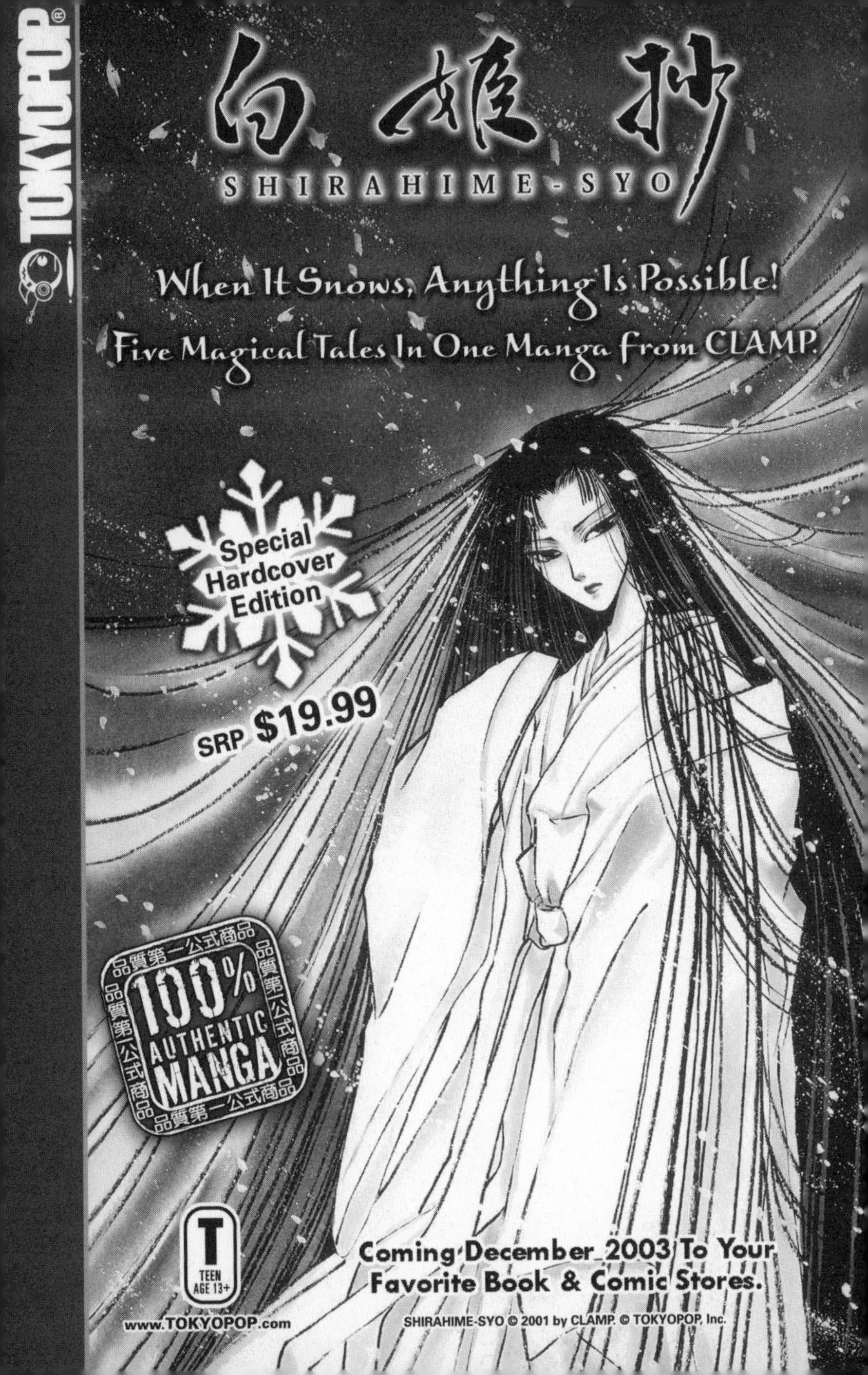
TOKYOPOP®
白姫抄
SHIRAHIME-SYO
When It Snows, Anything Is Possible!
Five Magical Tales In One Manga from CLAMP.
Special Hardcover Edition
SRP $19.99
品質第一公式商品
100% AUTHENTIC MANGA
T TEEN AGE 13+
Coming December 2003 To Your Favorite Book & Comic Stores.
www.TOKYOPOP.com
SHIRAHIME-SYO © 2001 by CLAMP. © TOKYOPOP, Inc.

kare kano

his and her circumstances

Story by Masami Tsuda

Life Was A Popularity Contest For Yukino.
Somebody Is About To Steal Her Crown.

Available Now At Your Favorite Book And Comic Stores!

Rank	Name	Class	Points
1	???		
2	???		
3	Tomohiko Ta	B	
4	Takumi	A	
5	Mieko T	E	
6	Nijo Watanab	C	
7	Akemi Imafuku		
8	Mizue Tanaka		
9	Yuki Honj		
10	Reiko Yokoo		
11	Hiroki Sato		
12	Akira Oshima		
13	Eri Yugawa		
14	Aiko Yama		
15	Shogo Ka		
16	Masami Ha		
17	Mizuho On		

KARESHI KANOJO NO JIJYO by Masami Tsuda
© 1994 Masami Tsuda. Copyright © 2003 TOKYOPOP Inc.
All rights reserved

100% AUTHENTIC MANGA

品質第一公式商品

boilerplate
TOKYOPOP

T TEEN AGE 13+

www.TOKYOPOP.com

STOP!

This is the back of the book.
You wouldn't want to spoil a great ending!

This book is printed "manga-style," in the authentic Japanese right-to-left format. Since none of the artwork has been flipped or altered, readers get to experience the story just as the creator intended. You've been asking for it, so TOKYOPOP® delivered: authentic, hot-off-the-press, and far more fun!

DIRECTIONS

If this is your first time reading manga-style, here's a quick guide to help you understand how it works.

It's easy... just start in the top right panel and follow the numbers. Have fun, and look for more 100% authentic manga from TOKYOPOP®!

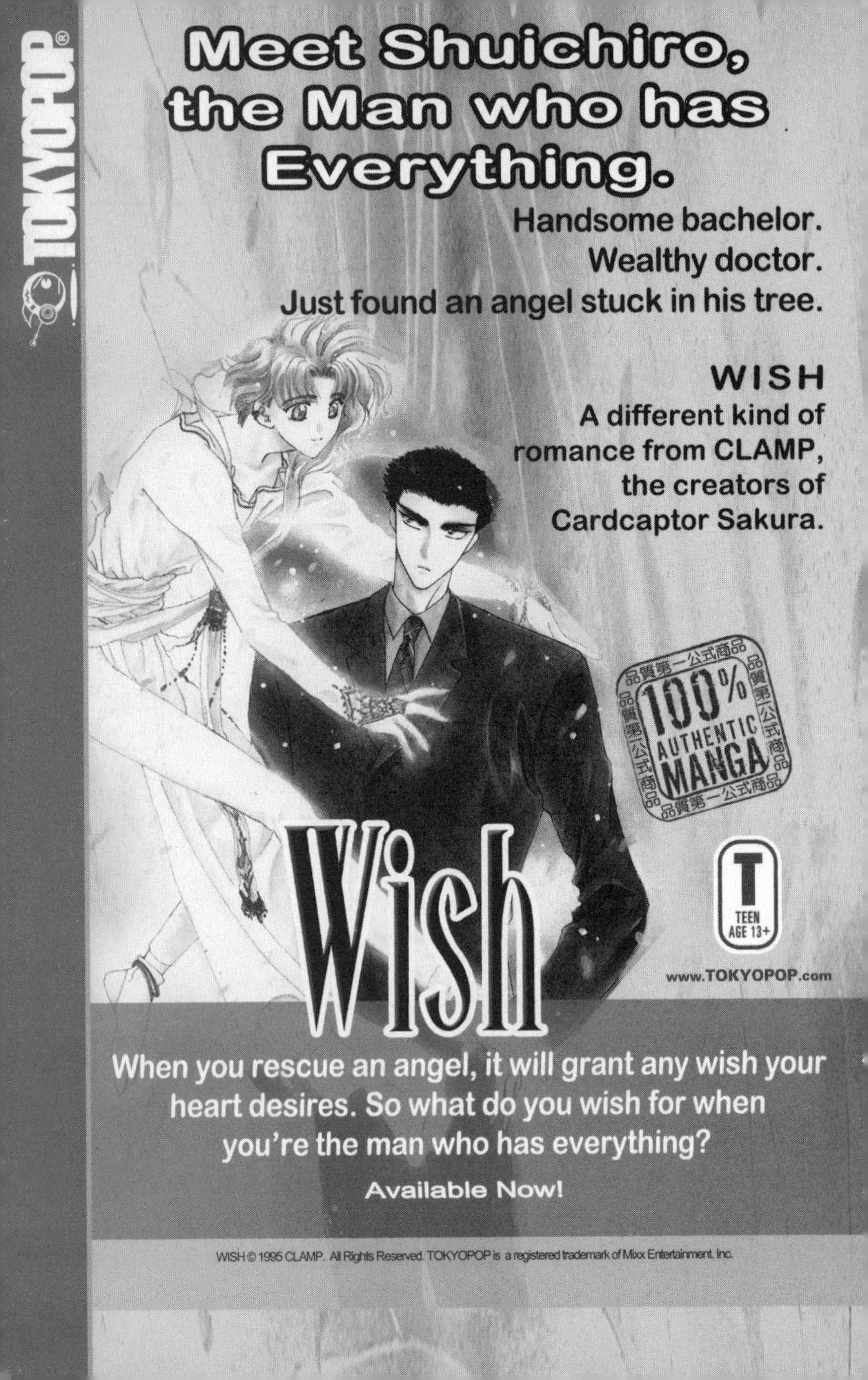
TOKYOPOP
Meet Shuichiro, the Man who has Everything.
Handsome bachelor.
Wealthy doctor.
Just found an angel stuck in his tree.
WISH
A different kind of romance from CLAMP, the creators of Cardcaptor Sakura.
100% AUTHENTIC MANGA
Wish
T
TEEN AGE 13+
www.TOKYOPOP.com
When you rescue an angel, it will grant any wish your heart desires. So what do you wish for when you're the man who has everything?
Available Now!
WISH © 1995 CLAMP. All Rights Reserved. TOKYOPOP is a registered trademark of Mixx Entertainment, Inc.